Utopian Feminism

Utopian Feminism

Women's Movements in *fin-de-siècle* Vienna

Harriet Anderson

Yale University Press
New Haven and London · 1992

Set in Ehrhardt by Best-set Typesetter Ltd., Hong Kong
Printed and bound in Great Britain by The Bath Press, Avon

Library of Congress Cataloging-in-Publication Data

Anderson, Harriet, 1957–
Utopian feminism: women's movements in *fin-de-siècle* Vienna / Harriet Anderson.
p. cm.
Includes bibliographical references (p. 282) and index.
ISBN 0–300–05736–9
1. Feminism—Austria—Vienna—History. 2. Feminist theory.
3. Utopias. I. Title.
HQ1610. V54A53 1992
305.42 '09436' 13—dc20 92–5739
CIP

Contents

List of Illustrations

Preface

'Oh, were there any feminists in *fin-de-siècle* Vienna?' is a response I often met with when I mentioned the subject of my research. This surprise and doubt strengthened my determination to show that indeed there *were* feminists in Vienna one hundred years ago, and that they are well worth getting to know. Viennese feminism has been relatively neglected during the revival of interest in modernism that has taken place over the last two decades. While the attitudes to women of male writers and artists like Freud, Kraus, Weininger, Klimt and Schiele have been elaborately documented, women's attempts to define their own identity in that modernist culture and to develop new institutions through which their needs could be expressed have been largely overlooked. The marginalisation they suffered around 1900 has been faithfully reproduced. One aim of this book is to correct that imbalance by bringing them into the foreground. I focus on aspects which have not yet been investigated and link these to known ones. And most important, I adopt a new, synthetic, approach which brings together the three main areas of feminist involvement: practical politics, feminist theory, and feminist imaginative literature. As this approach underlines, feminism was not limited to practical politics but was a much wider-ranging phenomenon.

It is very tempting when considering early feminism to follow either the hagiographic or the raised forefinger approach; both entail a one-eyed reading and a curtailed understanding. And both follow the leading question: well, how radical were the early feminists really? The first approach sweeps all hints of conservatism directly under the carpet. The second is out to judge and even condemn, to point the moralising finger at what might be seen to be lamentable examples of failed feminism. I follow a third approach by adopting the point of view of the feminists themselves, taking their understanding of what they were doing, their goals and their awareness as my starting-points. In this way I hope to trace a history of Viennese feminism from the inside. I do not wish to submerge myself uncritically in my subjects. But I do believe that it is only by first following them along *their* path that an insight can be reached which does the subject justice and which will permit a differentiated critique.

This approach means another way of seeing early feminism. It entails leaving the radical/moderate dichotomy which has explicitly and implicitly dominated the discussion so far. These terms are too sweeping to be really helpful once one takes a longer and closer look; they have a heuristic value but cannot function as more than guidelines. It means appreciating instead that the phenomenon was heterogeneous and personalised. It is question of several different feminisms, as I demonstrate in my discussions of each of the three main fields of feminist engagement. For each field, I believe, different types of feminism can be characterised mainly through their relationship to the impulse to propagate a vision which itself is not homogeneous. And in each type of feminism a small number of individuals were instrumental, individuals who left their very personal mark on Austrian feminism. Thus a handful of names frequently occur which also act as bridges between the various fields of feminist engagement. Yet although highly personalised, it is often the case that a feminist who was active, for example, in both political and literary activity might represent in the former a different kind of feminism than in the latter; the unity of person does not imply unity of feminism.

But who were the feminists I am talking about here? First of all, it is necessary to break with a widespread misconception that feminists were militant women who primarily campaigned for female suffrage *à la* Mrs Pankhurst. This perception is far too narrow. Secondly, the women I call feminist here were not those formally affiliated (however loosely and problematically) to a political party or church. This means that the Social Democratic and Catholic women's movements are dealt with only in so far as they impinged on those organised, usually middle-class, women who remained in this sense autonomous. Of these I have chosen to investigate those who called themselves progressive (*fortschrittlich*) – the term 'feminist' with its current meanings was hardly used – and whose support of progress, and therefore feminism, might be reduced to the lowest common denominator of the belief that women suffer systematic disadvantage on grounds of their sex and that it is necessary to rectify this, for that is progress. Progressive women's movements I take to be those women's organisations which adhered to this belief; they are the organisational face of autonomous feminism. This means that I do not consider merely unconventional or emancipated behaviour on the part of individual women to be feminist and for that reason worthy of inclusion in this study, quite apart from the problems of definition these terms themselves bring. And it also means that modern conceptions of feminism are not necessarily to be found in the organisations and texts I am calling feminist here. Cultural regeneration, and not necessarily a fundamental break with conventional notions of womanhood let alone merely women's rights, was the leitmotif of these women who called themselves progressive. This leitmotif did however for some women entail an attitude of moral mission and a rhetoric of pathos which some modern readers might find hard to sympathise with if these feminists' aims are not understood in nineteenth-century terms. Another corollary of my basic definition is that feminism does not become the prerogative of women; I also consider organisations and texts initiated or written by men. As far as selection criteria regarding feminist text production are concerned, I have taken as a rough guideline those texts of writers, born in the Habsburg Empire, who were linked to what are here being considered the Viennese feminist organisations either through membership or positive mention in the feminist journals at some time in the period 1890 to 1914. Although I have not slavishly followed this guideline, it does mean that the author and not the content of the text has been of more significance. In this way the distorting dominance of modern conceptions of feminism can be weakened and *fin-de-siècle* Viennese feminism critically understood on its own terms.

But underlying the main types of feminism dealt with here is a vision. It is this which guided these feminists, and this which guides this study of them. Being a feminist meant above all cherishing a vision of a new social order which was endowed with clear spiritual components. It is these women's idealism which marks their activities and their writings and makes them worthy of study. The demand for women's rights has since been largely overtaken by events, but the feminist vision is in many ways still of current relevance, as are the courage, commitment and critical thought which informed it. This book will, I hope, stand as a tribute and testimony to these feminists' struggles and beliefs.

Acknowledgements

Many people and events have contributed to this study, which brings together two long-standing interests: feminism and Vienna 1900. To them all I am very grateful. The foundations were laid by my parents, Olive and Matthew Anderson, who made me aware of some of the issues of feminism. Edward Timms also played an important role in bringing me in my student days to Vienna 1900. My interest in Viennese feminism in particular was first supported by Hanna Bubeniček, who also provided accommodation in Vienna from which in the early days of research I made my first forays into the Viennese libraries and antiquarian bookshops. My doctoral supervisor, the late Peter Stern, helped to guide that early interest, and an Austrian Government research scholarship which brought me to Vienna allowed it to flourish.

An oasis in what seemed at times to be the desert of research was offered above all by the Manuscripts Department of the Vienna City Library. My thanks go to the staff there for their inexhaustible patience and helpfulness, and for permission to quote from unpublished material. In the Wiener Settlement, directed by Frau Fleur Kretschmer-Dorninger, and the carefully guarded archive of the Bund Österreichischer Frauenvereine, entry to which was arranged for me by Frau Esther Wartburg, I also found out-of-the-way material. Access to material in private possession was kindly given by Dr Marianne Hainisch and Dr Cornelia Hainisch, the connection being established by Dr Gertrude Jackson. Herr Martin Lang generously helped me with written and photographic material of his grandmother, Marie Lang.

Christian Almásy, Robert Baldock, Cornelia Klinger, Brigitte Lichtenberger-Fenz, Sonja Rappold, Ritchie Robertson, Edward Timms and the anonymous readers for Yale University Press all read at least parts of the draft manuscript and supported me by giving their time, interest and critical comments. To them all I am most grateful. In addition, I thank Klaus Nellen and the Institut für die

Wissenschaften vom Menschen in Vienna for their help in technical matters. Special gratitude of a different kind goes to Christian Almásy and Gaby Bartuska-Thiede for their unfailing companionship.

The Fonds zur Förderung der wissenschaftlichen Forschung in Österreich most generously supported my research with a grant, which was kindly administrated by Professor Dr Ingrid Cella. I am grateful to both; this book is largely a product of the research financed by the Fonds. My thanks also go to Yale University Press for the careful editing and production, and in particular to Robert Baldock of the Press for his patience and encouragement.

Vienna, 1991 Harriet Anderson

INTRODUCTION

Moral Missionaries and Hysterical Hermaphrodites. Feminist and Anti-Feminist Perspectives in Vienna around 1900

In 1901 a number of middle-class feminists took part in the election campaign supporting the Social Democrat Victor Adler, much to the chagrin of the conservative and Catholic Christian Socials. 'In their impotent bitterness over [their] defeat', the leading feminist journal *Dokumente der Frauen* ('Documents of Women') later reported in an article with the title 'Rabble', 'and probably to frighten middle-class women away from further such activities, the Christian Social party leaders chose the most cowardly and dishonourable revenge thinkable. In all the Christian Social papers, above all . . . the *Deutsche Zeitung* . . . the women who had participated in the agitation for Dr Adler were insulted in the most lewd manner and called – prostitutes, whores etc. And . . . as a sign that this action was supported by the Party . . . the mayor of Vienna, Dr Lueger, repeated this abuse.' Whereupon two of the insulted women went to the office of the editor of the *Deutsche Zeitung*. 'When the two ladies asked the chief editor, the city councillor Dr Wähner, whether the article was written with his approval . . . he bawled and made a terrible scene, tore open the doors, called his editors into his office and shouted: "Just have a look at them!" . . . Dr Wähner declared his support "for the most lousy rascal" (his own words) in his office . . . and screamed at Frau von Langenau [one of the protesting women] that it was a scandal that she, the widow of an ambassador, campaigned for someone like Dr Adler.'[1]

This incident, which was by no means exceptional, indicates not only aspects of the feminists' morality but also, and more significantly, the force of anti-feminism and *its* morality in Vienna around 1900. As this account reveals, women who dared to enter the political arena and express their opposition to the forces of clericalism and conservatism could count on virulent opposition from elected politicians and their press, opposition which more often than not took the form of an attack on the feminists' sexual morals and private life. Anti-feminism was a widely accepted political phenomenon which lost no politician many votes and used a repressive sexual morality as one of its main weapons. Confronting anti-feminism was an integral part of the experience of being a feminist. Although anti-feminism was by no means a new phenomenon in Austria, it was given an obvious focus in the last decade of the nineteenth century by the rise of an organised political feminist movement in Vienna and by an increasing awareness that the social fabric was in ferment and being challenged by elements which had hitherto been marginal or subordinate, including women. This intimate connection of the feminist movement with a pervasive cultural change was interpreted in two different ways: for many, the movement was a *cause* or at least an *accomplice* in the collapse of the old order; for others, it was a *response* to that collapse.

For the former, the noted collapse and resulting ferment were due to a disrupted gender order rather than to social or economic factors. The masculine principle was succumbing to the feminine one, as the literary critic, dramatist and editor Rudolf Lothar claimed in 1891. 'It seems to us,' he pronounced, 'as if the striving of woman for power, the competition of woman with man shows itself in this feminine oversensitivity in looking, enjoying, thinking and feeling and is communicated to man and conquers him.' And to this 'nervous sensibility' he gave the label 'feminism'.[2] Following this analysis of cultural disorder as a smudging of the gender dichotomy, the supporters of the feminist movement were necessarily seen in terms of their relationship to that dichotomy. Here, three overlapping groups of attitudes can be distinguished: those of conservatives, of artists and of scientists.

Conservatives such as Dr Karl Lueger and his supporters who were concerned to uphold the shaken patriarchal moral order saw the female feminist (called *Frauenrechtlerin*, literally 'female women's righter') as quite patently over-sexed. For them she was a threat to both men and morality through her voracious – and unnatural – appetite for sex and power. The tracts of the self-proclaimed *Mannesrechtler* ('male men's righter', in obvious contradistinction to the *Frauenrechtler*, literally 'male women's righter'), one-time religious novice and mentor of Adolf Hitler, Lanz von Liebenfels, offer forceful evidence of this. For Liebenfels it was quite clear that at the heart of the organised feminist movement lay the degenerate sexuality of its female supporters. Combining a virulent racism with his anti-feminism, he claimed that their taste had been corrupted by the 'crude dark men of the lower races' who had made women dissatisfied with the refined sexuality of the men of the 'heroic races' (i.e. the Aryans), a process which had been promoted by the 'dark race women' who, according to Liebenfels, anyway dominated the women's movement. Thus the *cri de coeur* of the 'marriage slave' promulgated by the feminists was, in Liebenfels's opinion, nothing more than the cry of the Aryan woman abused by a husband of the lower races. Liebenfels had little pity for such women, for, as he remarked, 'these women always want to have pitch black gypsy, mongol and nigger rabble and at the same time men of noble disposition'.[3] The dark race woman, on the other hand, was in fact the tyrant of her heroic, long-suffering husband. Similarly, the feminist critique of double standards of morality was merely an excuse for increased and unlicensed sexual activity. Such behaviour coupled with the entry into the male preserves of the professions and politics would inevitably lead to even further degeneration and decline, Liebenfels declared. Developments like these represented a crime against nature for they eradicated gender difference, the disastrous consequences of which were already to be seen in those modern fools, the female feminists, who were bad childbearers, bad mothers, and dissatisfied and hysterical hermaphrodites.[4] Thus Liebenfels and his ilk, even if these latter were not overtly racist, declared that 'the emancipation of women, the penetration of women into male professions, woman's striving for social, economic and political independence is *hostile to culture* – yes, more than that! – it is *hostile to life*'.[5]

In contrast to such conservatives, many artists were concerned to overthrow patriarchal bourgeois sexual morality while still upholding women's oppression. They saw the 'women's righters' not as over-sexed but on the contrary as frustrated, jealous of the sexually 'free' woman, and supporters of the morality which attempted to bind her. They were collaborators in the dominant bourgeois-capitalist repression of sexuality. 'Let no one believe,' the cultural critic Karl Hauer proclaimed, 'that the so-called women's rights movement, because it talks about woman's right to self-determination, is anything other than organised sexual envy. As the sexual satisfaction of woman in democratic, capitalist cultures is tied to a repulsive bargain for social and financial advantages, the women's rights movement tries to make these advantages for the inferior type of woman as lucrative as possible.'[6] The '*esprit de corps* of the female mass'[7] was conning men into thinking that personal qualities were more important than physical ones and women into believing a 'phraseology of rebellion garnished with ethics'.[8] For such commentators women's campaigns against prostitution were merely a ruse to keep the bargaining prices of the less attractive women up by denying men access to the sexually satisfying ones. Furthermore, the concern of the women's movement for sexual morality, masquerading as high-minded social politics, was in reality a form of vicarious sexual titillation, as Karl Kraus also claimed in his comments on the excited scenes which had occurred in November 1906 when hordes of 'ladies' gathered at a rousing women's meeting to protest at the state toleration of brothels.[9] For all in this camp, women like these made the fundamental mistake of believing that man and woman could fulfil the same cultural tasks. Yet culture was clearly the work of man alone; woman's positive cultural role lay only in being the 'material of the male desire to create, a living work of art, or . . . the multiplier of male energy'.[10] Male intellectual and economic supremacy was to remain untouched and all attempts by women, and by men, to attain intellectual and social influence for women hindered the cultural process and were themselves symptoms of cultural decline. So the women's suffrage campaign, one of the issues which most claimed the popular imagination and became a (misleading) symbol of the women's movement, became in the minds of such commentators a symbol of cultural chaos brought on by female rejection of femininity.[11] Women's emancipation was, then, to take the form not of a forced entry into the male sphere which had corrupted enough men already, but of a celebration of woman's natural sexuality as the liberation from the constraints of culture.

This view of feminists as women alienated from their natural femininity was shared by those commentators who clothed an explanation of the feminist movement in the guise of science. 'Woman's need and ability to emancipate herself lie only in the elements of M [the masculine principle] which she possesses,' Otto Weininger, author of the bestselling and notoriously misogynistic *Geschlecht und Charakter* (Sex and Character) (1903) declared.[12] 'W [the feminine principle],' he continued, 'has absolutely no need and correspondingly no ability for this kind of emancipation.'[13] The women's movement was therefore supported by those women who were trying to liberate themselves from femininity; they were 'masculine' both in physical appearance – they are hermaphrodite, Weininger claims – and in intellectual prowess. But for the vast majority of women, emancipation was completely absurd and any mass women's movement doomed to failure. Weininger, while calling for the removal of obstacles placed in the path of this minority of 'masculine' women (*Mannweiber*), condemns all attempts at a widespread women's movement and complete equality as unnatural, artificial and dishonest.[14] The feminine will always remain incapable of real emancipation for this is the preserve of the masculine. 'The ultimate enemy of women's emancipation is woman,' Weininger concludes.[15] He makes transcendence of femininity the essence of emancipation, and for him this is the essence of the problem of humanity *tout court*. Weininger, like his admirer Kraus, perceived the women's movement to be a symptom of cultural decline, but unlike Kraus gave 'natural' femininity a highly negative evaluation and thus welcomed – as anomalies – exceptional women.

Weininger's contemporary, Sigmund Freud, although sharing the widespread interpretation of the 'emancipated' woman as equivalent to the 'sexually abnormal' one, did not share Weininger's evaluation. For

Freud the psychosexual development of female feminists had been arrested; they were bitterly jealous of men and above all the phallus, having failed to overcome penis envy. Yet like Weininger, Freud posits a close connection between commitment to women's rights and lesbianism. On this point they were joined by another Austrian sexologist, Richard Krafft-Ebing, who, however, sided with Weininger in seeing the ideal representatives of the 'virago' as 'outstanding female personalities of the past and present through their intellect and energy'.[16] But irrespective of evaluation they agreed that women like these were 'masculine'. And for none, in contrast to many conservatives, did the women's movement pose a serious threat to the patriarchal order for, as Weininger and Freud pointed out, the nature of femininity itself made widespread support an impossibility; such strivings would remain restricted to a small minority.

All of these anti-feminist commentators see the feminist movement in terms of a female sexuality which has in some way transgressed the bounds set by nature and which is invading the masculine domains of the intellect. None questions the equation of sexuality with the natural, none deconstructs the concepts 'masculine' and 'feminine' (although Weininger makes the attempt), and none considers the social and economic contexts of women's lives in their analyses. Weininger explicitly deals with the woman question only in so far as it is 'not theoretically a question of ethnology and national economy, that is, of the social sciences in the widest sense, nor practically a question of the legal and economic order, of social politics'.[17] Feminism and the women's movement are banished to the realm of ideology or indeed even metaphor and myth, while the very felt impact of the economic and social order on real women's lives is ignored.

This exclusion of the social dimension did not go unchallenged. Many commentators sought to explain the movement in terms not of disrupted sexuality but of fundamental social changes; they saw it to be less a cause than a product of a general cultural decline and, indeed, degeneration. The main impetus of the movement lay, according to their analysis, in the radical changes wrought in women's lives by industrialisation. In the pre-industrial age women, even if unmarried, had fulfilled central productive functions in the home, processing the raw materials for consumption. Woman was a 'universal genius',[18] responsible for kitchen and cellar, the fields and the domestic garden, and the production of linen and fine embroidery. 'In short,' one commentator claimed, 'it can be proved of every century that women honestly endeavoured to go forward step by step in all the kinds of work their social position demanded of them. That was how it was in the golden age.'[19] According to this view, the advent of widespread mechanisation put an end to this Paradise on earth as machines took over what had been women's work and the centre of production was transferred from the home to the factory. Women were relegated to exclusively reproductive tasks and a market economy arose which was to infiltrate even the life of the emotions. This change was lamented by many. Woman had been disinherited of the best that she had had, work in the home for her family, and sadly, 'these times of happiness and blessing are indeed gone for ever'.[20]

An even more important result, however, was that unmarried middle-class women of modest means were now forced out into the hard world of paid labour, for how else were they to survive? The extended households in which they had formerly carried out useful tasks at the side of female relatives had been dissolved; such women were without a social role and dependent, if they did not or could not enter the market, on what was tantamount to the charity of relatives. The woman question to which, for some, the women's movement was an answer, was then for many very much a spinster's question; married women, it was assumed, would not want – or need – to earn a living. Attention was directed towards the institution of marriage and it was discovered, to many commentators' consternation, that for various reasons men were unwilling to marry – in the 1860s just under 50 per cent of Vienna's population over the age of 20 was unmarried[21] – engendering or at least aggravating the woman problem. This observation sparked off a veritable literature on the subject, both cynical and serious. The respected middle-class newspaper, the *Neue Freie Presse* (New Free Press), for example, opened a debate on the subject, referring in a jocular article to a letter from a concerned mother who had bewailed the fact that neither in the theatre nor in the ballroom nor even any longer on the bicycle path was it possible to find suitable men for her two marriageable daughters. The journalist found the 'good' Viennese lady's desperation 'funny',[22] but others treated the problem with more gravity and suggested a number of reasons for middle-class men's reluctance to submit to wedlock. Many pointed the finger of blame at the poor economic situation of many men, who with the best will in the world could not afford to marry until relatively late (about 30–35), at which age there were fewer men than women in the corresponding marriageable age range for women (18–25). But, as was also observed, even those men who could afford marriage were reluctant to commit themselves. It was not merely a question of finance. The greater individualism of the age was one suggested explanation; men were no longer so willing to submit to the personal limitations imposed by marriage, particularly as the material benefits of the married state could be procured for money elsewhere. Men could afford to become more choosy.[23] From another perspective bachelors were seen as shirking their duties by preventing women from fulfilling their natural destiny and cheating them of their right to a husband. 'Real' men would marry. 'The man has the duty to take a woman, and the woman the right to get a man,' was one terse summary.[24] Tenacious bachelors were indulging in the egocentric desire for a life of ease and luxury. But even worse were those who married for money after leading a dissolute life and who polluted the race with the consequences of venereal disease.

However, as another commentator maintained, men were also likely to be nervous of making a mistake and contemptuous of those women too obviously out to catch a husband.[25] The behaviour and expectations of the young ladies were also subjected to investigation. Prospective brides should not be too demanding and above all not too clever or educated. A man would not fall for an educated woman. 'The real, true man loves the woman who needs his protection and who looks up to his intellectual superiority,' was one confident pronouncement, '... he does not love the masculine woman!'[26] And indeed, not only that. 'The woman who loves wishes to do nothing but – subordinate herself, be able to subordinate herself, and how gladly she does so!'[27] Nor were young women to be too frivolous and eager for luxuries. Indeed, an exaggerated emphasis on appearance and the symbols of social status on the part of middle-class women in general was lamented. Changing toilette five times daily, which involved spending a quarter of the day in front of the mirror, lavish and too frequent dinner parties, *décolleté* ball dresses and talentless piano playing were all attacked by these cultural critics as evidence of mindless expense.[28] The ideal woman was in their eyes the self-sacrificing companion and mother, faithful and forgiving, and with enough education not to bore. 'And yet it must and will come again,' one commentator comfortingly concluded, 'the time when men find their peace and refuge at the bosom of their women, forget the burdens and haste of daily life, when children learn the most important alphabet at their mother's knee, the alphabet of the heart and of love, when the sanctity of the family, the basis of a great and happy state, is cultivated and maintained.'[29] The set of values advocated with this analysis is one of a return to simplicity, seriousness, the genuine – that is, it was claimed, the natural – in contrast to the degenerate, unnatural and egoistic culture of the modern age. A new sobriety was to make itself felt, a process of personal purification had to be undergone and priorities set straight. And for young women that meant, above all, domesticity and modesty, true love and willing self-sacrifice.

Yet how was this desired return to married domesticity to be achieved? For many observers the answer to this was clear in one respect. Women should not strive for men's rights, for by storming the bastions of the male professions, or even entering the market, they would deprive men of a living wage and themselves of the chances of marriage and happiness in motherhood.[30] In addition, by promoting women's independence rather than dutiful dependence, female campaigners for women's rights posed a threat to the institution of the family and, of course, betrayed their own femininity. Instead of searching for viable alternatives to marriage, many commentators contented themselves with lamenting modern developments, praising marriage and motherhood, and implying that with a bit of luck a moderately good-looking and demure girl would get her man in the end. As Olga Waissnix bitterly remarked to the writer Arthur Schnitzler: 'Marriage is prescribed us as the only profession which can bring us happiness; if we don't find it, *tant pis*, calmly renounce and bear it is the message then! – But do you know that that demands a heroism of which not one single man in a thousand would be capable!'[31] Only a few searched for remedies, including methods by which intractable men could be encouraged to marry. Sidonie von Grünwald-Zerkowitz, for example, a flamboyant figure – from 1889–90 she was a member of the Association for Extended Women's Education in Vienna (*Verein für erweiterte Frauenbilding in Wien*),[32] but by 1899 had become anathema to the women's movement[33] – devised an elaborate system whereby girls who lacked the all-important dowry but were otherwise highly marriageable, that is, by her definition, healthy and likely to produce healthy offspring, might find marriage and motherhood. A tax on unmarried, childless and widowed men was to be imposed and paid into a state dowry fund, which would then be distributed in the form of a grant to those women excellently qualified to regenerate the race. If all else failed, women could be shipped out to far-off parts as governesses; there they would be almost sure to find a husband, such was the dearth of white women.[34]

Other commentators displayed a greater openness to some of the claims of the women's movement although they also maintained a critical distance. Women's need to have greater access to employment possibilities was the claim most widely accepted. This was, however, seen almost exclusively as a definite second best to marriage and in many cases sharply distinguished from any wider claims to women's rights, particularly political ones. A distinction emerged between 'working, struggling women and girls, striving to go forwards and upwards' and the '"emancipated" woman, seized by a sort of megalomania'.[35] The financial independence of the former was seen to make her both a regrettable but necessary victim of the system and one of the vanguard of liberation. The latter on the other hand was regarded as the promoter of the lamentable and unnatural state of marriagelessness and as a threat to the family and indeed the whole of the human race.[36] She was the *hors sexe*, the masculine woman who wished to bring other women down to the level of men, confusing equality with economic necessity.[37] Yet improved employment conditions and opportunities for working-class women were greeted as necessary; in this way the 'woman question' was conveniently reduced to a complicating aspect of the 'social question'.[38]

This group of commentators took up, then, a conservative position. Lamentably, the modern world of mechanisation, the dominance of the market, egoism and a craving for luxury were such that not all women could find marriage and motherhood and realise woman's role as the natural educator of humanity. A number had to remain alone and fend for themselves, and should be supported in their unhappy fate. Yet whether in the domestic or public arena, all women could play an important role in cultural development, namely through complementation. 'Like individuals, so too should the sexes exert a mutual influence and exchange and complement their abilities,' it was declared.[39] This, however, assumed that women remained women. 'In order to do justice to the tasks creation presents her, woman has only to preserve what is feminine about her at all times, that is, to be the seat of the sublime, the source of mildness and the focus of decency and morality.'[40] The women 'fighting for emancipation' were in danger of losing this prerogative, it was noted, and of succumbing to the socialist preachings of equality.

Yet who *did* perceive themselves to be supporters of the women's movement and how did *they* describe themselves? First of all, they were careful to say what they were not. They were not the 'emancipated women' feared by the conservatives for their transgression of prescribed cultural boundaries, either as the representatives of sexual libertinage or as the viragos who took 'pleasure in masculine habits', smoked, rode astride, cut their hair short, liked to travel dressed like men and lowered their voice to a bass.[41] And they were certainly not that most 'free' woman of all, the prostitute, even if the two merged in the popular imagination. Indeed, for the feminists, it was in the first resort not a question of emancipation or freedom at all. Nor were they the 'modern women' of the conservatives, the representatives of cultural decline, pampered hothouse plants, living in the lap of enervating luxury, bored and shirking their familial duties. Nor were they unfeminine women who did not take fright at exposing the 'ugliest and basest sides of the social question'.[42] And certainly they were not the representatives of a fad, jumping on to every bandwagon and parrotingly preaching women's rights and independence merely because it was 'the fashion'.[43] Yet neither were they primarily 'feminists'. The term 'feminist' (German: *Feminist*) was at this time usually reserved for male supporters of the movement by its opponents. It was applied to those men who supported a greater female influence in public life but were in the popular imagination often considered to be effeminate. The female counterpart of this (*Feministin*) was not used even moderately widely by the women of the movement until just before 1914.[44] And of course, in their own eyes they were not the one-sided eccentric ladies or militant campaigners for women's rights that even some unusually well-educated and independent women thought them to be.[45]

In their own opinion they were 'progressive women'. For these women, the feminist movement was above all about promoting the natural progression of culture to a higher level. They shared the analysis of their critics that modern culture was in need of regeneration; they agreed with the conservatives that the modern age was marked by egoism and a lack of leading ideals. But they differed crucially in their conceptions of that longed-for regeneration. And on this essential point the feminists themselves parted ways.

The main proponent of visionary feminism was the primary school teacher and leading figure of the General Austrian Women's Association (*Allgemeiner Österreichischer Frauenverein*) Auguste Fickert (see figure 1). For her, it was important to make a sharp distinction between campaigners for women's rights who merely wanted equality in the shape of the rights of men, and her view of political engagement in the women's movement which had more far-reaching goals. 'The attainment of rights is not the goal of the women's movement,' she firmly declared.[46] 'It is altogether a petty point of view to squabble for rights and has got middle-class women the name of "women's righters", a name which will always have an unpleasant ring of meanness and "I told you so". Let us not forget,' she warned, 'how closely right and force have always been connected, that the struggle for rights should always be only a means, never an end in itself. We do not want to imitate men who in the course of history have generally used their attained rights only to oppress those weaker than themselves. For us it is a question of something much higher.'[47] Although acknowledging the need for rights as armour in the struggle for existence that circumstances had forced upon women, Fickert was anxious to give the women's movement more of a visionary dimension. This can be most concisely summed up as a vision of the women's movement as a moral force. 'The women's movement . . . is the bearer of new moral ideals, and it expects women's entry into public life to bring the moral regeneration of civilised humanity.'[48] For Fickert this meant above all the abolition of relations of capitalist exploitation (wage slavery), and more particularly the abolition of the exploitation of women by men (sexual slavery). Both forms of exploitation were a matter of economics and psychology, and so it followed that changing external conditions alone would not suffice. 'People must undergo an inner change,'

1. Portrait photograph of Auguste Fickert, *c.*1890, Vienna. Österreichische Nationalbibliothek.

Fickert insisted, 'they must overcome the slave mentality which still holds them captive in the present order of things.'[49] 'A new social order is . . . not possible . . . as long as those who comprise it remain as they are,' she emphasised.[50] Yet it was above all the female individual who had to change if this moral elevation and the abolition of relations of exploitation were to occur, for Fickert was convinced that 'we women have a great ethical mission to fulfil, not because we are by nature better, more moral than men, but because brute strength, physical power is denied us and making human society moral is in our most personal interests'.[51] In contrast to that of many other active supporters of the women's movement, this vision was not that of a feminine but of a feminist culture. It was based not on a concept of a natural femininity, motherliness or motherhood, but on a social role woman could adopt in order to moderate or overthrow patriarchy.

A sound basis of this new moral social order freed from relations of oppression could be offered, according to Fickert, only by 'the merging of intelligence with morality'.[52] Woman was to become aware of her position in the existing system of power relations and of how she could help to change it. Intellectual awakening was, for Fickert, largely consciousness raising. It meant familiarity with a 'way of thinking and perceiving which corresponds to the development of modern science',[53] that is, according to Fickert's view of science, it was anti-authoritarian (primarily anti-clerical) and led by a belief in upward evolution. Some women, the so-called 'de-classed', middle-class working women, had already come to experience such changes. Driven by the 'furies of hunger', they had been forced to comprehend their suffering as 'a necessary phase in the history of the evolution of the human race'.[54] But as a result they were no longer sexual slaves; they were in fact released from the 'doll's existence' to which an exhausted cultural era had banished them. And it was they who could combine the two tendencies of the women's movement, the 'aristocratic-individualist' tendency with the 'democratic-altruist' one, not only to unsettle party political life but also to give politics itself a new content: 'It [the women's movement] turns to the mass of women and tries to make them enthusiastic for what is new, what is coming, by pointing out to them how they have been abused as a result of their intellectual abilities having been thwarted. It demands of them that they call their personal dignity to mind in order to intervene with awareness in the formation of human community.'[55]

Fickert however did not consider this 'tearing down of the barriers which have prevented the development of [women's] humanity'[56] to be restricted to middle-class working women. The new social order which was the goal of the women's movement was to be free not only of sex slavery but also of wage slavery under capitalism. This meant for the labour movement, as for the women's movement, not only external but also personal change. 'In both cases,' Fickert asserted of these movements, 'it is a question of a deepening . . . of individuals, of their awakening to become personalities aware of themselves and their position with regard to others.'[57] Following an easy symmetry, Fickert declared the abolition of sex slavery to be the concern of the woman question and the abolition of wage slavery that of the social question. In her opinion both movements were working towards the same ultimate goal and she enjoined both to invest their as yet unused intellectual and moral powers to the benefit of the community, for then 'a new and better order of present society, which is still so marked by power and the exploitation of the weak, will not be a quite hopeless utopia'.[58] Social Democracy was, she maintained, taking important steps in this direction. 'By making women aware of all the power games which the present order of things means for them, namely economic, social, sexual bondage, [it] therefore leads women . . . by a detour to the same goal that the women's movement attempts to reach directly.'[59] Working-class women and the abolition of capitalism played a central role in Fickert's vision, for, as she claimed, 'anyone who has recognised the private capitalist means of production to be the root of the economic and social misery of the bourgeois world will be anti-capitalist, will strive for a different organisation of society'.[60] And in her practical involvement she rarely forgot the working class.

However, neither rights nor socialism was the final goal of Fickert's vision, but aware, moral individuals. This goal could be achieved above all by women, who would then educate others for the coming age. 'Even if women's emancipation brings an extension of our rights,' Fickert declared, 'it is not external change but what we win in terms of personal development which will be decisive for the future organisation of our society. Our final goal is therefore not the acknowledgement of rights, but the elevation of our intellectual and moral level, *the development of our personality*.'[61] The moral society such personal development would help to foster was not an end in itself. It was desirable because it would bring happiness to all; woman's elevation meant 'an era of blossom, of growth, of happiness' for humanity as a whole.[62]

Fickert's vision of the 1890s unites various elements in an unusual mixture. It accepts the need for equal rights but relegates these to a precondition, a means to an end. The end is making society moral; yet Fickert, in contrast to many, does not see this as woman's mission by virtue of any natural feminine moral superiority or maternal qualities, but thanks to her social role and outsider status. Woman's motherly qualities are of significance but not in any extended sense of social motherliness. Her 'virtues' of self-sacrifice, love, devotion are not given primacy here, or woman as priestess in the temple of ideals, tirelessly nourishing the fire at the altar of the Good, the True and the Beautiful,[63] or woman as the protector of morality; instead the intellectual, politically aware woman is paramount. It is she who will bring morality. And it is not the family which is praised as the bulwark of the new moral social order but the working woman. She is not the pitiable creature denied its 'natural profession' but the pioneer of a new age. In Fickert's vision woman is not the complement of man, but the instigator of a social order which upsets the prevailing bourgeois masculine order instead of preserving it.

The feminism from which Fickert was so concerned to distance herself was represented in Vienna above all by Marianne Hainisch, wife of a cotton-factory owner and leading member of the League of Austrian Women's Associations (*Bund Österreichischer Frauenvereine*) (see figure 2). She was the figurehead of a visionary feminism which although preaching cultural regeneration through woman did not involve a challenge to the status quo of power relations as Fickert's feminist vision did. On the contrary, it was content to limit the challenge to some of the consequences of those power relations. Yet like Fickert – and indeed the conservatives – Hainisch took up a position which was critical of her times; she regarded these as degenerate, egoistic and lacking in real morality. And like these other com-

2. Portrait of Marianne Hainisch by Marianne von Eschenburg, *c.*1890. Oil on canvas, 65.1 × 50.2 cm. Österreichische Nationalbibliothek.

mentators she claimed to struggle for the elevation of humanity. This was to be achieved by the women's movement, for it was 'the most effective means of liberating women from their apathy, passivity and indifference so that they can perform their most specific tasks and the great tasks of humanity, it is . . . the means of raising the whole population to a higher level'.[64] Hainisch's vision of those 'great tasks of humanity' differed from Fickert's. For Hainisch it was not a question of removing 'brutal powers' and relations of exploitation, nor of seeing women and the working class as the restructurers of the social order, but of 'welfare initiatives for all those truly in need'.[65] Thus while Fickert emphasised that the women's movement was more than merely the struggle for rights and the integration of women into the masculine status quo, Hainisch defined the movement as 'the call of one half of humanity for its civil rights',[66] and the League asserted that its task was 'to promote the moral, intellectual and economic development of woman, to achieve for her a more influential position in society and the world of paid labour'.[67] 'Equal rights' and 'equality' are the key-words for Hainisch and the League in contrast to Fickert's leitmotifs of power relations and personal growth.

Not surprisingly, the arguments used by the two visionaries also differed. Hainisch's concept of justice rests on the balance between social roles and rights, the latter being a reward for fulfilled duties. In the case of women, however, it was clear that an imbalance pertained, duties outweighing rights. This imbalance, Hainisch claimed, was particularly blatant within the family, woman's particular sphere of activity. 'The most disgraceful injustice is done us at the side of the beloved spouse, at our own hearth. We, who know no bounds to our devotion to our child . . . we, who cease to wish, to strive for ourselves and live only in our child, we have no rights to our child! The greatest hardship is done us in the family.'[68] Not only was such a situation a crying injustice, the achievement of women's rights would, Hainisch argued, be in the interests of society as a whole for this would raise the general moral and intellectual level. Equal education opportunities for women would promote general development and protect society from the forces of reaction, 'for women's education is the bulwark against the oppressive remains of the barbarians and against the insane notions about woman which were rife in the nineteenth century. . . . What we achieve for the development and recognition of women's intellect we achieve for mankind.'[69] At the same time women's rights would promote moral progress. This they would do by bolstering the family, 'the highest thing that the moral world knows',[70] for woman as mother and wife was the educator of the coming generation to true morality. Yet although she was to have equal rights, woman was on no account to be considered to be the same as man: equal but different was the motto. The 'eternal feminine' would not vanish, Hainisch emphasised, allaying any fears. 'Nature sees to it that the eternal feminine does not disappear. Governing all relations, conquering all obstacles, levelling all divisions, something powerful works above us: love. . . . It [love] will remain for ever, it will make devotion, self-sacrifice, humility the highest bliss for woman for ever and ever.'[71] It was nature which would prevent women from doing anything that went against their femininity and their natural talents. 'There is in nature a law of selection,' Hainisch maintained, echoing a common argument of many liberal feminists, 'which sees to it better than all prohibitive measures that inability does not become rife.'[72] It was a matter of letting woman discover what her nature was and then attaining the corresponding rights. Granted, women were on average intellectually inferior to men, but this was a result of arrested development. It was not nature but the forces of barbarism that had weakened woman physically and intellectually.[73] So it was 'the duty of women not to rest until they have attained both the development and unfolding of their natural abilities and also the rights which correspond to their true nature'.[74]

For Hainisch, then, as for Fickert, the goal is to make society moral, but whereas for Fickert this means abolishing relations of power, for

Hainisch it means gaining power via rights. Like Fickert, Hainisch does not base women's moral influence on any natural superior morality leading to social mothering but above all on her familial mothering role, to which she gives greater emphasis than Fickert. In addition, again like Fickert, she couples morality with intellectual development, but again she interprets this differently. Unlike Fickert, Hainisch sees this more in terms of a conventional education which would equip woman for her social tasks either as wife and mother or as independent working woman and less in terms of personal development and moral elevation, as Fickert does. And although both are well aware of the 'social problem', Hainisch chooses to solve it by charity measures rather than undermining capitalism. In short, for Hainisch the women's movement is to shore up the status quo by extending women's range of influence there, mainly through rights. The well-being of society is to be increased but without altering the existing structure; there is no awareness that the structure itself might be harmful.

Yet although the visions differed fundamentally, neither entailed any gender struggle; these feminists were not the virago man-haters even supporters of the Social Democratic women's movement thought them to be, claiming that 'these women do not fight the whole ruling system, the cause of every oppression, rather they fight men'.[75] On the contrary, the writer, artist and feminist theorist, Rosa Mayreder (see figure 3), Fickert's right-hand woman from autumn 1893 to the turn of the century, declared in 1896:

> It is becoming increasingly impossible for me to see 'men' as the enemies of women's concerns. . . . I for my part think there are a number of people who belong to us – men and women. One can quarrel about the percentage of participation – according to my subjective experience however the male sex would be represented in much larger numbers. That is why I do not believe in the 'sisterhood' of women nor in the task of women to unite against men.[76]

Fickert was not prepared to go quite so far, maintaining that a degree of female autonomy was a necessary first step if the vision was to become reality. Women had first to become fully developed personalities before they could enter the male public arena and support any one political party. Yet she was also anxious to emphasise the union of interests of the sexes, explaining that 'the women's secession is not directed against man, it does not want to rebuild the old edifice which has become too cramped . . . ; it wants to erect a new building – roomy, high, spacious, light, for joint work between men and women, with rooms commanding an extensive view, with cosy, peaceful alcoves for shared happiness'.[77]

In accordance with this, men did play a significant role in the

3. Portrait photograph of Rosa Mayreder in a reform dress, *c.*1905, Vienna. Österreichische Nationalbibliothek.

middle-class women's movement. This they were allowed to do not only because the women involved were dependent on the support of men in Parliament, as they themselves had no direct representation there, but also because male support fitted the vision; as it was a question of the progress of humanity, not of women's rights alone, anyone who was prepared to support progress was welcome. Luckily, this vision was also shared by some men: social reformers, university professors, left-wing middle-class intellectuals and liberals. They were largely the male counterparts of the feminists in terms of social background and political beliefs and many had personal connections with the feminists. Together they created a loosely woven network, and formed the left-liberal, social reformist vanguard of Vienna at the turn of the century.[78] These men too believed in progress towards a more moral, reasonable society, and maintained that woman had a central role to play in that process. 'The level of education and choice of profession for women should in no way be restricted,' the physicist Ernst Mach declared, for the uneducated woman would perpetuate superstition and prevent progress; 'how is humanity to progress safely if not even half of it is walking on an enlightened path,' he asked rhetorically.[79] Friedrich Jodl, the philosopher, emphasised on the other hand woman's moralising role. 'We are of the opinion,' he declared at the constituting meeting of the Viennese Ethical Society (*Wiener Ethische Gesellschaft*) in 1894, 'that without women no deeper changes in the moral spirit are possible, that it is precisely woman who must be won for our ideas, and that once she is won, she will be their most effective exponent.'[80] As Hermann Bahr explained of these male feminists who, amongst other things, supported women's claims to suffrage, 'It is not so much out of liking for women that these men demand female suffrage as out of sympathy for men's politics, not for women's sake but for the sake of politics, because they hope that with women a new moral element will force its way into politics, an element which it [politics] needs in order to be up to the great tasks of the times.'[81]

This positive view of male feminists was by no means widely shared. Men who engaged in women's agitation were rejected and ridiculed by many and regarded as supporting the 'decline of the sexes'. Observers like Liebenfels considered these feminists – for him they could only be liberals or non-Aryans – to be castrated collaborators in what would be the 'legally regulated and planned extermination of the last remains of the heroic and aristocratic race'.[82] Socialists, unhappily married men, or starry-eyed adolescents who were running away from reality to seek comfort in the ideal of the woman of the future, petty-bourgeois men 'who have pledged themselves to a progressive programme *en bloc*'[83] and were out to emancipate everything, and those in love with an emancipated woman – these were all feminists, deluded creatures who mistook women's agitation, which was in fact aimed at sexual freedom and nothing else, for agitation for entry into the male world, and by so doing were contributing to the lamentable masculinisation of woman.

Despite these opinions, the male feminists remained true to their intellectual and moral support and played an important practical role in sustaining the movement. They supported the women's associations through donations, through offers of premises for meetings, and of course through membership. In some associations, for example the General Austrian Women's Association, men could not sit on the committee or be full members, but in others this was not the case. In 1900 the professor of law Edmund Bernatzik and the anatomist Emil Zuckerkandl were voted on to the committee of the Association for Extended Women's Education, the zoologist Carl Brühl and the classicist Theodor Gomperz were amongst its honorary members, and the physicist Ludwig Boltzmann was a full member.[84] Men also spoke at women's meetings, wrote for women's papers and, importantly, a few of the left-liberal politicians amongst them – particularly Engelbert Pernerstorfer, Ferdinand Kronawetter and above all Julius Ofner – brought the women's petitions to Parliament. Others founded initiatives aimed specifically at women, above all in higher education. The historian Ludo Moritz Hartmann and the Union of Austrian University Teachers (*Vereinigung Österreichischer Hochschuldozenten*) initiated the association, Athenäum: Association for the Holding of Academic Courses for Women and Girls (*Athenäum: Verein für die Abhaltung von wisssenschaftlichen Lehrkursen für Frauen und Mädchen*) in 1900. This organised lecture courses with the aim, declared in the statutes, of 'spreading education [and] leading women out of their intellectual narrowness'.[85] Several distinguished teachers, most of them with strong socialist leanings, participated. Karl Renner, later a leading socialist statesman, held a course on state theory, the social scientist Max Adler led one on social philosophy, and Carl Grünberg, a political economist, gave lectures on economic theory and history. Emil Zuckerkandl and Julius Tandler, who was an anatomist and influential local politician, also took part. The courses were well attended, although the traditionally female subjects of literature and art history still proved the most popular and the Association did not manage to achieve its goal of being accessible to working women; it remained largely restricted to the prosperous middle class. On a much smaller scale, Brühl held natural science lectures on Sundays which were free of charge and to which women were expressly welcomed – a fact not to be taken for granted; from 1863 to 1890 they were attended by a total of 4,262 women, about 12.5 per cent of the audience.[86] He also organised lecture courses in 1895–6 'for educated women and girls' in which he presented his theory on the central position of woman in the process of evolution, backing this up with examples from anatomy, philosophy and the products of the imagination: literature, art, sculpture and music. The lectures were illustrated by demonstrations and recitals.[87] Bernatzik for his part campaigned for women's admission to study law at university, while others defended women's study of medicine in the face of attacks from the medical profession, and in 1902 many university professors responded positively to a questionnaire on co-education at university level. Men's participation was not limited to higher education. The gynaecologist Hugo Klein was instrumental in founding the Austrian League for the Protection of Mothers (*Österreichischer Bund für Mutterschutz*) and also an association for the reform of women's clothing, and Ofner proved an indefatigable supporter of a wide range of women's issues and organisations.[88] This male support helped the women's movement in practical matters and also gave it a visibility and status in public political discussion that it would otherwise not have had.

Feminism was, then, not separatist in ideology; the autonomy the women strove for was limited and largely pragmatic. There was much co-operation on both sides, the women's movement being in the eyes of many one of a number of social reform movements with the same overall goal: the upward development of the human race. These progressive women also participated in the culture of their male counterparts. The Association for Adult Education (*Volksbildungsverein*) for example, necessarily appealed to these women's ideal of the union of education and individuality, and the names of many supporters of the women's movement can be found as signatories to a call for the foundation of an adult education centre: Bernatzik, Hartmann, Jodl, Mach, Ofner, Tandler and also Mayreder figure in the list.[89] Marianne Hainisch gave talks at the Association, and Fickert and Mayreder were at one time anxious to co-operate with it. As early as 1895 Mayreder was praising the Association, maintaining that 'this system of adult education classes seems . . . to point the way in which the future intellectual development of the female sex will be made possible'.[90] In 1907 Fickert thought of putting this into practice, suggesting the joint production of a women's paper which would have a wider circulation than one produced by the General Austrian Women's Association alone.

Initiatives by such left liberal organisations to bring about a change in morality were of course also supported by women associated with the women's movement. Grete Meisel-Hess, Camilla Theimer and Henriette Herzfelder, for example, were speakers at the enquiry on marriage law, instigated by the Cultural-Political Society (*Kulturpolitische Gesellschaft*) in 1905.[91] The Ethical Society, which propagated the spread of humanitarian ideas freed from religious morality and party political allegiance, also became a point of overlap for feminists and other social reformers. The first committee included Marianne Hainisch and Rosa Mayreder along with Jodl, Ofner and Arthur Gundaccar von Suttner (husband of Bertha),[92] and women's issues were given considerable attention. The move which perhaps drew most attention to the Society on that score was the women workers' enquiry it instigated in 1896. Representatives from almost all political parties in Austria took part as well as feminists: Therese Schlesinger-Eckstein, at that time a member of the General Austrian Women's Association, and Fickert were commission members along with Victor Adler, Michael Hainisch (son of Marianne) and Ofner.[93] To a commission of thirty men and five women, 300 women workers gave evidence of their working conditions and of the misery and sexual harassment they suffered. The enquiry remained, however, largely without practical results for the women workers, despite the hopes of the commission that it would disturb the bourgeois conscience. Moreover women were not welcomed by the progressive political parties at first. In the 1890s even the Social Politicians asked women to leave the room during an election meeting, and, as Fickert pointed out, largely neglected the concerns of women in their election programme.[94] However, by December 1900 the General Austrian Women's Association could proudly report that matters had changed: the successes of the Christian Social women in election agitation had opened men's eyes to women's political power.[95]

Yet as the incident with Dr Wähner and the *Deutsche Zeitung* indicates, matters had not changed enough. 'In France or Italy these people [Dr Wähner and consorts] would have been beaten to death . . . ; in England or America they would have been tarred and feathered,' the *Dokumente der Frauen* indignantly exclaimed, 'But in Vienna?! . . . Dr Wähner will remain a city councillor . . . middle-class women will . . . shake his hand. . . . We are not for lynch justice but such an uncontrolled reaction of outrage is a better sign of a healthy moral sense . . . than this putrid apathy.'[96] Although the supposed reaction abroad is no doubt exaggerated here, the point the anonymous writer is making is valid. Viennese feminists did have special problems to contend with. The Habsburg Empire was not only very Catholic and clerical, but also authoritarian, with no democratic, parliamentary tradition worth speaking of and still largely feudalistic with a relatively small liberal middle class, all elements which tended to make change particularly difficult.[97] In addition, a large proportion of women in the Habsburg Empire had certain rights usually denied their foreign sisters; some could, for example, vote in local and provincial elections, hold a job (except trade) without prior consent of their husbands, and had considerable rights over their own property. Many, above all married, women could claim to be satisfied with the status quo and saw little reason for change. This, combined with an inveterate conservatism, led to the apathy commented on in the *Dokumente der Frauen* and much lamented by the leading feminists. So not surprisingly, the Viennese feminist movement was late in getting going and the first wave of autonomous initiatives was to a large extent prompted by the question of how unmarried and impoverished middle-class women were to survive in an economic world dominated by the market. The initial focus turned largely to women as workers and the answer was sought in women's professional organisation, rather than in any wider vision.

PART ONE

AUTONOMOUS WOMEN AND VISIONARY POLITICS

CHAPTER 1

The First Wave

Vocational Initiatives

The autonomous women's association which is usually regarded as initiating the 'era of the organised woman'[1] in Austria was the Viennese Women's Employment Association (*Wiener Frauen-Erwerbverein*) which was founded in November 1866. The impulse came from the Association for Economic Progress (*Verein für volkswirtschaftlichen Fortschritt*), an all-male organisation which, following the tradition of economic Liberalism, promoted such a foundation for reasons of national economy rather than sexual politics and pragmatically recognised middle-class women's increased need to earn in the wake of large-scale industrialisation. More immediately, however, the Employment Association was a direct response to the events of 1866, which had brought the defeat of Austria by the Prussians in the Six Weeks' War and financial ruin to many middle-class families. 'Tragedy after tragedy,' ran the official version, 'occurred in homes in which women were used to receiving the means to sustain life from their caring spouse. Now these women had to think of earning those means in order to protect themselves and their loved ones from destitution.'[2] Thus initially at least, married as well as unmarried middle-class women were seen to need access to the market. That most were lamentably ill-equipped for its rigours became a *cri de coeur* of those concerned to alter the situation. Marianne Hainisch recounted how a married woman friend's plight on her husband's illness opened her own eyes to middle-class women's helplessness:

> As I saw her go, a beggar condemned to beg all her life in spite of her talents and so-called good education, an indescribable feeling overcame me. Now I, too, knew what my education was worth. I, who looked after my home well and conscientiously, what was I good for, what was I without it? And who guarantees every girl a

> household and husband and home for all her days!? . . . I suddenly clearly saw that woman, too, must be self-supporting. What use is an education which leaves us in the lurch when we need it![3]

The primary aim of the first large-scale and lasting women's organisations was to give those lower-middle-class women in need the training which would enable them to earn enough to support themselves and any dependants. After overcoming some reluctance on the part of women to take on the duties involved, the leadership of the Employment Association was entrusted to Iduna Laube. It was a decidedly genteel upper-middle-class affair, run by comfortably off women not themselves directly affected, who were of Liberal social reformist persuasion and fired by the Liberal belief in education as the path to self-help and independence. They lacked any aspirations to political rights or wide-ranging social change and had no intention of challenging the place of women's work in the social fabric or the class specificity of the various occupations. While fear of proletarianisation and even pauperisation made factory work unthinkable for such women, petty-bourgeois women were to learn petty-bourgeois female occupations and not strive for the opening of the professions, the prerogative of middle-class men. Thus, significantly, the first development was a school for sewing linen which housed, as a great novelty, four sewing machines.[4] Other initiatives of the Association subsequently included a commercial school and courses in embroidery, lace-making, hairdressing, dressmaking, cookery and housekeeping.

Yet as the problem of women's employment was seen to be also very much one facing the genteel but impoverished middle classes, the Employment Association was concerned, too, to build up an academic school for girls to ease their entry into female white-collar employment. This was founded in the autumn of 1871 in the form of a four-year *höhere Bildungsschule* where the emphasis was still placed on practical education, after a proposal brought by Hainisch for the foundation of a grammar school for girls had been rejected by the Association as too revolutionary. But it was only after 1908 that the school, which in 1889 became a *lycée*, that is, a glorified young ladies' college, was allowed to issue its own state-recognised leaving certificates.[5] Thanks to the support of Karl Lueger, the Association's various vocational schools and the *lycée* moved in 1910 to magnificent purpose-built premises, ceremoniously inspected by the Emperor in September of that year, complete with a large veranda, gym, science laboratory and swimming pool. A boarding school for thirty-two girls was also incorporated into the design. Although the vocational courses such as cooking, sewing and housekeeping were not abandoned before 1914, the academic school became increasingly important in the Association's activities, largely because a wealth of women's associations and vocational schools, some of them state-funded, emerged in the last third of the nineteenth century and took over the Employment Association's pioneering task of women's vocational training. Indeed, the Association was followed only a few weeks after its foundation by the Association for Girls' Support (*Mädchenunterstützungsverein*) with largely the same goals, in 1874 by a school for embroidery, and a year later by the Vienna Association of Housewives (*Wiener Hausfrauenverein*) with cookery and servants' schools attached.

The boundary line between these self-help vocational training initiatives and middle-class semi-charitable organisations was, however, not always completely clear. Although it was recognised that the needy had to learn to help themselves, the initiative was invariably taken by women of the upper middle class on behalf of their unfortunate – lower-class – sisters. The Women's Union for Social Welfare Work (*Frauenvereinigung für soziale Hilfstätigkeit*, 1896) did, for example, run cookery and housekeeping schools and after-school children's groups for working women, but it also lent second-hand children's clothing, undertook house visits in times of illness and offered various other welfare activities.[6] These initiatives were still partly in the time-worn tradition of middle-class ladies' charity work; class privileges were not touched, political awareness was as good as absent. Yet despite this these vocational associations did make a political statement, for they unwittingly challenged the hitherto private if not ashamedly secret nature of middle-class women's employment by making it public and professional. Women were acknowledged to be trained workers. Traditional female activities became professionalised.

This change is illustrated by a vocational initiative of a rather different nature which appealed to a more upper-class, genteel milieu, the Art School Association for Women and Girls (*Verein Kunstschule für Frauen und Mädchen*). Although it did not share the aim of direct alleviation of women's financial plight to quite the same extent as the vocational associations obviously intended for the impoverished middle class, it undertook to train women to be professional artists and commercial designers, thus stepping beyond the conventional bounds of ladies' artistic dilletantism, by which art was merely 'a harmless amusement for the young lady of good family in the time between leaving school and getting engaged'.[7] It was founded in October 1897 by Rosa Mayreder, herself the first woman member of the Vienna Club of Watercolour Artists, Olga Prager, and the writer and literary critic Karl Federn. On opening in December of that year it was attended by sixteen pupils and two teachers – the distinguished landscape artist Tina Blau and the painter and illustrator Adalbert Franz Seligman – numbers rapidly rising to 190 pupils by 1905.[8] One year after opening it was able to expand its teaching staff to include Emil Zuckerkandl, who in the winter of 1898–9 gave a series of lectures on human anatomy.[9] Following a contemporary trend which reached its acme in Vienna in the work of the *Wiener Werkstätte*, the school wanted to overcome the artificial divisions between the arts and crafts and to this end established courses in applied art and engraving. Indeed, some pupils of the school later went on to design for the *Wiener Werkstätte* while others became some of Kolo Moser's most successful students at his ceramics class.[10] From 1902 it began to complement this curriculum with some courses which went beyond the canon of feminine artistic activity: a chiselling course under Georg Klimt (brother of Gustav), wood-cutting, and two years later a calligraphy course led by Rudolf von Larisch joined one in art embroidery. In contrast to the other vocational women's initiatives, the Art School was on the whole attended by the daughters of the better off and the intelligentsia and supported by progressives such as Friedrich Jodl, its first president, who in 1906 was succeeded in that capacity by the distinguished architect Karl Mayreder, husband of Rosa. The school was regarded as expensive but from 1908 received a substantial yearly subsidy from the Ministry of Education and was able to offer twenty-five free and twenty supported places. It continued to flourish even after the winter of 1920 when the Academy of Fine Arts at last opened its doors to women, for the number of places there was strictly limited.

This trend to found vocational schools did not, however, escape critical comment from contemporaries. The lengthy training, which in some cases might last three years, was criticised on the grounds that most of the young women in need of the vocations offered were not in a position either to pay the fees or to spend so much time on a course which involved a great deal of theory. A shortened, more practical training was suggested instead, and attempts by the women's movement to extend the sphere of female employment and open it to higher-status jobs, particularly in commerce and the professions, were opposed. 'The women's movement has remained sterile,' one commentator exclaimed. 'As far as intellectual life is concerned, it has not increased the sum of things of cultural value, economically it has only depressed wages and supported the machine in its work which destroys the family.'[11] Girls should instead be trained in a trade or in agriculture – a training which represented the best dowry. Yet despite such voices, by the end of the first decade of the twentieth century the need for women's vocational training was no longer questioned by the authorities at least. In 1910 the Ministry of Public Labour ratified the opening of the vocational schools to women. It was a move which the League of Austrian Women's Associations greeted by publishing a vocational register in which the multitude of vocations now open to women were described and appraised in detail with the aim of helping women to choose a vocation,[12] but a move opposed by tradesmen and artisans, who saw their livelihoods threatened by female competition. Women's vocational training was, however, there to stay.

Educational Initiatives

The call, first made by Marianne Hainisch, for a grammar school for girls represented a potentially more subversive development than the vocational schools, for thus might the doors of the hitherto all-male professions be opened to women and a fundamental change in middle-class women's lives be brought about. At the same time, however, the revolutionary potential and proximity to women's emancipation which Hainisch's call implied were vigorously denied by its supporters. For many the – largely unacknowledged – fear of the breakdown of class barriers lay behind this denial. Just as the vocational schools were to prevent women of the lower middle class from slipping into the proletariat by offering them the skills necessary for appropriate occupations, so the girls' grammar school was to prevent the women of the upper middle class from slipping into the lower middle. Hainisch made this clear in her début speech at the third general meeting of the Employment Association in March 1870. Of the vocational schools, 'not one is suited to raise the level of education of girls from the middle-class intelligentsia and therefore to open profitable sources of income to them,' she maintained.[13] A girls' grammar school was necessary in order to prepare middle-class girls for an occupation appropriate to their social class; to earn a minimum wage was, she admitted, not difficult, but also not fitting for the bourgeoisie. It was necessary for *these* young women to receive a schooling which would enable them to enter the professions, and for this the schools traditionally reserved for such girls, the young ladies' colleges, were woefully inadequate; their aim, claimed Hainisch, was merely to train girls to please in order to catch a husband. Yet 'I was of course too progressive for the women of the committee,' she recalled. 'And thus I found that men were more favourably disposed to my talks than most women.'[14] A bank made a generous donation towards the foundation of a girls' secondary school, the Ministry of Education organised an inquiry, the state agreed to a subsidy – but the Employment Association's committee agitated not for a full secondary school as Hainisch had wanted but merely for a slightly more demanding ladies' college. The matter was allowed to slip until 1888, when the Association for Extended Women's Education was founded with the express aim of agitating for a grammar school for girls.

A petition signed by six women's organisations, including the Association for Extended Women's Education, for the foundation of such a grammar school and the admittance of women to a full course of study at the arts and medical faculties of the universities was handed in to the Imperial Assembly in 1890.[15] But the situation did not change until autumn 1892, when the Association for Extended Women's Education took matters into its own hands and opened the first class of a private *gymnasiale Mädchenschule*, a girls' school along the lines of a grammar school but without state recognition, the first of its kind in the German-speaking world. Several distinguished men such as Theodor Gomperz, the philosopher Wilhelm Jerusalem, Julius Ofner, the literary scholar Emil Reich and Ludo Moritz Hartmann as well as well-known women such as the writers Marie von Ebner-Eschenbach, Minna Kautsky and Emil Marriot (the pseudonym of Emilie Mataja), feminists like Hainisch and Fickert, and the pacifist Bertha von Suttner were active supporters of this project, but it was only when the director of Vienna's teacher training institute for grammar school teachers, Emanuel Hannak, recognised the role he could play as the school's director, that the project was really able to get off the ground. The special feature of the school was that the curriculum and standards demanded were equivalent to those of the boys' grammar schools. It took the significant step of asserting that there was only one education for both sexes and broke with the notion of gender-specific schooling. 'The general education of woman cannot be other than the general education of her time,' was the confident assertion.[16]

It was the first school in Vienna to bring girls up to the academic standards necessary for university entrance; this it did in the belief that if there were qualified women, and women's intellectual ability could be proved, resistancc to women's university entrance would wane. The girls were first taught by teachers from the boys' schools, for obviously it was only several years after the opening of Vienna University's arts faculty to women in the winter of 1897 that former pupils of the school could return as teachers. For many years the school-leaving examinations had to be sat at one of the boys' grammar schools, for the school was not allowed to hold the exams itself; it was not until 1906 that it was promised the right to set its own exams. Entrance was of course subject to examination, for high academic standards were the school's pride and it was conscious of being the élite school.[17] Results were about equivalent to those of the boys at the *akademisches Gymnasium*. The school could later boast several distinguished names amongst its old girls: the gynaecologist Dora Teleky, the feminist and pacifist Leopoldine Kulka, the writer and translator Helene (Scheu-)Riess,[18] all women who belonged to the feminist milieu. Despite many failings pointed out by the General

Austrian Women's Association – lack of a united administration, incompetent and rigid organisation, and lack of enough classrooms so that lessons had to be held in the Natural History Museum[19] – as well as opposition to the form of its foundation by some of the leading members themselves, the school flourished. There were twenty-eight girls by the end of the first year, with numbers rising to 131 by the end of the school year 1899–1900,[20] and by 1904–5 the school could boast the full eight classes of the state boys' grammar schools. In 1906, as the greatest accolade, it was allowed to call itself a *Mädchenobergymnasium* (upper grammar school for girls) in contrast to the much humbler *gymnasiale Mädchenschule* and received official state recognition for all classes. However, the school remained completely without government subsidy, so was restricted to those social classes which had the necessary means, and the view that a girl's education was worth paying for, although a number of aided places were available. Most pupils came from the families of leading businessmen, civil servants, army officers, teachers and of course the Viennese progressive intelligentsia;[21] between 35 and 40 per cent were Jews.[22]

The success of the school was due not only to parental support but also to the tenacity of the Association for Extended Women's Education in the face of numerous difficulties. Mistrust of women's secondary education was rampant. Many male teachers and examiners, and the authorities, proved sceptical. At the beginning the school had no premises of its own and was dependent on the unusual generosity of the Vienna City Council for permission to use the rooms and equipment of the teacher training institute. This permission was given only for one year at a time and was by no means to be taken for granted. A crisis occurred in 1903 when it was refused and the school was forced to look for new premises. It was only thanks to the generosity of the highly successful writer Marie von Najmájer, who had donated 40,000 crowns in 1901,[23] that the school was able to rent new premises, this time on a ten-year basis, and so at last had a more secure foundation.

That female secondary schooling was perceived as the greater potential threat was evident in the authorities' constant refusal to grant a subsidy to the grammar school as opposed to the (albeit modest) grant given to the school of the Employment Association or to the foundation of vocational training institutes.[24] To be sure, the authorities had often talked of the need for girls' secondary education – in Vienna in 1895 there were only five academic secondary schools for girls, all fee-paying, of course[25] – and in May 1900 the Ministry for Culture and Education organised an inquiry into the state of girls' secondary schooling to which women were invited to give their opinion. However the results were considered by those like Hainisch to be highly disappointing.[26] Grammar schools for girls were rejected by the Minister of Education, Wilhelm von Hartel, who reasoned that it was neither in the interests of the population as a whole nor in those of young women themselves to 'tear a large number of girls out of the sphere of their natural vocation and entice them to the learned professions'.[27] So the girls' *lycée* was introduced as the established form of secondary education in December 1900. The view of the government had been made clear almost a decade earlier: a sharp distinction was to be made, it had been stated, between the indisputable need to prepare women for employment and something more. On no account was the boys' school system merely to be transferred to girls. The *lycée* was to give girls a higher, general education fitting to what is 'specifically feminine'. For 'the first and highest task of educational administration as regards women's education will always remain that of educating woman to be the educator of her own children'.[28]

In view of such patriarchal attitudes on the part of the government it is not surprising that although the supporters of girls' grammar schools put up direct opposition, they explicitly dissociated their concern from the women's movement and everything which could be brought into connection with contemporary notions of women's emancipation and the politics of the woman question. They argued less in terms of women's emancipation or rights than in terms of morality. In a talk given in 1870 Hainisch emphasised the apolitical nature of her suggestions, declaring that secondary education would enable women not only to earn if need be but also to think and thus to lead more moral lives; they would spurn the frivolities of the average modern woman who forgot her housewifely and motherly duties and reject the craving for luxury of the emancipated women of the upper classes who had no, or refused to have any, family duties. On the contrary, the thinking woman of greater personal happiness and value would, she claimed, make moral and harmonious marriages more likely and would raise the general moral level of society. Of course, Hainisch did want to see women gain independence and a satisfying sphere of action, but only through work.[29] She joined those cultural critics who condemned the degeneration of modern life and propounded an ethics of bourgeois Enlightenment-Liberalism centring on work, which however, in the context of women's work, represented a transgression of the boundaries imposed on femininity.

Similarly, the Association for Extended Women's Education quite explicitly distinguished its demands from 'that St Simonistic' idea of emancipation – which it interpreted as a lack of attachments and making the sexes the same.[30] The Association went so far as to suggest that it was economic need and an empty life which caused otherwise high-minded women to turn to the women's movement. It thereby implied that recognition of the Association's demands would act as a bulwark against women's political demands.[31] Its declared aim was, in contrast, simply the promotion of the harmonious natural unfolding of femininity to its perfect completion, which meant the nurture of the independent personality and its adornment with knowledge. This aim it cherished for the sole reason that it is only the woman who is a person in her own right who can be of value to her husband and sons, and this after all was still the main duty of woman. Girls' secondary education had a very pragmatic *raison d'être*: it would 'make woman more useful to the state, more valuable for society and more indispensable in the home'.[32] Indeed, an education equal to that of men of the same social class acted as the best form of security and moral protection of the family, for it promoted marriage and refined the moral and intellectual link between parents and children.[33] Yet the spectre of middle-class proletarianisation, which particularly threatened the daughters of civil servants and army officers, was very real for both petitioners and petitioned, so the argument of morality and general benefit to society was interwoven with that of the burning necessity for education as a preliminary for suitable paid employment. Employment as opposed to education was, however, seen to be regrettable and primarily the – prosaic and personally limiting – domain of men.

A number of strands of argument intertwine here, none of which radically challenges the status quo. These women were concerned to show that they were conservative, no doubt partly from genuine belief but also partly for purely pragmatic reasons. The women's petitions and speeches were after all directed at a specific audience and intended to achieve a particular purpose which was dependent on the favour of those in power. That these women could also think along somewhat different lines is indicated by other arguments which are unobtrusively woven in. Women's right to education quite independent of the benefit gained by society was, for example, also asserted and justified in terms of women's contribution to the national wealth. Copious statistics were presented which demonstrated women's significant tax contribution. These were then contrasted with figures which showed how differently the state treated boys and girls in secondary education. Women paid 2/7 of direct taxation, it was claimed, while girls had to make do with about 1/15 of state finance of education (including vocational training). The injustice was apparent. As it explicitly said in an annual report, the Association was very well aware of the need to see the struggle for girls' secondary education in the context of that for women's rights and women's entry into the cultural sphere from which they were excluded.[34] But quite apart from this, as both Hainisch and the Association made clear, attempts to hinder women's struggle would necessarily fail, for the 'powerful tide of change'[35] was in their favour. Their demands were in accordance with the process of natural evolution, and thus endowed with almost superhuman qualities which made arguments superfluous. 'It is here no longer a question of the wish and will of the individual but of accomplished, inescapable facts,' the Association pronounced.[36]

And that did seem to be the case, for slowly but surely the bastions of male academic privilege were whittled away.[37] In March 1896 the first important step was taken by granting girls permission to sit the *Matura* (school-leaving exam) in a form which would entitle them to university study. In the same month medical diplomas gained abroad were allowed to be submitted to the authorities for official recognition, a long and trying process but one that did open the medical profession to women. These two concessions paved the way to the piecemeal opening of the universities to women, in which they had been tolerated only as guest auditors and denied the right to sit exams. In autumn 1897 the arts faculties of the universities were opened to women to follow a full course of study; at Vienna three women took advantage of this innovation in the first semester. Women wishing to study law had to be more patient. In spring 1899 Bernatzik asked the Law Faculty to appeal to the Minister for permission to open its doors to women.[38] The Faculty thereupon demanded a report, which Bernatzik duly supplied and which was published in its complete form by the Association for Extended Women's Education in its annual report for 1899–1900. The women were confident: 'We are convinced that this application will be granted; if not now then later. Men cannot remain passive when women are moving forwards in the spirit of the times.'[39] The times moved slowly however, for although the Faculty submitted the request to the Minister in 1900, by 1909 it had still received no reply, whereupon the Association again took matters into its own hands and itself submitted a request to the Minister. As it hinted, the reason why the Minister was so reluctant to grant this request was because it would open the door to the higher civil service, one of the status professions.

The Association for Extended Women's Education was defiantly concerned to promote the advancement of women; in addition to agitating for girls' state secondary education, running the grammar school and campaigning for women's university study, it organised a range of talks on related issues: Emil Reich on Ibsen and women's rights,[40] Carl Brühl, 'one of the most eager advocates of the equal competence of the female sex intellectually speaking',[41] on 'the gifts nature has endowed woman with and the consequences of this for the significance, place, tasks and rights of woman in human society', an anatomical, sociological report which used preserved brains as illustrative material,[42] the poet Richard von Kralik on Roswitha von Gandersheim,[43] and the writer Ricarda Huch on the influence of study and professional life on the female personality.[44] The Association flourished. In the year 1903–4 it could count a total of some 650 members, most from the intellectual, social reformist groups of Vienna.[45] Many supported the Association in financial terms, and Najmájer made her contribution not only through a donation in 1901 but also by setting up the first annual grant in 1898. This was earmarked for women students who followed a full course of study at Vienna University, although preference was to be given to old girls of the Association's grammar school and above all to the daughters of state officials and army officers.[46]

Representational Initiatives

Women already in paid employment were also very much a focus of attention, for their exploitation was all too apparent. Self-help organisations were initiated, to represent those working women's interests to the employers and government authorities, a need doubly felt not only because women were subject to sex discrimination at the workplace but also because their special interests were ignored by their male colleagues in the existing professional representative bodies. Indeed, women were often excluded – or even ejected – from these. In 1901 the Association of Postal Officials (*Postbeamtenverein*), for example, expelled its female members (a grand total of six), claiming that they were 'dangerous' – a move which earned the male postal officials ridicule from the feminists.[47] As in the case of the vocational schools, a very real need was seen to be met by these initiatives and so they multiplied. By 1914 a host of such organisations existed: women music teachers, midwives, actresses, writers and artists, and those female officials not in public service, to name just a few, had their own representative bodies.[48] These women's occupational groups brought together above all middle-class rather than working-class women, who found representation either in the Social Democratic or the Catholic groups.

Yet what did such groups really achieve for their members? Working conditions in the two main areas of employment open to middle-class women in the final third of the nineteenth century – teaching and governessing, and public service (above all in the Post Office) – were without doubt appalling. The organisations of these professional groups, the Association of Women Teachers and Governesses (*Verein der Lehrerinnen und Erzieherinnen*, founded in 1870) and the Association of Women Postal Officials (*Postbeamtinnenverein*, 1876), were, unsurprisingly, amongst the first women's occupational groups to be founded and were not sparing with their complaints. Attempts to alter working conditions remained tentative and piecemeal and were limited to alleviation rather than cure. The organisations offered women a support network, which although it might have made life more tolerable for them did not fundamentally change it. The Association of Women Teachers and Governesses, for example, professed in its statutes that the maintenance and promotion of the intellectual and material interests of its members was its goal.[49] It organised lectures, discussions, a library, and even excursions and visits to art institutions at reduced rates. It also published a newsletter, the *Mitteilungen des Vereins der Lehrerinnen und Erzieherinnen Österreichs* (from January 1893 *Die Lehrerinnen-Zeitung. Organ des Vereins der Lehrerinnen und Erzieherinnen Österreichs*), which acted as a platform for the exchange of views, tips and complaints, and as a noticeboard for events. As far as material interests were concerned, these were to be fostered by a free job agency service, a home for members, membership of a health insurance fund and, in cases of extreme need, interest-free financial support.[50] No mention was made at this stage of campaigning for equal pay or for equal promotion prospects: in Vienna in 1898 there was one headmistress, Marie Schwarz, compared to 90 headmasters of primary and state secondary schools, while 387 women and 476 men worked as temporary teachers.[51] No mention either was made of the abolition of the celibacy clause which in some provinces, although not Lower Austria, demanded of the woman teacher that she resign her post when she married or at least made her intention to marry *and* continue teaching dependent on the favour of the school authorities.[52] Not until just before the outbreak of the First World War was the demand for equal pay vociferously raised by women outside the General Austrian Women's Association at a solidarity meeting attended by women from socialist and Catholic women's organisations as well as the League of Austrian Women's Associations.[53]

The Association of Women Teachers and Governesses and its newsletter went no further than other initiatives and independent papers that emerged in the late 1880s and that originally focused on women teachers. The most important of the latter was *Der Lehrerinnen-Wart*, founded in 1889, which in 1891 attempted to extend its range and changed its name to *Neuzeit* and then three years later to *Frauenleben*. Yet criticism by female teachers who did not voice that criticism under the auspices of the General Austrian Women's Association was limited to remonstration when women teachers were slandered by members of Vienna City Council[54] and ineffectual, infrequent meetings protesting, for example, at the discrimination against Jews in the allocation of posts.[55] The most important aim, according to the *Lehrerinnen-Wart*, was 'tactfully' to represent women teachers' interests to all parties concerned.[56] No attempt was made to raise these women's consciousness. The articles focused on the school routine; school hygiene, praise and scolding in the kindergarten, gym in the girls' school, punishment and even a typology of schoolgirls were all given attention. The ideal woman teacher was to be 'selfless, amenable, always ready', the assistant to the male teacher just as the married woman is the helper of her husband; in short, a good colleague.[57]

This reservedly critical attitude and concentration on pragmatic measures was the characteristic feature of these early initiatives of working women. The Union of Working Women (*Vereinigung der arbeitenden Frauen*, founded in 1901), for example, an organisation which had an exceptionally wide circle of potential members – women officials in banks, at the railways, and in insurance and legal offices, secretaries, typists and commercial employees as well as those in lower-status jobs such as shop workers, seamstresses and tobacco sellers[58] – concentrated on vocational training facilities, pension rights, health insurance and a free job agency, as well as producing a paper and organising talks and discussion evenings. Yet at the same time, although recognising the need for organisation, the Union included in its statutes the 'maintenance of class interests'.[59] Class differences were not to be tampered with. The Association of Women Writers and Artists in Vienna (*Verein der Schriftstellerinnen und Künstlerinnen*, 1885), which was founded because women were excluded from the male equivalent organisation, also saw its goals as primarily humanitarian and supportive, in both moral and practical terms, and realised these in similar ways – through cultural events, a library, price reductions, for example for the Danube steamer and a range of hotels and spas, and above all through a pension and health insurance fund.[60] Only in second place did it see its function as helping to support and stimulate women's artistic activity by offering the opportunity for intellectual and creative exchange in the form of readings by well-known actresses of texts by women, the performance by women of music composed by women and organising exhibitions of women's art.

As in the case of the vocational schools, further evidence of the quiescence of these organisations is given by the approval shown them by the authorities, above all the monarchy, and also by the patriotic stance taken by the organisations themselves. The Emperor, for example, made a donation to the pension fund of the Association of Women Writers and Artists, members of royalty and leading statesmen such as Eduard Taaffe and Nikolaus Dumba were also donors, and in *Neuzeit* the women teachers were enjoined to regard fostering 'an Austrian patriotism which springs from the innermost feelings' as 'one of the most beautiful duties of those who shape youth'.[61] Such timidity on the part of these women's organisations did not pass without critical comment. The Association of Women Writers and Artists for example was criticised for not campaigning for a training scheme open to women which would be state funded and enable them to compete as artists and writers on the same terms as men.[62] Likewise the Association of Women Teachers and Governesses and its paper were the target of a sharp attack by those with more militant views, who wanted to see female and male teachers struggle together against the school authorities instead of against each other.[63] But these elements had had to wait until 1893 before they found in the General Austrian Women's Association a broadly based organisation which would represent their views. The first wave of Viennese feminism was partial indeed.

CHAPTER 2

Personal Politics. The General Austrian Women's Association

A Political Women's Association

'The existing women's associations, although so numerous, could not satisfy our need to grasp the woman problem in its entirety, to uncover its roots, which extend to all spheres of human community, and to acknowledge the need to give the whole movement a theoretical basis. Our association therefore had to emerge.'[1] Thus the committee of the General Austrian Women's Association presented its *raison d'être* and at the same time pointed out the three ways in which it was to differ fundamentally from the women's associations that already existed. It was not to be confined to any one concern as its predecessors had been, but would encompass all issues which touched on the woman problem; it would not limit itself to alleviating symptoms but was to go to the roots, to be 'radical' in the true sense of the word; and it was not to focus only on economic problems but would consider ideological elements as well, for, as was also explained, 'whoever . . . is familiar with the history of culture knows that . . . however much one acknowledges the material in human motivation, ideals have always been the main motors of progress.'[2]

The circumstances of its foundation foreshadow these different aims, for it emerged indirectly from the first calls for women's *political* rights rather than from any desire to administer immediate practical aid to women in need as the other associations had done. In 1888 the right to vote for the Lower Austrian Provincial Assembly (*Landtag*), gained in 1849, was withdrawn from women with the pseudo-reasoning that as women's suffrage in Austria was not uniform – women in neighbouring Vienna, for example, were excluded from the provincial vote – in the interests of uniformity it would be more desirable also to deny Lower Austrian women the right to vote for that assembly. At the same time it was suggested that Lower Austrian tax-paying women be deprived of the right to vote for the local government as well. This motion stimulated two protest meetings, the first since 1848 to deal openly with women's suffrage in Austria. They took place on 3 October 1890 and 14 May 1891, and both were organised by the schoolteachers Marie Schwarz, President of the Association of Women Teachers and Governesses, and Auguste Fickert. As a result of the first meeting a petition to the Provincial Assembly containing about a hundred signatures was drawn up. This requested that the female vote for the local government be retained and the vote for the Provincial Assembly regained. And indeed, the move to deprive women of the local government vote was rejected.[3] Two petitions emerged from the second meeting. In the first, addressed to the Imperial Assembly, the vote for that body was daringly demanded for all Austrian adults regardless of tax status, sex or rank, as was the abolition of paragraph 30 of the Law of Association (which forbade female membership of political associations), the opening of the secondary schools and universities to women free of charge, and the extension of female professional opportunities.[4] The second petition, to the Provincial Assembly, requested once again, amongst other things, the return of the provincial vote to women in Lower Austria.[5] Although little attention was paid to either of these petitions by the law-making bodies, the women had indicated their range of concern and radicalism. Apparently some agitational effect was achieved, too, for plans were made to organise the first Austrian women's day, to take place at Whitsun 1892 as a response to the questions raised. This event was ambitious in conception and pioneering in its goals. The issues to be covered encompassed women's education, employment (including the servant question, prostitution and women's factory work as well as the middle-class professions), politics (the call for the right of free assembly, suffrage for both sexes without property qualification) and also the founding of a political women's association to push through the resolutions of the women's day.[6] The organisers thus explicitly took up the rights of working-class women, and indeed men as well, making it clear that they considered the woman problem extended beyond the middle classes and involved wider-reaching issues of social and economic organisation.

Precisely because of this, however, the plan was doomed never to get off the ground. At short notice four of the billed speakers, including Marie Schwarz, withdrew, explaining that they could not identify with the spirit of the meeting and were unable to collaborate with some of those involved, for Social Democratic women had been invited to speak as well. Obviously the goals had been too radical, as Fickert commented in her speech to the women's meeting which was then called instead of the women's day in May 1892.[7] For the Social Democrats, however, they were not radical enough.[8] After some debate, participants at the meeting decided to postpone the women's day to some more propitious date and to found a general Austrian women's association, which was slowly to prepare Austria's women for the goals of the women's movement, goals for which, as they had just demonstrated, they were still lamentably immature.[9] The tensions which were to mark the activities of visionary Austrian feminism were already evident.

Officialdom was also to prove uncooperative in the face of these women's radicalism. The provisional committee of the Association was voted in at the meeting of May 1892 and the constitution of the Association planned for the autumn of that year. Yet it was not until 28 January 1893 that Fickert could call the constituting meeting of the Association. The delay was due to her over-optimism regarding the relaxation of paragraph 30. In Parliament voices had been raised for the abolition of the paragraph and Fickert had, by her own admission, been so naive as to believe that the paragraph would be relaxed within the year,[10] so she had put 'foundation of a political women's association' on the programme of the women's day. This, of course, was forbidden by the authorities and so she was forced to found a 'general women's association' instead, which had to confine itself in its statutes to 'the promotion of the economic interests and intellectual education of the women of Austria as well as the elevation of their social position' and to state explicitly that it would exclude politics. These officially accepted goals were to be achieved, according to paragraph 2 of the statutes, by organising and educating women and by founding sections and subsidiary groups in other towns and cities. This represented a victory for the authorities, for the preservation and extension of women's civil rights as citizens had occupied a prominent place in the first draft of the statutes.[11]

The official exclusion of political goals did not, however, mean that the Association would in practice ignore these issues. Fickert made this clear in her opening speech at the constituting meeting by pointing out the double standards which informed the Liberal constitutional laws of 1867. Article 2, for example, claimed that before the law all citizens were equal. Fickert had no difficulty in pointing out that some – men – were more equal than others, as paragraph 30, women's exclusion from higher education and many other handicaps illustrated. In addition to such verbal criticism, she announced practical measures. In order to subvert paragraph 30 political meetings would be called by private persons rather than the Association and, above all, courses and talks would be held to show women how far they were all already involved in economic and cultural life while being excluded from the legal rights that should go with that involvement.[12] This awareness was, according to Fickert, absolutely central, 'for it is above all a question of declaring ourselves of age, then our maturity will find adequate expression in the law, too,'[13] she confidently asserted.

At this constituting meeting the committee was elected. Joint vice-presidents were Ottilie Turnau and the teacher Marie Mussill (the office of president was not filled), Fickert was voted secretary. Full membership was restricted to women over 16 on payment of annual dues. Amongst the full members at the end of the first year were Minna Kautsky, who was the mother of Karl and *the* socialist popular writer of the day, Rosa Mayreder, Marie Schwarz and the provocative feminist writer and theorist Irma von Troll-Borostyáni in Salzburg. Men could be supporting members on payment of the same dues; on foundation these included Engelbert Pernerstorfer and Emil Reich. Both women and men might be classed as founders of the Association on payment of a single lump sum irrespective of whether they were actually involved in the founding of the Association. Thus Rosa Mayreder was classed as a founder although she was not present at the constituting meeting. All in all the Association could count at the end of its first year 5 founder members, 207 full members and 12 supporting ones.[14] The membership numbers subsequently fluctuated between 200 and 300. Six years later it had 6 founder members, 298 full members with 34 supporting ones.[15] This was, however, sadly meagre in comparison to the rabidly anti-Semitic and anti-emancipatory Viennese Christian Women's League (*Christlicher Wiener Frauenbund*) whose president, Emilie Platter, in the same year proudly boasted a membership of 14,000.[16] In spite of Fickert's repeated calls for solidarity, the apathy and indeed also fear of radical politics of those middle-class women impervious to feminism, who, according to Therese Schlesinger-Eckstein,[17] were largely resigned housewives or the self-satisfied wives of wealthy men, was a constant source of disappointment and anger to the leaders of the General Austrian Women's Association. Two years after its foundation Fickert was forced to admit that the Association's handling of the servant problem and sexual matters had frightened many away, although she did not miss this opportunity both to chastise such timorous women and also to explain again that education in the widest sense was necessary: 'We are fighting, you see, for ideas which are still new and as a result unsettling for the mass of women. We must therefore not tire of discussing them time and again until insight grows and public opinion accepts them.'[18] She was particularly concerned to reach young women, insisting, for example, that discussions even on a subject such as prostitution were to be open to them.[19]

Yet the Association always remained a select band, and even of the members only a handful were really active. The goal mentioned in the statutes of extending to other cities seems to have come to grief on this apathy. By far the majority of members lived in Vienna. In the membership list for July 1905, for example, only 14 out of 223 full members have addresses outside Vienna, these ranging from Prague and Kassel to Klosterneuburg, so that in one sense the name General Austrian Women's Association hardly seems justified. Judging from the known names in the list, the social composition of the Association seems to have been that of the wives of some of the progressive intelligentsia with probably a large element of teachers and other white-collar working women. In so far as it is possible to judge, there is a significant Jewish element. The aristocracy and the artistic avant-garde are hardly represented. As her correspondence indicates, Fickert was in touch with a wide range of personalities on Association business. Women in Germany ranging from the left-wing feminist Minna Cauer, the eugenicist Agnes Bluhm, the socialist Clara Zetkin and conservative Gertrud Bäumer wrote commenting on the Association or responding to invitations, while men such as August Bebel, Carl Brühl and Victor Adler could be counted as well-wishers.

Publicity

Various events were organised in order to raise women's consciousness in the sense intended by the Association. Courses were run on human anatomy and law, meetings for Association members and the general public were held, as were lectures and discussion evenings on a wide range of subjects, the latter also being used to encourage women in public speaking. The Association managed to build up a library, too. But the most effective means of making the mass of women politically aware were the Association's journals. At the beginning of its existence it was prepared to co-operate with a political party to gain newspaper space. From 5 March 1893 the Association produced *Das Recht der Frau. Organ für die moderne Frauenbewegung* (The Right of Woman: Organ of the modern Women's Movement), a supplement to *Die Volksstimme*, the newspaper of the small Democratic Party. This arrangement was negotiated with the help of Kronawetter, a leading member of the Party and sympathiser of the Association, for he and his Party, like leading members of the Association, above all Fickert, were critical of the Liberal betrayal of the spirit of 1848, anti-clerical, opponents of all forms of anti-Semitism and sympathetic to the socialists. *Das Recht der Frau* normally consisted of two to three pages including a leader. This could be a transcript of a talk given at the Association, the report of one of the discussion evenings or an article reprinted from another feminist paper, for the Association had exchange agreements with, for example, *Neue Bahnen* (New Paths) (Leipzig),

4. Portrait photograph of Marie Lang, *c.*1888 (in the private possession of Herr Martin Lang, Vienna).

The Englishwoman's Review (London) and Clara Zetkin's *Die Gleichheit* (Equality) (Stuttgart). It also included Association news and announcements of forthcoming events. This arrangement continued peaceably until November 1896 when difficulties arose between the leadership of the Democratic Party and the Association. As a result the supplement ceased to be published; only the column 'Zur Frauenbewegung' appeared instead until 15 January 1899.

In 1898 the Association's announcements appeared in the Berlin paper *Die Frauenbewegung* (The Women's Movement) edited by Minna Cauer, who followed very much the same visionary line as Fickert. But an independent organ was vastly preferable and already in the summer of 1897 plans for such a paper were being discussed.[20] This was not finally launched until March 1899. It bore the title *Dokumente der Frauen* but was not to be the official mouthpiece of the Association, as Mayreder, one of the editors, made clear to Fickert when she insisted that the committee members were to have no say in its editorship.[21] In practice, however, it was closely linked to the Association as its three editors, Mayreder, Fickert and Mayreder's friend Marie Lang (see figure 4), were also leading lights of the Association. The magazine was received with encouragement and enthusiasm in the Liberal and socialist camps. The *Neue Freie Presse* foresaw the most lively interest in the paper on the part of women in all circles if the editors followed the programme outlined in their preface,[22] and Emma Eckstein positively reviewed the second number along with the first number of Karl Kraus's satirical periodical, *Die Fackel* (The Torch).[23] Her sister, Therese Schlesinger-Eckstein, who had left the Association to join the Social Democratic women's movement, wrote to Fickert to express her approval of the first number.[24] Three years later she made her opinion public. 'The political attitude of this magazine can certainly be called sound,' she declared, 'and in the three years or so that it has existed it has more than once found the opportunity to shame the whole of the liberal press of Vienna by its uncompromising exposure and condemnation of existing wrongs as well as by an intrepid partisanship for the injured or those threatened in their rights.'[25]

The line to be followed by the three editors was made clear in their preface to the first issue. They intended the paper to act less as the partisan battle-cry heard by Schlesinger-Eckstein than as a means of making women aware of reality, of liberating women from constraining fantasies, and thus helping them to become autonomous, the goal which formed the basis of the feminist vision. The paper would, the editors claimed, include politically objective, sober, factual evidence – documents – of the actual conditions of women's working lives, and would show women how they were to set about defending their interests and demanding economic, social and political equality. The paper would bring together women who worked and those who did not, and give them a sense of solidarity and real power. 'For women have a social mission to fulfil,' the editors pronounced. 'It is they who will leave a mark on the culture of the future. In the unused strength of women lies the best hope for the civilised world; the entry of women into public life will completely change the social organism and above all be able to heal those ills which were bound to emerge from the one-sided dominance of the male sex.'[26] This tone is very different from that of other publications aimed at middle-class women. These appealed only to women in the private sphere or, as the editors pointed out, to specific professional groups' need for entertainment and socialising; the links between women's working conditions and questions of politics, including sexual politics, were ignored. The *Dokumente*, unlike these papers, included outspokenly frank, often anonymous, articles written by those involved – women tobacco sellers, temporary teachers, telephonists – which showed just how bad those working conditions were, and was concerned to emphasise how so-called bourgeois women workers were as exploited as their working-class sisters, how they were also members of the proletariat. The paper was of an extremely high intellectual standard; it shunned the usual columns on cooking, dress, health and so on and instead included many politically aware articles ranging from philosophical essays, articles on female suffrage and women's wages to those on the youth movement. Most pieces were written by women although some by men were also printed. Cultural themes were not forgotten; there were book reviews as well as serialisations of suitable novels. Notices concerning the progress of the women's movement all over the world were included, as were notices confined to the Association. The only concession was the advertisements, which included those for children's fashion, cosmetics, and even the abominated corset.

The choice of articles and financial arrangements was largely the responsibility of Marie Lang, who was able to interest many notable contributors through her numerous contacts. She was, for example, a great admirer of the Vienna Secession, a group of artists which in 1897 separated from the Viennese art establishment. She regarded the Secession as representing the striving for freedom on the part of modern man 'who cannot bear comedy and old mummery any longer and naked as he is, even if at the price of beauty, steps out before us'.[27] She had contacts with artists such as the Secession's leading spirit Gustav Klimt, Adolf Loos, Alfred Roller and Gustav Mahler, as well as supporting Hugo Wolf both financially and emotionally and being acquainted with Lou Andreas-Salomé. She was also in touch with social reformers such as Karl Renner and Ludo Moritz Hartmann and with the Hofmannsthal and Wittgenstein families. The paper was financed by subscriptions, collections amongst the members of the Association and by advertisements. It was a moderate success and could count 1,281 subscribers just under six months after the first issue appeared.[28]

Editorial difficulties soon arose, however, as had been feared by Mayreder right from the beginning of the undertaking. 'It would be for my inner life a catastrophe of indescribable consequences,' she had confessed to Fickert, 'if my relationship to Marie or to you were to break down because of this paper. I feel quite sure as far as you are concerned – but with regard to Marie I feel at the back of my mind something threatening which fills me with a painful dread. . . . But we must, we must remain on good terms whatever happens – that is no less a problem than the paper itself.'[29] By July of the same year the magazine had become the '*enfant terrible*'. Lang, according to Mayreder, lacked business sense and was unreliable in her decisions.[30] She apparently agreed to divide the work on the paper along the lines that Mayreder be responsible for the literary contributions, she herself for the general articles, and Fickert for the articles and notices on the women's movement, only to renege on this agreement four days later to say that she could not work with Fickert.[31] The break came quickly. On 19 October 1899 Mayreder and Fickert sent their resignation to Lang, although the parting was not officially announced in the *Dokumente* until January 1900. In the Association's annual report the committee explained that 'the motives for this decision lay in deep differences of opinion as to the goal, as well as to the editorial and financial organisation of the paper. In addition, Frau Lang, as she told some persons involved in the launching of the paper, had right from the beginning intended to exclude Auguste Fickert as much as possible from the editing of the paper.'[32] In July 1899 Mayreder had suggested another explanation. She saw the real roots of the tension between Fickert and Lang as lying in Lang's contempt for Fickert's attempts at literary writing, pieces that Lang would consider publishing only after she herself had altered and, in her opinion, improved them.[33] None appeared in the *Dokumente*.

As Mayreder had sensed, it was personality clashes that played the largest part in the failure of the three editors to work together harmoniously. Lang had a tendency to throw herself into projects with an ebullient enthusiasm which bordered on the artificial. In a letter to Fickert she spoke of the *Dokumente* thus:

> Beloved Bille! We come Thursday at 5 o'clock to you be good and work at your annual report *brilliantly*. I am also as diligent as I can be – often with tears of pure distress and anguish, for the paper is my youngest child. After pains which are really to be compared to those of labour we decided on 'Dokumente' I hope almost in desperation that you agree. Oh Bille how I am suffering! Oh Bille how I sometimes rejoice![34]

She had been a great admirer of Fickert since meeting her at the end of 1893,[35] and had through her enthusiasm and energy attracted Fickert's attention to herself. She frequently spoke at meetings, chaired discussions, and in July 1898 was sent as the Association's representative to the International Abolitionist Congress in London, the only Austrian to participate in this congress dealing with prostitution. As late as June 1899 Lang was still an extravagant admirer of Fickert. But this cooled rapidly as Lang's impulsiveness jarred with Fickert's more sober approach when they came to work more closely together, so that by August of the same year Lang was complaining to Mayreder: 'I have written umpteen letters to Fickert and torn them up again. But I must at least tell *you* that I am suffering hellish torment because of her . . .'[36]

The *Dokumente* also spelled the end of Mayreder's friendship with Lang, which had begun in the late 1880s and had also been characterised by an excessive admiration for Mayreder on Lang's part.

Mayreder, for the first time in her life, found in Lang a woman friend. 'With her fervent imagination which drew on dreams and symbols, her overflowing emotional life against which reason was powerless . . . she captivated me so much by her warmth and the immediacy of her feelings that under a kind of spell I submitted to her entirely,' Mayreder recalls.[37] Mayreder, on the other hand, was chiefly characterised by her intellect. Even as a young woman she was considered by outsiders to be a 'scholar and profound thinker'.[38] She had a strong personality in her combination of 'clear, connecting, logical understanding'[39] with courage and idealism, 'for the intellectual joy of thinking and creating did not completely satisfy her soul. Just as strong in her was the revolt against the baseness of our age and the longing to fight for a better world.'[40] As Mayreder herself remarked of Lang, 'she was the absolute opposite of my own nature!'[41] Nevertheless, in the years before the founding of the *Dokumente* the friendship between the two women was so close that Mayreder lent Lang clothes and cutlery when needed as well as giving her money and acting as godmother to Lang's sons Heinz and Erwin (who later married the dancer Grete Wiesenthal).[42] Lang expressed her gratitude in her usual excessive style: 'Dear Röslein! . . . [I] must tell you that I have transformed all the material goods I have received through you into the immaterial, into pure ecstasy, into a thousand joys, whether it be that I dress my children in your exquisite fresh underwear, eat your sardines, whether it be that I, with your money, roam through woods and over meadows . . .'.[43] Yet as Mayreder drily remarked, 'such a relationship, naturally, cannot last'.[44] On Lang's death many years later, in 1934, she commented: 'An obituary . . . celebrates her as a public speaker and writer who played an important part in the women's movement – quite wrong. Her significance lay only in the originality of her personality through which she became an experience for everyone who was receptive to it. What she was to me remains inextinguishable in my life.'[45]

After the breach concerning the *Dokumente* Lang wrote to the committee of the Association to announce her resignation, and her exit from the Association (she had joined in 1894, was voted on to the committee in 1896 and became co-vice-president with Mayreder in 1897). The Association for its part officially cut its links with the paper. Lang's main problem after the breach, as before, was to find adequate finance. In the number of 1 January 1902 she appealed to subscribers to recruit new readers and otherwise to support the paper as best they could. Marianne Hainisch, too, was asked to help by becoming a permanent contributor. She refused, limiting her help to an annual donation. The financial crisis worsened, and came to a head the next month when the publisher demanded the immediate payment of debts. Lang was forced to look for another publisher. None willing to take on the risk was found, and the *Dokumente* were forced to fold at the end of September of that year.[46] Relations between Lang and Fickert were never restored. Indeed, it seems that Fickert publicly polemicised against Lang, for Therese Schlesinger-Eckstein felt called upon to protest at a note in *Die Gleichheit* which suggested that the *Dokumente* merely served the editor's material interests.[47] She asked Fickert to publish a correction, making it clear that if Fickert did not, she herself would. Obviously Fickert was not prepared to do so, for on 5 March 1900 Schlesinger-Eckstein wrote again, protesting this time at Fickert's 'laconic' card to herself.[48]

Fickert's antagonism took on another form at the beginning of 1902 when she launched *Neues Frauenleben* (New Woman's Life), a rival paper to the *Dokumente* and the formal successor to the innocuous *Frauenleben*. It was the official organ of the General Austrian Women's Association and thus fulfilled a goal Fickert had cherished since starting her agitational activities. However, criticism was not absent. Schlesinger-Eckstein publicly expressed her regret at the competition this meant for the *Dokumente*, and Aristides Brežina, Director of the Natural History Museum, a leading member of the Ethical Society and supporter of the women's movement, who saw Fickert's move as the attempt to harm 'a useful weapon of the modern women's movement', presented a heated defence of Lang's role in the quarrel.[49]

These criticisms did not deter the iron-willed Fickert. The paper published articles on a wide range of social questions, on the state of the women's movement, literary essays, and also reviews of books, art and music as well as presenting poetry and literary extracts or serialised fiction by the best modern authors. It thus followed roughly the same format as the *Dokumente*. After Fickert's death in 1910 it was edited by Leopoldine Kulka, the literary historian; the first woman university teacher of German in Austria, Christine Touaillon; and by Fickert's brother Emil. Auguste Fickert's preface to the first issue clearly indicates that she regarded the paper as an important tool in her efforts to spread awareness amongst women. She declares that the paper is dedicated to all struggling women, whether they are struggling for existence or for the highest good of existence: insight. She goes on to hope that the former will find refreshment in the pages of the paper by thinking of other women struggling to create a new social order which gives the individual room to develop, and the weak protection. She also enjoins those who carry a happy message to declare in the paper's pages what they have seen and thought. 'And if their thoughts have been born in pain, they will lead us all the more surely "through insight to freedom and happiness",' she comfortingly pronounces, repeating the motto of the Association.[50] So, like the *Dokumente, Neues Frauenleben* aimed to breach the gulf between employed and unemployed women and foster solidarity between them, emphasise the importance of personal experience, and articulate the search for a new form of human organisation. And both, in contrast to other papers for middle-class women, were concerned to show how white-collar women workers were in fact members of the proletariat. Yet the tone of the much shorter preface of *Neues Frauenleben* differs from that of the *Dokumente*. The popular Darwinian element of women's struggle for existence is particularly brought out in the former. In the *Dokumente*, however, women are presented rather as responding to an almost metaphysical force, for 'a great movement is sweeping through the countries of Western civilisation. New forces are emerging from the earth; life is seeking to take on a new form, and a promising stirring of minds heralds the coming century.'[51] The leader of *Neues Frauenleben* on the other hand suggests that in Fickert's eyes by 1902 the coming century had already disappointed that promise of natural change.

Eight years later the tone is different once again. The visionary elements have disappeared altogether. The editors of *Neues Frauenleben* now see the paper as primarily preparing women for their social and political duties and supporting them in their struggle for their rights. No longer is there any talk of the dawning of a new age and of a new social order. Education and employment opportunities are to be extended and women's position in the family, professions, society and the state improved. Nothing more. In addition, the appeals to the reader to communicate her experience have disappeared. Instead, the contributors to the paper are proudly listed; the 'experts' have taken over and reader participation has been reduced to encouraging new subscribers. *Neues Frauenleben*, particularly after Fickert's death, may in one sense have remained what it had been on its foundation – 'a middle-class paper which represents the most extreme wing of free thought and stands close to Social Democracy in its social opinions without completely agreeing with it'[52] – but in another it had renounced the feminist vision that had informed its early years.

Passion and Politics

Yet it was a vision which had always been clouded, above all regarding co-operation between the feminists. Expectations were set high, for these women acted largely out of a very personal commitment and entered the public arena with their whole personalities. Politics was for them a matter not of tactical considerations but of personal passion. This Mayreder early on applauded: 'Isn't it in fact a promising quality of women that they appear in public as whole personalities without regard for other things, unlike men, who are "matured" in public life, and who just play a part which is well-considered and therefore devoid of all impulsive force?'[53] These women formed a tight network woven out of personal relationships. While this may have given them the support needed in their outsider position, it led to personal friction which could not be separated from political work, as the *Dokumente* episode had shown.

Mayreder herself soon illustrated this problem, for tensions between her and the Association arose early. In May 1894, just over six months after her election on to the committee, she was commenting to Fickert on her own unsuitedness to her position in the Association. 'I would just like to emphasise one thing,' she remarked, 'it is not contempt or boredom which the Association's business makes me feel but increasingly that I am just not really suited to it. . . . If I recognise any generally valid duty, then it would at the most be the duty not to pretend to be what one is not. And it is against precisely this commandment that I sin badly enough by my position in the Association.'[54] At the beginning of October 1895 she openly asked to be released from her position in the Association and suggested that Schlesinger-Eckstein take over, arguing that she, Mayreder, would perhaps be of more use to women if she concentrated her energies on one activity, instead of dabbling in many.[55] Fickert was obviously reluctant to agree to this plan and apparently offered to release Mayreder from certain functions as a compromise, for Mayreder in a later letter attempts to negotiate with Fickert on this point.[56] She asks to be released from the meetings of the legal aid committee, as well as the Association meetings where no important decisions were to be taken. Whether all Mayreder's wishes were respected is unclear, but probably they were, for in later letters she does not voice much direct complaint of her position in the Association. This changed in the summer of 1902 when problems arose concerning the Association's membership of the newly founded League of Austrian Women's Associations. Mayreder's view of the matter becomes clear in June 1902 in a long and bitter letter to Fickert. At a meeting of the Association in April 1902, Fickert seems to have promised to extricate the Association immediately from the more conservative League, as membership would impair the Association's freedom.[57] Fickert, however, did not keep this pledge, a breach of trust which deeply upset Mayreder, who had been opposed to membership right from the beginning and was also angry about personal intrigues in the Association, particularly those involving Ida Baumann, Fickert's companion. In May she asked to be released from her duties for a year. 'I must forget recent events if I am ever to regain my goodwill and belief in the Austrian women's movement,' she maintained. 'At present I am of no use to it. My belief is destroyed. And someone without belief is brittle wood, a naked tree on which no leaf can again grow green.'[58] She did not declare the open break she now felt with Fickert until 26 June, and it was not until February 1903 that Mayreder officially resigned from the committee, giving as her reason her wish to devote more time to her artistic activities and apparently convinced of her unsuitability for practical life.[59] She remained, however, highly ambivalent, for she continued to speak in public and play an active role in a number of pressure groups, ruefully noting in January 1908 that she was a member of five committees,[60] after having a year earlier cursed the fact that she had founded an anti-prostitution association and declaring, 'I'm a "scribbler"; practical life bewilders and confuses me.'[61]

Yet the roots of Mayreder's difficulties with the Association lay not only in her self-proclaimed unsuitedness but also in what she herself called her 'heretical' ideas about certain premisses of the women's movement.[62] She rejected the dogma of female submission and male egoism,[63] and refused to have anything to do with the 'morality question' in the form in which it was presented by supporters of Christian ethics. She called the moral purity movement 'immature', 'nebulous' and 'injudicious', and declared to Fickert 'the word "morality" is an empty vessel into which first a content must be poured; for the majority however it is still the term used for traditional morality. The "morality" that average women understand is not a morality for you or me; we must therefore avoid the word.'[64] The automatic sisterhood of all women against the universal enemy 'man' was another point of disagreement,[65] as was the glorification of female self-sacrifice, of which she exclaimed that 'every sacrifice which leaves bitterness behind in the soul is worth nothing at all. No, nothing is more unbearable than this old women's morality with its eternal unappreciated sacrifices.'[66]

It is perhaps hardly surprising that Fickert, Mayreder and Lang should have parted in disagreement, for the backgrounds of the three differed widely, as did the brands of feminism each represented. Fickert seems to have come to the movement for a mixture of reasons. Disappointed both in her deeply felt adolescent wish to become an actress and to find a husband who would meet her ideal, she looked for substitute fulfilment on both scores and also a surrogate religious belief as she turned away from her Catholic upbringing and convent school education. As her diary indicates,[67] she saw the stage to be the prime place of moral uplift and missionary activity, the platform from which the word of human emancipation could be spread: 'Oh, the playwright's art is the most noble gift God has given man,' she effusively recorded on 29 April 1872 after seeing a performance of Schiller's *Wilhelm Tell*:

> it is through it alone that I have become aware of what man *is*, what he *can* be, and what he *must* do. He *is* the being created free by the

> highest master's hand, put into this world to govern it with his free spirit; he *can* achieve what is highest with his soaring thoughts and deeds; he *must* break the bonds which bind him to what is base, must liberate his spirit from its chains . . . must strive to achieve a goal higher than that of this world's miserable transiences.

Similarly, the marriage of romantic love was to liberate and redeem. 'Love is the most certain protection against the atavistic desires of the bestial in human beings,' she has an emancipated woman say in an unpublished sketch, 'Ahnungen', which clearly represents Fickert's own view, 'and the more it extends its bright empire, the more it takes possession of the hearts of people and sets them free from narrowness, limitation and pettiness, the freer, stronger and therefore nobler those human hearts will beat, the happier they will be.'[68] Woman's true love would, she maintained, bring collective salvation, but it is a love which can come only from the 'new woman'. This path of love is that of the new woman's pilgrimage: 'By this path those queenly women will emerge . . . by this path humanity will be redeemed for a second time, not for the world beyond, but for this world.'[69] The yearning to spread the word of love and freedom, which was a substitute for unfulfilled emotional needs, combined with the constraints of her own material situation – as an unwilling primary school teacher she was forced on her father's death to support not only herself but her family and was also exposed daily to discrimination on grounds of gender – acted as the motor for Fickert's feminist commitment. The women's movement offered her the only public platform other than the stage from which she could preach her message of the new woman's ethical mission. And this she combined with a sharp eye and feeling heart for the injustices done the middle-class working woman. It was a quasi-religious belief that inspired Fickert to champion a cause which was in her eyes the 'holy and highest good'.[70]

Mayreder's background and motives were very different. While Fickert's family was of the humble lower middle class and it was clear that Fickert would have to work, Mayreder's was of the *nouveau riche* lower middle class, where women's earning power played almost no role. Her path to feminism was therefore not paved by keenly felt material disadvantages as Fickert's partly was, but by an awareness of the constraints tradition placed on her personal, and above all intellectual, development. 'My intellectual development occurred at a time when the bourgeois family was still completely governed by unquestioned traditions. Rebellion against them forms the decisive experience for me as far as my personal fate is concerned,' she later recorded.[71] Rather than being a moral mission, Mayreder's feminism was a rebellion and an assertion of personal freedom from all collective constraints which ran counter to individualism. Yet, like Fickert,

Mayreder did have a sense of religious mission. In her own eyes she was a symptom of a particular stage of human evolution,[72] namely of a new femininity by virtue of her intellectuality. And this intellectuality was divine, the voice of God in man, and the path to personal salvation and freedom.

In contrast to Fickert and Mayreder, Lang's feminism was a product more of adult enthusiasms, above all the attraction she felt to Fickert and her interest in theosophy, than of any long-standing conviction or personally felt disadvantage. An excessive admiration (in which erotic elements probably played a part) drew her to Fickert. But it is an admiration which again reveals the religious component of these feminists' commitment. By Lang's account Fickert appears as a conquering, triumphant archangel with raised sword; Lang was converted on the spot.[73] A contributing factor may well have been Lang's theosophical leanings. In the late 1880s she was at the centre of a circle of young people 'all of whom admired her and delighted in her spirit and silvery laugh'.[74] They met informally – guests were to bring their own refreshments – and included Julius Mayreder (brother-in-law of Rosa), later also Hugo Wolf, Rosa Mayreder herself and the theosophists Rudolf Steiner, a close intellectual friend of Rosa Mayreder for several years, Franz Hartmann and Count Carl zu Leiningen-Billingheim. It was the latter who introduced Lang to theosophy, into which she then threw herself with her usual *élan*.

From Lang's later agitational speeches it is clear that she considered that feminism offered the possibility of uncovering the mysteries of nature and the powers that lay latent in human beings, two stated goals of the Theosophical Society.[75] Feminism, she believed, could restore nature to its mystical and mythical splendour through its criticism of governing sexual mores and motherhood. The subject of Fickert's speech when Lang was converted, the celibacy of women teachers, appealed precisely to this creed, and no doubt contributed to Lang's enthusiasm. The mother of four, Lang revelled in her maternal role and was concerned to impress the sanctity of sexuality and procreation on her children. Thus, for example, she insisted that they should not 'desecrate' the parental bed by romping on it, for it was the place of birth, love and death.[76] For Lang, therefore, feminism was closely linked to spiritual and sensual fulfilment. She was inspired to join the women's movement by an experience similar to religious conversion centring on an adored leader (Fickert), reinforced by a belief in the holy mysteries of nature. Yet, it was a personal bond which could easily be broken when constant commitment was called for. In addition, her spiritual leanings brought her to seek the mystical in feminism. This contrasted sharply with Fickert's and Mayreder's awareness of power relations.

Fickert's personal qualities, too, made co-operation difficult. She might have liberated her mind from her convent school education 'but in her manner she embodied the best aspects of a religious education and always distantly reminded one of a nun of a strict order,' Emil Reich remembered, commenting on her 'almost fanatical love of truth, her immovable resolution, her ascetic self-discipline'.[77] Mayreder, he remarks, appeared on the other hand 'more able to enjoy life, more open to things of the world, genuinely Viennese'.[78] In her memoirs, Mayreder conjures up the military aura surrounding Fickert, who is 'heroically determined' to 'fight' for what she thinks right, regardless of the obstacles in her path, and gives Mayreder orders 'like a commander-in-chief to his adjutant'.[79] Fickert's authoritarianism was commented on by Leopoldine Kulka, in many ways Fickert's right-hand woman after Mayreder and Schlesinger-Eckstein had left the committee of the Association and a key figure in the editorship of *Neues Frauenleben* even before Fickert's death. But as Kulka remarked in an obituary, 'Many called this woman tyrannical because she was intransigent. But how can someone who carries the strictest law of action in themselves give way? . . . However, she did think "Anyone who is not with me is against me" and acted accordingly.'[80] It was probably Fickert's dedication and enthusiasm to the cause which led her to demand of herself total personal involvement, but it was this commitment that the Association depended on if it were to exist at all.

This exclusivity which bordered on fanaticism also led to a certain cliquishness, caustically commented on in *Die Fackel* by a former member of the Association. She accused it of being class-bound and elitist, to which the Association responded by dismissing the reproach as 'childish nonsense'. This of course aroused Kraus's ire. He in turn patronisingly noted that the Association had not taken up his offer of space in *Die Fackel* for an objective response and criticised a would-be defender of the Association for offering mere sentimentalities instead, a retort which set the tone of Kraus's further comments on the 'general Austrian women'.[81]

Kraus was not the only public figure in Vienna to take exception to the Association and the *Dokumente*. Attacks also came, if for different reasons – and more trenchantly – from the anti-Semitic, Christian Social camp. Such attacks were hardly surprising, given the political orientation of the *Dokumente* and the Association. What was more surprising was the degree of hostility the women's actions aroused. Obviously they were proving successful in unsettling masculine self-confidence. The most public and virulent of such outbreaks came from Karl Lueger in the Lower Austrian Provincial Assembly in July 1899. There he slandered Fickert for her anti-clericalism. This aroused a wave of protest, both during the sitting from Julius Ofner, who leapt to

Fickert's defence only to be showered himself with anti-Semitic abuse, and afterwards from the progressive intelligentsia, some of whom expressed their condemnation of Lueger and admiration for Fickert in an open letter. Fickert paid dearly for her convictions, for in addition she was continually harassed by the Christian Social school authorities. And she risked losing her job when she left the Catholic Church in protest at the Liberals' stipulation that schoolteachers of the same confession as the pupils were to participate in religious prayers.[82] On top of such brushes with the authorities, commitment to the women's movement often meant becoming a stranger in one's own family. Fickert's mother showed no understanding of her daughter's activities, and Mayreder's family chose to ignore her intellectual achievements. 'For them I was and remained unknown as a personality,' Mayreder bitterly remarked.[83] Indeed, after she had spoken in public opposing the state regulation of prostitution one of her brothers denied his relationship with her to an acquaintance.[84]

Who then were these feminists who were prepared to lay themselves open to such treatment and why did they do so? One linking feature is that all came from middle-class families although some, despite this middle-class background, were forced to earn. Fickert and Ida Baumann, for example, belong to this group, and like so many women in their position, both took to primary school teaching. Fickert's father died when she was twenty-five leaving his dependants unprovided for and forcing her to give coaching lessons in addition to her regular salary.[85] Baumann came from an even poorer family. Her father was a village teacher and cantor whose salary had to support a family of eight; Ida was dependent on the charity of a brother to receive an education at all. Her situation, in a highly insecure profession, was made even more difficult because she was a Jew; when she wished to open her own kindergarten in Saxony the city authorities refused to give her permission for precisely that reason. She spent many of the early years of her life going from one insecure and badly paid appointment to another.[86] Others such as Schlesinger-Eckstein, Mayreder and Lang never experienced these constraints. All came from prosperous backgrounds; Schlesinger-Eckstein's father was a wealthy Jewish parchment manufacturer from Bohemia, Mayreder's a publican who had made his fortune with Schwechat beer and the family pub in Vienna which acted as a cultural venue, while Lang came from a highly successful Viennese joiner's family.

External influences – whether family and friends or books – played a large role for all these feminists. Mayreder may have tenaciously claimed to have discovered emancipation and individualism of her own accord, but this was not true in every sense.[87] Certainly, as a child and adolescent she had no strong role models. Her mother led what appears to have been a largely conventional marriage of convenience; she was subordinate to her husband who was twenty-eight years older than she and held highly traditional views on women, particularly his own wife. 'Blue stockings' were considered by those with whom Mayreder grew up to be

> degenerate creatures [who] haunted far-off places – in Zurich, where they attended the university as ragged, rowdy, unwashed scarecrows, or in Russia, which anyway bordered on the land of Thule of the sagas, somewhere at the end of the world. The whole disgust of the family for a power which was to shake its foundations was reflected in the literature written for the family circle and settled in the hearts of the posh young ladies who had turned out well.[88]

But it did not, of course, settle in Mayreder's heart and her reading matter played a significant, positive role in influencing the type of feminism she was to represent. Her father, who was a supporter of the ideals of the Revolution of 1848 as far as his views on education were concerned and certainly not the family tyrant Mayreder makes him out to be in her memoirs, was, in contrast to many a father, willing for his obviously gifted daughter to read to her heart's content. Schiller, Goethe, Richard Wagner and later Nietzsche made up her diet and, for reasons which will become clear later, left their lasting mark on her feminism.

For Schlesinger-Eckstein (see figure 5) the path to feminism was prepared by parental interests. Unlike Mayreder's parents, Schlesinger-Eckstein's were enthusiastic attenders of Carl Brühl's Sunday popular science lectures on comparative anatomy and basic questions of Darwinism. Her brother Friedrich Eckstein, a polymath and the friend of many distinguished figures such as Kraus, Mahler and Bruckner, recalls how the children often had to wait hungrily for their parents' return from Brühl's courses.[89] Their father was a member of a group of friends which included the social reformer Josef Popper-Lynkeus, Mach and Brühl.[90] He was a free-thinker, introduced regulations to protect the workers in his factory, and displayed a social awareness which, claimed Friedrich, rescued his children from that 'sad blindness' to social questions which afflicted most of the middle class.[91] Lang's parental background can also be seen as creating a favourable climate for feminist involvement. Her father, like Mayreder's, was a supporter of the 1848 Revolution and an enthusiast of freedom,[92] and perhaps this as well as her interest in the occult helped to make her so receptive to Fickert's presence.

For all these feminists the personal was intimately intertwined with the political. For all, commitment to the women's movement meant a great emotional investment and satisfied fundamental human needs,

5. Portrait photograph of Therese Schlesinger-Eckstein. Österreichische Nationalbibliothek.

above all that for conscious personal growth. For those women, such as Mayreder and Fickert, who came from families which they experienced as stultifying, involvement in the women's movement meant a very lived liberation; it was a means of demonstratively going their own way and achieving an individual identity otherwise denied them. For others, such as Schlesinger-Eckstein and Lang, although political involvement was not connected to a rebellious struggle against family constraints, it was still a path to inner development and expansion. Schlesinger-Eckstein confessed of her political commitment that it was a source of strength, 'psychological rescue',[93] which sustained her through a life full of personal tragedies and difficulties. It enabled her, she claimed, to rise above the poverty of a merely personal circle of interest and to mature emotionally. These were sentiments shared by Lang, who also regarded her own involvement as opening up a new world to her, the world of social politics.

The personal sphere played another role, too, for the leadership of the Association was largely a result of a network of friends. Mayreder was introduced to the Association by Friedrich Eckstein,[94] Lang by Mayreder,[95] and Schlesinger-Eckstein by Lang.[96] The distinguished Eckstein family – in addition to Friedrich and Therese there was also Emma, better known as the subject of Freud's dream of Irma's injection, and Gustav, the Marxist theorist – seems to have played a key role. Lang was on friendly terms with Friedrich, having been introduced by Hugo Wolf who had shared a flat with Mahler and Lang's second husband, the lawyer Edmund Lang (a distant cousin of Hugo von Hofmannsthal), while Mayreder was a close friend not only of Lang but also of both Emma and Friedrich, the latter of whom she had met when she was a 'blooming . . . young girl with long, flying plaits' and was bound to in an 'unshakeable friendship'.[97] This personal network extended to other supporters; personal contacts altogether played an important role. Often married couples were supporters. Karl and Rosa Mayreder are a case in point, as are Friedrich and Margarete Jodl and the left-wing economists Otto Neurath and Rudolf Goldscheid and their wives Anna Schapire-Neurath and Marie Goldscheid. Other family connections were important too; as well as the Ecksteins, the Federn family was significant here. Karl and Else, brother and sister of the psychoanalyst Paul, both supported the movement in different ways, Karl through his journalism and Else in the Settlement movement.

Commitment to the women's movement was not a matter which could be divorced from other aspects of life but was all-encompassing; the political and personal were inextricably interwoven. Political work merged with the search for the fulfilment of emotional needs and it was probably this very personal investment which gave these feminists the courage and strength to flout the norms in which they were enmeshed. It might, however, along with the heterogeneity of the personalities involved and the brands of visionary feminism they represented, also be considered a cause of the frequency and force of the conflicts with which the Association was plagued. Yet despite these, under the leadership of Fickert the Association did attempt to realise the three cornerstones of her vision: women's consciousness raising; the union of political awareness with morality; and the abolition of relations of exploitation.

CHAPTER 3

Practical Politics. The Activities of the General Austrian Women's Association

Women's Public Sphere

It was an absolutely central belief of the Association's leadership that women needed to be politically educated and not only accumulate knowledge or undergo vocational training. Unlike other women's groups it offered a wide range of events for its members, which were intended to widen their horizons and encourage critical thought. By the end of its second year, for example, it had organised amongst other things a talk on girls' upbringing, a reading by Karl Kraus from Gerhart Hauptmann's play *Die Weber* (The Weavers), a talk by Julius Ofner on the struggle for civil marriage, and a lecture on the female brain, specially written for the Association, by the doctor and philosopher Ludwig Büchner, the brother of the playwright Georg Büchner. In addition it had run courses on the structure and care of the human body, on law, and on female anatomy and physiology. As part of its claim to enlighten, a library with initially 140 volumes was set up for members, special attention being given to works concerning the woman question. Those who donated books included Ebner-Eschenbach, Suttner and Minna Kautsky.[1] Reading was given high priority as a main means of bringing women to the critical consciousness which was systematically denied them by conventional young ladies' literature, which, as Mayreder remarked, was 'in its essence hypocritical and false, [and] makes a prudery which is hostile to life . . . its supreme law'.[2] Conventional upbringing thwarted the thirst for real knowledge which was a natural attribute of woman, Fickert claimed. In order to give guidelines on quenching this thirst she drew up a list of books which, she maintained, 'would be able to communicate a comprehensive world view which corresponds to the state of modern science'.[3] The list was divided into five groups. Titles in the first, dealing with natural science, were prefaced by two works – Ernest Renan's *Leben Jesu* (The Life of Jesus) and David Friedrich Strauss's

Alter und neuer Glaube (The Old Faith and the New) – which, claimed Fickert, proved that religion and dogma are the products of human psychology. These were followed by books propounding evolutionary ideas, including Charles Darwin's *Origin of Species* (1859). The next two groups, on cultural history and philosophy, and social science, were dominated by materialist, evolutionist works and socially critical ones respectively. The fourth group, on the woman question, included books by August Bebel, Irma von Troll-Borostyáni, Emile Zola and John Stuart Mill, and the fifth, concerning *belles lettres*, placed special emphasis on authors who dealt with modern women's concerns (a knowledge of the classics was assumed): Henrik Ibsen, Björnstjerne Björnson, Leo Tolstoy, and also Suttner and Ebner-Eschenbach. An upbringing along these lines, which promoted interest in cultural as well as artistic matters, one which included intellectual challenge and encouraged awareness of current affairs too, would, claimed Berta Zuckerkandl, a journalist, art critic, and wife of Emil, also lead women to support the women's movement. Joining the *cri de coeur* of the leadership of the Association, she claimed that it was girls' inadequate upbringing which led to their indifference to public affairs.[4] However, Fickert's selection did not go unchallenged by members of the Association. Flora Carnegie for one regretted seeing Zola, Ibsen and Tolstoy on the list. The former's works incited, she claimed, the very vice they were supposed to expose and reform, and anyway the majority of Zola's readers were licentious, lascivious men. Ibsen and Tolstoy did not fare much better for they, according to Carnegie, were 'unhealthy reading. In a sensitive mind they are liable to create an unwholesome, morbid pessimism.'[5]

This central question of upbringing, and the wider one of the relative importance of nature or nurture, of course also raised the problem of how far the feminists' ideals could be made reality at all. As Mayreder pointed out in a letter to Fickert,

> the problem which occupies us is probably so difficult mainly because we do not have any reliable criterion which tells us what is unchangeable in the conditions of human society, that is, what belongs to the essence of life itself... and what is merely imperfection, inability, a lower stage of evolution, that is, changeable and capable of improvement. One cannot fight against the former; to remove the latter as far as we can, to work together for the elevation of the social level is our noblest task.[6]

The Association's supporters were divided into two groups on this question: the interventionists and the non-interventionists. Both, however, saw the problem in terms of the relative claims of nature and culture, in which nature was seen more positively than culture, and both emphasised how conventional upbringing perverts woman's nature, to turn her into a 'physically degenerate creature'[7] with undeveloped muscles, who is highly strung, anaemic and trained to be lacking in independence in competition with men from childhood on. The natural woman, on the other hand, had the same potential as man, potential which could either be brought to fruition or stifled according to upbringing, which in turn was largely dependent on social norms.

As an alternative to this lamentable state of affairs the interventionists suggested an upbringing and education similar to that enjoyed by boys. This, which was seen to be 'natural', included vigorous physical exercise, a proper and sufficient diet, and clothes which did not hamper movement. Co-education in school was suggested as the best method of counteracting the existing cultural imbalance, for this meant that girls would obtain a boy's education. The joint education of the sexes would have other generally beneficial consequences; a mixing of the positive personal qualities of each sex would be achieved and the boys, too, would change to take on the positive feminine qualities of selflessness, tact and sympathy for others.[8] As a result, the general moral level would be raised and also, it was hoped by some, a less one-sided education in boys' secondary schooling introduced.[9] This desire to strengthen women intellectually, morally and physically for the demands of the future social order went so far that some suggested that women do a year's social service in analogy to men's obligatory military service.[10] For some others such as Mayreder, training women for reality meant early sex education. This was, she claimed, vital armour in the struggle for existence in which women had to fight like men, for it reduced their need for male protection; and it was also vital if women were to fulfil their maternal role which demanded not the features fostered by the conventional upbringing but courage, fearlessness, tenacity and toughness, women's natural qualities.[11] Intervention was seen as necessary to counteract the harmful influence of cultural forces. Liberation from culturally imposed degeneration would give women power in the struggle of the fittest, prepare them for their future tasks, and raise the moral and physical standards of coming generations.

The non-interventionists wished to see girls (and boys) allowed to develop without education as far as possible. They placed the emphasis on individuality rather than any preparation for life's tasks. They claimed to reject ideals of personal growth, preferring to let nature really go its own way for 'the stature and value of a person does not consist in his trying to be an "ideal" . . . but rather in his being true to himself, following the impulses of his true nature and taking the consequences'.[12] And in contrast to the interventionists' programme of physical strengthening, the non-interventionists advocated a more relaxed attitude which honoured the body and sexuality as divine and beautiful. Those responsible for upbringing were, then, merely to allow each individual child's unique essence to develop rather than to channel it in any particular direction. 'Let each one be what he is! Helping each one to discover the place which is right for him – that is the art!' enjoined Marie Lang.[13]

But of course formal education was also to play a role. This, it was hoped, would enable women to enter the public sphere, which they could then influence through their feminine qualities. The Association thus here joined its voice to that of other women's associations that wanted to see girls have access to educational establishments other than the *lycée*.[14] However, it concentrated more on the campaign to open university study to women, probably having recognised that enough other organisations were active on the school and vocational training fronts. Until the winter of 1897 the University of Vienna did not permit women to study for a degree, although since 1878 it had been possible for a few to sit in on lectures with special agreement from teacher and faculty. Women who wanted to study formally were forced to go abroad; most chose Switzerland, and particularly Zurich. With the slow growth of girls' secondary education and the activities of the women's movement, voices demanding women's regular university study in Austria began to be raised, but it was not until the end of 1895 that the Ministry of Education was forced by a parliamentary resolution to take some form of action. The official recognition of medical doctorates gained abroad was the easiest path and the one the Ministry chose to take first. This was long and tortuous for the few women who ventured on it, for not only did all the examinations taken abroad have to be repeated in Vienna but even the *Matura* had to be sat again at a grammar school in Austria. Nevertheless, in 1896 Baroness Gabriele Possanner von Ehrental became a doctor of medicine along this path, the first woman to gain an Austrian medical doctorate.

The campaign for the opening of women's university study centred on medicine rather than the arts, perhaps partly because it was easier to argue the need for women doctors and partly because the issue was particularly topical. In 1895 a slim volume violently condemning women's study of medicine was published by the distinguished Viennese surgeon and university professor Eduard Albert. In it he claimed that it was quite patently the case that women were intellectually and emotionally ill fitted for the medical profession and that they could at best be useful assistants to male doctors.[15] This caused a storm of reaction both *pro* and *contra* and stimulated many meetings, speeches, pamphlets and articles. The Association organised a meeting in October of that year at which Fickert pointed out the logical inconsistencies of Albert's arguments and soundly refuted them;[16] others also eagerly jumped at this opportunity to express their enlightened views.[17] As a result the Association handed in a petition to Parliament in which it requested that women be allowed to study medicine,[18] and in April of the following year the petition was supported by a letter from Mayreder in the name of the Association.

How far the agitation of the Association had the desired effect must remain uncertain. What is certain is that it was the Faculty of Arts which was first opened to women for the simple reason that, unlike medicine or law, an arts degree did not automatically open any professional doors. For of course what was really at the bottom of men's opposition to women's university study was not so much their ideal of 'true femininity' as their fear of later loss of their own professional livelihood. Despite this, the Medical Faculty along with pharmacy did eventually open its doors in the winter of 1900. Yet although the case of Professor Albert seemed to have been thereby laid to rest, and not even the most hostile observer could have maintained that the universities were overrun with women (in the winter semester of 1900–1 only 2.3 per cent of students at Vienna were women),[19] his spirit lived on; in winter 1900 the leading Viennese professor of medicine and specialist in internal diseases Hermann Nothnagel was still refusing to allow women to attend his lectures,[20] and in 1907 Karl Kraus printed Fritz Wittels's essay on female doctors (which appeared under the pseudonym Avicenna) in which hysteria is made responsible for women's wish to study medicine and the 'threat' posed by women doctors outlined.[21] That attitudes like these were by no means beyond the bounds of respectability is indicated by the fact that the essay was given serious although largely critical attention at a meeting of Freud's Wednesday Club.[22] However, by 1904 many Viennese university teachers, including such distinguished names as Mach, Jodl and Grünberg, were in principle supporters of co-education at university level as a questionnaire organised by the Association made plain, even if many suggested that it was still too soon to make a firm judgement. The only sharply dissenting voice was that of Theodor Gomperz. He proposed a separate university for women; after all, surely no one could expect him to discuss the sexual customs of the Ancient Greeks before a mixed audience. Others, such as Ludo Moritz Hartmann, the Germanist Jakob Minor and Emil Reich were on the whole in favour but lamented the lack of an adequate school education for girls; this sometimes made itself felt in the quality of the female students, it was claimed, and gave women's study a bad name.[23]

Although the Association was in principle in favour of the expansion of women's secondary and higher education, some of its members did not uncritically accept that this was beneficial in every case. Complaints were soon voiced about those female students without intellectual ability or dedication who studied merely because it was the fashion to do so. They were the daughters of the wealthy who could pay for the expensive secondary school education or private coaching necessary for the *Matura* but who did both the women's movement and women's study a disservice. This tendency became increasingly marked during the first decade of women's university study, so that by 1914, the prominent socialist Käthe Leichter recalls, the first generation of 'great pioneering spirits' had already disappeared and those dedicated to scholarship were swamped by those others who, 'thoroughly despised by me and others who took scholarship seriously and thought it to be something holy, soon became the characteristic feature of the university'.[24] Mayreder, in contrast to her public support as a leading member of the Association, privately displayed some scepticism about the benefits of university study altogether, declaring to Fickert that 'we can hope for nothing from those Byzantine institutions of the grammar school and university, in which the male sex grows to become state cripples'.[25] Women, such commentators implied, were not to become obedient teacher's pets as so many men were; they were on the contrary to retain a subversive attitude to the system. 'We do not need handmaids of the law but rather only handmaids of people in need of their rights,' Kulka declared, referring to the debate concerning women's study of law.[26] Unlike most other associations concerned with women's formal education, the Association took the opportunity to suggest the need not so much for women's meek adaptation to university study as for a change in the system altogether. It was to become more practical and to open professional doors to a large number of women rather than merely pamper to the intellectual and social ambition of a handful of wealthy and/or gifted women. For the Association it was not a question of increasing the privileges of an already privileged minority of women. Nor was it one of women's entry into the male sphere for the sake of equality *per se*. It was a question of raising the general level of women's education and increasing employment possibilities, of promoting women's awareness, strength and independence, and in this way contributing to general human progress.

This ideal, and the reality of slowly increasing numbers of women in white-collar professions, eventually raised the problem of the possible combination of professional life and motherhood. This debate reached a climax in 1910, catalysed by a pamphlet, *Mädchenerziehung und Rassenhygiene* (Girls' Education and Racial Hygiene), written by the Association's one-time supporter but by then renegade, the university professor Max Gruber. In this he declared that giving women an academic education damaged the health of the race by diminishing women's desire to have children. A storm of protest similar to that sparked off by Professor Albert's tract fifteen years earlier swept all camps of the women's movement. The Association countered with the arguments for women's education used by the earliest associations and emphasised the movement's support of those women who chose to have children not out of a sense of duty to the race but out of a joy for life and love. As a retort to Gruber's accusation of feminists' lack of a social conscience, it also drew attention to its concern for social questions by pointing to its support for anti-alcohol groups, the youth movement and women's social work.[27] But more important was its assertion that the ideal to be pursued was the combination of family and professional life, not the (false) choice between the two.[28] It therefore supported initiatives which attempted to organise both, although it was less concerned with the professional women of the middle classes, who were in any case less in need of such measures, than with the working-class women, neglected by Gruber. The suggestion that women should go back to the family hearth was forcefully rejected.

At the constituting meeting of the Association Fickert had already made it abundantly clear that gainful employment was essential if women were to become self-determining beings. Indeed, as early as 1892 she had joined the discussion in feminist circles provoked by Theodor Hertzka's bestselling utopia *Freiland* (Freeland) (1889), in which women, maintained by the state, are relegated to reproductive and aesthetic tasks.[29] Fickert challenged those who supported *this* vision of femininity and human progress. Such an arrangement of state provision, she maintained, merely exchanged the dependence of women on one male worker, as in the typical marriage, with dependence on all males, and anyway only work could endow women with true human dignity.[30] This high evaluation of paid labour remained a tenet of the Association. Indeed, some went further to declare that work was the only path to self-fulfilment, salvation and therefore immortality.[31] Of course, this attitude does display the ivory-tower religiosity of some of these feminists, for the self-annihilating slavery of the vast majority of working women is completely ignored. Yet some others, such as Anna Schapire-Neurath, although claiming that they saw 'in women's gainful employment not only an economic necessity but also an ethical and intellectual elevation of woman',[32] still managed to extend this to the working class. The haggard, drained working woman may seem to deride these words, Schapire-Neurath conceded, but improved living conditions would achieve this elevation and lead to solidarity, a feeling of social responsibility, and the awareness of having a place in human culture. As far as the union of family life and paid labour was concerned, this meant introducing measures to protect women workers and mothers, and a number of other initiatives such as communal kitchens.

In Vienna, family communal kitchens never became a reality before 1914 and although the Association wholeheartedly supported agitation for the protection of working women of the working class, it did not make this its priority. Probably it realised that the Socialists were in a far better position to do so. The protection of mothers, however, *was* an issue it directly dealt with. And this led the Association away from the concern with women's consciousness raising and with making women's public sphere a political matter straight into a concern with the politics of the private.

Women's Private Sphere

In the first phase of the feminist movement, women's entry into the male-dominated public sphere of civil society was the main concern. Giving the private sphere of domestic life and thus also woman's maternal role a political significance increased in importance only towards the end of the first decade of the twentieth century. So although Grete Meisel-Hess, for example, had called in 1901 for social measures for every mother-to-be in need, it was not until April 1914 that the Association founded a special section for maternity insurance. This was mainly to set up a maternity fund to which those women not covered by compulsory insurance were to contribute a small monthly sum which, after one year's contributions, would entitle them to claim when they gave birth or had a miscarriage. Yet although such measures were intended, according to Adele Gerber, one of the organisers, to bring the 'difficult question of how a profession and motherhood are to be combined, this basic problem of the women's movement, closer to a solution',[33] it transpired that the fund would be needed primarily by working-class housewives, for women in gainful employment would be covered by the new social insurance law.[34] Various arguments were used in the course of the discussion. It is noticeable that Schapire-Neurath's perception of maternity insurance as a means of easing the union of paid labour and motherhood and thus of organising femininity in the interests of women does not dominate the debate. Instead, two other perspectives are central: humanitarian individualism and racial hygiene.

Around 1900 it seems that sex reform for humanitarian reasons dominated the discussion, which at that time centred on the unmarried mother from the working class – the 'fallen woman' and victim of middle-class double standards.[35] The cruelty and injustice of Austrian law was pointed out, as was that of prevalent morality under which the joys of motherhood were permitted only within the context of marriage, while the unmarried mother who cared for her child was ostracised. For the prosperous, lack of rights and moral prejudice presented few problems as the illegitimate child was given away in care. But for the working-class women who, it was maintained, made up the majority of unmarried mothers, they could mean physical and moral ruin. A double standard was in operation which was, as Mayreder for one pointed out, obviously directed against those women who transgressed against the patriarchal code of male possession of offspring and who asserted their mother-right.[36] And it was clearly seen that unmarried motherhood, and also abortion, were not merely moral but also economic issues (although abortion was very rarely discussed by Viennese feminists before 1914).[37]

Although Meisel-Hess had in 1901 supported maternity insurance because it would benefit society, 'for then it [society] will have harnessed those torrents of *healthy*, *happy*, *motherly* strength which now so often seep away or die for its communal, social reservoir of strength',[38] just a few years later the argument for a relaxation of the tie between marriage and maternity for humanitarian reasons was usually linked to considerations of the health of the race. Thus the call for membership of the German League for the Protection of Mothers issued in 1911 condemned, for example, the marriage which merged money and love, 'at the cost of the health and fitness for life of the offspring'.[39] Signatories included Rosa Mayreder, Meisel-Hess, Julius Ofner, Wilhelm Jerusalem and Rudolf Goldscheid, all supporters of the Association, as well as Freud and Hermann Bahr, to name other distinguished Austrians. Pleas based on humanitarian arguments, although still articulated, became increasingly uncommon. Interest had shifted away from undermining patriarchal morality in the hopes of promoting the interests of women and thus creating a *new* and higher moral order, towards support for a social structure in which women's particular interests were subordinate.[40] The vision had faded.

At the turn of the century the intimate link between money and marriage at the expense of emotion had been very much at the forefront of the feminist debate and feminists' efforts to realise a new morality. The Association claimed that only love could make a sexual union moral and condemned a union formed for any other reason. Using the lonely hearts column of the middle-class press as illustrative material, the callous attitude to marriage was dissected in an article in the *Dokumente*.[41] The number of advertisements for marriage partners demonstrated that such a method of finding a partner was not unusual, and an analysis of the content revealed that the column was used above all by the petty bourgeoisie. Money was the main motive for seeking matrimony, a fact which some advertisers did not even trouble to disguise. Giving the analysis a materialist turn common to Fickert's arguments but not to many other autonomous feminists, the writer, Fritz Winter, commented: 'It is economic need in all its forms, it is intellectual need which enslaves people. It is our world of buying and selling which finally has reduced people themselves to objects to be bought, to products, and which forces them to place their own humanity on the market and to give it to the person who offers most.'[42] And he took the opportunity to condemn the fact that it was precisely those who advertised in that way who were the first and most vociferous to attack the fallen woman and to preach the sanctity of marriage. He also stressed the differences in attitude to marriage between the working class and middle class. The former did not marry for money, and if motives other than love prevailed, these were usually the working capacity of the woman or the desire of the man for a stable household.

The direction of this critique is clear: the marriage morality of the bourgeoisie is hypocritical and the marriage of true love is the superior form of union. Indeed, the leading members of the Association went one step further to claim that such a sexual union even without formal marriage was moral. With the agreement of her co-editors, Fickert reprinted in the *Dokumente* an article by the Swedish feminist Ellen Key which pleaded exactly that point, and at the same time spelled out how the morality Key advocated contrasted with both conventional morality and with the morality of 'free love'. The supporters of the former, those who adhere to the Christian view of life, demand celibacy from both sexes equally and deny the significance of sensuality, emphasising the importance of social duty instead, she explained. Supporters of the latter deny the existence of deep feeling and commitment, even condemning this as conventional. But both moral codes, claims Key supported by Fickert, are atavistic, forget the realities of life and stand in the way of the higher goal, the new religion of humanity: happiness.[43]

Yet although emotion was praised and seen to be the guarantor of happiness, it was also clearly realised that women's changed economic situation made changes in marriage and family law essential. Belief in true love was mixed with a dash of silent scepticism. However, the femininsts were not alone; they found the times were moving with their discussion of marriage law. An Imperial Government Commission for the revision of the Civil Code was set up and the Cultural-Political Society conducted an inquiry into the issue. In addition, the Association of Catholic Separated Marriage Partners was campaigning for legalisation of the dissolution of marriage for Catholics.[44] Several parties were, then, interested in change.

This widespread dissatisfaction led the Association to draw up a petition in December 1904 for the reform of the Civil Code.[45] The general tendency of the suggested reforms was to extend forms of sanctioned sexual cohabitation, to whittle away the control of men and patriarchal institutions such as the state and the Church over such cohabitation, and at the same time to protect women and their children and to extend their rights. The Government Commission was prepared to consider some of the proposals, such as that the illegitimate mother be allowed to become the guardian of her own and other mothers' children, and that illegitimate children be able to inherit from each other. Yet many were rejected outright, such as the suggestion that cohabitation without marriage be legally recognised and that illegitimate children have a claim to inheritance from the father, for such changes were considered to be destructive of the family, the apparent basis of society and the state. The points of agreement and disagreement were commented on by the Association when the proposals were presented to the Upper Chamber in December 1907. The Association recognised that the points which had been rejected threatened not only the patriarchal family but also the interests of the ruling classes, particularly where inheritance was concerned. It emphasised however that justice and unprejudiced humanity should demand that the natural connection between father and child be acknowledged in inheritance law. By 1913 the proposed changes accepted by the Commission had at last got near to becoming law, whereupon, in order to exert pressure, the Association organised a series of lectures by distinguished lawyers at which many of the women's claims were repeated. After so much investment of energy and such a long wait, the outcome when the laws were finally passed must have been bitterly disappointing. In October 1914 an emergency law was passed which amounted to merely minimal changes.[46] Not even civil marriage and divorce for Catholics were introduced. The only change of consequence was that the illegitimate child was given the same inheritance rights as the legitimate child to its mother's and her relatives' estate.

The Association's attempts to realise Fickert's vision centred on sexual morality, its intimate links with patriarchy and class structure, and of course the exploitation of women as sexual and economic beings. These attempts thus struck right at the heart of bourgeois sexual politics. Yet although marriage law reform and unmarried motherhood aroused feminist passion, the most exposed field on which the battle was fought was the issue of prostitution. Not only was it there that the interweaving of sexual and economic power relations was most apparent, the very fact that women concerned themselves with the topic at all was enough to be scandalous; by venturing on to this hitherto forbidden territory the Association set a precedent. And not content with that, its leadership did not lose itself in moralising arguments but maintained a clear perception of the power relations involved.

Observers concerned with the issue around 1900 can basically be divided into two camps. The first group regarded prostitution as an inevitable evil, the negative effects of which, namely venereal disease, could be controlled by the authorities through hygienic measures. This group divided into two wings. The first wished to see the introduction of compulsory medical check-ups for the prostitutes, the second the establishment of state-controlled brothels. The other main group demanded that the state, instead of condoning prostitution, should do all in its power to stamp it out as a disgraceful and dehumanising institution. The supporters of this second main attitude also divided into two camps. The first, the Abolitionists, called for a return to Christian ideas of chastity and the revival of religious feeling. The second rejected this and regarded the roots of prostitution as lying in economic conditions and moral views. It was this second approach which was taken up by the leading members of the Association and above all by Mayreder, who made her first public speech on precisely this subject in January 1894 and came to be considered the Association's spokeswoman on the issue.

Certainly, the feminists had every reason to be concerned. Prostitution was rife, and it also penetrated into their own most private lives. Josef Schrank, one of the leading police doctors and a Viennese authority on the subject, estimated that there were 2,400 registered prostitutes in Vienna in the summer of 1896 but at least ten times as many unregistered ones in a population of just over 1.5 million.[47] Most of these women were poverty-stricken; many were unemployed servants, seasonal workers, actresses and chorus girls. Only a sprinkling came from a middle-class background. It was quite *de rigueur* for young men of all classes to be initiated into the 'arts of love' through being taken to prostitutes by an older male relative – if, that is, the often preferred alternative of a servant girl was not so readily available. The medical profession colluded too, prescribing a prostitute as the solution to many ailments. As a young man, Rosa Mayreder's husband had, for example, been advised by a doctor to seek his first sexual experience in this manner,[48] and her platonic lover regularly visited prostitutes. Prostitution was a phenomenon which could not be avoided and yet had been systematically ignored.

This contradiction was supported by the mass of police decrees which had been passed in Vienna by the 1890s, for these worked in two conflicting directions.[49] On the one hand the *Sanitätspolizei* (police concerned with public health) was concerned to lift the veil of concealment surrounding the trade, for its task was to control the spread of VD. This it did by introducing compulsory health checks for the prostitutes in January 1873 in direct response to the increased demand expected as a result of the World Exhibition held in Vienna in May of that year. The other set of regulations, from the *Sittenpolizei* (police concerned with public morality), by contrast aimed to thicken the veil of concealment by means of a morass of restrictive decrees. Brothels with the name were not permitted in Vienna (according to paragraph 512 of the Penal Code of 1852) although 'tolerated houses' were. And of course the prostitutes themselves remained silent and without rights. It was not until 1923 that a self-help group was founded to promote prostitutes' interests and call for solidarity amongst them – but without success.

It was the projected introduction of brothels (*Kasernierung*) by the local government in Vienna in winter 1892 which prompted a women's protest meeting in December 1893. This in turn commissioned the Association to present a petition to Parliament. The Association duly produced one with a long preamble (which bears the marks of Mayreder), which was handed in to the Imperial Assembly in April 1894 by Pernerstorfer. It made four demands: that no brothels be introduced by the police in Vienna; that those houses with a licence have their permit withdrawn; that the system of health checks be abolished; and that the police limit its actions to the suppression of excesses and public scandals connected with prostitution.[50] These demands were supported by an impressive body of statistical material and quotations from the leading male authorities on the subject. The Association, well aware that it was breaking with the conventions of women's silence and ignorance on the subject, condemned the state regulation of prostitution first as hypocritical in that the state claimed it was a necessary evil yet refused to give the prostitutes the status in that case due them, secondly as atavistic, and thirdly and most importantly as mistaken in concept and inefficient in execution. It attacked the arbitrariness of the police in whose discretionary power the matter largely lay, the fact that the system could not cope with the large amount of clandestine prostitution, that brothels would merely promote the white slave trade, and pointed out the absurdity of examining the prostitutes and not the clients and also the irony that prostitutes in brothels were more likely to be infected than those freelancing. In addition, the collusion of those institutions supposedly controlling prostitution was roundly condemned.

In her capacity as the Association's representative, Mayreder claimed that the cause of prostitution was not only the economic need of the prostitutes but also the taboos on pre-marital sexual relations. Men, she claimed, did not marry until they were financially secure, which inevitably occurred at an age much later than the beginnings of their sexual activity. Thus they were driven by social-sexual mores into the arms of prostitutes instead of being able to live with a woman without getting married. By using this argument, pre-marital sexual relations for women were also implicitly claimed. This was a position which contrasted sharply with the ascetic Christian moralising of the Abolitionists,[51] and the promotion of concubinage for the middle and upper classes as well as for the working class (where it was more rife and accepted)[52] proved too much for some members of the Association. Flora Carnegie wrote a series of indignant letters to Fickert accusing the petition of encouraging sexual licence in men, and emphasised that such an arrangement could be nothing but degrading for women as long as social conditions remained unaltered.[53] She herself also wanted to see the introduction of a new moral code, not that of Christianity but of reason along the lines propagated by Herbert Spencer, in which human passions were controlled rather than fired. But it was precisely this last which she accused the Association of doing by condoning cohabitation without marriage and, so she thought, sexual pleasure rather than mutual love and esteem.

Carnegie was not alone in her indignation and rejection. The Association asked twenty other women's associations to sign the 1894 petition. Of these only two responded positively. In her reporting speech to the Association, Fickert divided the replies of the others into four categories: politely regretful, conventional, impolite, and downright coarse. The last two categories were filled by the Association for Extended Women's Education and the Vienna Association of Housewives respectively, the latter of which replied on being approached a second time that it did not concern itself with *that* kind of thing.[54]

The authorities were hardly more supportive; the petition was rejected – after it had been kept waiting for nearly three years – without a proper discussion. The feminists were accused of citing male authorities out of context, misusing statistics and generally coming to false conclusions. The conclusion for the two referees of the Health Commission (*Sanitätsausschuss*) was that the inefficiency of the system the women pointed to was not due to the system as such but to its execution, and advised the women to concern themselves with finding work for their impoverished sisters, for in this way they could do more for their sex than through getting the vote.[55] This offhand rejection led to a protest meeting in February 1897 at which Mayreder and Schlesinger-Eckstein spoke. After justifying the attention they paid to the report of the Commission, 'not because we think it is so unique, but precisely because it is typical of the way in which our people's representatives think they can come to terms with the gravest social problems',[56] Mayreder demonstrated how the report was itself full of illogicalities, irrelevancies and errors and stated again that the women's movement could on no account applaud an institution which reduced women to mere objects. State regulation was not only inadequate to fulfil the task it set itself, it was also unjust and hampered attempts at fundamental change, which had to begin with economic and social measures. And that also meant the struggle for the rights of the individual. Schlesinger-Eckstein emphasised the economic roots of the phenomenon, the unemployment and starvation wages of vast numbers of women – a problem which could not be solved by shouting for the police – and stressed the necessity for women's suffrage if there were to be laws that considered women's interests. The meeting closed with a resolution which condemned the authorities' treatment of the petition and the hygienic measures in operation, which repeated that only the economic, social and sexual emancipation of women would solve the problem, and which called again for social reforms, above all women's suffrage. The whole series of events was documented by the pamphlet *Zur Geschichte einer Petition* published by the Association in 1897, which included the original petition of 1894, the response by the Health Commission, and the speeches and discussion of the protest meeting.

This failure did not dampen the women's concern and anger, which focused on the behaviour of the state authorities rather than the prostitutes or their clients. A particular point of attack was the discretionary power of the police to drag off any woman without credentials to be examined by a police doctor. Cases of wrongful detention, above all of servants, were brought to public notice in the *Dokumente*, giving the feminists once again the opportunity to condemn the regulations and point out their brutality and inefficiency in the hope that public pressure could bring about change. Matters reached a crisis when it became clear that it was not only working-class but also middle-class women who could thus be degraded; a conspicuous hat was reason enough for a respectable woman to be arrested, it was claimed.[57] This harassment culminated in 1901 when a young Frenchwoman with connections in high places was arrested by an over-eager policeman and examined without the necessary precautions being taken to establish her identity first. A storm of indignation blew up, not least because the French ambassador intervened on the woman's behalf. As the Association was quick to point out, a similar scandal would not have been raised in the case of an Austrian woman who had no embassy to represent her interests.[58] The case was reported in detail in the *Dokumente* and found supportive mention in the *Neue Freie Presse*, provoking an agitated but perhaps representative response from one female reader who exclaimed: 'Let these humanitarian men, those energetic women who serve the "woman problem" in word and deed here raise their voices, here apply pressure. What use are a girls' grammar school, women doctors, philosophers, if we can be treated like this.'[59] A protest meeting was held on 11 March 1901 at which working women were also present in large numbers. The resolution which closed the meeting contained the following points: the punishment of the officers, the introduction of women police officers and doctors, and the payment of damages to those women wrongly arrested. The authorities remained, of course, unmoved and unmovable. The Minister responsible expressed his regret at the incident and stated that the officers were being subject to a disciplinary inquiry – a response which was hardly adequate for the women, for, as was remarked, a disciplinary investigation was as good as useless as it would not lead to punishment and hardly to the prevention of further such incidents.[60]

The feminists remained tenacious, ready to present their arguments at the next opportunity. This promptly arose with the Riehl scandal.[61] Frau Regine Riehl had kept a tolerated house in Vienna but was brought to trial, accused of gruesomely mistreating the prostitutes in her care with the collusion of the police. The press made heavy weather of the story, the journalists gloating eagerly over each unsavoury detail and adopting a pose of innocence, ignorance and moral outrage. The case also aroused the moral outrage of the Association, although this was directed not so much at Riehl, and certainly not at the prostitutes, as at the police and the prevailing system which made the behaviour of the police possible and indeed acceptable. As a result a meeting was held on 16 November 1906. There Mayreder made a speech which largely repeated her position of 1894 and 1897. She pointed to the atavism, degradation and inefficiency contained in state regulation and called not only for economic and legal measures but also for sex education. She showed here, however, less criticism of the Abolitionists and engaged less in a discussion of mores. The state is the main object of her attack.[62]

Prostitution remained an issue of political and personal importance for the feminists. The state, however, remained firm and continued to deal with the phenomenon by issuing police decrees, adhering to the view that it was its duty to intervene, as prostitution hindered 'the execution of the concept of the state . . . by undermining the bodily well-being of its citizens and destroying their sense of morality. The state must reckon with it as it is a social evil which cannot be removed.'[63] For such commentators it was not a question of women's dignity, nor a question of sexual politics, but of the power of the state. Yet for feminists such as Mayreder it was precisely this state power which they wished to undermine and thereby introduce a more moral and humane social order.

Undermining Relations of Class Exploitation

Raising the moral level of society as a whole was, as Fickert had seen, also dependent on undermining relations of exploitation, whether the exploiters be the state, men, or indeed bourgeois women. The Association thus took a critical look at conditions of working-class women and sided with them on a number of issues, even if this meant going against its members' own class interests.

The selfless adherence to the vision of progress to a juster, more humane society became apparent in the Association's commitment to a reform of the regulations concerning domestic service. This was, of course, essentially a female occupation: according to a contemporary observer, Fritz Winter, every eighth woman in Vienna in 1890 was a servant, and of the servants in the city 94.27 per cent were women.[64] Most had come from the eastern outlying parts of the Habsburg Empire in order to go into service and were alone in Vienna. The majority were in their twenties, and many entered service at 14, the earliest possible age. The regulations on their working conditions dated from 1810, and were brutal and anachronistic. The servants were subject to police control and were issued with service books in which a note of posts and performance was kept. They had no set working hours, no claims to a proper sleeping place or food, and no guidelines were laid down on wages.[65] Any disputes emerging from their work were assumed to be the servants' fault, terms of notice were correspondingly unfair and there were no provisions for health insurance or a pension. The regulations were, claimed Fickert, 'a remnant of the Middle Ages which extends into our time which is so rich in progress of all kinds'.[66]

These terms of employment were re-examined in 1891 on the initiative of the City of Vienna. A new set of regulations concerning domestic service was suggested, but the Association considered this woefully inadequate. Supported by the Ethical Society, it called a meeting on 22 March 1895 at which Ofner and Johann Herrdegen spoke, the first on the regulations and the second on the servants' employment exchanges and old age pensions. As a result, the Association was commissioned to prepare petitions to the municipal bodies concerned asking for improvements in the regulations. In April of that year the points to be made were further discussed and the petitions were handed in soon after. These called for the suspension of police supervision and the abolition of punishment for servants; the introduction of more care for minors; a juster distribution of duties and rights which were to include eight hours' sleep a day, an appropriate place to sleep and free time at midday and in the evening for adequate meals, acceptable wages, and humane treatment; the introduction of a compulsory accident and health insurance on the part of the employers and an old age pension contributed to by both parties and perhaps also the state; and the introduction of an inspector of servants' living conditions. The petitions were of little effect, however, for in February

1902 Fickert lamented that matters had come to a standstill and suggested that a petition be handed in to Parliament which would again put forward many of these suggestions.[67]

Of course, in keeping with Fickert's emphasis on personal change as the path to social change, these feminists were concerned not only with approaching the legislative bodies and altering the regulations, but also with changing the attitudes of housewives to their servants. In most cases a battle was waged between mistress and maid, the former lamenting the laziness and faithlessness of the latter and she in turn the former's meanness and harshness. The problem was given special attention in an issue of the *Dokumente* in which the contributors emphasised the plight of servants rather than the dissatisfaction of employers. Ofner once again raised his voice, commenting on the negative reaction from housewives to his 1895 speech, but noting that the reforms he suggested were also in their interests; contented servants would work better and be faithful and reliable.[68] Schlesinger-Eckstein – in an article that displays not only a humanitarian concern but also an attention to detail which reveals these women's very real contact with the problems of coping with everyday domestic life – also underlined the need for housewives to change but based this on claims to humanity rather than self-interest. She stressed the delicacy of many young servants and explained how the housewife could lighten the servant's burden by, for example, doing without a few trinkets or other articles of dress and thus saving the money to pay a second maid to do ironing or the basic cleaning. Such consideration was usually taken to be a sign of a bad housewife, but, as Schlesinger-Eckstein declared, 'I would rather be in the eyes of others a bad housewife than in my own a bad person.'[69]

This emphasis on humane treatment went several steps further in two other articles in which the authors were explicitly concerned to treat servants as family members rather than employees:

> '. . . We [housewives] . . . want to conciliate and reconcile, lead, and gradually educate others to have higher and more noble views and habits,' one claimed. 'We must therefore take a quite different path, the path of infinite patience and love. Above all we need love, indulgent, long-lasting, deep love like a strict but just mother bestows on her children. . . . Housewives who have merely a work and wage relationship with their servants . . . do not know and feel that such a relationship receives the correct sanctity and makes mutual satisfaction possible only when one gives and receives beyond a work and wage relationship.'[70]

Ofner's view that servants have rights because they are employees was here explicitly relegated to a secondary position; the patriarchal perspective proved tenacious – as was critically pointed out by others in the Association.[71] The feminists therefore displayed two conflicting aims: to expose the relationship of power between housewife and servant; and to promote the patriarchal familial relationship which in fact obscured that relationship of power.

The Association's concern for the exploited found a more practical outlet in the legal aid centres it set up to advise married and unmarried women without means on all disputes emerging from social, business, marital and extra-marital relations. The first was established in February 1895 in the workers' district of Favoriten after the authorities in middle-class Wieden had refused to give it a locale, claiming that such an institution would promote women's 'addiction to quarrelling and court cases'.[72] A rota of volunteers from the Association worked one evening a week trying to solve the clients' problems. If the case was too complex, then professional lawyers were called in – often the husbands of Association members – who offered their services free of charge. These included such prestigious names as Julius Ofner and Eugen Ehrlich. In the first year there were 216 clients on 33 days. The most usual cases concerned disputes about money (73 cases), alimony (47), and divorce and family quarrels (32). Typical cases were, for example, a servant who with the Association's help was able to reclaim money she had lent her employers; an impoverished widow who got back the pension out of which she had been cheated by her landlady; the divorce of a woman married for twenty years to a drunkard who battered her. Casual workers such as servants and washerwomen were the most common clients (46) with factory workers coming a close second (40) and independent tradeswomen third (32).[73] Those who could not pay for advice obtained it free of charge. This legal aid side of the Association's activities, which was made a separate section of the Association in 1902, was successful and so obviously met a deeply felt need that in 1897 the Association opened another, similar office in Währing and in 1901 a third in Mariahilf. By 1913 on a total of 115 days there had been altogether 1,410 cases of which 448 were referred to lawyers and 957 settled by the volunteers themselves; in some cases contact had been made with similar institutions in Dresden and Munich so that problems which involved parties abroad could be dealt with.

The Association's concern for relations of power and the exploitation of the socially weaker did not blind it to the fact that these were not only to be found among the working class and ostracised, but included many of middle-class background, particularly women in the relatively new white-collar professions. These women, themselves often reluctant to admit it, made up a new, female proletariat which suffered not only from exploitative working conditions as the factory worker did, but also from petty bourgeois mores which were a major obstacle to the growth of a political consciousness.

Nevertheless it was above all such white-collar working women, neglected or rejected by the Social Democrats and unions, whom the Association took it upon itself to politicise. Such concern was of particular urgency around 1900 as the traditional spheres of employment for impoverished single middle-class women – teaching or governessing – were rapidly expanding and new ones were becoming accessible. For example, although secretarial work had first been the domain of men – when courses in Gabelsberger shorthand were opened in Vienna in 1842, this was, by stipulation of the Ministry of Education, only permitted if women were excluded[74] – in the last third of the nineteenth century this area of employment in industry and trade was increasingly opened up to women.

More important for the Association, however, was the introduction of state service, above all in the Post Office, for women at this time. In 1872, as an experiment, the first forty women were employed as telegraph operators and two years later the first women not belonging to postmasters' families – these had been employed at minor post offices since 1869 – were employed by the Post Office. The age of the female civil servant had begun.[75] Their conditions of employment were disgraceful, as the *Dokumente* did not cease to point out; it frequently published detailed accounts, written by the women themselves, which brought the reality of the situation to life in a way no official report could. In 1899 telegraphists worked long hours (including Sundays and holidays), did a job which taxed nerves and body, earned an average monthly wage which, as the *Dokumente* worked out,[76] was not enough to cover even the most modest living expenses of the single woman, were not covered by any state health insurance, and were entitled to a two-week holiday only every two years. In addition, only unmarried or widowed (if childless) women were considered for this job, and then only if they could prove a clear criminal record and pass an entrance exam, the preparation for which they were expected to finance themselves. Preference was given to relatives of male civil servants, and marriage was considered to be tantamount to resignation. As a response to these appalling conditions, in 1901 the Association founded a special section for female civil servants which, inspired above all by Fickert, organised these women politically. 'Thus the spell which still lay in the word "organisation" for the women civil servants was broken,' it reported, 'and a small enthusiastic band, conscious of its dignity and strength, followed the call of the noble leader.'[77] In the same year an inquiry into their working conditions was conducted by the Association, and the ever-willing Ofner (and others) asked Parliament to intervene to improve the horrific working conditions of female clerical workers at police headquarters.[78] The practical results were a pay rise and increased public attention, which the women civil servants' day organised by the Association's section in November 1904 did its best to promote.[79] Indeed, by 1918 the Association could proudly announce that women civil servants' position had completely changed.[80] In 1908 the women civil servants' section of the Association made itself independent – a tactical necessity, the Association claimed – calling itself the Central Association of Female Postal Officials (*Zentralverein der Postbeamtinnen*) and in the following year it was able to fund its own newsletter, the *Postanstaltsbeamtin* (from 1904 the Association gave the section its own supplement in *Neues Frauenleben*). Like the Association, it came to be regarded as radical and was attacked not only by men's organisations but also by other women's organisations. It saw itself as closely linked to the women's movement, for they had the same basis, namely the emancipation and elevation of woman.[81] The vision persisted here, at the coal face, too.

In 1907 when the government announced that it had 4 million crowns to spend on accommodation it seemed that matters were to take another upward turn for the women civil servants. Fickert immediately suggested that a home for female postal workers be built in co-operation with the Central Association. It was pointed out that white-collar working women earned such a low salary that they could not afford a home of their own and were forced to live in squalid lodgings, dependent for food on expensive and poor eating places, and without care when they fell ill. In order to offer these women cheap and healthy board and lodging, a home, 'Heimhof', with a central kitchen was planned in 1909.[82] In addition to furnished and unfurnished rooms for about a hundred women, it was to offer a library and a common-room. The project was supported in the form of gifts by the leading middle-class reformers of Vienna whose names often appear in connection with the initiatives of the Association: Goldscheid, Herrdegen, Jodl, Karl Mayreder, Eugen von Philippovich and of course Ofner. Artists and writers also made donations to the building fund: the writers Goswina von Berlepsch and Eugenie delle Grazie, Rosa Mayreder, the architect Max von Ferstel, and the artists Olga Wisinger-Florian and Tina Blau. The project was to be organised as a co-operative based on the principle of self-help and self-organisation. Ninety per cent of the finance was to be given by the state and the home was to be open to women in a variety of white-collar professions: to teachers, artists, writers. Yet, much to the dismay of the Central Association, it soon transpired that the co-operative form of the initiative limited participants to those women with a more than minimal income and thus excluded many in need, above all the retired civil servants. And indeed, when it was officially opened in October

1911 – the first women's purpose-built home on a co-operative basis – it was discovered that annual board and lodging alone came to more than the annual salary of the vast majority of those for whom it was primarily intended. The occupants of the home were therefore those women in the upper income and social status bracket – some teachers, students and those in the liberal professions. The Association interpreted this failure to fulfil the original goal as proof of the state's exploitation of its female employees.[83] 'Heimhof' indicated once again how the Association and the state conflicted. Even if the state co-operated as it increasingly did as regards the self-help initiatives of the Association, it did so in a different spirit. In the eyes of the Association, the state's representatives wished to give 'Heimhof' the aura of a government charity; at the opening ceremony they did not even mention the Association's and above all Fickert's part in the project, and the Association's representative was not allowed to speak. After all, the spirit of 'solidarity, mutual help and self-confidence on the part of working and thinking women',[84] which was promoted by Fickert and which the Association wished to see realised in 'Heimhof', was hardly welcomed by the state.

Femininity and Power

Fickert did not equate femininity with the traditional middle-class woman's roles of housewife and mother. However, her wish to make women aware of their position in society increasingly came to mean teaching women to see how these traditional roles could give them power. This development was in part fired by a rapid rise in the cost of living and by a meat shortage, particularly after about 1910, both of which helped to make women aware of the politics of food distribution and consumption.

It was assumed by the General Austrian Women's Association that the state could be compared to a large household and an extended family.[85] Women could thus enter public life as housewives and managers of the household, and as mothers and nurturers of the family. They could change the basis of the state to that of the home; equal care for all members, the organisation of production and consumption, mutual consideration, mutual help, the offer of security and protection were to become the principles which governed the running of the state.[86] Yet, significantly, woman's caring role was not to maintain the status quo but to upset it. Thus the conservative housewives' movement represented by the Imperial Organisation of Austrian Housewives (*Reichsorganisation der Hausfrauen Österreichs*) was greeted with caution by the General Austrian Women's Association. It was recognised that measures which gave women more power in the home could confine them even more inescapably to the domestic sphere. 'The women's movement,' Kulka maintained, 'cannot renounce the postulate of the union of a profession and marriage.' And this union was vital if women were to become economically independent, have equal educational opportunities and wages, and also develop intellectually.[87] Yet this did not mean that the housewife was ignored, for as a consumer she had political power. Pointing to the English movement as a model, the Association explained that the aim of the consumer movement should be not only to enable housewives to buy more cheaply, but also to put pressure on producers to make production conditions more humane. By displaying consumer solidarity and refusing to buy goods produced under exploitative conditions, organised consumers, and above all women, could plant the seeds of a new, non-capitalist social order.[88]

It was not only as housewives that women were to enter public life. They could change society as the representatives of maternal qualities too. So the enforced celibacy of women teachers was fought on the grounds of women's maternal gifts, which, it was claimed, found their natural expression in teaching. Similarly, women *qua* women were to enter certain professions, for example to become factory inspectors in branches which employed a high proportion of women, as they could better empathise with the problems of women workers. Femininity itself was made a strength.

But only 'natural' femininity. As in the discussion on girls' upbringing, culturally imposed norms of femininity were regarded by some members of the Association as degenerate. Thus women's fashion was seen by some at least to be an expression of women's dependence on men. In an issue of the *Dokumente* devoted to the subject of women's dress, the architect Adolf Loos delivered a cogent feminist critique, pointing out how women's fashion was woman's attempt to gain power over man by appealing to his sensuality which had, itself, been corrupted by civilisation. The absurd excesses of fashion would disappear as women achieved economic and intellectual independence.[89] Yet the clothing of the 'new woman' should still be beautiful, if now also practical. 'Not because we women feel made to be the "decorations of the male sex" do we want to be beautiful, but out of a deep need to please ourselves. . . . But no longer do we want only to *please* ourselves and others; we have become too clever, too self-centred, and too comfortable for that,' was one summary.[90]

Women and Party Allegiance

Although the mingling of intellectuality and morality was to initiate real change, it was also recognised that women's suffrage and direct party agitation were necessary if this much higher end were to be reached. In the early years of the Association's activities the demand for women's suffrage, the main immediate impetus to its foundation, was an extreme demand and met with little serious consideration. Yet undeterred, the feminists persisted in submitting petitions to the law-making bodies and often linked the demand for suffrage with other issues, such as prostitution, indicating how suffrage was seen as a means to an end, not a goal in itself. The demand for political rights was supported by a mixture of ideological and practical arguments. Largely as a result of their changed economic position as workers, women had, Fickert maintained, become responsible, self-determining beings. They therefore deserved the vote. In addition, through their presence in political life, they would bring 'purer and more noble forms' of living: justice rather than force, one morality for men and women, a living democracy in schools rather than rigid bureaucracy.[91] Quite apart from that, Marie Musill claimed, it was only in this way that women could obtain laws suited to their particular needs and concerns. Anyway, the principle of female suffrage had been accepted, for some women (the large landowners) already had the vote – albeit by proxy – for all three representative bodies. It was simply a matter of justice being done to half the population.[92] Although the Association used women's tax contribution as an argument for their right to vote, it constantly emphasised that it was demanding suffrage for all, irrespective of tax position or rank.[93] Indeed, at a general women's meeting held in April 1896, at which a petition for suffrage for tax-paying women was to be discussed, Fickert and Lang refused to support the petition precisely because of its class bias.[94] The Association was careful not to make the vote issue a class issue, and representatives of the socialist women's movement were invited to speak at the first meetings organised by the Association. The socialists were, however, always concerned to indicate the differences between the socialist and autonomous women's movements.

Agitation by the Association continued during the 1890s; but it did not bring about any changes and died down around 1900. The subject was given renewed consideration after 1906 when it became clear that the introduction of universal suffrage for men was almost inevitable. This was partly due to socialist women's willingness to renege at least temporarily on their own claims to the vote, a move which was supported by the Association. In 1907 another petition for women's suffrage was handed in on behalf of the Association, this time by Pernerstorfer.[95] It was coolly received by the middle-class parties, who pointed to women's political immaturity and the threat female suffrage presented to Liberal parliamentary groupings. The Social Democrats supported it, however, as the Party itself was in the process of preparing an application for female suffrage.[96]

The phrasing of the Association's petition indicates that although women's legal situation as regards the vote had not changed since the first agitation in 1889, general political awareness had. The partly apologetic, explanatory tone of earlier petitions had disappeared. No longer did the fear of appearing ridiculous ring through, as it had in the 1896 petition. The call for women's suffrage was no longer the prerogative of a handful of eccentric radicals but had become an accepted topic for discussion in the political establishment. It was to be taken seriously, as indicated by an inquiry conducted by the Association in 1913 in which 'a number of highly esteemed men and women' were asked whether they thought women's suffrage was just and necessary and a promoter of culture. As was proudly noted in *Neues Frauenleben*, all gave a considered reply, proof of how the matter had progressed; previously the question had been greeted with scorn and ridicule. Almost all those asked – including Georg Brandes, Ricarda Huch, Ernst Mach and Frank Wedekind – recognised the principle of women's right to vote; only one – the zoologist Ernst Haeckel – gave a categorically negative reply.[97]

This concern for women's suffrage necessarily went hand in hand with agitation for alteration of paragraph 30 of the Law of Association of 1867. Although the feminists had circumvented this obstacle by calling political meetings as private persons, the paragraph was still a hindrance to the development of a strong political women's movement. Agitation for change on this point ran parallel to that for the vote – and with the same lack of real results. Similar arguments were used, the main one being that change was in the interest of both women and society. In 1907, in one of the Association's petitions, it was claimed that political education of women, which the paragraph prevented, was necessary, for 'in a constitutional state, those who are ignorant and inexperienced harm not only themselves but also prevent the progress of the whole'.[98]

Women's lack of the right to vote and legally to join political associations did not mean that the feminists were inactive in party politics. Quite the contrary. The leading members of the Association were very concerned to point out how party politics mattered to middle-class women and influenced their daily lives. Not only the wages and conditions of working women were affected by what was decided in Parliament, they explained at their meetings; wives and housewives, who paid direct and indirect taxes, and mothers, whose children's schooling was determined by politics, were also concerned. The Association took an active part in election campaigns and enjoined others to do so. In 1901, when the election for the Imperial Assembly was held, Fickert vigorously encouraged women to participate in the election effort on the side of the progressive candidates, in particular the Social Democrats.[99] Her call did not fall on deaf ears, for after the election, which brought defeats for the Christian Socials and victories for the Social Democrats, Leopoldine Glöckel could proudly report that the progressive women of Vienna had held numerous meetings, distributed agitatory material, collected money, organised carriages and telephones, and done a lot of administrative work. This participation also had more far-reaching consequences, Glöckel emphasised, for if women could prove their political power in this way they would obtain political rights.[100]

In the eyes of the Association's members the Christian Socials were the enemy *par excellence*. 'Six long years lie behind us in which the Christian Socials wielded their lash,' these women exclaimed, 'the blackest clericalism, the most inflated demagogy, the most blatant corruption and an unheard-of protectionism have devastated schools and our local and provincial government in the most harmful way possible.'[101] No opportunity was missed to launch an attack which would expose the Christian Socials' reactionary tendencies. Even when Lueger died, the Association – in contrast to many critical groups – did not join the chorus of eulogies. On the contrary, it remained true to its opinions and even expressed regret at the change of heart of Lueger's one-time opponents. Fickert took the opportunity to repeat her conviction that 'the general good . . . can only be based on inner, moral culture', a culture to which Lueger had contributed nothing and which he had even tried to prevent.[102]

But although Lueger was dead – and Fickert herself soon after – the Association's hostility to clericalism and the Catholic women's movement did not abate.[103] The large-scale women's meetings organised by the Catholic Imperial Women's Organisation (*Katholische Reichsfrauenorganisation*) in 1910 and 1914 were exposed in *Neues Frauenleben* as clerical propaganda exercises prompted by fear of the free-thinking women's movement and of Social Democracy.[104] Discussion of social issues at these meetings merely illustrated how the Catholic women were unwilling to envisage real change and preached Christian charity and obedience to the Catholic Church instead of political action. Women themselves were not the pillars of society, no – Kulka maintained, invoking Ibsen – 'the spirit of truth and the spirit of freedom, those are the pillars of society', implying that precisely these qualities were absent amongst the Catholic women.[105]

Criticism was not directed only at the Christian Socials and Catholics. The Liberal Party was also a popular target, for it had betrayed the spirit of constitutionalism when it deprived Lower Austrian tax-paying women of the vote for the Provincial Assembly in 1888. 'A petty politics of self-interest had suffocated liberal principles,' Fickert later explained, 'and instead of the principle "Equal rights for all", the protection of the owning class had become the motto.'[106] The Liberals had, in short, sold out. Half-heartedness, Fickert had previously declared when the provincial elections were held in 1896, 'was the curse of the Liberal party, the Party was destroyed by this half-heartedness which always came to the fore when total commitment was necessary'.[107] Yet the left liberals – the Fabians and the Social Politicians – also ran this risk, as Fickert remarked on the same occasion. She enjoined these men to 'personal firmness and the fearlessness which is necessary if they want to make what they have recognised to be right come true in the self-interested struggle of public life'.[108]

Of the political parties in Vienna around 1900 it was the Social Democratic Party which was the most attractive to the Association. Indeed, there was even talk of affiliation. To some this seemed only right and proper in view of Fickert's criticism of the capitalist form of production and Schlesinger-Eckstein's criticism of it as a form of production which oppressed the middle-class woman.[109] The possibility of affiliation was also indicated by Fickert's open support for the Social Democrats and the labour movement; this extended from helping the Social Democrats at election time and supporting strike calls, to working as a teacher together with the Social Democrats Otto Glöckel and Karl Seitz and giving talks for the Viennese Women Workers' Education Association (*Wiener Arbeiterinnen-Bildungsverein*). Indeed, after condemning the 'senile state', 'a bourgeoisie, which... has become incapable of expressing forcefully its dissatisfaction' and 'women who participate in all these public and private abuses', Fickert in a letter came to the conclusion that 'the only good thing in Austria is the labour movement which is developing and making progress'.[110] In addition, it was to August Bebel that Fickert first turned when seeking advice on how to found a women's association,[111] and his *Die Frau und der Sozialismus* (1889) remained a Bible for the feminists in the Association; according to them, it made the intimate connection between questions of ethics and economics apparent.[112]

Yet despite this open and strong sympathy and shared goals, and even a shared experience of exploitation in the world of paid labour, Fickert always resolutely rejected any kind of formal link between the Association and the Social Democratic Party or indeed any political party at all. 'The women's movement... does not need a political party, it is itself a driving force in political life and perhaps destined not only to transform party politics but to fill politics altogether with a different content.'[113] Women might here and there use political groupings to push through partial demands, Fickert conceded, but no political party could help women reach their final goal of personal development and cultural moral renewal. 'This task,' she claimed, [women] can only achieve when they are free from one-sided party interests, when they stand above the political daily fray, survey the whole with an unclouded gaze, delve down deeper into themselves and study human nature and the needs of society with an examining mind and a just heart.'[114] The autonomous individual dominated, even at the expense of practical politics. In addition, Fickert maintained, although the interests of white-collar women workers were in the last resort those of the proletariat, various factors – male resistance, dependence on the state as the employer – meant that their tactics had, temporarily at least, to differ from those of the Social Democrats.[115] For the latter, the protection of women from exploitation was paramount, for the former, women's cultural mission had to take precedence. The final goal might in each case be the same, but the means used to achieve it differed greatly and this made a clean division necessary.

Not all members of the Association were of Fickert's opinion. Minna Kautsky protested at the Association's decision not to align with the Party. She argued:

> As Social Democracy in its programme guarantees woman the same rights (political and social) as man and only Social Democracy can see such a revolutionary idea through . . . I had taken it for granted that those women who have committed themselves to struggle for their economic independence would join this party, that they would have to join it . . . if they wanted to reach their goal. I was wrong and therefore want to leave you.[116]

And leave she did.

Therese Schlesinger-Eckstein also made her exit from the Association after serious conflicts with Fickert on the question of party allegiance. A leading committee member, she had voiced her views to the Association in October 1896 when reporting on the international women's congress which had been held in Berlin. There she had suggested that the *leaders* of the women's movement could already join the Party, for they had recognised that the goals of the Social Democrats and the women's movement were the same and that their paths would inevitably meet. However, she maintained, for the majority of women such alignment was impossible as the Social Democrats neglected the plight of the new proletariat – middle-class working women.[117] This speech aroused Fickert's ire. In her concluding words at the meeting she adamantly asserted that women wanted to go their own way and in a letter apparently threatened to expel Schlesinger-Eckstein from the Association unless she 'returned'. Schlesinger-Eckstein strongly protested.[118] After this disagreement there seems to have been co-operation for about a year. Schlesinger-Eckstein, while lamenting the lack of a coherent organisation in the movement and the diversity of views of the members of the Association, even still felt able to suggest that only she and Fickert were of one mind and to express to Fickert her wishes regarding the Association:

> I would like to make our Association a Social Democratic organisation which we could run quite autonomously . . . with our own meetings, our own paper etc. The organisation of those women who are active in the several liberal professions would be the economic task of the Association, the intellectual one would be the spread of propaganda amongst middle-class women. Thus we would be in close contact with the working population, be of use to it and stimulated by it.[119]

Obviously Schlesinger-Eckstein failed to understand the distinction Fickert insisted on between supporting socialism and the Social Democratic Party as a 'very imperfect expression' of socialism in practical matters,[120] and becoming affiliated to the Party in any more formal and permanent way. Matters inevitably came to a head. The result was that Schlesinger-Eckstein left the Association and joined the Social Democratic Party, still confident that Fickert would shortly join her, a hope in which, however, she was disappointed.[121] Yet despite this difference of opinion, Schlesinger-Eckstein and Fickert remained in friendly contact. Schlesinger-Eckstein not only occasionally contributed to *Neues Frauenleben* but also admitted to Fickert that she had encountered difficulties in the Party. She commented that since their ways had parted she had been forced to acquire a thicker skin, no longer being encouraged and supported by considerate friends as during her days in the Association.[122] And to Karl Kautsky she confided: 'In the most extreme left wing of the middle-class women's movement . . . I in no way had to subordinate or disguise my socialist convictions and worked there under the most pleasant conditions. . . . Now I am among strange people who do not yet trust me.'[123]

Rosa Mayreder was less favourably disposed to the Social Democrats. She publicly expressed scepticism about their support for women's demands, commenting that 'men recognise women as equals only for as long as they themselves are oppressed' and that it was a conspicuous phenomenon that as soon as they laid their hands on power, men were only too ready to ignore women's issues.[124] Mayreder, an even stronger believer in individualism than Fickert, criticised the socialists for their dogmatism and intolerance: 'The socialist terror is today already so great that every word of criticism is considered to be *lèse-majesté*. If it continues like this then we will witness the funeral pyres of the Giordano Brunos . . . of a future anti-socialist world view.'[125] She became increasingly convinced that any form of mass movement would necessarily have to indulge in power politics. 'The means [used by the powerful] are quite the same irrespective of whether it is a question of the old powers in the shape of social rank and the Church or of the new powers which are emerging in Social Democracy or in any other up-and-coming, so-called "movement".'[126] Power politics meant appealing to the masses, with all that that implied, for 'wherever the masses are involved, where the intellect and taste of the masses are counted on, whether that be in art, politics, science, there shallowness, empty phrases, baseness rule'.[127] The exceptional individual would be forced to come down to the level of the masses, something Mayreder found intolerable and culturally damaging.

Of course, the question of the Association's relationship to the Social Democrats was not only a matter for the Association but also for the Social Democratic women. And they made no bones about their unwillingness to contemplate formal co-operation on any terms, despite Victor Adler's admiration for Fickert. Such women may claim to be anti-capitalist, a leading agitator, Charlotte Glass, commented, directly referring to Fickert and the Association, but, she went on to remark, 'It is only strange that the Association far more often emphasises its negative "anti-capitalist tendency" than that tendency's logical consequence: socialism.'[128] Even Schlesinger-Eckstein was attacked for her speech to the Association about the international women's congress in Berlin. She was, claimed Glass, blind to the class character of the Social Democratic women's movement and played off the suffering of middle-class working women against that of working-class women.[129] In the eyes of the Social Democrats, the autonomous women's movement could at best be reformist, not revolutionary. The Association rejected this judgement and defiantly proclaimed, 'The women's movement is at its heart revolutionary, for it aims at a fundamental reorganisation of all forms of human living together, a reorganisation that perhaps even Social Democracy does not dream of.'[130] The primacy of the vision remained unquestioned.

CHAPTER 4

Equal but Different. The League of Austrian Women's Associations

The League of Austrian Women's Associations (see figure 6) emerged in circumstances which immediately indicate the difference in political direction of the two main faces of autonomous Austrian feminism. While the General Austrian Women's Association was a direct response to women's lack of political rights, the League emerged as part of the feminist network, more as a public relations body of the Austrian women's movement than as a vehicle of campaign. It had its origins in a call from the politically moderate International Council of Women (ICW) to send a delegate to the second general meeting of the Council to be held in London in 1899. Fickert invited various women's associations to select a joint delegate; their choice alighted on the *doyenne* of the movement, Marianne Hainisch. According to her, she was very impressed by what she saw in London. 'I knew immediately that I wanted to return to my country with the mission of organising Austrian women through their associations, that is, of forming a league of Austrian women's associations which was to be attached to the ICW.'[1] The idea was slow to catch on and on its foundation in May 1902 only thirteen associations joined the League.[2] In the spirit of the ICW, all associations had been invited to join irrespective of confession, nationality, goal or class. In practice the national women's organisations refused even to answer the invitation and the socialist and Catholic organisations did not join either.

At the constituting meeting on 5 May 1902 Hainisch was careful to explain that the goal of the League, which in 1903 became a member of the ICW, was merely to support the individual associations in their activities, not to compete with them. She also emphasised the League's wish to represent all the member associations, although she rightly saw that their variety would greatly limit the practical work the League could do. 'We may aim only for what all want and that is why we should proceed slowly and circumspectly,' she cautioned.[3] As a result, the League's main aim at first was merely to open women's eyes to

6. The first general meeting of the Bund Österreichischer Frauenvereine, in front of the house of Marianne Hainisch in Vienna on May 21st, 1903. Marianne Hainisch is marked by a cross. Österreichische Nationalbibliothek.

social problems and how they were personally affected by them. This timid approach meant that at the constituting meeting the League limited its goals to the admission of women, to the care of the poor, orphaned and sick, and to the foundation of vocational schools for girls.[4] It concentrated on women's contribution to the well-being of women, the family and the populace at large; women's work in the public sphere remained confined to social work. The League's emphasis on doing – and being – good was underlined by its (and the ICW's) motto 'Do as you would be done by'. However, as Hainisch claimed, for the organised women of the League this philanthropy had further consequences, namely the final goal of the 'woman equal in value and rights: as daughter, wife, mother, worker, citizen, everywhere striving for the highest and demanding the highest, not the same as man, but equal'.[5] She thus pointed to the demarcation lines between her vision and Fickert's demand for a fundamental restructuring of social and gender relations. Both talked of upward striving, but while Hainisch made changed women the goal, Fickert saw that goal to be a changed society.

Despite its modest beginnings, the number of member associations grew so that in 1914 the League could boast a total membership of around 40,000 women (not taking overlaps into account) in eighty associations, which ranged from the Athenäum, the Art School, the Austrian Peace Society and the Settlement to the Association for the Improvement of Women's Dress.[6] It was divided into commissions, each with a chairwoman. Its declared goal was now 'to bridge social contrasts, to exclude conflict as far as possible and to awaken the striving for high, moral goals in all its members'.[7] In November 1905 in an effort to draw its disparate constituting elements together, the League had launched the paper *Der Bund* [The League]. *Zentralblatt des Bundes Österreichischer Frauenvereine*, which was edited by Henriette Herzfelder. In the leader to the first issue Hainisch explained that it was to report on the women's movement in the whole of the Habsburg Empire and to promote the League's ideal of the equal woman.[8] It focused on equal education opportunities for women, on the family, paid employment, and the law. There was no talk of searching for a different social order as there was in *Neues Frauenleben*, nor of the gender one-sidedness of the status quo or of the potential power of women's solidarity as in the *Dokumente*. How then did the League attempt to realise its declared goal of the 'moral, intellectual and economic development of woman'[9] and how did its activities in each of these three spheres differ from those of the Association?

Women's Moral Development

Like the Association, the League often touched on questions of moral education and public morality. According to Herzfelder, the former could be achieved by the introduction of co-education in schools, for then 'man and woman get to know each other in their true form, not in those drapes and masks which the mimicry of love gladly makes use of'.[10] 'In the place of secrecy comes trust, in the place of curiosity the unquestioning acknowledgement of natural difference. What an exceptional lifelong moral footing is given to a person with such a childhood!,' she declared.[11] In 1910 the League requested that secondary schools turn co-educational, which in practice meant girls' entry into boys' schools; in this way girls, it argued, could get a proper academic schooling, free. The request fell on deaf ears.

The League also concerned itself with public morality and by necessity with its darker sides. On the occasion of the Riehl trial it handed in a petition protesting at state-controlled brothels, which was signed by all but four of the member associations. Feelings had changed considerably since the débâcle experienced by the Association when it had asked the women's associations to sign a similar petition over a decade earlier.[12] This change of heart may have been a result of the campaign to bring the issue into the realm of subjects acceptable for discussion by women which the Association had waged since 1894; it may also have been a result of the scandal aroused by the Riehl trial. But more probably it was the rather different tone and content of the League's petition that made it more acceptable. For here attention is directed to the evil of prostitution as a force which undermines the health of the individual, the family and the population in general; and its existence is claimed to be evidence of a cynicism which undermines the family and marriage by corrupting young men, these women's sons. These women petition expressly as the mothers of families, concerned to protect their sons who are encouraged to licence by state measures which were intended to control prostitution but did quite the opposite. Thus unlike the Association, which pointed to the degradation of the prostitutes and the inhumanity of the system which protected the public from the prostitutes but not the prostitutes themselves, the League banished condemnation of prostitution as a 'demoralising, unnatural, inhuman degradation and exploitation of woman'[13] as an afterthought to the end of the list of reasons for its petition. Some of the demands made there are indeed those made by Mayreder in her handling of the case. Common to both are the condemnation of measures of state toleration, the demand for stiffer penalties for colluding with the white slave trade, the limitation of police power in the matter and the introduction of sex education classes in school. But one important cause of prostitution – the plight of female workers – is left unmentioned by the League. Nor does it appeal for improved working conditions and extended working opportunities for women. Instead, it emphasises women's familial, maternal role and particular concern for young people by demanding that women be allowed to become legal guardians, that the age of consent for girls be raised, and that existing provisions for court orders over minors be fully implemented. Also in contrast to Mayreder, the League takes a far more punitive line, calling in the same petition for the severe punishment of the transmission of VD. It does not suggest solutions which would confront the phenomenon at a deeper level, as Mayreder and members of the Association do in their support of concubinage. In contrast to Mayreder's angry outrage, the tone is conciliatory towards the authorities, for as the League placatingly declares, 'We know that the struggle against prostitution is an unsolved problem and that this grave social evil can be confined only when all the relevant state institutions co-operate with voluntary social workers', that is, according to the League's vision, when the state co-operates with women.[14]

This emphasis on women as the guardians of the moral good of society and the family, which, as the primary unit of human organisation, must be protected but simultaneously given power, is a feature which runs through the League's discussion on sexuality and morality. It was only in the family, Hainisch declared, that sex education could take place; only there could the 'wonders of nature, of becoming, growing and declining' be adequately communicated, for sex education in school neglected the moral aspects and undermined natural shame.[15] In *Der Bund* Hainisch supported calls for film censorship in the name of the moral protection of young people and the struggle against increasing moral decline.[16] In addition, the 'new ethics' of the mother protection movement were condemned by the League for they encouraged women to give way to their own and others' desires. The monogamous marriage which imposed on both partners the same responsibilities was the only ideal for the League.[17] And so the unmarried mother was looked on askance and the sex reform side of the activities of the League for the Protection of Mothers rejected. The other side of this organisation's activities, the campaign for more maternity regulations, was, however, gladly acknowledged. Yet such regulations were not primarily intended to emancipate women by making it easier for them to combine motherhood and professional life, but to protect mothers so that they could leave paid employment and increase the birth-rate. However, these demands were also given an obvious political thrust, for, it was claimed, women would only have children and become aware of the important social role they could play as mothers if they were given rights which they had been hitherto denied. 'Only through active participation in the life of the state will women come to understand its most vital interests and be willing to satisfy them even if this means making sacrifices; the female citizen with full rights will be a mother who is better fitted to her lofty task and an educator of better citizens.'[18] The family and woman's position in it were to be paramount but were also to be used as a lever to demand equal rights for women. The private was indeed made political, but in a way that shored up woman's maternal, familial role.

Women's Intellectual Development

Women's intellectual development, the second element of Hainisch's vision, was approached by the League along the conventional lines already followed by associations such as the Association for Extended Women's Education. It supported demands for equality in women's secondary and higher education for largely the same reasons but also saw the devaluation of university study by dilettante young ladies to be a danger. A university education, claimed Hainisch, was to be restricted to gifted women who studied from an 'innermost calling';[19]

the university would thus become an elitist institution for women, not a place of general higher education or vocational training. So although educational establishments were to be open to both sexes equally, higher standards were set for women than for men, large numbers of whom certainly attended university without any sense of inner calling. But the real task of formal education for these feminists was character building. And this was also a matter for mothers 'free of frailty and feebleness', who were to exert their salutary influence on (boys') schools, 'for no one is more appointed to judge what promotes or inhibits the development of the child than the mother'.[20] Hainisch was therefore an active supporter of moves to reform secondary schools which were initiated by left liberals in 1898. These took the form of an inquiry organised by Robert Scheu and the magazine *Die Wage* in which men such as Bernatzik, Karl Mayreder, Jodl, Gomperz and Philippovich took part.[21] Ten years later this was followed up by another inquiry, this time organised by the government authorities.[22] Hainisch, like her male colleagues, lamented the emphasis which the existing system placed on dry knowledge as opposed to a general education. She called again for the viewpoint of mothers to be heard and for the abolition of gender-specific school education.[23] After about 1914 this found support in suggestions by some women for a year of compulsory social service for women. This, they claimed, would prepare women for their domestic, maternal and social duties and counteract the conventional upbringing that fostered dilettantism in practical matters.[24]

Women's Economic Development

By its commitment to women's vocational education the League eagerly continued in the tradition of the first response to the woman question and on that score it achieved most. In 1910 it finally achieved a long-standing goal by forcing all state vocational schools to be opened to girls. This aroused considerable opposition from a number of parliamentary representatives, who argued that women would deprive men of a livelihood and push many male artisans down into the proletariat.[25] The foundation of numerous schools for domestic training, of a careers advice bureau for girls and the secured continued existence of the women's agricultural school were also achievements of which the League was proud.

The well-meaning but limited nature of the League's commitment to working-class women's interests is revealed in its discussion of the servant question. An extreme illustration of the narrow-mindedness of housewives, so lamented by the Association in its discussion, is offered by Louise Hackl. She indignantly remarks on the increasingly demanding attitude of servants, which had apparently culminated at a meeting in Paris at which 'it is said that there was hardly any talk of duties, but only of rights'.[26] In her view the problem was compounded by men who meddled in housewives' business and excluded the housewives themselves from a discussion of the issues which were their central concern. A German doctor had even had the temerity to suggest that immediate dismissal should not be the lot of servants with syphilis although this was a disease, Hackl insisted in a graphic depiction, which could be spread even by using the same handkerchief. Such liberal attitudes were, she asserted, merely the thin end of the wedge which would ultimately lead to the dissolution of the patriarchal household and the establishment of – *horribile dictu* – communal kitchens. Although this extreme view is not representative of the views of the League as a whole it is remarkable that it was given serious consideration at all.

In October 1910 on the occasion of the much-delayed reform of the regulations governing domestic service *Der Bund* printed an article which lamented the inadequacy of the new regulations and remarked that the two groups of women immediately concerned, namely the housewives and the servants (whose interests Hackl had also completely forgotten), had not been consulted by the men who made the laws. Yet although the League was critical, calling the new regulations 'merely a simplifying summary of the 166 paragraphs which make up the regulations concerning servants',[27] the motives behind the criticism ultimately display solidarity not so much with the servants as with the housewives, women like the League's own members. To be sure, bad working conditions are acknowledged but primarily because they make service unattractive, lead to a scarcity of servants and therefore higher wages. 'Is it then not more advisable,' these women rhetorically asked, '. . . to aim at an agreement which can bring both parties advantages and peace, than to submit one day to the dictatorial force of Socialist power?'[28]

Here the fear which lurked behind the League's attitude to class relations has come out into the open: social reform is necessary in order to appease the workers and avoid socialism. Talk of an anti-capitalist social order was not part of the League's discussion as it was part of the Association's. Of course, this did not in practice mean that the Association supported revolutionary change, nevertheless its attitude to class relations was based not primarily on philanthropy but on laws and regulations that might indeed go against these middle-class women's own interests. The League, while condemning and lamenting workers' poverty, did not go even this far, but contented itself with calls and plans for help which were not, however, to threaten existing power relations.

This class bias becomes apparent in the League's treatment of women's rights. In 1904 in its petition for the reform of the Civil Code the Association demanded the legal recognition of cohabitation and the rights that would go with it, and also the equality of illegitimate children with legitimate ones, both issues which would benefit the lower classes more than the middle classes. The League, on the other hand, concentrated on improving the position of women within marriage and the family by, for example, pressing for the financial security of the divorced wife, an issue which affected working-class women less, as many of these earned their own money.[29] Women's political rights, too, became a class issue. 'While a large number of men in our country were still without political rights,' the League explained when universal male suffrage was introduced, '... women's demands for the franchise could be rejected as untimely. The exclusion of all women from the right to vote while giving this right to all men, illiterates included, must however be felt by every woman to be discrimination and a grave limitation for her sex as a whole.'[30] The catalyst for the League's renewed agitation was the fact that men of all classes had the vote, not that the vast majority of women were still excluded.

The League was not only class-bound, it was also, despite its at times rousing comments, concerned not to overstep the boundaries of propriety. *Der Bund* does not indulge in the sarcasm, wit and unabashed criticism of the *Dokumente* and *Neues Frauenleben*. Thus when the respected *Österreichische Rundschau* published a piece by Princess Stephanie of Belgium condemning women's emancipation as 'the wild torrent of millions of immature wishes' which threatened 'to drag states, societies into a deep chasm',[31] the League demurred, insisting that feminists were privileged women who were nobly fighting for better conditions for their less fortunate sisters.[32] The Association hardly deigned to take the Princess's outpourings seriously, caustically pointing out in *Neues Frauenleben* that her social position was the only reason why her tirade had been published at all.[33] Similarly, according to the League, government ministers spoke in a ceremonious and sympathetic manner, the concerns of female public employees were greeted with 'well-meaning understanding' (if little else), and the speeches of superiors were described as 'warm words' with which 'the diligence and sense of duty' of working women were 'praised'.[34] Obviously the League was intent on avoiding conflict. It also tried to paper over the divisions between the different wings of the women's movement. It did not, for example, condemn the first Catholic women's day in May 1910 as the Association did. On the contrary. Although the League and the Catholic Imperial Women's Organisation parted company on the questions of Catholic propaganda in schools, female suffrage and woman's 'God-given' subordination to man,[35] the League welcomed much of what the Catholics said, for the Catholic women were perceived to be following the same goals as the ICW.[36] And as Hainisch generously explained, 'every achievement by those working for society, regardless of who that is, must become part of the general good'.[37]

A 'Guerrilla War'

To mark its first anniversary in 1903, Marie Lang welcomed the League as proof that Austrian women, after earlier mutual intolerance, had at last seen that there were common interests at stake and acclaimed Hainisch as the only woman able to unite them. As a one-time insider of the General Austrian Women's Association Lang should, however, have known better, for it must have been clear that co-operation between the two organisations would be almost impossible. Mayreder had with greater perception obviously intimated as much to Fickert on the League's inception, remarking to her after the first wrangles, 'you know I am no believer in the League and have never expected the least thing from it'.[38] It is hardly surprising that the history of the Association was chequered with conflict with other women's groups. After all it had been born in an atmosphere of dissension and suspicion in the wake of disagreement over the women's day, and even within its own ranks there was little unity. Generally, the Association was, in its early days at least, regarded as breaking too many taboos concerning middle-class women. This was particularly true with regard to the two most sensitive issues – prostitution and the working class – for both, unlike the struggle for women's rights, necessarily involved contact with groups marginal to middle-class society. In addition, the clearly unladylike tone of the Association's discussions was too much for members of other middle-class groups, who accused the Association of turning to methods of agitation: its members, it was noted with alarm, insulted other middle-class women and flattered the socialists, talked of the most momentous social questions with impunity, but were at the same time unable to conceal their true colours as well-heeled middle-class ladies, the deserved object of ridicule of the true working class.[39]

This early criticism and mistrust of the Association and of Fickert in particular on the part of other autonomous women's organisations as well as the internal tensions within the Association immediately made its position within the League difficult. It was abundantly clear that the League and with it the majority of such groups on the one hand and the Association on the other were inevitably straining in opposite directions. The protection of mothers, for example, was a cause supported by the League, but only if motherhood occurred within marriage; prostitution was to be condemned and eradicated, but by repressive legislation; domestic servants were to be treated better, but not given their due as employees; and marriage law was to be reformed, but to the benefit of the middle-class wife. Fickert, by contrast, was concerned to challenge the power relations the League wished to uphold. For her the protection of mothers also meant moral reform; prostitution was also a product of the capitalist system of production and bourgeois system of morals; domestic servants were to be employees with rights; and marriage law was to be reformed also to the benefit of unmarried mothers and illegitimate children. Of course, this fundamental political difference did not go unnoticed and without comment, and Fickert made no bones about what she thought the League really wished to achieve. 'Nothing new is to replace what has become an anachronism. What exists is to be merely improved, merely cobbled together with new repairs,' she lamented. In addition she noted of the League that 'not ability but property, being a member of a certain social class, is still what matters', and asked, 'would it not be a task worthy of a women's movement to help overcome this form of society?' But instead of this, the League stopped short, for 'where ... middle-class needs end, there is at most mild goodwill'. The women's movement as represented by the League was 'bourgeois through and through and therefore exclusively a movement for women's rights,' she pronounced.[40]

Difficulties between the two organisations became apparent very early in the League's history. The last-minute decision of the League when it was founded that the president of an association could not be voted on to the committee was undisguisedly directed at Fickert's exclusion and immediately sowed the seeds of dissension.[41] In addition, the committee of the Association, even before the League's decision, had elected Mayreder to be its representative; this made her the League's third vice-president. This decision had obviously hurt Fickert's feelings; she felt she should have been asked to take on the position. And it was a decision which Mayreder herself did not welcome, chastising her acceptance as 'typical short-sightedness and weakness of will' and remarking that the position itself would demand 'a horrendous sacrifizio dell' intelletto' on her part.[42] She was surprised that Fickert consented at all to the Association's membership of the League. Mayreder reacted to the situation by reneging on her own agreement to take over the post of third vice-president.[43] Fickert, however, instead of promptly executing the Association's exit from the League as agreed at the meeting in April 1902, responded to the tensions by initiating what Mayreder called a 'guerrilla war',[44] much to the latter's dismay and anger. This Fickert launched on 24 May 1902 when she sharply criticised the League both for inept organisation and lack of a clear line in a progressive direction, a two-pronged line of attack which was subsequently to be sustained.[45] A year later when the second general meeting of the League was held, she compared the women of the League with children overwhelmed by excessively generous Christmas presents:

> Unfortunately this impression cannot be avoided by even the most favourably disposed observer when he follows the superficial activities of the society ladies, sees how they approach great social problems with such modest means and think they can solve them by founding a new association which has a high-falutin name, unattainable goals and often no more members than it has committee members.[46]

A pervasive dilettantism, general muddle-headedness and personal animosity could be observed, she caustically remarked. She even insinuated that it was more a case of a class-bound lack of interest than a lack of understanding. 'Did the ladies leading sheltered lives simply not understand or did they lack interest in the interests of the unmarried mother?' she disingenuously asked when the suggestion that unmarried mothers be assured maintenance from the father before the child's birth was greeted with apathy.[47] The question of dress reform, on the other hand, had managed to arouse lively discussion.

Inevitably, it soon came to a confrontation. The trigger was a notice which appeared in January 1906 in the *Staatsbeamtin*, the supplement of *Neues Frauenleben* which represented the women civil servants' section of the Association.[48] Under the heading 'Betrayed' it commented on a notice in *Der Bund*. This announced the foundation of a new organisation for female post office and telegraph workers, the Imperial Union of Female Post and Telegraph Workers (*Reichsverband der Post- und Telegraphenmanipulantinnen*), which had been guaranteed support by high-ranking officials. In response, the Association asked the League to justify its implicit support for a post office workers' organisation which would represent a rival to the Association's own section, an organisation which was notoriously not supported by high-ranking officials. An extraordinary general meeting was held by the Association at the end of March of the same year. It was called by twenty-one members of the Association, including Hainisch, Leopoldine Glöckel and Henriette Herzfelder. In turn they asked the editors of *Neues Frauenleben* to justify their negative stance towards the League. A heated discussion ensued during which Hainisch welcomed the

Association's threatened exit from the League, while Julius Ofner and others emphasised the progressive and dynamic role of the Association in preventing the League and the Austrian women's movement as a whole from stagnating. The majority voted that the Association should leave the League.[49] At the same time twenty-four members (including Hainisch, Glöckel and other leading women in the League) left the Association, convinced that the differences between the two organisations could not be bridged. They protested that they could no longer belong to an association which continually attacked the League, although the League had the solidarity of all women as its guiding principle and wished to struggle along with women of all political persuasions against their legal discrimination.[50] But this showdown did nothing to curb the Association's criticism. It persisted in attacking the political ambivalence and bad organisation of the League.

CHAPTER 5

The Feminist Fringe

While the two main women's groupings were locked in a war of attrition, organisations on the feminist fringe followed a calmer course. These were those organisations run by women which concentrated on one specific activity but which were at the same time concerned to bring about cultural regeneration. It was less the areas of practical concern they touched on than the two main ideological driving forces which informed them that brought them together. These forces were the belief in the primacy of individual change and its leading role in collective moral renewal, and involvement in a women's network.

Changing the Individual

The Viennese Settlement Association (*Verein Wiener Settlement*) like the General Austrian Women's Association was based on thc creed that individual change was the path to social change. The idea behind the Settlement movement was that middle-class helpers would live in a working-class district, get to know proletarian poverty from the inside, make friends with the local inhabitants, and organise activities for them. They would give spiritual and intellectual rather than material help. In this way class barriers would be overcome and the poor given a taste of the delights of middle-class culture. The Viennese movement was initiated by Marie Lang, who while in London attending the International Abolitionst Congress in July 1898 had had the opportunity to visit the Passmore Edwards Settlement. Greatly impressed, she returned to Vienna eager to found a similar establishment, gave several talks and tried to stimulate interest in her project, particularly among the women of the General Austrian Women's Association. She had a measure of success, for after one talk about thirty women including Hainisch offered their services.[1]

The idea was given hopes of realisation in February 1901 when Karl Kuffner, owner of a large brewery in the working-class district of Ottakring, placed a house at Lang's disposal. In that month the Settlement Association was constituted under Lang's direction; it was supported by members of the socially progressive intelligentsia. The building in Ottakring was fitted out by the Secessionist artists Josef Hoffmann, Kolo Moser and Alfred Roller amongst others,[2] and opened in October of the same year. Karl Renner, who much admired Lang, held the post of president of the Association from 1901 to 1903, and Else Federn became the dedicated chief organiser. After just over a year the Association could boast a morning kindergarten for forty toddlers, afternoon play-groups for schoolchildren, and evening events for apprentices and mothers. These included musical soirées and literary readings.[3] The Settlement extended its activities to include the provision of a cooked midday meal to the children of working mothers, advisory groups for mothers and mothers-to-be and a summer holiday camp for which children were selected not according to the traditional criterion of how obedient they were but according to social and physical need. In many cases these were the first initiatives of the kind in Austria. A conscious effort was made to integrate all religions and nationalities. Following the principle of not offering charity but cultivating friendship and respect on both sides, a small membership fee had to be paid in order to be entitled to take part in the Settlement's activities.

The supporters of the Settlement emphasised that the individuality of both Settlement workers and recipients was central. Not alms but the personality was to be given by the former – 'Give not your money but yourself' was the motto of the Settlement movement. And individuality was to be cultivated in the latter, particularly in the children – 'Each is treated as an individual,' its supporters proudly announced.[4] They believed that a 'regeneration of the totality of political and social life'[5] could be achieved by treating people as individuals and understanding the circumstances in which they lived. Self-help, harmony, evolution and the promotion of the individual's own strength and diligence without regard for class prejudice were the leitmotifs. But in practice this meant the transmission of the values of the 'highly cultured, free-thinking bourgeoisie' to the 'circles newly striving for elevation',[6] and this indicates the Settlement's limitations. It was tacitly expected of the working class that they would adjust to middle-class cultural values, and that this would suffice to bring about the envisaged social harmony. The working class was to be raised to the level of the bourgeoisie, yet without the material basis being touched. As Else Federn wrote: 'Within the limitations set by economic need, so many intellectual pleasures, so much refined cultivation is possible.'[7] A

7. Portrait photograph of Eugenie Schwarzwald by d'Ora Benda on November 30th, 1923. Österreichische Nationalbibliothek.

personal commitment which would bring about individual change on both sides was to suffice.

A number of other women's initiatives emerged as a result of this belief in individual change as the precondition of social change. Many of these dealt with education, for education was seen as the main path to effecting this sought-after development. In contrast to the educational foundations of the pragmatic, first-wave feminists, the initiatives of these later feminists were not primarily intended to equip women to earn in a way fitting their social station and to adapt to an existing education system, but to bring new elements into this system. One of the largest initiatives was the complex of private educational establishments run by Eugenie Schwarzwald (see figure 7). An imposing, dynamic figure, she was a Jew with a doctorate in German literature from Zurich University, and a friend and confidante of a range of distinguished people. At various times these included the writers Elias Canetti, Egon Friedell, Rainer Maria Rilke and Robert Musil (who used her and her husband Hermann as the prototypes for Frau and Herr Tuzzi in *Der Mann ohne Eigenschaften* [The Man Without Qualities]), as well as those more closely connected with Schwarzwald's schools, such as Loos, Oskar Kokoschka and Arnold Schönberg. The friendship with Loos did not, however, secure a similar relationship with the writer Peter Altenberg or with Karl Kraus, and Eugenie – like so many others – became a target for the latter's pen. She and Hermann unwittingly served as the models for the busybody Hofrat and Hofrätin Schwarz-Gelber in Kraus's satirical *Die letzten Tage der Menschheit* (The Last Days of Mankind).

Schwarzwald's educational establishment resembled a *Gesamtkunstwerk* as it embodied a vision of harmony in multiplicity by bringing together several different types of school under one roof and administration. The core was the *lycée* for girls founded in 1901 which maintained six classes for ages 10 to 16.[8] The range of the school was extended in the first year by the foundation of the first of the grammar school classes, which were intended to enable girls to sit the *Matura* (taken at the *akademisches Gymnasium*) after four years. Further education courses were also offered to those girls who already had a *lycée* education; these lasted another two years but were in no way equivalent to university study. In 1903 a junior school was started, the first in Vienna to be co-educational, and in 1910–11 a secondary school for girls was founded with equal weight being placed on the natural sciences and modern and classical languages. The whole complex grew steadily over the years, from 180 pupils in the first academic year (1901–2) to 470 by the end of the academic year 1912–13. It moved to new premises in the centre of Vienna in 1902 and again ten years later, the rooms of the second building being redesigned in 1913–14 by Loos. This commission of twenty-two classrooms, the headmistress's room, library, staff room, a caretaker's flat, a roof garden and an assembly hall which doubled as a gym was the only project of the Schwarzwald schools given to Loos to be actually carried out, although even then the original plan was more impressive than what eventually had to be settled for. Yet even if economy measures thwarted the original plan for the assembly hall, which was to include walls half covered with marble, it was still an impressive room with wood panelling, a pea-green felt carpet and yellow silk-shaded lamps.[9] In addition, a school for about 200 pupils on the Semmering, a mountain near Vienna, was planned in 1912–13 with Loos as the architect.[10] The outbreak of war, however, forced this plan to be abandoned.

Some of the teachers Schwarzwald employed came from the group of artists she and her husband promoted. Loos was a case in point. Not only the school's interior designer, he was also a good personal friend and was responsible for the interior design of the couple's flat in the Josefstädter Strasse.[11] In addition, he was allowed to hold a private architectural class on the school's premises in the years 1912–13 and 1913–4 and taught history of art in 1911–12 as one of the further education courses. Loos was a pivotal personality for Schwarzwald and the school, for he introduced both Kokoschka and Schönberg to Schwarzwald. At the time of meeting, Kokoschka was being hounded by the press and regularly fired from his posts as art teacher in state schools and evening classes. He thus took on a post as art teacher at Schwarzwald's *lycée* where officials and the press had – so he thought – no say. But even there, the rumours of the gossip-mongers reached him.[12] And the officials did intervene; in 1913 he was forced to give up teaching at the school, unable to prove a teaching qualification.[13] In the case of Schönberg, Schwarzwald found it demeaning that he was forced to search for private pupils and so offered him rooms on her premises at the school in the afternoons, when there was no teaching, so that he could hold a free seminar. The composers Alexander von Zemlinsky and Elsa Bienenfeld acted as colleagues. In 1904–5, the first year when courses were held, Schönberg taught harmony and counterpoint, Zemlinsky theory of form and instrumentation, and Bienenfeld the musical history of the nineteenth century. The courses were poorly attended and in the following year the composer Egon Wellesz and the pianist Rudolf Weirich were the only participants.[14] Schönberg's links with the school did not break with the cessation of the courses. From 1918 to 1920 he held a seminar in composition for the Schwarzwald school in his flat and the first concerts of the Association for Private Musical Performances (*Verein für musikalische Privataufführungen*) were held in the assembly hall of the school. Schwarzwald remained active on the musical scene, giving the young Egon Wellesz, whose fiancée Emmy was a pupil at the school, the opportunity to run a course for the school's musically gifted pupils. These included Helene Weigel, later a distinguished actress and wife of Bertolt Brecht, Alice Herdan(-Zuckmayer) and Elisabeth Neumann(-Viertel), later the wives of the writers and theatre directors Carl Zuckmayer and Berthold Viertel respectively. Even after the war, Schwarzwald was still supporting avant-garde musicians, such as Josef Matthias Hauer.

The precept of Schwarzwald's pedagogy can be summed up by her own term 'creative education'. For Schwarzwald this meant child-centred teaching, the release of the creative artist in every child, and the activation of all its powers of feeling and thinking. Education was not to be merely a means to an end, and nor was childhood a preparatory stage but a phase of life in its own right, with its own claims to satisfaction and recognition, and a phase during which a child learnt of its own accord, out of necessity.[15] In order for children to develop, a 'purified atmosphere' was needed, an atmosphere in which there was no war and no class struggle. The teacher was not to be an authority figure who inspired fear or imposed discipline, but a friend who allowed each individual child's talent to have a chance and encouraged the child to have the courage to go its own way. School was to be a place of joy, a paradise for children.[16]

The precepts governing Schwarzwald's establishment were, then, very different from those of, say, the grammar school of the Association for Extended Women's Education. Schwarzwald shared the non-interventionists' attitude to education, represented amongst the feminists above all by Lang and Mayreder. Indeed, Mayreder acted as an unknowing mentor to Eugenie Schwarzwald, who confessed to having been deeply influenced by two sentences from Mayreder's collection of essays *Zur Kritik der Weiblichkeit* (Towards a Critique of Femininity; English title: A Survey of the Woman Problem) (1905): 'One educates with what one is, not with what one knows', and 'In order for people to become themselves, they must above all overcome the influence of their education'. These she copied out and placed on her desk at the school. Thus, she claimed, many thousands of Viennese children had reason to thank Mayreder for a happy youth and undisturbed development.[17] In accordance with this belief in non-intervention, Schwarzwald, like Lang, emphasised naturalness. For her this meant the recognition of the significance of the body, of humanity's place in the natural environment, and above all the awareness of the alienation from the foundations of physical and spiritual health which city life imposed; it would be the highest task of culture to reunite humanity and nature, to find the way back to the primal mother.[18] This could be achieved in a country spot, where practical, physical outdoors work combined with intellectual work and the observation of nature would achieve the harmonious development of all talents and strengths[19] and promote health, uprightness and strength of character.[20] It was precisely this paradise on earth that Schwarzwald wished to achieve with the Semmering school. That Loos was the right architect for such a job was clear, for his was also a struggle against unnaturalness, untruth, excess and lack of authenticity, Schwarzwald maintained.[21] Loos's own precepts become clear in his essay 'Rules for He Who Builds in the Mountains' ('Regeln für den, der in den Bergen baut'), published in the school's annual report in 1913, in which he enjoins the architect above all to truth.[22] With this emphasis on honesty, simplicity and sometimes also puritanism, Schwarzwald was joining a *cri de coeur* of the feminists. It is the same rebellion against social hypocrisy as can be found in the feminist condemnation of, for example, the double morality, women's upbringing, and convention.

Although the Semmering school project could not be realised, the ideas underlying it could to some extent be applied in the daily running of existing schools. That school was fun for pupils and also teachers is demonstrated in the tenth annual report by Clara Reiss, a teacher in the primary school, who wrote a contribution on amusing grammar lessons.[23] The spontaneity of both teacher and children can be clearly felt as can Reiss's concern that the children really understand and do not merely repeat by rote. To this end she obviously played a lot with the children, stimulated their imagination and let them talk. The same lively freshness is found in a contribution on the 'School Essay of Our 8-Year Olds', with 132 original examples,[24] essays that indicate the school's policy of letting the children express themselves freely without regard for orthography or grammar, rules or conventions. The aim of promoting character development shown clearly in Schwarzwald's appeal to parents not to help their children with homework, which should anyway be kept within limits. She underlines the need instead for creative relaxation, by which she means reading a good book, meeting boys and girls of the same age, enjoying masterpieces at the *Burgtheater* and the opera, going to good concerts, visiting museums, enjoying walks outside the city, and now and again going to a jolly dance which does not go on until past bedtime. She warned against all late-night amusements and frivolous gossip, as these would infect the pupils with the heady society morality she was so opposed to. She appealed to parents to dress their daughters in simple practical clothing, to abandon the corset, jewellery and lavish pocket money. Schwarzwald justified this call to the family for help in carrying out the school's work by claiming that 'the school in turn serves to strengthen family life in so far as it is what it should be, that is, not a school which merely teaches but a school which educates, not the place which merely transmits knowledge and skills . . . but that which wishes to promote the growth of personalities by the strengthening of the will'.[25]

These ideas on child development and education did not necessarily mean that conventional notions of femininity were abandoned. Schwarzwald's views become clear in a report of her talk on the Swiss author Gottfried Keller. Keller's female figures were to be a model for the pupils, she declared, for they are diligent, cheerful, good, loving, industrious and warm-hearted, the opposite of the society coquette and pampered lady on the one hand, and the masculine woman on the other.[26] For Schwarzwald, this is what woman should be. Above all she was still to find her main fulfilment in marriage and motherhood. True emancipation for women would not be found in imitating men in external manners and appearance, but in adopting a masuline intellect and combining this with feminine sweetness and warmth of heart. These views on femininity, fully shared by many visionary feminists, find further confirmation in the article 'Household, Fashion, Politics' ('Haushalt, Mode, Politik') by Hermann Schwarzwald, whose views may be taken to have been applauded by his wife.[27] Here he laments women's struggle for the vote as a false emancipation. True emancipation lies in the liberation and promotion of specific feminine qualities, not in the docile imitation of masculinity, he declares. One prime sphere in which women could use their feminine qualities to achieve liberation is that of the household, he suggests, echoing the attitude of the General Austrian Women's Association to the consumer movement. The home is by nature a woman's realm, and should on no account be despised. On the contrary, it could be used as a foothold to political power if women would band together to protest at price rises, shoddy goods, and so on. This only women of knowledge, character and action can do. Yet the majority of women are not on this level as is shown, Hermann Schwarzwald argues, by their weakness for fashion, which lays them open to exploitation by producers. It is first of all necessary to give women an awareness of economic and social reality, and this can be done in the family. The inference is that the family as well as the school can educate girls to be better women, freed from the trappings of a morally corrupt society. Girls would then grow up as women and as human beings in free, self-attained and aware morality and thus open up the prospect of a society which is a community, and of a general renewal of femininity. Hermann Schwarzwald advocated an ideal very similar to that of the visionary feminists. It posits moral regeneration above all through changing the female individual. In view of this ideological agreement it is not surprising that both Eugenie Schwarzwald and the feminists should have extended their involvement to a variety of other – seemingly unrelated – areas, all of which were to allow individual and thus collective moral change.

Two areas which immediately affected the individual and were taken up by reforming women were drink and clothing. Schwarzwald, who, according to Robert Musil, embodied the 'co-existence of doing good and doing oneself good',[28] was, like many feminists, also active in the teetotal movement. As early as 1904 she tried to set up a simple restaurant in which there was no compulsion to drink,[29] although this did not really get off the ground until the war.[30] On the organisational level, the anti-alcohol movement was promoted mainly by the Association of Abstinent Women (*Verein abstinenter Frauen*) (of which Schwarzwald was a committee member) and the League of Abstinent Women (*Bund abstinenter Frauen*). The former founded teetotal restaurants and organised a non-alcoholic drinks cart in Ottakring; the latter gave aid to alcoholics.[31] This activity did not, however, go without critical comment from other visionary feminists, such as Mayreder, who here, as so often, took up an outsider position. She maintained that the teetotal movement was an attack on the freedom of the individual 'and the involuntary admission that human beings are senseless beasts if their hands are not tied. And I see in it a hateful symptom of what threatens the free and independent person if this culture based on the rule of the people continues.'[32] Yet the teetotallers insisted on their proximity to the women's movement, claiming that both aimed at the 'liberation of humanity from ancient chains of slavery' and the 'realisation of the modern ideal of culture',[33] and that this was particularly a woman's task because of her place in the family. As far as anti-alcoholism was concerned this meant offering men an attractive alternative to the pub, but more importantly it meant education. And here women as mothers, 'the natural educators of the nation', could take on the leading role, it was maintained.[34]

Dress also came in for feminist attention, taking on a symbolic significance as an expression of achieved change. The driving force behind the Viennese movement for dress reform was Hugo Klein, founder of the Association for the Improvement of Women's Dress (*Verein für Verbesserung der Frauenkleidung*). He emphasised not only the increased comfort of reform clothing, which abhorred the corset and the wasp waist, but also its appropriateness to the new lifestyle of the independent working woman who dressed and undressed without a maid, and jumped on and off trams. The new dress was both emancipatory and an expression of emancipation.[35] By dressing differently women could live differently. Berta Zuckerkandl went one step further by insisting that women should not allow themselves to be dictated to by artists on point of dress.[36] Dress had become a symbol of women's emancipation from norms established by men. And emancipation was also to be achieved through the reform dress movement's emphasis on individuality and naturalness. 'The reform movement will never demand homogeneity from its aficionados,' Klein assured. 'It wants to fit fabrics, shapes and colours to the natural form of the body; it wants to harmonise them with [the body's] colouring . . . with its external appearance and individuality with the seasons etc.'[37] Reform dress was a protest against the tyrannies of fashion, and an assertion of women's determination to be healthy, natural, and individual, three important goals of visionary feminism.

These were some of the initiatives undertaken by women to change individuals, particularly women, and thus to change society. Seemingly disparate initiatives were informed by the same ideal, while seemingly similar initiatives, for example in the field of women's education – the first girls' grammar school, the Schwarzwald schools, the Athenäum – could be fired by differing motives. But one thing all had in common: all were to serve the spirit of progress and to promote the special role women were to play in bringing about that progress.

The peace movement also incorporated these elements, so may be considered to have made a contribution to feminist culture in Vienna around 1900, even if it itself was not a feminist organisation. It was supported by the women's movement right from the beginning. Fickert reported to Bertha von Suttner (see figure 8) that the foundation of the

8. Portrait photograph of Bertha von Suttner in Vienna, 1891. Österreichische Nationalbibliothek.

humanitarian, apolitical Austrian Peace Society by Suttner in 1891 had been greeted in her (Fickert's) circle with great enthusiasm and went on to praise the fact that Suttner had followed 'the deepest urge of her genuinely feminine sensibility' and was at the forefront of a movement 'to liberate humanity from the last remains of a barbaric age'.[38] She pledged women's support for the Peace Society and at the same time seized the opportunity to invite Suttner to contribute to the struggle for women's suffrage. Although professing her support for Fickert's endeavours, Suttner felt obliged to refuse, pleading lack of time. Marianne Hainisch, too, although much admired by Suttner, met with a refusal: 'It is not prudery which stops me from joining the struggle against VD,' Suttner explained, 'but because it is just as important . . . as a dozen other things: mother protection, child protection, marriage reform, anti-alcoholism, tuberculosis . . . etc. etc. No, I cannot manage all that.'[39] Yet although Suttner was a convinced supporter of the women's movement, she did not join those feminists who regarded woman as having a special regenerative function. Women were to play an important role, but only those who were personally progressive, and that for Suttner meant rational: 'Modern women do not shake at the institution of war because they are daughters, wives and mothers,' she explained, 'but because they have become the rational half of a humanity which is becoming more rational and see that war represents an obstacle to cultural development.'[40] Women were, then, to enter the peace movement as the representatives of a higher level of evolution which was characterised by the rule of reason and embodied in the women's movement.

This widespread emphasis on the evolution of a progressive collective culture, and woman's vital role in this evolution, meant that woman in her capacity as mother became a focus of attention. Hers after all was a vital role in the reproduction of the race and health of the nation. The movement for mother protection had two main concerns: the protection of the mother's (and therefore the child's) health, and moral elevation. With both goals in mind the Austrian League for the Protection of Mothers was founded in 1907. The founding declaration, extracts of which appeared in *Neues Frauenleben*, maintained that the League aimed to protect married and unmarried mothers and their children from material and moral decline, and to remove the prejudices against unmarried mothers and their children.[41] These goals were to be achieved through helping those mothers who were willing to work and bring up their children to become economically independent, by creating homes for such mothers and pregnant women, by introducing a general maternity insurance and a fund for needy mothers, and by providing medical help and legal aid. The constituting meeting was held on 22 January 1907, led by Hugo Klein, at which Ofner, a Dr S.R. Friedjung, Marianne Hainisch and Wilhelm Jerusalem spoke. They divided into two camps. Ofner and Friedjung emphasised the plight of the unmarried mother and the need to help her by fighting the prejudices against her and her child. Hainisch and Jerusalem underlined the need to abide by conventional morality. Unmarried mothers were to be protected but not more than that, Hainisch declared, while Jersualem warned against an ethic of free love. This difference of emphasis seems to have led to a vigorous debate at the meeting, for *Neues Frauenleben* reports strong opposition to the second view; the distinction between married and unmarried mothers was declared to be incompatible with the demands of the mother protection movement.[42] In terms of practical achievements the League, within a year of its foundation, managed to establish a home for unmarried pregnant women in which, at a very moderate price, they could live immediately before and a few months after the birth, and an information office for any mothers and mothers-to-be.[43] In addition to numerous discussion evenings and lectures, by 1911 it had also submitted various petitions to Parliament. Most of these pleaded for paid maternity leave, the free use of midwives, and the introduction of breast-feeding breaks for female factory workers, as well as the payment of extra money to those mothers who breast-fed for more than three months.[44] The League was, however, unsuccessful.

The Women's Network

Progress, woman's role in achieving progress, and personal change were the key-words of these feminist initiatives. They by no means implied hostility to men *qua* men, or any automatic sisterhood of women. Yet female networking was significant, particularly because it managed to cross class barriers and also met women's needs in a male-dominated social scene. To this end social clubs for women were founded, ranging from swimming clubs to the more adventurous Vienna Women's Club (*Wiener Frauenclub*). The latter was intended to act as a community centre for women from all walks of life. The president, Margarete Jodl, described the club as a place of culture and pleasure where women could find solitude and be spared curious gazes, could enjoy reading, conversation or games. It was to be open to cultured women and those striving for culture, without regard to social class or status; the only qualification was that all were to be real 'ladies', that is, with an unspoilt reputation and perfect social manners.[45] As Meisel-Hess pointed out, it took steps towards realising one of the most important goals of the women's movement: the bridging of class differences.[46] In practice, however, it was closed to the mass of working middle-class women, who had neither the time for such pleasures nor the money for the relatively high membership fee. The list of the club's supporters, which included Marie Lang, Emma Eckstein, Eugenie delle Grazie, Emilie Mataja, Gabriele Possanner and Berta Zuckerkandl, that is, primarily women from the prosperous upper middle class, makes the point.[47]

The club was founded in May 1900 and opened in November of that year (see figure 9). A lavish launch party was thrown to mark the event. The gentlemen of the press took this unique opportunity, for otherwise men were refused entry, to comment on the buffet and above all on the interior design. The club offered various comfortable rooms, including a writing and reading room, well stocked with local and foreign papers and journals, a billiards room, a dining room where light refreshments were served at moderate prices, a games room, and a salon as well as a bathroom where baths could be taken. The interior décor was the work of Adolf Loos, who perhaps received the commission through Karl Mayreder in whose architectural office he had worked in the autumn of 1896.[48] The style was welcomed as 'secessionist'.[49] It combined functionality and honesty in materials with colourfulness. Most of the ceilings were white, the walls either

9. The committee of the Wiener Frauenclub in the billiards room on the day of the opening of the club's premises, designed by Adolf Loos. Photograph taken from the Internationales Blatt of November 22nd, 1900. Österreichische Nationalbibliothek.

light green or pale red; the furnishings had a bold pattern of 'large, questioning flowers' eyes'[50] and were in harmonising tones except in the dark-green games room where the chairs were vermilion. The armchairs into which one could sink as into 'apple purée'[51] posed, however, a problem. Loos, when ordering these deep English gentleman's club armchairs, had forgotten that the elegant ladies had different sitting habits; it was considered particularly good manners for them to sit on the edge of chairs; on Loos's chairs this meant that the ladies tipped off forwards.[52] The club could boast 400 members at its inaugural meeting and ambitiously planned to hold talks and musical evenings while excluding all political matters. Its life was too short, however, for in July 1902 it was forced to close its doors and leave its premises. The struggle for an organisational basis at the expense of other concerns was, the *Dokumente* analysed, the cause of the trouble.[53] A year later the New Vienna Women's Club (*Neuer Wiener Frauenclub*) was opened in other, more modest premises, offering roughly the same facilities but at more reasonable prices and without the avant-garde aura of Loos's setting. It managed to develop more of a calendar of events and became a popular venue for women's meetings. Its modesty made it attractive to single working women, who after all were those most in need of such a women's space, so it enjoyed a longer life than its predecessor.

These basic elements of feminism – individual change, social progress and female networking (while co-operating with men) – found their most publicly noticed expression in the suffrage movement. Although the campaign for women's political rights had been one of the main reasons for founding the General Austrian Women's Association, strictly political goals were not represented by specifically suffrage organisations until December 1905.[54] The catalyst to their foundation was the prospect of universal male suffrage which was to be gained at the expense of votes for women. In 1906 autonomous agitation was taken up more vigorously and the first organisation which was to campaign solely for women's political rights, the Committee for Women's Suffrage (*Frauenstimmrechtskomitee*) was founded under Nini (Ernestine) von Fürth, Marie Schwarz and Marianne Hainisch. In January 1911 the *Zeitschrift für Frauenstimmrecht* was launched. In March 1912 the first Austrian conference on women's suffrage was held in Vienna with the aim of organising a supranational association which would become a member of the International Women's Suffrage Alliance.[55] The German-language organisations of Vienna, Opava (Troppau) and Brno (Brunn), the Polish ones of Cracow and Lvov (Lemberg), and the Slovenian organisation from Ljubljana were represented. The Czechs had, however, refused to take part, as they objected to the use of German as the negotiating language. Yet although the women's suffrage movement was unable to secure unity on the supranational level within the Austro-Hungarian Empire, it did achieve a measure of co-operation with the Social Democratic women. The committee on occasion joined forces with them, and while emphasising the different means each had chosen, it was anxious to stress their unity by virtue of gender. 'The shared experience of our motherliness, our femininity joins us women of all classes, all professions,' Nini von Fürth declared in a tone Fickert would have rejected, and, she continued, it 'unites us beyond all that could divide us, in our common struggle for our most important right, a really universal, equal suffrage'.[56] In March 1911 the Committee took part in the Women's Suffrage Day, which was organised by the Social Democrats and accompanied by Vienna's first street demonstration for the female vote – 20,000 women and men marched together to Parliament. This event was repeated in 1912 and 1913.

In June 1913 the committee, not to be outdone, organised an international women's suffrage meeting;[57] participants at the conference included many leading figures is the women's movement – Rosa Mayreder, Marianne Hainisch, Yella Hertzka, Dora Teleky. As at the Social Democrats' Women's Suffrage Day, great emphasis was

10. The logo of the *Zeitschrift für Frauenstimmrecht* (*Journal for Women's Suffrage*), Vienna, 1913.

placed on femininity. Not only was it pointed out how the delegates themselves personified the ideal image of the modern woman, uniting feminine charm, motherly warmth and devotion with interest and understanding for all economic and political matters,[58] it was also emphasised that femininity was the driving force behind women's agitation. By virtue of the vote, women were to help to bring about cultural regeneration, for they could complement the work of men and bring womanly and above all motherly qualities to bear on the social fabric. The older ethical and economic arguments used by Fickert over twenty years earlier were not completely forgotten: the need for women of all kinds – civil servants, teachers, factory workers, housewives, mothers, wives – to represent their own interests was still recognised. But the emphasis had markedly shifted from the creed of human equality and the demand for rights and self-determination to what women as women could contribute to society. The suffragists, it was claimed, 'want rights only in order to give their womanly and motherly activities a social dimension which will benefit the whole'.[59] Women were to shake off their subservience but also their apparent privileges in order to reach the peak of human development and so to enrich culture. But both Fickert and her successors were convinced that women's suffrage and their entry into public life were in harmony with the spirit of the times, and that such changes would lead humanity onwards and upwards. For both it was a question of progress. Through suffrage, woman was to be liberated from her silence, as the logo of the *Zeitschrift für Frauenstimmrecht* intimates (see figure 10). Having broken the chains which had kept the lips of woman as she used to be locked together, the new woman would, it was suggested, emerge into a new age. In contrast to her predecessor, she would look the world in the eye, strong as the eagle and wise as the owl, a priestess bearing a message and a blessing.

CHAPTER 6

Coda: 1914–18

Patriots and Pacifists

Even before the outbreak of war some feminists claimed to notice that mores were changing in a way they had wished. In 1914 Henriette Herzfelder, for example, remarked with satisfaction that real or affected ignorance of life, above all of its darker sides, lack of independent thought, judgement and action, and an uncritical respect for men by women were now nowhere to be found except amongst the *ingénues* of remote provincial towns.[1] Four years earlier, the writer Erich Holm (the pseudonym of Mathilde Prager) in a piece for *Neues Frauenleben* had asserted that young women were enjoying the fruits of a taxing struggle waged by their elders against tenacious resistance, irrationality and ridicule:

> The youngest girl nowadays has more freedom of movement than the matron ever did. The principle that woman is not a person with a free will but a being determined by nature has been broken with in many respects although still by no means overcome. Education and employment are being opened to her although still accompanied by all kinds of limitations and difficulties. The censorship which constantly encircled her life has been greatly loosened.[2]

The old system was obviously crumbling. Personal appearance was no longer the main criterion of judging a woman, Holm remarked, and remaining unmarried, whether voluntarily or not, had ceased to be a source of shame, in the eyes of the educated at least. Woman, she explained, who could now stand on her own feet and be a useful member of society in many fields, commanded a new respect. Although queried by the editors of *Neues Frauenleben*, Holm went so far as to assert that even pre-marital or extra-marital sexual relations, if they emerged from the 'highest of moral laws which alone really makes the union of the sexes holy'[3] were no longer greeted with pitiless condemnation. This process of loosening the old bonds which the feminists had helped to untie before 1914, gathered force and momentum after the war, which acted as both a caesura and a stimulus. The new woman had been born, the old patriarchal order in the family and the state had collapsed, and the war had brought with it the 'fatherless society'[4] – or so it seemed to some contemporaries. In the eyes of the conservatives the emancipated woman was no longer the scarecrow student in Zurich or Russia she had been for Mayreder's family, but the self-possessed, independent woman, in 'a blouse with a high, turn-over collar and long, masculine tie',[5] who smoked and wore her hair cropped.

After 1918, this new spirit of emancipation found partial if inadequate expression in the law. In November of that year women's right to vote for the National Assembly and the provincial assemblies was granted, as was the right to stand for office. Significantly in view of preceding agitation, only women's war work and not any pre-war agitation by feminists was regarded as directly connected with this change. 'The achievements of women in the war are well known,' it was declared, 'and they had to lead to a change in the law as regards the participation of women in public life. As a result of the war, the permanent co-operation of women in all the material and intellectual work of the nation has become a historical fact and we must therefore of course acknowledge this fact in terms of the law by involving women in public life.'[6] The events of 1914–18 had wiped out public memory of feminist agitation of the years before 1914 and blotted out the authorities' previous acknowledgement of the principle of female suffrage.

This neglect did not prevent feminists like Hainisch from declaring female suffrage to be 'our greatest achievement',[7] even if they could not greet it with the jubilation it deserved, due to the pressing need caused by the war and its immediate aftermath. Of course, with the vote came the abolition of paragraph 30 of the Law of Association. Women now had two of the rights which some feminists at least had regarded as the most important. In December 1918 twelve women entered the Vienna City Council, one of the two Liberal progressive women elected being the veteran of the women's movement, Marie Schwarz.[8] In March 1919 ten seats in the Provisional National Assembly were occupied by women (as against 170 by men),[9] and in 1920 seven Social Democrats, two Christian Socials and one *Grossdeutsche* (German nationalist) were elected; the Social Democrats included Schlesinger-Eckstein and Adelheid Popp.[10] This is not to say that all resistance to women's political activity had disappeared.[11] Politicians' vehement opposition to female suffrage had died by 1918 but unease was betrayed in several suggestions put forward to supervise women's voting patterns, including manipulation of the voting age and compulsory voting. Female suffrage was a political risk for all parties; the new voters – over half of those eligible – were an unknown quantity. And for some who tenaciously clung to the ideas of such as Weininger, the introduction of women's suffrage was an opportunity to point out once again the cultural decline that threatened. 'The emancipation of women is a sign of the decline of the populace and accelerates the advance of this decline; it promotes the end of every true freedom,' one commentator declared as late as 1927.[12]

Other long-standing demands were also at least partly met. Indeed, the exceptional needs created by the war brought women a number of rights for which they had long wished. They were permitted to become guardians and witnesses in court on the same terms as men,[13] and improvements in the law of inheritance were introduced. 1920 brought full legal equality of women on paper; the Constitution now declared that 'all federal citizens are equal before the law. Privileges as a result of birth, sex, rank, class and confession are excluded.'[14] Institutions formerly closed to women were forced to open their doors. The Faculty of Law welcomed its first female students nineteen years after Bernatzik's first appeal, and the Colleges of Technology and Agriculture did likewise. In addition, the state began to become responsible for some girls' secondary education and girls were admitted to the boys' secondary schools. Other piecemeal reforms followed, many being brought to Parliament by the female representatives. Adelheid Popp brought a motion concerning improvements in working conditions for domestic servants, Schlesinger-Eckstein pushed through women's right to represent others in court; she was also, as all were, active in the expansion of girls' secondary education. The *Grossdeutsche* Emma Stradal was successful in achieving state aid for private girls' secondary schools, while the Christian Social representative Olga Rudel-Zeynek, later the first woman president of the Federal Assembly, was responsible for laws securing women's right to maintenance and forbidding the sale of alcohol to minors.[15]

But although these reforms were certainly not without practical significance, they were highly limited in range and effect, as some women were quick to point out. Women's legal equality may have been proclaimed in the Constitution, but in practice matters looked rather different. Women still had to fight for their rights, even in relatively petty matters: the League of Austrian Women's Associations, for example, found itself having to wage a war with the Corn Exchange for women to be admitted even as visitors.[16] Women were still discriminated against at work and in the political parties, the number of women students at the universities was tiny, legislation concerning maternity insurance was obviously concerned to remove or exclude women from the workforce rather than to promote their interests, and Austrian women had to wait until the 1970s to see reform of marriage law along the lines suggested by the Association and the League in the first decade of this century. And not only that. The new woman was expected to play the double role of the professional and the lovable woman. As the otherwise irrepressible Hedy Kempny pointed out to Arthur Schnitzler: 'I'm expected to balance the books as a bank official and afterwards be well turned out and play the sweet young thing, stay fresh until far into the night and not have a flat of my own in which at least to sleep without being disturbed and collect strength for the morning.'[17]

Austrian women's legal position may in fact not have been so bad – largely because they had enjoyed an exceptional degree of freedom compared to women in other European countries even before 1918 – but they still remained subservient, mainly, it was claimed, out of ignorance of their rights[18] and because of their general apathy concerning politics. In 1927 only six women were elected to the National Assembly, it was sadly noted, and the hope was expressed that this 'loss [would] teach women voters to stand behind their female candidates, to cultivate an interest in politics and to form a public opinion, a united will which cannot be overlooked. . . . Perhaps this bitter experience will help women recognise that woman can be a cultural force only when she is also a political one.'[19] Consciousness raising, the fundamental goal of the General Austrian Women's Association, had obviously still not been fully achieved.

Mayreder immediately recognised the absence of this precondition of effective political participation, remarking with justification in 1918: 'Female suffrage has been accepted in all the new republics. And with it a right, for which only a tiny group fought, falls into the laps of the huge majority of women. Thus it is to be feared that most women of the urban middle class and rural population do not know what to do with this right.'[20] It was precisely this widespread fear which forced others in the women's movement at last to recognise the central importance of political consciousness raising for women. In view of the changed circumstances many women had to be given a political education, it was widely conceded; the *cri de coeur* of the Association – politicisation of women – had finally been appreciated even if it was now interpreted more narrowly. Thus the Committee for Women's Suffrage – which on the abolition of paragraph 30 had become the Association for Women's Suffrage (*Verein für Frauenstimmrecht*), and, on finding itself deprived of its original *raison d'être*, had changed its name once again to the Association of Austrian Female Citizens (*Verband Österreichischer Staatsbürgerinnen*) – turned to the education of middle-class, liberal women in their civil rights and duties. This was the most neglected group of women politically-speaking, for Social Democratic women had already been prepared for political involvement and the Christian Socials were used to participating in election campaigns anyway.[21] The League, too, joined this work, Hainisch declaring that 'the education of woman has always been the highest goal [of the League]; now it is a question of educating women to be citizens, and of declaring repeatedly that women who now do not exercise their right to vote sin against their homeland'.[22] Yet at the same time these autonomous women's organisations were very restrained as far as party political agitation or allegiance was concerned. Hainisch seems to have disapproved of the fact that the League officially called itself a political association even after the relaxation of paragraph 30. She was anxious to emphasise that its task was to educate, saw party politics as divisive and threatening to the existence of the League,[23] and declared that it would be difficult to unite all members under one political banner anyway. She was obviously in conflict with the committee of the League, which felt obliged to draw up a set of guidelines for those women who had no definite political opinion. These guidelines were dominated by the creed of a democracy which favoured neither the Social Democrats nor clericalism, and the League enjoined its members to support the democratic middle-class parties;[24] it remained independent of any official party link. Indeed, so seriously did Hainisch and the League take their political independence and their vision of social motherliness that the Austrian Women's Party (*Österreichische Frauenpartei*) emerged from its ranks, founded by Hainisch in December 1929.[25] This was to offer women an independent political forum and focus, as well as acting as a link between the male-dominated political parties and the Peace Party, and it called for the reduction of both the *Heimwehr* and the *Schutzbund*, paramilitary groups on the right and left respectively. However, in 1933 this impartiality was renounced as the League reported without comment on the co-operation of most of the women's associations in Germany with the regime there, and two years later leading members of the League became members of the women's commission of the rightist *Vaterländische Front*. Yet despite these concessions the League itself was still deprived of its formal existence in the general enforced disbanding of political parties in 1934–5.[26]

Hainisch may have felt able to call the introduction of female suffrage 'our greatest achievement', but other feminists were not so jubilant. Mayreder for one expressed a more negative attitude. Women may have got the vote, 'but the realisation of the higher purposes and goals of female suffrage, the realisation of the ends to which female suffrage was to be merely a means, we have hardly come any closer to that,' she remarked.[27] The feminist vision largely promoted by the

General Austrian Women's Association had, she recognised, been obliterated. By 1928 Mayreder was even discussing the question of whether one could talk of decadence in the women's movement. She stressed that the two practical goals of the movement – the vote and improved education – had been achieved, but that its two main ideological goals – women's right to self-determination and a new sexual morality – had not, largely because of a lack of leading personalities in the postwar women's movement. Modern women, Mayreder claimed, had not used their newly won freedom in the way intended by those who had struggled for it. Legal equality, she insisted, was by no means the be-all and end-all. On the contrary, its achievement had robbed the movement of its most effective lever and led to the neglect of the ideological aims. 'Not until experience has shown women that social equality has not furthered even the material let alone ideological interests of the female sex can a women's movement emerge,' she declared.[28] Social equality of the sexes could mean real equality only if woman was relieved of the extra reproductive burden placed on her by nature. As it was, 'equality' had meant that women had become doubly burdened. Not only were they expected to have the physical energy to be successful professional women and also mothers and wives, but they were also trapped in an emotional conflict:

> The renunciation, suffering, waste of emotional energy brought into women's lives by the conflict between the so-called natural calling and the intellectual calling is indescribable. Supposed equality has altered nothing on this score; on the contrary, extending women's possibilities of practising an intellectual profession without at the same time organising institutions to relieve natural inequality has only made the conflict even more widespread.[29]

Furthermore, sexual equality had in practice meant women's acceptance of the morality of masculinity, a development which ran quite contrary to the intentions of the women's movement. The double morality of the pre-war era might have been abolished or have disappeared, Mayreder conceded, but the morality of 'soulless promiscuity'[30] which had taken its place was no better. This she regarded as a threat to woman: 'To descend to the level of soulless sexual intercourse . . . that means for woman merely that she is once again the object of male sexual aggression without having the possibility of appropriating the natural advantages of masculinity.'[31] Woman's experience of sexuality differed from man's, Mayreder claimed, not only as a result of her greater burden in the reproductive process but also because of her psychosexual development. As part of the process of cultural evolution woman was developing a sense of being a self-determining subject, 'which means . . . that equality with man can be achieved only through deep love in which each partner is both subject and object, not through a merely sexual relationship in which the natural superiority of the man will always lower the woman to the level of mere object'.[32] The vision of a renewed moral order in which relations of power were absent and of a new social order in which human rather than masculine values would prevail had proved elusive.

The elusiveness of this vision had already become apparent during the war, which taxed even the most committed of visionaries. It was then that the docility of the League of Austrian Women's Associations became apparent in contrast to the genuine opposition displayed by members of the General Austrian Women's Association. Before the war the League had supported the peace movement and was proud to have Bertha von Suttner as the chair of its peace commission, but on the outbreak of conflict this pacifist enthusiasm was promptly forgotten in exchange for solidarity in the face of a common foe. Ironically, it was the war which finally brought together the League, the Social Democrats, and the Catholic women's movements, who in the previous twenty years had themselves been fighting a war against each other. They pooled resources to form voluntary aid organisations, co-ordinated by a central committee with a heterogeneous seventeen-member board. This central committee organised twenty-three women's sub-committees in the twenty-one districts of Vienna. Their most important task was to help solve the unemployment problem caused by the war. Sewing and knitting groups were formed to occupy the many unemployed seamstresses and to train women made redundant in other fields, and by 1915 the Social Democratic *Arbeiterinnenzeitung* reported that up to 800 women knitters and 3,000 seamstresses had found employment producing clothing and blankets for the army and hospitals.[33] The committees were also to supply information, to collect and distribute food to pregnant women and mothers with young children, to distribute coupons to working women, and to act as job agencies. Advice centres were set up for mothers, children's groups run to relieve working mothers, station refreshment buffets organised, and the League launched a campaign to encourage women to preserve fruit and vegetables. By the end of 1914 it announced proudly that in Vienna 40,000 kilos of preserves had been made to be sent to the military hospitals.[34] The women's organisations, which before the war had campaigned for particular goals, were now eagerly involved in the war effort and rallied round. The New Women's Club became not only a centre where women could relax, as before 1914, but also one for plucking lint, 'which shortens the day of many a lonely woman';[35] the League for the Protection of Mothers extended its maternity home and established more toddlers' play-groups; the Association of Women Teachers and Governesses abandoned its special concerns to take up cooking in hospitals, and the inmates of its home worked away at garments for the winter. The Austrian Peace Society, however, did not participate. 'Deeply moved by the War and the death of its President Bertha von Suttner, [the Society] could not take part in the war effort,' it was announced.[36]

For the women gladly involved in the war effort it was a matter of helping those who were fighting at the front, 'for the inheritance of our ancestors, for the earth holy to us, for the survival of what is uniquely ours, for the conditions of its continued development, we are fighting for the security of our existence, for the assertion of our position in the world, for freedom of action, for prosperity'.[37] Much as the war had shaken and pained women, to campaign for peace would, Hainisch maintained on behalf of the women of the League, be a betrayal of their menfolk and of the fatherland. For these women it was clear that Austria was waging a war of survival. The Tsar's pan-Slavism, French chauvinists' desire for revenge and English envy of Germany were, according to Hainisch, the causes of the conflict forced on Austria.[38]

Not all feminists were of this opinion. Some, from the ranks of the General Austrian Women's Association, did make pacifist moves with the conviction of ending the war and thus helping to bring about the higher moral order which was at the heart of Fickert's vision. Before 1914 the Association, like the League, had proclaimed its support of peace initiatives. And even then it had indicated its rather different position: one of greater critical analysis and less emotional posturing. Thus on the occasions of the peace manifesto signed by Tsar Nicholas II in 1899, which was greeted by Bertha von Suttner as 'the most lustrous peace document that had ever been proclaimed . . . a new leaf of history had been turned'[39] and of the Peace Conference at the Hague in the same year, at which, according to Suttner, 'words were spoken, which even if today are ignored by many, are to resound, and remain engraved in the tablets of the histories of the states',[40] Fickert took up a rather different position from the jubilant Suttner. Fickert pointed out that most of the states participating in the Hague conference were sick and certainly did not uphold the genuine rule of law. Unlike Suttner, she gave the phenomenon of war a materialist analysis, claiming that militarism was fed by injustice at home and expansionist colonial policies abroad in the mistaken attempt to further domestic industrial growth. This, however, said Fickert, could best be guaranteed by raising the material and intellectual level of the populace at home and spreading awareness that the interests of all classes went hand in hand. Peace would be achieved by changing the individual and power relations, not by international courts as Suttner suggested.[41] This attitude, which was shared by members of the Association, came to the fore in the years immediately before 1914, at a time when food

11. Portrait photograph of Christine Touaillon in 1927. Österreichische Nationalbibliothek.

prices were rising rapidly, meat was scarce, and the Balkan Wars were being waged. A direct connection was established between domestic power relations, war and inflation. Not until all rather than just a small minority had the power to use technological and intellectual developments, Kulka argued, would war and inflation be avoidable.[42]

On the outbreak of war the differences between the League and the Association became even clearer. While the League underlined women's contribution to the relief of suffering, the Association, although also drawing women's attention to what they could do in the war effort, gave more emphasis to the bitter revelation that its vision of an international human culture of spirit which transcended the material was based on an illusion. 'The world had not acquired a new face; it was just that we saw it for the first time with the right eyes,' Christine Touaillon (see figure 11) sadly explained. 'Material interests had always ruled everywhere. . . . The World War has made it obvious that there is no world culture. What we took to be culture is only the personal embellishment of a few.'[43] This is not to say that nationalist sentiments were taboo for the Association. In Touaillon's eyes Austria was quite clearly the victim of, above all, England's petty shopkeeper's greed which had betrayed Europe to the Tsar, the white race to the yellow, and had abandoned 'the achievements of thousands of years of culture to the mercy of aliens devoid of culture'.[44] But although right and truth were unquestionably on the side of Austria for both the League and the Association, both still indulged in self-reproach. The League did so in a nationalist manner, chastising Austrian women for overestimating anything foreign.[45] The Association on the other hand found Austria's citizens guilty of placing material gains over spiritual ones. 'We should at every opportunity have fought the materialist attitude, by word and example, and because we neglected to do so we, too, are responsible for its hegemony,' Touaillon declared in self-chastisement.[46]

Even during the war the Association, unlike the League, maintained an openness to internationalism and professed the will to peace, adjuring women not to glorify their work in the war effort but to see it as imposed on them by human imperfection. It also drew their attention to the fact that how they set about that work was decisive for the future:

> Woe betide us if now only hate and contempt between nations is deepened, if we do not, 'in spite of everything', still recognise what unites them and are not able to see in the enemy people who are just as aware of their nationhood, striving for the same goals, feeling the same as we are. Woe betide us if we believe that the prosperity and interests of one state can emerge only at the cost of another, if we do not understand that each part of the present cultural world is dependent on the others.[47]

The Association thus maintained the internationalist tradition it had fostered in its pre-war activities and journals, and also its previously propagated belief in mutual help as a leading evolutionary principle. In response to Peter Kropotkin's *Mutual Aid: A Factor of Evolution* which appeared in German in 1904, Kulka had suggested that of the two evolutionary principles – the survival of the fittest and mutual help – it might be possible to see the former as the masculine and the latter as the feminine principle. 'In any case there is no attitude to life which women could serve better than that which is freed from all master morality, all power of the stronger, that of mutual help,' she concluded.[48]

It was in this spirit that a group of Viennese women, largely drawn from the Association, banded together in 1915 to unite all women 'who fight every form of war, exploitation and oppression, who strive for the solution of conflict on the basis of human solidarity, co-operation and the establishment of social, political and economic equality for all without distinction of sex, race, class and religion'.[49] They followed in the footsteps of an international initiative, the International Women's

Committee for Lasting Peace, which in April 1915 organised a women's peace conference at the Hague. Six Austrian women were present at the conference and supportive telegrams were sent by Marie Lang, Rosa Mayreder, her close intellectual friend Rudolf Goldscheid, and the Committee for Women's Suffrage, amongst others.[50] In Vienna, the Association organised a meeting to mark the occasion. Mayreder gave the opening speech. She implied that the importance of the conference lay not so much in its practical demands as in the fact that it bore witness to women's opposition to the masculine values that informed public life. According to Mayreder, the 'permanent glory of the conference' was guaranteed by three features: it confirmed the international solidarity of the women's movement; it demonstrated that this solidarity was independent of all external factors; and it proved that subjective passion with its corollaries of blinkered vision and partisanship were not inseparable from femininity, as opponents of the women's movement maintained.[51]

In Zurich in 1919 at a second women's peace conference, which was attended by four Austrian women probably including Kulka, the International Women's League for Peace and Freedom officially emerged from the International Women's Committee for Lasting Peace. The Viennese feminist pacifists promptly also established themselves as the official Austrian branch of the League, with Mayreder as the nominal president. In 1936, however, this Austrian branch came under suspicion of communist infiltration and in August 1938 was compulsorily dissolved by the Nazis.[52] It supported the practical goals of the International Women's League for Peace and Freedom which included female suffrage, the establishment of a League of Nations, and the self-determination of nations, and was a sharp opponent of the Versailles Treaty. Following in Fickert's footsteps, it took up a materialist position, emphasising the need for 'economic freedom', 'for without economic freedom, that is, a share in the raw materials of the earth, in production and manufacture, there is war', and also for 'social freedom', 'which lessens the danger of war between the classes'.[53] For these Viennese feminists, public relations work reached its climax in 1921 when the third conference of the International Women's League for Peace and Freedom was held in Vienna itself. 'For someone like me who experienced the beginnings of the women's movement thirty years ago, this women's parliament appears impressive in spite of everything,' Mayreder could at last remark with satisfaction.[54]

This pacifist engagement during the War was, however, not welcomed by all feminists in Vienna. In 1915 the League openly distanced itself, explaining that its absence from the Hague meeting was an expression of its elemental, passionate feeling for the fatherland which forbade international discussions with women of the enemy. Such a refusal to participate was neither lack of moral courage as had been claimed, the League retorted, nor renunciation of the struggle for women's rights. It was merely the case that 'women are voluntarily subordinating their claims in favour of service to the fatherland, they now want only to do their duty'.[55] Yet even after the war had ended, the League proved unwilling to be active in the international women's peace movement. It agreed to publish an article by Kulka on the resurrection of the idea of internationalism, of the simple feeling, as Kulka put it, 'that we are all . . . poor, small, tortured creatures who have nothing to reproach each other for and have enough on our hands helping each other; it should not be so difficult to implant that in our own souls, in those of our children'.[56] But the editors of *Der Bund* made it clear that they did not share this opinion and prefaced Kulka's article with the remark that 'we are not of the opinion that it can be our task to meet presumptuous and cruel victors . . . with confessions of belief in ideas which are quite strange to them'.[57]

The history of the attitudes to pacifism and the war displayed by the Austrian women's movement is symptomatic of the conflicts that had already divided the Association and the League years before. The Association proved visionary in trying to change the status quo through internationalism and in believing in woman's special role as bearer of the natural evolutionary law of mutual help. The League on the other hand demonstrated its obedience to the status quo by its involvement in piecemeal reforms which would alleviate the suffering the war caused but would not help to abolish war altogether.

This history is also typical of the emotional investment that marked the Association's visionary feminism. Like the Association, the Austrian branch of the International Women's League for Peace and Freedom was torn by personal intrigues and squabbles. 'From 10–16 July International Women's Congress of the League for Peace and Freedom. Amongst the foreign delegates many distinguished and pleasant figures . . . amongst the Austrian ones nothing but wrangles and quarrels,' Mayreder wearily recorded in her diary.[58] And like the Association, the League for Peace and Freedom was fired by emotions. 'Sitting on the Austrian committee. . . . The gulf between the inadequacies of the individuals and the force of events appears almost grotesque – and yet the certainty with which a few women defend the right to their feelings in the face of overwhelming circumstances impresses me,' Mayreder confessed.[59] Indeed, her own attitude to the League for Peace and Freedom was similar to her attitude to the Association. It was marked by ambivalence regarding 'practical life' and therefore reluctance to occupy a leading position, and by increasing scepticism about her own ideals. She commented on her speech concerning the Hague women's conference: 'Spoke in public for the first time in three years . . . I spoke of cultural ideals which could shape the future – but they sounded to me like hot air. Do I still believe that any cultural movement can assert itself in the face of the vile bestiality of human nature? Individuals yes, of course. But they will always remain individuals.'[60] The discrepancy between public image and political reality which dominated the Association made itself apparent here, too.

Private Tragedies

The gulf between the feminists' ideals and their reality proved unbridgeable, as regards not only their public commitment but also their private lives. Mayreder described Fickert as embodying the ideal of the 'fully rounded personality, the complete and free individual who has transcended the one-sidedness of gender. She had as many good qualities which one usually calls feminine as those which are considered to distinguish masculinity.'[61] Fickert apparently advocated true love as a leading moral force, and was above all what Mayreder called a 'moral genius',[62] believing in justice and insight as the paths to human freedom and happiness. Her private life, however, stands in some contrast to this publicly promoted image of the feeling, morally aware feminist who put the human first. It seems her life ran along more 'masculine' lines: she was a workaholic and put things above persons and her own personal comfort, a trait which appeared to others to be 'self-denial', a 'willingness to make sacrifices which had something heroic about it'.[63] Fickert herself shed a rather different light on this when she frankly admitted to Kulka: 'I do not serve any concern but myself, I find my full self-expression in what I do, and in fact so much so that I have little remaining interest for personal relationships. You see here immediately the great disadvantage of what may appear to you and others to be a good personal quality.'[64] The love and human regard she preached was hardly put into practice in her private life even if she 'felt so clearly, so bitterly the injustice, the suffering which others bore, as most other people feel only their own'.[65] She invested her whole personality and all her energies in the work of the Association, but at the expense of personal relationships. Her companion for many years, Ida Baumann, was neglected in favour of political agitation. Shortly after Fickert became intensely politically active, the two women seem to have separated. 'This morning Ida Baumann moved out,' Fickert recorded in her diary on 15 July 1893,

> after we have lived together for twelve years. What remains can at best be merely the superficial communication of friendship, like that

> one has with childhood companions who have become estranged, with blood relatives who are not related in spirit – living with and for each other, the comforting certainty that we will be understood, the certainty of encountering interest for everything which moves us – that has gone for ever.[66]

Fickert was perhaps slightly pessimistic, for the two appear to have subsequently taken up close contact again, but personality conflicts continued to play an important part in the difficulties between the two women. Baumann was the more introverted and domestic of the two, but Fickert's enthusiastic political involvement seems to have played an even greater role in the tension between them. 'There was one point,' Baumann recalled, 'on which we could not agree: work in the public eye, in which Auguste now revelled like a fish in its element.'[67] This led to estrangement. 'On Sunday, do go to your inquiry which commands all your attention now,' Baumann bitterly wrote to Fickert. 'I cannot come. I've already arranged my programme for Sunday. I won't expect you on Tuesday either, I've withdrawn from society and from now on no longer want to be so egoistic as to deprive humanity *twice* a week of your strength and your so sought-after personality and to bore you at the same time.'[68] Three years after Fickert's death Baumann drowned herself in the Danube.[69] For Fickert, the cause came before human emotions. She had betrayed her own vision of love and the importance of human needs.

Yet it was perhaps the vision of a 'naive idealist', as Mayreder called Fickert. It was doomed to clash with reality, not only because of Fickert's own limitations but also those of others.[70] As Kulka analysed the situation, Fickert had joined the movement inspired by the injustice and need she had seen and the belief that women could help to bring about change. 'She thought they [women] would bring feminine kindness where harshness now prevails, motherly love and sacrifice where now petty egoism rules, pure morality where there is dirt and coarseness, a natural love of freedom where now oppression is. One only had to give women freedom and the right to participate.' In this she was, according to Kulka, painfully disillusioned, for 'hardly had she taken the first steps, hardly had women gathered around her, than she had to recognise how many had brought vanity instead of self-sacrifice, pettiness instead of generosity, falsity and self-interest instead of purity, a cowardly readiness to make compromises instead of a courageous thirst for freedom. It was a bitter disappointment.' At the end of her life Fickert no longer believed in women's mission, Kulka declared, even if she still maintained it was her duty and kept her courage to continue struggling.[71]

The ambivalence of Fickert's attitude to her vision is indicated by her very last diary entry of 7 March 1910, which takes the form of a poem with the title 'Mein Wiegenlied' ('My Lullaby'). Here Fickert talks to the son she had wished for, not so that she could have kissed the child's sweet mouth or have felt the warmth of its small body, but so that she could have borne the creator of a new world, have given him healthy blood and strong nerves, a child who would have been fathered by 'the king of all men', an ideal, perhaps of the future, perhaps of distant parts. Fickert still maps out a new world as the ultimate goal, but now transfers it to the 'what might have been' which is to be achieved by a man, her offspring, begot of a man. Yet the whole is immediately subverted by the subtitle to the poem: 'Grössenwahn' ('Megalomania').[72] By Fickert's own admission, the vision has in essence become a pathological fantasy.

The same contradiction between lived reality and public vision marks Mayreder's life. While Fickert lived counter to her creed of love and humanity, Mayreder on important occasions lived counter to her belief in female self-determination and individuality. This became apparent even to her on the occasion of her second extra-marital attachment which lasted from 1902 to 1909. This was with a man who, as she clearly saw, was incapable of attaining her erotic ideal of the synthesis of sexuality with personality, an inability which, as she confided in her diary, was 'the typical fate of men, the sight of which I cannot bear and from which my inner being turns away in pained desperation'.[73] Without a trace of remorse her lover regularly visited prostitutes. This was particularly painful for a woman with Mayreder's opinions on the subject, opinions which after all she had even expressed publicly, as it ran counter not only to her ideal of masculine sexuality but also to her assumptions concerning the role of this conflict in men's lives. She had to recognise with horror and pain that pleasure played a part: 'The great mistake which leads me to make so many blunders is precisely that I thought he suffered from the conflict in his inner nature. But in fact he feels quite at home like that or at least thinks that he can find strength and enrichment in it.'[74] At the same time such a personal encounter with prostitution reveals aspects of Mayreder's attitude to the prostitutes themselves which are not revealed in her public utterances. In her diary she calls them 'the basest elements' and in emotional torment exclaims:

> The salvation which was my dream quite different women achieved by quite different means than those which were at my disposal! And a burning, unbearable shame filled me because I had kissed and caressed the face which only a few hours before had glowed from the touch of those women.... More clearly than ever did I feel his being to be a poison which had poured itself into my inner being

> and corroded it. My love appeared to me in this mood of deepest self-contempt as dishonouring evidence of the poverty of my intelligence and my character.[75]

Her most private emotions remained trapped in a condemnation of prostitution in contrast to the public, intellectual position she took, during this love affair, on the Riehl trial. For her on that occasion the most important words in her speech, which she copied into her diary, condemned prostitution as the lowering of woman to an object and 'where this attitude prevails then the woman in *every* woman is lowered, and however high a woman may raise herself as a person, woman per se, woman as a sexual being remains degraded in her', words she intended her lover to realise referred to their own relationship.[76] Not the predicament of the prostitutes but the predicament of the 'respectable women' turns out to have been Mayreder's real driving force.

This gulf between the intellect and the emotions, the public and the private, is symptomatic of aspects of Mayreder's thought and life other than her attitudes to prostitution. Mayreder clearly recognised the inadequacy of this lover and the disharmony of their personalities, yet was unable to liberate herself from the relationship, which certainly compromised not only her public position but also her position in her family, as a sister pointed out to her.[77] She legitimised her infatuation in ways that once again demonstrate the complexity of her attitudes and her inner contradictions. She justified the pain she submitted herself to by claiming that it was necessary to her productivity: 'I find my relationship to him and also all the suffering it brings legitimate, indeed in the highest sense something reasonable, as long as I can at the same time feel it is contributing to my productivity',[78] for 'without pain one cannot be productive. The life of the mind is the same as the life of the body: everything which is born emerges from pleasure and pain.'[79] It seems that this affair took on a symbolic significance for Mayreder. This is indicated by the profusion of diary entries it gave rise to (over 1,000 pages), by the fact that she copied out passages many years later, and above all by the literary character of the entries. Some extend for over twenty pages and contain passages of dialogue; they do far more than merely fulfil Mayreder's professed goal of improved insight and keeping a note for the future. Suffering caused by love became a surrogate for life; Mayreder revels in it, recording every detail and elevating it to the springs of her productivity, letting it dominate her emotional existence. In this she complies with the tradition of the centrality of romantic love, in women's life in particular, and the hegemony of self-destructive emotion over intellectual insight. Mayreder's ideal of the new woman, who is self-determined and achieves a synthesis of sexuality and individuality, remained caught in the contradictions and ambivalence that mark every lived life.

That the ideal of a permanent monogamous partnership publicly advocated by Mayreder and other feminists could also severely backfire is indicated by Mayreder's own marriage. In her memoirs she conjures up the public image: 'A kind star did however shine over the unfavourable circumstances into which I was born,' she comments. 'It let me find early in my youth the man who belonged to my inner being and in whose love that inner being found itself justified. No greater happiness than finding this self-affirmation through love can befall someone who has grown up struggling against their environment.'[80] The marriage was supposedly harmonious, largely because Karl Mayreder supported his wife in her political activities. 'In the few years that we worked side by side in the middle-class women's movement,' Therese Schlesinger-Eckstein recalls, '. . . it became clear to me that one of her most vigorous sources of strength is to be found in the deep and understanding love of her husband and that the limitless affirmation of her actions and essence by her high-minded husband helped her over difficulties and disappointments which she, without this support, would hardly have been able to overcome.'[81] Another side to this harmony is revealed in Mayreder's diaries, which tell a rather different story to that presented to the public. The marriage was by no means always harmonious. Indeed, problems arose very soon, increasing after 1912 when Karl began to suffer from severe depressions and bouts of insanity. These lasted with only a short break until his death in 1935 and put the marriage under a great strain. Rosa saw Karl's personality change and his love dwindle, but was unable to question the primacy she accorded marital love. The couple sought help from a total of fifty-nine doctors, and tried one remedy after another, ranging from psychoanalysis by Freud (to whom they had been introduced by Paul Federn) and Alfred Adler, hormone treatment from Julius Wagner-Jauregg to quack cures. Freud's diagnosis is particularly revealing as it scratched painfully at Mayreder's vision of marital love. Freud suggested that Karl's depressions were the expression of a sense of inferiority in the face of a strong, intellectual wife who dominated her husband, a diagnosis Rosa was completely unable to accept, as she admitted in her diary:

> 'I have written my obituary,' said Lino [Rosa's endearment for Karl] at breakfast. And after a pause he added: 'It has the heading: Rosa Mayreder's husband dead'. At first I laughed but then I saw that it confirmed Freud's view that he suffers from my personality because I suppress his masculine prerogative [the need of men to feel superior to women]. . . . If I had to admit that it would be the

ultimate martyrdom for me, the complete loss of everything which made our life together valuable.[82]

And indeed, what she wrote during this long period of great difficulties and also during the time of her unhappy love affair ran counter to her lived experience. Ideology proved stronger than reality; the ideal remained an ideal and was not modified by experience. In both episodes her ideal of self-determined femininity found itself in a head-on collision with emotional facts. The main elements of Mayreder's vision – the freedom of the intellectual woman, the merging of sexuality and personality, the primacy of intellectual values – proved incompatible with reality.

Marie Lang's experience also illustrates how difficult it was for these women to live according to their beliefs. For Lang, as for Mayreder and Fickert, it was precisely that aspect of her vision which was paramount which also proved hardest to realise and caused most grief. Lang's emphasis on a freer attitude to sexuality and her ideas on children's upbringing proved fateful. Lang had early indicated her attempt to live according to this freer attitude to sexuality by leaving her first husband, the respected jeweller Theodor Köchert, after she had fallen in love with Edmund Lang, the brother of her sister-in-law; she had even added to the scandal by attempting suicide before leaving Köchert. She flew in the face of decorum, not only by her adultery but also by the fact that she left behind a child by Köchert and bore Lang a son (Heinz) six months before her second wedding. (Remarriage was possible only because Marie was a Protestant.)[83] Her ideas on upbringing she also put into practice. The children of her second marriage were allowed to participate in all the conversations of the adults, permitted to read any book they chose, and at an early age displayed an interest in all the problems of the adult world.[84] Once a week about twenty young people gathered in Lang's home to talk about social matters, the guests including Egon Wellesz, a schoolfriend of Heinz's, and Fritz Adler, son of Victor. Lang emphasised how happy her children made her, how important motherhood was to women, and seemed to friends to embody maternal feeling. 'The dominant feature of her inner being was motherliness,' Else Federn recalled, '. . . we all felt her to be a mother and motherly and honoured her for that.'[85] So the suicide of Heinz Lang in 1904 at the age of 19 must, in view of her attitudes, have been even more shattering for her than the suicide of any child must be. It transpired that Heinz had been having an affair with Lina Loos, the wife of the architect. On Adolf Loos's discovery of this, he, Loos, wrote to Heinz renouncing his wife.[86] She, however, decided to end the relationship with Heinz and also wrote to him to that effect. A desperate Heinz then turned to Peter Altenberg for

12. Portrait photograph of Marie Lang with her son, Heinz, *c.*1900 (in the private possession of Herr Martin Lang, Vienna).

advice who, according to Hugo von Hofmannsthal, is reported to have said: '"What you *should* do? Shoot yourself. What you will do? Go on living. Quietly. Because you are just as cowardly as I am, as cowardly as the whole generation, inwardly scooped out, a liar, like me. And that is why you will go on living and perhaps later some time become the third or fourth lover of the woman."'[87] While on holiday near Birmingham Heinz shot himself, perhaps as a response to these words. The tragedy was to inspire Schnitzler's uncompleted tragi-comedy *Das Wort*, in which a Frau Langer appears as the loving, sensible and sensitive mother of the suicide victim (see figure 12).

Marie Lang never really got over this blow and reproached herself for failing to protect her son better, reportedly saying to Else Federn, '"I could no longer work at the Settlement with mothers – how was I, who could not protect her own child better, to advise other mothers?"'[88] She must have been forced to a bitter recognition that a new form of upbringing without a new social context was as good as impotent or indeed even a danger. The force of the status quo was stronger than the vision. Change could only be achieved little by little by dedicated, committed individuals. And Lang proved herself to be one of these, for on discovering that Heinz had fathered a child with a servant, she adopted the child.[89]

Of the leading feminists it seems that only Marianne Hainisch managed to some extent to live according to her ideals. She was the model daughter, wife and mother and presented the acceptable face of feminism in both her vision and her lived reality. Unlike that of Mayreder and Fickert, her childhood seems to have been free of rebellion. In her memoirs Hainisch describes her family life as 'the best possible life for us children'.[90] Her experience of family life as a child taught her, she claims, the significance of the mother in the family, a central aspect of her vision. 'Like so many I learnt how important the mother is in the life of the individual. It is said that the nursery remains with one and that is the case,' she asserts.[91] She put this insight into practice by introducing Mother's Day into Austria and by raising her children herself. 'My organisational activities of course did not prevent me from bringing up my children,' she exclaims.[92] Hainisch was always concerned to underline the positive importance of her family in her life in sharp contrast to Mayreder, who found herself wondering in 1914, 'When I consider how much female energy the family consumes, then in fact it seems to me to be an infamous form of living together. May someone be torn out of her path just because she is a sister, daughter, wife –?'[93] Hainisch's courtship and marriage were also largely conventional by the standards of the 1850s (she married in 1857). It was a marriage based on quiet companionship without any deep emotional demands and expectations, quite unlike Mayreder's. At the wedding the priest reminded her that 'the wife should be a valuable friend to her husband',[94] words which, Hainisch claims, remained with her for life and which she advocated in her political work. Hainisch knew how to realise traditional feminine humility and at the same time to combine this with dedication and hard work. She managed to live her vision – but largely because it demanded so little that presented a fundamental challenge.

PART TWO

PHILOSOPHERS OF FEMINISM

CHAPTER 7

Autonomous Feminism and Feminist Theory

Theory and Practice

One of the most significant achievements of the autonomous women's movement was the stimulation of the production of women's theoretical writing. Before visionary feminism became a political force, women's writing had been largely restricted to *belles lettres* and marginal forms such as letters, diaries and memoirs. Only when an organised movement developed did women writers emerge from this enclosure in significant numbers to enter the arena of political debate, intellectual exchange and cultural criticism. On the one hand, the movement created a new need – for a theoretical foundation to and justification of women's practical political demands. On the other, it contributed to and was itself in part a product of the discourse about the nature of woman and sexuality which was widespread at the turn of the century. The women's movement brought together these two spheres – the public and the private – to feminise and politicise both; and to do this it needed theoretical back-up which was to come primarily from women, who would speak as women, with a voice essentially different from that of men.

And speak they certainly did, even if not always in the terms desired by the movement. Else Asenijeff, for example, a novelist, poet, and companion and model of the artist and sculptor Max Klinger, gladly takes up the pose of feminine sacrifice in her self-acclaimed prostitution of her innermost feelings *Aufruhr der Weiber und das dritte Geschlecht* (The Women's Revolt and the Third Sex) (1898). There she claims to find it necessary on behalf of all 'true women' to speak naturally as a woman and not as a philosopher, an artist or an *hors sexe*, that is, a feminist.[1] 'I wanted,' she explains, 'to render quite naturally that which rises up from within.'[2] However, she then uses her seemingly reluctant voice to revel in an elitist invective, woman to woman, against 'degrading' feminist demands for equality with men. Similarly,

Felicie Ewart (the pseudonym of Emilie Exner) emphasises that she writes as a woman, albeit giving her voice legitimation in the shape of a fictional male authority figure, 'Dr Amicus'. He claims that her voice is that of a 'woman living in a happy marriage, who has raised a bevy of mentally and physically healthy children and observes life with open eyes', and compares her favourably with those other female commentators on the problem who are girls, spinsters or unhappily married women.[3] So it is not surprising that Ewart sees only the married state as offering women a source of permanent and deep happiness and that she overlooks or misrepresents the achievements of the women's movement, as Auguste Fickert caustically pointed out in a review of Ewart's *Eine Abrechnung in der Frauenfrage* (A Personal Settlement of the Woman Question) (1906).[4] Others such as Clara Schreiber openly dissociated themselves from the feminists. 'I have nothing in common,' she proudly asserted, referring to Irma von Troll-Borostyáni and August Bebel, 'with any champions of *that* kind of "womens rights" ';[5] she came to the conclusion that as women could not be real men, they had the task of remaining real women, putting morality and convention above personal happiness, which was in any case limited by the will of nature.

Yet voices more critical of the status quo were also raised. Most such commentators concentrated their attention on certain issues, the favourites being girls' upbringing and marriage. And for most the fact that they were talking as women was seen to be a strength, either because they talked from personal experience, which gave them privileged insight, or because they thereby defied the male monopoly. Else Jerusalem brought the two concerns of upbringing and marriage together in her *Gebt uns die Wahrheit* (Give us the Truth) (1902), a plea for an education to marriage and motherhood which would allow the free and honest development of the union of the emotions and sexuality. She speaks, she asserts, from her own particularly female experience as one who has suffered the farcical fate she describes, who herself was made one of the 'dumb actresses of our naive-sentimental roles'.[6] Thusnelda Vortmann, on the other hand, claims to approach the subject 'medically' and to expose courageously the painful wounds of society, but like Jerusalem she attacks the institution of marriage strongly. Based on female submission and male egoism, marriage is, she claims, immoral, inefficient and out of date.[7] She suggests temporary marriage (to last between five and ten years) as a preliminary step to the final desirable state of free love and state maternity protection.[8] In this way, she says, women would be released from sexual slavery, there would be only one code of morals for both sexes, and humanity would on the whole become happier.

Vortmann's tone is often strident and her view dogmatic. Yet she is not quite as extreme as the philosopher Helene von Druskowitz, an acquaintance of Nietzsche, Ebner-Eschenbach and Lou Andreas-Salomé. She indulges in a veritable tirade against man, whom she reviles as a 'logical and moral impossibility and curse of the world'.[9] In addition she suggests that cities be divided into male and female sectors[10] and enjoins women to hate men and marriage and to feel themselves to be higher natural beings, 'a more noble, aristocratic sex, surrounded by a natural, priestly aura'.[11] Also along man-hating lines although on a less elevated level, Ella Haag paints lurid pictures of domestic oppression, making the modern man the sole cause of woman's suffering. 'He is the originator,' she expostulates, 'of a long chain of suffering to which he condemns these innocents [his family]; but he does not think of that; he thinks only of himself, his ego is his god, his egoism the pivot around which his whole life revolves.'[12] However, the 'real man' remains the ideal for Haag: 'For where does woman blossom with more beauty than in the tender care of the true, upright man! – He remains the ideal protection and the refuge to which she can flee.'[13]

Not all adopted such an embittered, nostalgic tone. An evolutionary optimism is also contained in much of this analytical writing by women on woman and her problem and is most clearly expressed in the work of those who stood closer to the women's movement than Haag and her ilk. It is particularly apparent in Bertha von Suttner's *Das Maschinenalter. Zukunftsvorlesungen über unsere Zeit* (The Age of the Machine. Future Lectures about Our Time) (1889). This is a series of fictional lectures, held at some time in the twenty-first century, which look back at the primitive and lamentable conditions at the end of the nineteenth. Woman then, argues the fictional lecturer, was regarded as made merely for man. She was intellectually and materially dependent on him, and in love relationships and marriage was reduced to the role of object. And she was the victim of double standards of morality which denied her sexual pleasure.[14] Yet, it is confidently explained, the irrepressible natural force of upward human evolution manifested in women's emancipation was later able to change that and to achieve the ideal of autonomous womanhood that is described as the dominant reality of the lecturer's present. So women of various political persuasions joined the debate on woman, in most cases speaking consciously as women. Women as a sex had for the first time found a voice and become in their own and others' eyes the legitimate object of interest.

It was not only the need of the autonomous women's movement for theoretical justification which sparked off this increased production of analytical writing. The movement's respect, indeed veneration, for learning, and its deeply held conviction that ideas can bring radical change were also important. Education and with it the cultivation of the intellect and the widening of horizons may themselves, it was thought, have generated the woman question, at least according to the widely shared opinion expressed in Marie von Ebner-Eschenbach's oft-quoted aphorism, 'The woman problem was born when a woman learnt to read.'[15] But education was also seen as a path to the solution of the problem, for the visionary feminists believed that the real instigators of change were to be found in the word and the idea, rather than in material conditions. As Fickert had made clear, the General Austrian Women's Association was different from other women's groupings precisely in its desire to grasp the woman question in its totality and in its recognition of the need for a deeper concern with questions of theory on the part of the whole movement. And so, while acknowledging the lack of clear boundaries between the ideal and the material and the undeniable significance of the latter, Fickert maintained, obviously in response to criticism, that the conviction that the former is the main motor of progress was justification enough for the Association's conspicuous concern with questions of theory. These self-justificatory sentiments were shared by Rosa Mayreder, who also emphasised the importance of ideas as against economic factors. She did not, she maintained, wish to diminish the significance of the economic upheaval brought by mechanisation, without which the ideological demands of the women's movement would hardly have been realised, but 'I do,' she declared, 'nevertheless still set great store by the fact that it was not the material but the ideal side of the question which historically speaking was its starting-point; and however highly one values the influence of economic factors in practical matters, the ideal postulates of the women's movement are still its most important component.'[16] For, as Marianne Hainisch had declared as early as 1870: 'Ideas are powerful if they are rooted in deepest conviction and meet the needs of the age.'[17]

For these feminists, theory and practice could not be separated along the lines that first comes an identifiable theory and then it is put into political practice. On the contrary, ideas were to be the substance of the practice; they were to be inextricably linked to it as its internal driving force. And so the leading visionary feminist theorists – Rosa Mayreder, Irma von Troll-Borostyáni and Grete Meisel-Hess – were also activists in the movement. They saw their work in both spheres to be work for the women's movement. As Mayreder explained to Hainisch when she resigned from the committee of the Association:

> You know, I am not actually made for real and practical life, I am not a politician but an artist; that is why I can on the whole deal only with the theoretical propaganda of the woman question. And that I

am doing as best I can and hope that I can do my bit with my book [*Zur Kritik der Weiblichkeit*], on which I have been working for so long.[18]

Conversely, the women's movement was receptive of their work. Their writing was reviewed – not always uncritically – in the feminist periodicals, which also gave space to public critical debate between these writers.

The visions of feminism's politicians and those of its philosophers had to differ. The autonomous women's movements were by necessity dominated by the changing politics of the day. The politicians of feminism were forced to concentrate on piecemeal reforms although they refused to make concessions regarding the inspiration which informed their work. Their writings are marked by pressing concerns and the need to legitimise demands; there is little scope for the open and detailed discussion of wider-ranging questions. This the philosophers of feminism managed to achieve by designing systems of social ethics and philosophies of culture, by seeing sex, gender and gender relations as central to culture and any cultural renewal, and by giving that renewal a spiritual dimension.

Three Feminist Philosophers

Although many Austrian women wrote on the woman question around 1900, only three created a coherent visionary feminist theory. Troll-Borostyáni, Mayreder and Meisel-Hess, all at one time connected with the General Austrian Women's Association, are remarkable because they envisage a social order which gives central significance to, but is not limited by, women and gender relations. They outline a vision in which the woman problem is only one – albeit central – element. But just as the autonomous women's movements did not share a single vision, neither do these philosophers of feminism. Despite common features each vision has its own individual character. Troll-Borostyáni's is one of a new morality which is to be based on nature, seen by her to be an essentially reasonable force; Mayreder's is that of a culture of *Geist* based on a synthesis of polar opposites;[19] and Meisel-Hess's is based on equating the natural with the sexual instinct.

These differences in vision are underlined by differences in these women's styles of thought and the influences they proved receptive to. Troll-Borostyáni, one of the first generation of feminists, remains a Liberal of the old school, a believer in the self-regulating powers of society and the individualism of the bourgeois citizen whose goal is political self-determination. Reason is one of her key-words. Nature in her view is benign, rational and unproblematic. In the context of this intellectual heritage she sees science, not religion, as the path to emancipation and progress. Clearly, her intellectual context is that of the Enlightenment; her style of thought that of the utilitarians. Amongst Troll-Borostyáni's formative literary influences were Ferdinand Freiligrath and Heinrich Heine.[20]

Mayreder's thought is rooted in other traditions. Her individualism is not that of the bourgeois citizen with rights and duties, but that of the remarkable personality. It is the individualism not of Liberalism but of neo-Romanticism. It was the early Richard Wagner and Nietzsche rather than the writers of 1848 who influenced her. Before he turned to Christianity with *Parsifal*, Wagner the heathen, as Mayreder called him, played a significant role in her intellectual development.[21] Bayreuth was in her eyes a monument to the great individual who triumphed over the masses,[22] and Wagner himself she regarded as an advocate of the individuality and self-determination from which a new humanity would be born. Particularly attractive was his creed of the purely human, 'that liberated and ennobled humanity', which could be reached through sexual love.[23] Wagner, as Mayreder recalls, confirmed with his divine authority 'the destination of the path which I had taken in my lonely darkness'.[24] Nietzsche on the other hand fascinated her by the 'overpowering magic of his language' and the 'brightness of total intellectual freedom',[25] although she was by no means his uncritical follower, as Hugo Wolf suggested when he called his maternal friend a 'Nietzschean of the purest kind'.[26] But in this neo-Romantic context it was Goethe who proved the most influential of all. His synthesis of a cult of the personality with an evolutionist world view became a pillar of Mayreder's thought. She, like the young Auguste Fickert, had first been influenced by Schiller, although it was not so much Schiller's political texts as his ideal of inner culture represented in 'Anmut und Würde' which attracted her and remained a model for her all her life.[27] Yet she turned increasingly to Goethe; Schiller's 'image gradually retreated into the background, it was overshadowed by the appearance of him to whom I have been bound since I first became acquainted with him, bound by a mystical feeling which comes closest to the adoration of God as the highest example of humanity'.[28] The religious nature of Mayreder's thought already becomes apparent here. Goethe is her divinity, the intellectual pole according to which her artistic activity and dealings with people orientated themselves, although, she hastens to add, not as a gesture of submission but as a gesture of discipleship which sprang from a sense of fundamental agreement.[29]

Born in 1879, Meisel-Hess belongs to a younger generation than Mayreder and Troll-Borostyáni, who were born in 1858 and 1847 respectively. Hers was a generation more influenced by a metaphysical-cum-scientific world view than by the grand old men of German Idealism and humanism. Instead of the political rights and reason of Troll-Borostyáni, or the individual and synthesis of Mayreder, healthy evolution and monism are the key-words for Meisel-Hess, an adherent of the mother protection movement. Ernst Haeckel rather than Goethe is her model. Haeckel openly challenged Christianity by the monist rejection of the established dualisms of body and soul, matter and spirit, and replaced them by a religion of evolutionism based on natural selection. This proved particularly enticing for feminists as it claimed to dissolve the network of patriarchal dualisms within which women had been trapped, and gave woman as mother, freed from patriarchal bondage, a new status as promoter of the upward evolution of the human race. Yet Meisel-Hess's context is not only that of monism. She, too, is an individualist of the Nietzschean brand, and a less critical one than Mayreder. Mayreder's ideal of the 'new man' (meaning human being) conflicted in some respects with Nietzsche's 'superman'. She proved reluctant to accept what she considered to be his glorification of power and aggression which put what is over what should be and thus negated the process of organic development. Meisel-Hess focused more on Nietzsche the moralist, the champion of a freer sexual morality and the rebel who undermined the dogma of the invariability of moral species, just as Darwin had shaken the dogma of the invariability of physical species.

Freud also had more intellectual influence on Meisel-Hess than on Mayreder. Meisel-Hess saw in psychoanalysis and Freud's theories concerning sexuality scientific support for her own belief in women's need for an active sexual life if they were to be healthy in mind and body, and for her view of the largely pathological nature of much of modern sexual life. It also confirmed her psychologising explanations, for Meisel-Hess, like Freud, thought in terms of a libido which comes into conflict with moral norms and of a resulting repression; sexuality is for her, too, an eminently psychological matter. Neurosis and psychosis are seen by Meisel-Hess, who directly refers to Freud's work, to be the results of a pathological social-sexual order.[30] And as for Freud, so too for Meisel-Hess 'where id was, there shall ego be' is a slogan, even if she expresses it in other, more spiritual terms. As she explains, 'every possibility of the inner rebirth of an individual is conditional on his relation to sexuality. And he will be granted redemption and renewal only when the foul air of the instinctual retreats, and the bright, white light of awareness streams in where it was once fetid, dark and ghostly.'[31]

Mayreder is also a psychologising thinker who in many ways – probably unwittingly – shares aspects of Freudian thought. This is particularly true of her idea that culture demands a repression of and distancing from natural sexuality, called by Mayreder man's 'animal essence' (*Tierwesen*) as opposed to his 'intellectual essence' (*Geisteswesen*). Yet she was sharply critical of Freud. Quite apart from her private contretemps when she bitterly called him an 'outstanding dialectician of psychology and in addition a monomaniac of his system' on the occasion of his brief treatment of her husband Karl,[32] Mayreder was also unsympathetic on the scholarly level. The Oedipus complex came in for attack. Why, Mayreder asks, should sexual jealousy between father and son explain the opposition between them? Social jealousy would be a better explanation – and anyway, she adds, 'Oedipus slew his father unknowingly and not from conscious rebellion as a son; he is therefore not a typical representative.'[33] These comments provoked the ridicule of the psychoanalyst and faithful Freudian, Theodor Reik,[34] but Mayreder's first point deserves consideration and forms the kernel of some recent criticism.[35] Yet for all her private and public criticism of Freud and the misunderstandings between them, Mayreder obviously did find some of Freud's work interesting, for according to the notebooks which record her reading she was familiar with *Totem and Taboo* and *The Future of an Illusion* at least.[36]

Around 1900, then, these feminists were by no means intellectual outsiders even if, like Mayreder, they may have adopted such a pose and later really have become anachronisms, as Mayreder bitterly sensed. But at the turn of the century, at the peak of early feminism, they stand squarely in a number of intellectual contexts shared by other Austrian thinkers. Mayreder's own background is in many ways unremarkable for a young intellectual growing up in the Viennese culture of the 1870s and 1880s. The psychologists Freud and Christian von Ehrenfels, like the Social Democrats Victor Adler and Engelbert Pernerstorfer, were all at one time aficionados of Wagner and Nietzsche. Freud, Mayreder's almost exact contemporary, was also a deep admirer of Goethe. What *is* remarkable is that these feminists managed to enter the intellectual arena at all. Unlike their male contemporaries they were outsiders in terms of formal education and could not avoid being aware of their exclusion on grounds of gender. Troll-Borostyáni and Mayreder were autodidacts by necessity; in Troll-Borostyáni's case formal education was confined to a convent school near Salzburg, and a Viennese young ladies' college had to suffice in Mayreder's. It was books which were the real educators for both. Thus Troll-Borostyáni was able to report that her reading, which included Goethe's correspondence with Schiller and Frau von Stein, and plays by Corneille and Racine, was 'formative and beautiful',[37] while Mayreder's notebooks reveal an eclectic thirst: in the years immediately after 1890 her reading included Meister Eckhardt and Jakob Boehme, Aristotle and

13. Irma von Troll-Borostyáni, frontispiece to *Ausgewählte kleinere Schriften* (Leipzig: Spohr, 1914).

Cicero, the cabbala, Schopenhauer, Nietzsche, Emerson and Byron. Neither had any kind of formal higher education and both suffered from the monotony of the dreary existence of the young lady of good family. 'I sometimes envy the people who complain that they have so much to do that they do not know what to do next,' Mayreder remarked of the boredom of her existence. 'I for my part have so little to do that I also do not know what to do next.'[38] And Troll-Borostyáni confessed, 'I feel incapable of being active in a feminine way . . . I will suddenly decamp to Vienna and give lessons there . . . I would rather die [of hunger and exhaustion] than live drearily and without a goal – in spiritless renunciation or unintelligent resignation.'[39] And decamp to Vienna she did, to study music and dramatic art, write her first articles and dress as a man, and visit red-light districts, only to be forced by financial necessity to be active in a 'feminine' way after all; she accepted a post as governess in Budapest, married, bore a child who died in infancy, separated and returned to Salzburg to write, joined the circle around the poet Georg Trakl and lived the life of a sickly but eccentric recluse (see figure 13).[40]

Meisel-Hess's case is a little different for she belonged to the first generation that was able to profit from the laboriously won changes in women's education. She was a pupil of the school of the Association for Extended Women's Education and later attended lectures at Vienna University, although she did not follow a regular course of studies. It is hardly surprising that university-educated women feature more frequently in Meisel-Hess's writings than in Troll-Borostyáni's, or in Mayreder's where they are absent altogether. But it is likely that the wide reading she displays in them was gained through her own efforts rather than thanks to educational establishments.

No doubt a complex combination of factors in addition to their intellectual curiosity made these women enter the arena of theoretical debate and led each one to make the specific contribution she did. Personal experiences probably played a role, although it is difficult to establish a causal connection between life and works. This is particularly true in the cases of Troll-Borostyáni and Meisel-Hess, for whom there is very little autobiographical and biographical material, while Mayreder's thought often seems to have run counter to her life. The basic ideas of her feminism, above all her individualism, date from her teens and twenties. They emerged from her awareness of her own exceptional intellectuality and educational disadvantage, and from her disobedience to the norms of femininity. Later personal experiences were used where possible to bolster these ideas. Those which might have challenged them, as for example her experience of love, were, however, relegated to her diary; they did not find a place in her works or lead to a revision of her feminism.

Yet for all three, despite the changes enjoyed by Meisel-Hess, entering the arena of public discussion meant overcoming a considerable gender barrier and being forced to compete with men on unequal terms and on unfamiliar territory. And indeed, it meant not only competition but also a direct challenge to male authority as offered, for example, by Mayreder and Meisel-Hess in their open criticism of Weininger's *Geschlecht und Charakter*. Mayreder's comments are subtle and succinctly point out where Weininger's theory of sexual gradation has to fail, namely in his tenacious connection of primary sex characteristics with psychological ones.[41] Meisel-Hess's comments constitute a heavyweight onslaught which may lack Mayreder's perception but demonstrates the energy and conviction with which some feminists could set to work to demolish misogynist writings. 'Weininger's work,' she summarises, 'has rushed past the facts and his arguments have shattered at the first impact with reality. It has in truth nothing to do with "woman and her question".'[42]

Such trespasses on male territory did not pass without censure. Troll-Borostyáni and Suttner came in for opposition. As German and Austrian publishers proved unwilling to take the risk of accepting their work, both were forced on occasion to go to Switzerland.

Troll-Borostyáni's most important work, which appeared in the second edition as *Die Gleichstellung der Geschlechter und die Reform der Jugenderziehung* (The Equality of the Sexes and the Reform of the Education of Youth) first appeared in Zurich (in 1884), as did Suttner's *Das Maschinenalter* which she chose to publish under the obvious pseudonym 'Jemand' (Someone). As she explains in her memoirs,

> Cowardice was not the motive behind this pseudonym; but because 'Das Maschinenalter' deals with scientific and philosophical topics in a completely free way I feared that the book would not reach those readers I wished for it if it were signed with a woman's name. For in scholarly circles there is so much prejudice against the capacity of women to think that a book signed with a woman's name would simply have remained unread by those for whom it was intended.[43]

It soon became clear that Suttner's caution was justified, for even close intellectual companions such as the Darwinist philanthropist Bartholomäus von Carneri jumped to the conclusion that only a man could have written it.[44] Similar prejudices dogged Troll-Borostyáni's *Gleichstellung*. Published under her real name, the book was accused of plagiarising a man – none other than August Bebel, whose *Die Frau und der Sozialismus* (Woman and Socialism) had appeared from the same publisher fourteen days earlier; that a woman could independently have such ideas was considered impossible by many critics. Fortunately Bebel was not one of those. It was clear to him that Troll-Borostyáni's book could not have been written and published in fourteen days and he responded by expressing his pleasure to Troll-Borostyáni that two people who had grown up in such different circumstances could have the same opinions.[45] But the double bind remained. Women were expected to write according to conventions of women's writing and this was judged inferior to that of men. If they transgressed these boundaries their achievement was denied. Provocative work could only be men's work. Women were forced to deny their sex and gender if they wished to step beyond the territory mapped out for them. For her first forays into the world of writing Troll-Borostyáni assumed the male pseudonym 'Leo Bergen', thus defying her brothers who were 'caught in the prejudices of their time and station',[46] and went so far as to wear a suit and tie and have her hair cut short. For this she became a figure of note within the women's movement, 'the highly gifted woman who so completely leaves the confines of the conventional "feminine"',[47] and the object of attack by those outside it.

Yet despite this unconventionality, *Gleichstellung* became one of the classics of the German-speaking women's movement. In her obituary of Troll-Borostyáni, written almost three decades after the publication of the book, Mayreder could assert that the measures Troll-Borostyáni suggested in order to create a new social order were still among the guiding ideas of the women's movement. The debt the present generation of women owed Troll-Borostyáni may not be adequately appreciated, Mayreder lamented, but Troll-Borostyáni's contribution to the Austrian women's movement would remain forever undiminished.[48] Mayreder's own *Zur Kritik der Weiblichkeit* also became a classic. It was even translated into Czech, Swedish and English, and in England apparently caused a 'real sensation'.[49] However, despite her personally felt disadvantages as a woman, Mayreder's work has none of Troll-Borostyáni's polemic, as she herself pointed out, claiming that 'the value of this book is more that of insight than of propaganda'.[50] It did not arouse the opposition Troll-Borostyáni's work did, but on the contrary was positively received, not only by the militant feminist press but also by the less militant and those quite outside the movement. Published by the ideologically inspired and respected German publisher Eugen Diederichs, it was not surrounded by the Amazonian aura of Troll-Borostyáni's book, although it goes further towards unsettling established notions of the relations between sex and gender than Troll-Borostyáni does. However, like Troll-Borostyáni's work, it was well received by some socialists, and was called 'a book whose unassailable objectivity and illuminating analysis cause the gloom of all this fog of opinions concerning the sexes generated by preference and dislike to appear to disintegrate into nothing'.[51] The same positive reception greeted Meisel-Hess's major study *Die Sexuelle Krise* (English title: *The Sexual Crisis*) (1909), of which the Soviet revolutionary feminist Alexandra Kollontai claimed that it offered 'Ariadne's thread through the labyrinth of sexual relationships'.[52] Yet although Meisel-Hess went on to complete the extensive trilogy of which *Die Sexuelle Krise* was the first part with the studies *Das Wesen der Geschlechtlichkeit* (The Essence of Sex) and *Die Bedeutung der Monogamie* (The Meaning of Monogamy), published by Diederichs in 1916 and 1917 respectively, and although *Die Sexuelle Krise* was translated into English in 1917, these books failed to achieve the canonic status of Troll-Borostyáni's and Mayreder's contributions. Middle-class feminism had already passed its heyday.

CHAPTER 8

A Champion of Reason. Irma von Troll-Borostyáni

'The supreme law of all life is development,' Irma von Troll-Borostyáni declares in her 'book for parents' *So erziehen wir unsere Kinder zu Vollmenschen* (Thus We Educate Our Children to be Fully Developed Persons) (1912), '. . . forwards and upwards, but always in league with nature and in full understanding of the inviolable forms it takes and its inviolable laws.'[1] Just as nature never stands still, so too does society constantly change and humanity stride forwards to a higher stage of development. In addition, nature is the foundation of a moral civilisation, for it is governed by reason, and only 'reason freed from all prejudices, and the recognition of the laws which govern man in his relation to the social organism',[2] and not any metaphysical 'moral instinct', constitutes an acceptable foundation for a system of morals. Only independent thought which leads to understanding can bring man to the knowledge of good and evil, the basis of his morality. This system of morals, Troll-Borostyáni emphasises, takes account of human nature as it really is, rather than designing an ideal and expecting people to live up to that. Her morality has its foundations in what emerges when the distortions imposed on people by an unnatural and sick civilisation have been eradicated. And this true human nature is, according to her, determined above all by the drive for personal happiness. 'Whenever a person asks himself: why do I live? – then his natural instinct answers: in order to experience pleasure!'[3] she asserts, and draws attention to how this differs from the Christian and Buddhist religions in which suffering is propounded as the answer to this question.

At the same time she is careful to consider the social dimension, suggesting that ethics could be called 'the science of those laws which govern individual and social life in the striving to achieve the greatest possible perfection and happiness of the individual through the social whole and of the social whole through the individual'.[4] Pleasure-seeking human nature is at the same time altruistic, since concern for others or for the collective good is also fired by the natural drive for personal happiness. However, this is found only in people who have reached the highest evolutionary level. 'That person whose ability to experience emotionally does not extend beyond his nerves, who is deaf, blind and insensitive to all pain and all joy which does not immediately affect himself . . . belongs to the lowest level of humanity,' she claims. 'To the highest belongs that person whose heart beats for all humanity, whose love extends to all. . . . And yet the fundamental motive which gives rise to the actions of both is the same: the natural instinct to find a basis for one's own happiness.'[5] The main message is clear: human beings will always be driven by the desire for happiness and this drive is natural. It is also amoral, for it is in its essence the instinct for the promotion of one's own well-being, the instinct for survival. Good and evil can thus be redefined according to what Troll-Borostyáni calls the ethics of the 'mechanistic-materialist world view', as striving which promotes the happiness of others, and striving which is detrimental to the happiness of others respectively. Likewise, inanimate objects can be categorised as good or bad according to whether they are useful or harmful.

In addition, Troll-Borostyáni asserts, this ethics, unlike the ethics of convention, leads to truth, justice and love. It leads to truth because what actually is is accepted rather than what should be or is thought to be by social convention. This is a truth which includes that 'first and foremost duty' of being honest to oneself.[6] It leads to justice because reason will make humanity see that only equal rights can bring about happiness, collective well-being and the intellectual and ethical progress of the human race.[7] This is a justice which Troll-Borostyáni regards as anchored in equal rights for the two oppressed groups of society: women and the working class. It leads to love because the acceptance of self-love will lead to the love of humanity, including true sexual love, endowing the latter with its 'natural sanctity'.[8]

Nature, Reason and a New Morality

Yet how is this vision of a natural moral culture to be achieved? And how does it relate to feminism and the women's movement? For Troll-Borostyáni, the central conflict to be solved is that between the demands of nature represented by the individual and those of civilisation represented by society; and the arena in which this conflict is most openly and bitterly fought is that of gender relations. The general happiness and well-being of society can be promoted by allowing people to satisfy the natural drive to sexual union and to enjoy the happiness which goes with it; it can be hindered by those social institutions which present an obstacle to that union. Seven fundamental changes, Troll-Borostyáni claims, are necessary to achieve a moral culture: the social and political equality of the sexes; abolition of prostitution as a tolerated institution; the possibility of the complete and unconditional dissolution of marriage; the reform of education and upbringing; state control of education; and abolition of inheritance rights. Her solution is, then, despite disclaimers, a highly interventionist one.

For Troll-Borostyáni it is clear that the equality of the sexes 'would of its own accord lead to a reorganisation of the social order which would infinitely favour the ethical and intellectual development of human society'.[9] This is not, as commonly supposed, because women are by nature more virtuous than men, she hastens to add, supporting this statement with some statistical detail and information. The fact that women commit fewer crimes than men can be traced back to quite different reasons: social constraints and upbringing demand that women keep a tighter check on their instincts and passions. In addition, social measures offer a greater protection to young female innocence than to male, although much harsher measures are meted out by society to the woman who strays from the path of conventional virtue. Morality comes to be based on gender difference; a double morality with one code for men but quite another set of values for women emerges. Relaxing the moral censures imposed on women would not, Troll-Borostyáni claims, lead to the state of immorality feared by many opponents of feminism. The fear of unbounded female sexuality which underlies this double morality is unfounded. Both sexes have strong sexual drives and both sexes suffer when forced to be celibate. She paints a lurid picture of the consequences of the suppressed sex drive: hysteria, depression, catalepsy, insanity, congestion of diverse organs, cramps, epileptic fits, hallucinations and apoplexy as well as various ailments of the glands and sexual organs lurk in wait for the celibate woman.[10] Yet this need is not recognised by social mores and laws, for these are made by men for their own benefit and pleasure. Man is concerned to make woman his servant and the means of the satisfaction of his needs, so he seeks in woman primarily those qualities which make her particularly suited to this double task: humble subservience, faithfulness and beauty. For this reason he also seeks to confine woman sexually and prevent her political and social equality with man. It is this protection of men's own interests which lies behind the double morality and male resistance to attempts at change. Yet, Troll-Borostyáni emphasises, change is possible. Releasing women from the constraints of this old, corrupt morality would enable a new, natural morality to emerge. This would be based on the recognition of the natural law that only those sexual unions are immoral which are detrimental to the general good and do not offer adequate provision for the care and rearing of offspring.[11] Further results would be the recognition of women's sexuality and an improvement in the social position of illegitimate children.

The further ramifications of this are clear to Troll-Borostyáni, for she takes it for granted that sexual equality also implies women's economic and intellectual emancipation and their entry into the public sphere. Thus she also demands equality between the sexes in education and employment. In this way sexual relations can be made nobler, she argues; men would have a higher opinion of women and they would gradually learn to see them as human beings with the same human rights. The intellectual exchange between the sexes, made possible by the change in women's position and education, would have a moderating effect on male lust and would cultivate women's ethical consciousness and strengthen their character. The moral quality of marriage and family life, and the general state of society regarding sex and morality would be raised and human happiness thereby promoted.

Yet Troll-Borostyáni is anxious not to appear to condone reckless pleasure-seeking or revolution. Indeed, women's emancipation, she claims, is the best way of counteracting all 'unhealthy socialist dreams, excesses and subversive meddling', for 'woman in her whole essence is opposed to socialist (or communist) principles and theories'; it is only frustration which makes her turn to such ideas.[12] Woman's traditional role does not come under Troll-Borostyáni's fire. On the contrary, she emphasises how it is 'beautiful, genuinely human and fitting to nature'.[13] 'Woman does not wish to be emancipated from her own, innate nature,' she asserts.[14] But the law should not exploit that nature and shore up women's tendency to loving self-sacrifice in the form of female submission. Neither should woman be confined by a socially imposed, and for Troll-Borostyáni unnatural, role. Revealing the Enlightenment and Liberal tradition in which she stands, she declares women's emancipation to be necessary in order to allow nature to show what woman is and is not capable of. It is the basis for the emergence of her own innate nature: women's emancipation, far from heralding an era of sexual anarchy, would mark the beginnings of a true, natural morality.

This would make itself felt particularly as regards prostitution. The emancipation of women from the limitations governing their legal, social and economic position is, claims Troll-Borostyáni, the precondition for the eradication of prostitution which, far from protecting the virtue of 'decent' women and girls, merely incites men to unnatural sexual excesses at the expense of one group of exploited women. 'If prostitution did not exist,' she explains, 'then all opportunities and invitations to debauchery which it offers men would be removed . . . the control over his desires which man has as yet never attempted would be made easier and his sense of morality purified.'[15] The natural consequences of this would include an increase in the health and strength of the human race and in the incidence of marriage.

Yet Troll-Borostyáni is not a supporter of conventional marriage. She regards it as eminently unnatural, irrational and immoral and, pointing to the hypocrisy of the institution, openly opposes the widespread view that the prevailing form of monogamous marriage is a precondition of civilisation. 'He who has seen even only a little of life and has the courage openly to admit to his experiences must agree with us,' she asserts, 'when we declare that our so-called monogamous marriage is nothing but a wretched hypocrisy, a lie, with which one individual thinks he can dupe another, society thinks it can dupe the individual, and the individual thinks he can dupe society.'[16] This type of marriage is based not on physical, spiritual and intellectual attachment but on quite different factors – the desire for sexual satisfaction and/or for material profit or indeed subsistence. But it is precisely this kind of marriage which presents an obstacle to the evolution to higher and nobler forms of human existence. The happiness and well-being of the individual and of society, which is after all the goal of evolution, can be achieved only in a marriage which is based on love and which can be easily and completely dissolved once the feelings that should have been its motive have changed or died. Anything else is unnatural, for 'if a union of love which does not have the sanction of marriage is called a transgression of the dominant moral laws, then a marriage without the sanction of love is a sin against nature which takes its terrible revenge in the consequences'.[17] Troll-Borostyáni is quite explicit about these consequences: 'Anaemia and weak nerves, weakness of mind and body, absence of high-mindedness and idealism, joyless addiction to pleasure, inability to experience any noble passion . . . such emotional and physical devaluation of human material is the fruit of a nature which has been cheated of its inalienable right – the right to love –'.[18] Children emerging from the 'womb of love' receive on the contrary 'fresh strength and health of mind and body'. Yet Troll-Borostyáni's exposition is not a plea for promiscuity or 'free love'. She retains marriage as the ideal form of sexual partnership. It is still 'the most holy and sublime bond . . . in its lofty purity the divine bond which unites two souls . . . through love'.[19]

As these suggested reforms could be made superfluous if human nature were allowed to develop without the distortion and corruption imposed on it by civilisation, Troll-Borostyáni turns her attention to education and upbringing. This, like society as a whole, is to be guided by nature and to work in harmony with it. 'The more natural an upbringing is, the better it is. Its goal cannot be nature's suppression and crippling but nature's ennoblement,'[20] she concludes. This, like the other reforms she propounds, is governed by reason. It requires a holistic approach, one which sees the individual not only as an intellectual, but also as a physical and moral being. Thus physical exercise and personal hygiene are to be cultivated. Suitable gymnastic exercises and cold baths daily, plenty of fresh air and sunshine, and a sensible diet are amongst Troll-Borostyáni's prescriptions. Obedience to such a regime would promote not only a joy in mental and physical health but also keep young people from wishing to follow an unhealthy lifestyle. 'It is a well-known fact,' she asserts,

> that the more people follow a suitable diet and take pleasure in gymnastic games, swimming, rowing, mountain climbing and so on . . . the less they tend to an excessive and premature sexual and therefore softening life. . . . Only by means of such natural measures can young people remain truly young and thoroughly protected from forcibly grasping, while still immature, at pleasures which can give real satisfaction only when one is in full possession of manhood or womanhood.[21]

A natural physical upbringing leads to moderation in sexuality. It also fosters inner harmony and the promotion of feminine and masculine characteristics in both sexes, for example strength in women and delicacy in men. Equipped with such a physical upbringing the children of such children will also profit by inheriting 'higher natural predispositions' and thus contribute to the increasing perfection of human society.[22]

Similarly, young people's moral education should be natural and therefore also rational, for 'the only real basis of morality is reason . . . the most highly developed morality is synonymous with highest reason and clearest recognition'.[23] This means shunning convention and teaching young people to think independently and to see for themselves what is moral and what not. Insight must be fostered as 'every kind of immorality is a product of inadequate insight'.[24] The 'Thou shalt' of authority is to be abolished, for 'intellectually gifted and alert children do not submit to an unmotivated order based on power. They want to know why they should do this, are not allowed to do that.'[25] This insight is the source of humanitarian love, which in turn is based on the identification of one's own good with that of others. This is the highest form of morality, and the highest form of insight. It is the task of a moral education to achieve this purification of natural self-love and the harmonious merging of egoism with altruism. This can be done by appealing above all to the rational recognition of the need for a moral social order and by cultivating the identification of the pain and pleasure of others with that of oneself.[26]

Young people's intellectual upbringing, too, should be natural and based on independent thought and observation rather than drill and rote learning. It should be more purpose-orientated than the conventional education, encompassing a wide-ranging general education as well as vocational training for a profession that is chosen according to talent and interest. These opportunities are to be offered to both sexes, for 'the only just, the only reasonable division of labour because it fits its purpose is one organised not according to the social station or sex of society's members but solely according to their individual suitability'.[27]

To put these ideas into practice, Troll-Borostyáni suggests, the state should shoulder the responsibility for both education and upbringing, for only in this way can it do its duty of looking after the interests of the general good in the face of the threat presented to society by the 'moral and intellectual neglect of a large part of the young generation'.[28] Troll-Borostyáni proposes the foundation of institutions for pre-school children in which they would be fed and supervised by trained teachers, who would be far more competent than the usual hordes of run-of-the-mill governesses and nannies. This work would be done above all by progressive women, for who, she rhetorically asks, 'is better suited to this pioneering work than women who are in the vanguard and who concern themselves with the cultural tasks which the new era will impose on the female sex. The maternal feeling credited to women, which consists of nothing but glad sacrifice and submission in the service of others, naturally entrusts them with the mission of raising the human race.'[29] All children were to go to such institutions, exceptions being made only for those whose parents could prove that they themselves could offer a good education and upbringing. But, asks Troll-Borostyáni, how is such a state undertaking to be financed? She answers this by suggesting that in addition to imposing fees on wealthy parents, the monasteries and convents and with them the priesthood be phased out by the state and the income gained from the property formerly owned by the Church be used to finance these educational institutions.[30]

This firm belief in the potential emergence of true human abilities when freed from the constraints imposed by a deforming social order also leads Troll-Borostyáni to a critique of inheritance capitalism, which, along with the oppression of women, she calls the 'basic sickness of our social organism, from which the sexual misery of our time with all its various illnesses springs'.[31] It is a cause of social sickness as it obstructs the 'natural, free flow of national property, and just as in animal life all influences which disturb the circulation of the blood make the body ill, so too it is quite natural that the right of inheritance which obstructs the circulation of economic values, the blood of the social body, should make this ill'.[32] For Troll-Borostyáni there is not the 'shadow of a right or reason'[33] to justify the state's permission to the individual to dispose of his property on death as he sees fit. Justice and collective well-being, on the contrary, demand that property be returned to the 'great stream of the people's property'[34] and that property be earned as a reward for individual achievement and abilities. The abolition of inheritance rights would promote the hard-working and capable and thus contribute to the upward evolution of the human race.

Troll-Borostyáni's vision is clear; sexual equality and changes such as those she suggests regarding education and inheritance rights are to lead to a natural civilisation in which human happiness, justice and freedom prevail. It will be based on reason and a recognition of how things really are, and not on the irrational ideals which make up the basis of the present prevailing – and ailing – civilisation and its morality. But, as she is anxious to point out,

> this recognition of the real is not the enemy of idealism . . . rather it is this which leads man upwards to the highest level of ideality, for so he learns that those divine qualities of love, kindness and justice, with which he has endowed his imagined creator, have been given him by nature. . . . This recognition is the philosophy and religion of the future; it is this which allows what is purely human to develop most beautifully and nobly and allows humanity to find that happiness, harmony and peace which no religious confession up until now has been able to give.[35]

A natural civilisation means for Troll-Borostyáni one which allows human nature to develop freely and which accepts human nature as the only viable basis of a new morality. This insight is the precondition of the inner growth of human beings and indeed of the development of the world order as a whole, of the relations of organic beings to each other and to the inorganic world. This order is, claims Troll-Borostyáni, what man has instinctively called Paradise.[36] Her suggested reforms are, then, to lead humanity to that place of perfect happiness; not back to the Garden of Eden but forwards to a new Paradise.

Nature and Civilisation

Troll-Borostyáni is clearly a visionary feminist. Women's emancipation in the form of the political and social equality of the sexes is for her only one aspect of a far more comprehensive design for human emancipation from the deforming constraints and moral corruption of an unnatural civilisation. This emancipation is seen as bringing salvation, above all in the form of a new, natural morality. Her vision focuses on a dichotomy between nature and civilisation. Yet precisely here lies one of the main problems, for Troll-Borostyáni never questions her concept of nature and the natural. She assumes, for example, that there is a true human nature which will emerge of its own accord once the distorting norms of civilisation have been removed. At the same time, however, she emphasises the importance of intervention in the form of a natural education and upbringing. What then are 'nature' and 'natural' to mean? Which criteria does Troll-Borostyáni use to distinguish certain characteristics as those of true human nature from those she considers to be the product of civilisation? This question is never addressed, and no answer emerges in her writings. She maintains quite happily, for example, that femininity is a relative concept[37] and that there are no sex-specific virtues but only generally human ones, which become increasingly manifest the more humanity progresses. But she also asserts the special role of the mother–child bond for women,[38] and thereby the 'natural' psychological as well as physical differences between the sexes. Yet it seems to be clear that for Troll-Borostyáni a human nature does exist, which, at loggerheads with the present status quo, has been deformed by civilisation, but which, when freed, will lead to an improvement of society. But yet again, the question of where nature and society begin and end is not discussed. Might not nature itself be just as confining as its supposed opposite, civilisation? Might not nature itself lay down norms and deny the creative potential of human intervention? These are questions Troll-Borostyáni does not consider. In addition, she assumes a beneficent nature which wishes what is right of its own accord – and what that is is again remarkably straightforward. It seems that nature is defined as a negative quantity: that which is not civilisation. Yet it can at the same time apparently be fostered by human measures, that is, by that very same civilisation. This means that Troll-Borostyáni is able, for example, to propose eugenicist measures in the name of a rational nature.[39] The truth of the matter is that the natural is used as a metaphor for what in Troll-Borostyáni's eyes furthers upward evolution – whether this be intellectual, physical or moral – which is in turn a metaphor for her own system of moral values. Nature and the natural in the last resort merely legitimise Troll-Borostyáni's own moral vision.

This unquestioned primacy of morality also sheds some light on Troll-Borostyáni's other fundamental concept: that of rights. Again displaying her Enlightenment heritage, she considers it to be an inalienable human right for each individual to strive for increased perfection. But in her design this seems to exclude personal freedom and individualism; when there is a clash between the individual and society, the latter is paramount. Troll-Borostyáni's individualism is restricted to what she considers healthy; talents are to be exercised for the good of humanity not for self-fulfilment. Like her concept of nature, rights are primarily seen as healing a sick civilisation and not in the usual terms of autonomy and self-development. It seems that rights, too, are to be subordinate to her moral system.

How politically cogent are the reforms Troll-Borostyáni suggests? In essence she sees women's emancipation as consisting of their integration into the status quo, which in turn means for her legal equality between the sexes. She neglects other forms of sexual equality and also the questions of class, racial and religious equality, and their significance for radical social and individual change. Troll-Borostyáni's assumption that equality means legal equality, which means justice, is both false – for justice can be based on gender difference – and also too weak for the function she gives it – for when all is said and done it is the 'innate moral concept'[40] that turns out to be the basis of all ethics and the precondition of full freedom. She is concerned with the need to change customs, conventions and laws, and seems in places to sense that change in these areas alone is too little to achieve the vision she proposes. She also emphasises the need for inner, personal change, but displays little insight into how this might be achieved other than suggesting a natural upbringing and education. Indeed, it is altogether unclear how the evolution of society is to occur. Is it an inevitable natural process as she would suggest in *So erziehen wir unsere Kinder*? Or is it a process which must be helped along, especially by progressive women struggling for their rights? In neither case does Troll-Borostyáni fully see the political dimension; she has little sense of the fragmentation of society and the clash of interests it contains caused by the differences in means of access to power. For her, people have merely to 'see reason', to activate their rational faculty, in order to bring about change. She overlooks factors other than lack of reason which might lead to resistance to change and neglects to consider that reason itself might well be guided by (self-)interest. Troll-Borostyáni's psychology is highly simplistic; the workings of the unconscious play no role for her.

Yet Troll-Borostyáni's vision of the goal of human development as the full development of an innate rational and moral nature is significant for a study of early feminism even if it is not completely politically cogent. Some of its significance lies in the fact that it indicates that the division made by several commentators on early feminism into radical, political, rationalist feminism on the one hand and moderate, cultural, romantic feminism on the other might be too rigid.[41] Troll-Borostyáni certainly represents a political feminism, that is, she sees changes in the legal and institutional structure of society as paramount to women's emancipation, and wishes to see women integrated into the public sphere. She also represents a rationalist feminism. She emphasises the role of reason in this emancipation, as for example in the superior importance she gives reason over passion in her advocacy of a natural moderation in sexual matters and in her support of rational sexual companionship over passionate love. In addition, she consistently asserts that morality is what is natural and thus rational. There is no room for the irrational, for the unconscious, passionate, and sensuous in her vision. And there is also no room for the particular and unique; the universalism of human rights and human nature dominates, threatening to obliterate difference and deprive the individual of the freedom of self-determination. Yet Troll-Borostyáni's rationalist and political feminism does not exclude a cultural vision; it is not only a question of rights. Rights are merely one path to wider and fundamental cultural change, which embraces change in the individual and in human relationships to lead to a new, moral civilisation. Troll-Borostyáni represents a rationalist cultural visionary feminism as opposed to a Romantic one. To restrict radical feminism to the struggle for women's political rights, especially women's suffrage, as some commentators have done, is surely too restrictive.[42] As shown in the analysis of the practical politics of the autonomous women's movements in Vienna, the struggle for women's emancipation in the form of rights, that is political feminism, was intimately bound up with a struggle for human emancipation in the form of individual change, that is cultural feminism. It was precisely those organisations and individuals that were regarded as radical which most strongly forged this bond. Here Troll-Borostyáni is no exception.

CHAPTER 9

The Synthetic Ideal. Rosa Mayreder

'Everyone has to wrestle for a god . . . in order to give his existence a meaning,' comments Rosa Mayreder as a concluding flourish to her memoirs, 'and so I have chosen the synthetic god, who overcomes the division between the suffering in the world and its joys, between its horrors and its beauty. I have remained true to him regardless of what fate has brought me; may it be granted me that I show him honour to the end of my days.'[1] This god is Jesus Apollo, 'the god of a new world order, who in his superhuman manifestation forms a synthesis of two great cultural epochs',[2] namely the Judaeo-Christian and the classical-pagan. Man's adoration of this god expresses

> the deepest human longing, a longing which struggles for expression in infinitely many forms, which is reflected in the most manifold ideas [and] speaks a clear language in religious and profane dreams. . . . It is the longing for a higher existence, for a more perfect state in which the inadequate old humanity is to find uplift and transfiguration.[3]

Synthesis, then, is the substance of Mayreder's design for a new, divine humanity.

Mayreder proposes a number of syntheses, both individual and collective. Those on the individual level, which mainly deal with the relationship between sex, gender and psyche, form the focus of *Zur Kritik der Weiblichkeit* (see figure 14); those on the collective level form the substance of the essays making up *Geschlecht und Kultur* (Sex and Culture) and deal mainly with the relationship between sex, gender and culture. (This volume of essays appeared in 1923, although most of the essays were already written by 1915.) In their fundamentals, however, all the syntheses Mayreder proposes represent 'the contrast between the intellectual and elemental, [a contrast] which may be regarded to be an essential characteristic of the human species, the

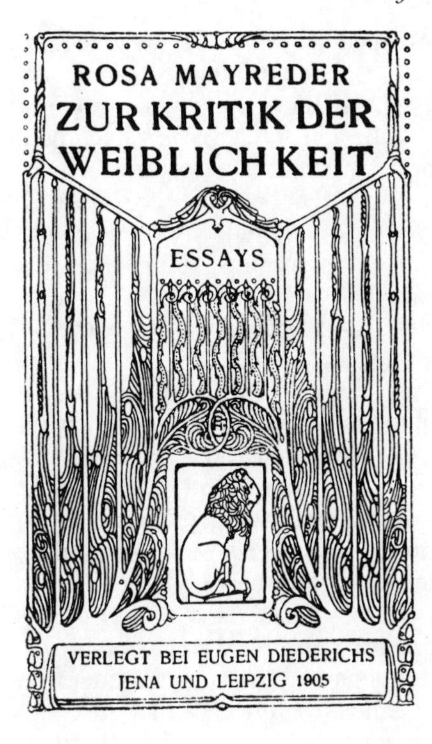

14. Title page of *Zur Kritik der Weiblichkeit* (Jena: Diederichs, 1905).

motor of its whole evolutionary history'.[4] It is the synthesis of this dialectic which dominates her vision.

Intellect and Sex

The primary synthesis Mayreder proposes is that between *Geist* and *Geschlecht*, a polar pair which can be roughly translated as intellect and sex. By *Geist* she understands that which is individual to each person, those 'characteristics which, each regarded on its own, could equally well belong to the one or the other sex', and which 'as a complex in their special combination make what is individual about the person'.[5] *Geschlecht* on the other hand is characterised by those psychological qualities needed for reproduction, the teleological function of humanity. For women, Mayreder suggests, these qualities are weakness of will, patience and passivity, for these best equip woman for her generative tasks of conceiving, bearing and bringing up children. Aggression, enterprise and violence are the teleological qualities of men, as these favour sexual conquest, man's role in the reproductive process.[6]

As *Geist* is individual and not sex specific, it stands on a higher evolutionary level than *Geschlecht* and is a distinguishing feature of the present level of evolution. 'At the stage of development of modern people,' Mayreder claims, 'individual differentiation has reached such a high degree that it is no longer possible to make statements about the psychology of individuals which are based on their physiological characteristics [for example physical sex].'[7] So all generalisations about men and women are misleading, and all assertions of an essential difference between the sexes unfounded. Personal and collective development are directed precisely towards overcoming the sphere of teleological sexual nature so that entry into the sphere of what is purely human and therefore individual can be achieved.[8] Such purely human qualities do not originate in any evolutionary process of adaptation to sex teleology, Mayreder emphasises, but have their roots in a religious struggle, the highest goal of which is to overcome gender difference. At the same time, however, changes in the typical image of the sexes are a result of changes in the economic and social position of men and women, and it is a task of modern life to discover which characteristics of the traditional image can still be used as ethical directives.[9] But it is certain that one goal of culture must be the adaptation of sexual relations to those external conditions and at the same time the acknowledgement of the individual qualities of the self that struggle for free development. Only in this synthesis can the individual regain a lost harmony between self and the external world.[10]

By seeing humanity in this way, Mayreder adopts a form of Darwinism only to overturn it for her own, feminist, purposes. She subscribes to the idea of evolution via adaptation of sex characteristics but, in contrast to Darwinists, sees this as evolution towards greater heterogeneity within the sexes and greater homogeneity between them. The Darwinist premiss of 'adjustment of powers to special functions',[11] cited by most commentators to justify women's subordination, Mayreder uses to legitimise those 'unfeminine' feminists who fought against that subordination. She also subverts the evolutionist dogma of culture's natural progression from primitive homogeneity to advanced heterogeneity, which in the context of sexual selection implies the increasing differentiation of masculinity and femininity. This, for conservatives, provided excellent justification for the ideal of separate spheres. Mayreder applies the assumption that increasing heterogeneity implies cultural progress to reach the opposite conclusion: that decreased sexual differentiation implies an increased differentiation of character, that is, a higher level of personal culture.

Yet this evaluation of *Geist* over *Geschlecht* does not mean that Mayreder condemns the latter. On the contrary, for her it is the potential basis of individuality, although not its measure or boundary.

'The motherly instincts of the female and the warrior instincts of the male sex are the soil on which, in certain circumstances, the most admirable elevation of the individual flourishes,' she concedes.[12] And indeed, the reproductive instinct promotes individual development. 'The former, which most threatens the freedom of the personality, at the same time most provokes the strength on which the latter rests,' she explains.[13] It is not a matter of asceticism, but of achieving a synthesis in which *Geist* leads and dominates *Geschlecht*. For women this is a harder task than for men, as women are more limited by and closely tied to their reproductive function; unlike men, their teleological sexual nature does not favour independence and the development of the personality. This injustice is reinforced by culture, which creates a conflict in the individual of both sexes by creating an opposition between the duties to the species and the duties to the personality and by devaluing the former as the latter gains in importance and status.[14]

Despite these obstacles, the synthetic person Mayreder envisages, who has achieved that harmony of *Geist* and *Geschlecht*, is already a reality even if an exception.[15] What is lacking, however, is general acceptance of this exceptional individual. Instead, the extremes of the 'real man' and the 'real woman' are still propagated as ideals. But through the synthetic person, the human race is, Mayreder optimistically claims, indeed progressing, for 'every individuality appears as a new possibility of existence, as an extension of the species'.[16] The female synthetic person is the herald of the new woman who transcends the norms of average femininity without adopting the negative aspects of masculinity.[17] For women, such a synthetic, new femininity means perceiving and experiencing the self as an active, self-determining subject, not solely as the passive object of male desire; it means experiencing love not as self-renunciation but as the freedom found in two beings complementing each other;[18] it also means the rejection of overly masculine men. On the level of cultural evolution, the development of a synthetic female sexuality means that woman has overcome the two earlier evolutionary stages of seeing herself as the possession of a man, and of regarding marriage as the only permissible basis for a sexual relationship. She has reached the third evolutionary stage of recognising that only emotions can justify a sexual union.[19] Marriage is thus no longer a matter for the state, Church or society and need not be sanctioned by any of these. It concerns only two individuals of the opposite sex.

Synthetic masculinity is characterised for Mayreder not so much by self-determination and individuality (for these qualities do not conflict with man's teleological sexual nature as they do with woman's), as by the transcendence of both primitive masculinity and dyscratic masculinity, that is, a masculinity characterised by over-intellectuality.[20] This means for the former not the elimination of primitive masculine drives but the elimination of all the prejudices and weaknesses which belong to that primitive masculinity. It means above all the insight that the glorification of masculine physical strength and courage in war is an anachronism. The fitting male role model is no longer the warrior but the intellectual; modern life in a large city and the now typical male professions of office worker, lawyer, and businessman do not demand the qualities of primitive masculinity.[21] Clutching at this anachronistic ideal merely leads to a conflict in men between social reality and the relation to their own sexuality, a conflict which hinders the evolution of humanity. Yet the excessive importance which the intellect is given in modern life is equally harmful. Only when the modern man can combine intellect with a refined sexuality will he again become a harmonious and imposing figure and be born again as the 'phoenix of a new humanity'.[22] Thus men, like women, must go through three evolutionary stages. From a primitive state of inner harmony with the sexual drive because there is no consciousness of individuality, they must pass through a transitional stage of conflict between a growing sense of personality and the demands of sexuality, to reach a third stage, of harmony again, but this time because the claims of sexuality have achieved a synthesis with those of the personality.[23] These changes will affect both sexes for, as Mayreder rhetorically asks, 'how could one part lose or gain without the other being affected?'[24] And for both sexes love is to play an important role by offering the possibility of overcoming the limitations of sexuality without denying it.

Masculine and Feminine

This synthesis of *Geist* and *Geschlecht* implies another one: synthesis of those intellectual qualities which are masculine or feminine.[25] Only by transcendence of what is intellectually gender specific can the tasks of a 'higher humanity' be realised.[26] These tasks include creative work by both sexes, for the mind of the creative genius is androgynous. Here Mayreder does not restrict the creative genius to the artistic world, but considers any outstanding achievement, be it in the world of politics, love or social life, to be a sign of creative genius. Mayreder claims that the predominance of intellectuality in itself brings an androgynous element into the human personality. 'The genius is not to be understood as an intensification of masculine nature but as an extension across the boundaries of one-sided sex differentiation, as a synthesis of masculine and feminine nature,' she explains.[27] To support her case she cites how the male genius displays greater emotionality and lability than the average man; Goethe, for example, was well known for crying easily.[28]

In *Zur Kritik der Weiblichkeit*, however, Mayreder restricts her remarks to the male genius; only once, in an unpublished article written as late as 1918, does she appear to have dealt with female creative genius. In that article she denies average femininity any creative ability, for women without a strong sense of personality can, according to her anthropology, see themselves only as the object of male desire: 'the typical woman can basically say about herself only that which she perceives in the mirror of the subject; the average poetry of female authors treats woman just as male authors do – only with the difference that . . . the female author remains limited to herself'.[29] It is clear that 'Only when the female personality is mixed with a masculine strain, by which she gains the ability to experience herself as subject and no longer only as object, only then does she gain in a higher sense the suitability for communication, for aesthetic shaping.' And so Mayreder comes to the conclusion that 'the genius of the female sex does not essentially differ from that of the male'.[30] The female genius, however, does, or potentially can, bring something new into creative life, namely a new perception of masculinity, for, as Mayreder explains, the genius symbolises his or her inner life, which means also the androgynous elements of that life. The female creative genius, unlike the average woman, will be able to experience the opposite sex as object and herself as subject, and to give that experience expression, something only men had been able to do so far.

Mayreder's visionary synthesis of the masculine and the feminine has far-reaching consequences at the collective level of politics, above all social politics. For her it is clear that modern society is made by and for men and that consequently women and their special needs are neglected. In primitive societies, she claims, motherhood does not present any kind of obstacle to woman. It is modern society which makes childbearing and rearing such a burden and which devalues woman, as intellectual life – which in the status quo is only with great difficulty compatible with motherhood – rises in value. Mayreder emphasises the necessity for change in that status quo so that women are able to combine intellectual work and motherhood.[31] It is the exceptional woman's mission to bring this change about, for 'the task of achieving a different position for the female sex in a future social order must be carried out by women themselves. That is the great social mission of every woman who through disposition and action rises above the traditional sphere of her sex.'[32] These are the women who do not have to subordinate themselves to the leadership of the masculine intellect, as they are themselves intellectually independent. Average women, on the other hand, are confined by their teleological sexual nature and will, assures Mayreder, continue to concentrate on the family sphere, incapable – and unwilling – of playing a role in cultural life outside.

In *Geschlecht und Kultur* this synthesis of the feminine and the masculine on the collective level takes on a further dimension. Here Mayreder makes a distinction between civilisation, a society, she explains, in which control over nature with the aim of making life easier is primary,[33] and culture, a society in which ideals are all-important and in which technology stands in harmonious relation to those ideals and ideologies.[34] In this distinction Mayreder joins the 'progressive reaction'[35] of many anti-materialist German-speaking intellectuals at the turn of the century, whose protest against the increasing dehumanisation and depersonalisation brought by the mechanised society of the urban masses often gave way to a glorification of pre-civilisation organic community and its traditions.[36] Mayreder, like these intellectuals, laments the influence of the metropolis, which leads to an imbalance between productivity and receptivity. She too rejects one-sided specialisation and laments the decline of a harmonious, many-faceted intellectual life concerned with values and questions of spirit, but in which the emotions and subjectivity are not neglected. She also shares with her contemporaries the reaffirmation of personal ideals and the charismatic leader in the face of the materialistic, impersonal tide of the times. The exceptional person who is a productive cultural force and initiator of communal tradition is to oppose the prevalent mass anti-culture of over-specialised science and rampant technology which neglect the intellectual and spiritual needs of the human beings they supposedly serve. What was formerly culture has, Mayreder agrees with the sociologist Ferdinand Tönnies, been converted into a state-ridden civilisation in which culture is at risk of total suffocation.[37] She also shares the progressive reaction's reservations about 'proletarian socialism'. Socialism raised the spectre of state-enforced uniformity and the suppression of self-determination in the name of an equality which (in her eyes) was merely a denial of unavoidable natural difference. The mass of average individuals could never rise to the level of the exceptional, and to lower the exceptional to the level of the average would represent the end of culture.

In these ways Mayreder's contribution to the debate is representative of the progressive reaction. Yet her attribution of gender to culture and civilisation is unusual. The latter is for her masculine through and through, characterised above all by immoderation and hubris, the result of man's reproductive role which allows a freedom to excess now that the strict religious paternal morality of earlier times has been relaxed. Symptoms of the masculine nature of civilisation include the overrating of intellectual productivity as against feminine receptivity;

the rapid production of superfluous goods and the accompanying wastage in contrast to the long gestation period needed by feminine culture; bellicosity and militarism; and the exaggerated importance attached to science and specialised knowledge at the expense of human wholeness. This one-sided masculinity, Mayreder claims, is in urgent need of a counterweight – the feminine. This gendered distinction comes closest to that of the German philosopher Georg Simmel. Mayreder recognised this herself, and on 22 October 1915 confided to her diary that his distinction between objective and subjective culture is exactly hers between civilisation and culture – except that she has expressed it better.[38] Her refusal to attribute culture or civilisation to any one race or nation, thus avoiding any hint of nationalist sympathies or social Darwinism, is also unusual. In addition, she avoids the glorification of a pre-urban past in which community and national traditions dominate. Instead, Mayreder's contribution to the debate continues her forward-looking ideal of the world's essential equilibrium and the harmony of polarities. The inner and the outer, the personal and the social, the ideal and the material, the masculine and the feminine are to be united. The crisis of overly masculine civilisation is no exception.

But how is this union to be achieved? It cannot, Mayreder warns, be reached by means of a division of labour along the lines that women are responsible for the tasks of culture and men for those of civilisation. Neither can it be achieved if women enter the public sphere to adopt masculine norms and goals. On the contrary.

> Not until women in general realise that their mission in the life of society must be quite different from that of men, not until they oppose the dominant male values with their own which are orientated according to the natural inequality between the sexes, will they turn a new leaf in the book of world history when they enter political life.[39]

It follows from woman's greater generative burden and the dominance of masculinity in civilisation 'that it must be woman's task to defend the specifically feminine interests which go with her being sexually tied down, that is, the duties and rights of motherhood, and to assert these in the face of dominant masculine values'.[40] Women then are to remain women, for that is their strength; it is now precisely their sex-specific qualities, which Mayreder had rejected in *Zur Kritik der Weiblichkeit* when talking of the exceptional woman and her mission, that are needed by a civilisation which has lost touch with nature. Yet this does not mean that average women are now progressive. It is still the case that only those women who are self-determining personalities and have a fully developed sense of individuality can contribute to cultural progress. Armed with these values, differentiated women are to enter spheres previously closed to them and there bring about change.

It is this awareness of being a female personality with specific needs which leads some women to focus their struggle on prostitution and war, for these phenomena epitomise the social dominance and anti-evolutionary nature of norms made by and for men. The precondition of abolition of prostitution is woman's sense of being a person, for as long as some women reduce themselves to the status of object and are seen as such by men, women as a whole cannot and will not be able to change their position in society and obtain the rights of the free personality.[41] 'All relations, organisations, conditions in which the concept of woman as a thing or a mere means continue to function, obstruct in some way the equality of rights and thus also the possibility of making specifically feminine influences dominant in social culture.'[42] For this reason it is important that attitudes to sexuality are changed, either by appealing to the intellect and spreading knowledge on sexual matters, or by appealing to the emotions and altering sexual behaviour. The former has already been put into practice, claims Mayreder, and she praises the achievements of men on this score. But she also points out once again that the first impulse to talk came from the women's movement. And 'it was also woman who first found the courage to oppose the injustice, bias, and secrecy with which the authorities treated the victims of prostitution [the prostitutes themselves].'[43]

Similarly, war, like prostitution, is in its very essence contrary to the existence of the fully developed female personality and the leading role of feminine values. For Mayreder it is clear that war is a phenomenon with not only political and economic roots but also instinctual ones, and those instincts lie deep in primitive masculinity. 'Theoretically, war represents the most extreme product of masculinity, the final and most terrible consequence of absolute masculine activity. The naturally feminine cannot assert itself as something with equal rights beside this greater external intensification of natural masculinity.'[44] The inner essence of war is conquest through destruction, while the most fundamental and general function of the feminine is the sustaining of life. Woman as childbearer and nurturer must value human life more than man. But war confines woman to her reproductive role alone, prevents her participation in social life, and allows male sexual unrestraint to run riot. A militarist society in which the values and sexual instincts of primitive masculinity are dominant can never offer any hope of an improvement in women's social position. This is dependent on the growth of a state based on law in which individual freedom is a precondition.[45]

Mayreder represents a pacifism which recognises relations of power as central. 'All problems of how the world is to be shaped can be traced back to one thing – the problem of power. . . . War is inseparable from the striving for power; whoever wishes to combat war as such would first have to devalue the principle of power,' she comments drily.[46] Here she clearly if implicitly sets herself apart from women like Suttner, who represented a rational pacifism. But the women's movement is instrumental for Mayreder as for Suttner. It has seen that the values of militarism rob it of any foundation and has therefore made the struggle against war one of its goals, although this, for Mayreder, means internationalism rather than rationalism. 'Without internationalism every form of resistance to war is utopian, indeed senseless,' she asserts.[47] This means putting the feeling of community with humanity as a whole above other forms of collective feeling such as family, sex or race. It is only in a culture guided by such a sentiment that women can hope for any real equality.[48] And it is only in such a culture that they will be able to bring their genuine values to bear. The women's movement once again becomes the cultural pioneer of Mayreder's vision, for 'after the experiences of the World War one can surely say: European culture . . . will either be organised internationalism or it will not exist at all'.[49]

Intellect and Instinct

Mayreder, then, sees instinct as playing an essential role in cultural organisation. In the case of the male aggressive instinct this is diametrically opposed to woman's interests. However, another male instinct claimed by Mayreder – that of fatherly feeling – is in women's interests and so, suggests Mayreder, can be joined to intellectual considerations to produce another synthesis, between instinct and intellect. For Mayreder, fatherly feeling has two dimensions: feelings of property and authority (the social dimension), and feelings of identity in blood bondage (the instinctual dimension). The first set of feelings is an accompanying phenomenon of the social status of fatherhood, not of its biological status, as the second set is. It is the dimension more commonly acknowledged, for

> the great majority of men know fatherliness merely as an accompanying phenomenon of the social position of the father which rests on property and dominance . . . in only a smaller number does fatherliness also have the character of instinctive affection as a result of the physiological bond . . . a complex of feelings which in its instinctual strength is in no way inferior to that of motherly feeling.[50]

The first set of feelings is therefore dependent on intellectual recognition of the biological bond, rather than any instinct, as the second set of feelings is. Intellectual recognition is given altogether a greater significance than instinct in social life, Mayreder remarks, referring to the institutions developed in order to ascertain the legitimacy of paternity. These are so important in bourgeois society, she explains, because on that legitimacy of offspring depends also the legitimacy of the inheritance of property. And for precisely that reason, society has developed a complex double morality, denying the sexual freedom to woman that it concedes to man.[51]

Yet it is Mayreder's concern to counter that exaggerated social significance in order to claim that there is indeed a paternal instinct, just as there is a maternal one. The earliest human societies were based on mother-right, and the biological bond between father and child was unknown, she claims, and points to 'primitive' peoples and folk customs (particularly that of couvade) as evidence of how a paternal instinct has existed in other cultures quite independent of the intellectual recognition of biological paternity and the social status of fatherhood. This instinct, like all instincts, is pre-cultural, for it represents nature's consciousness – called by Mayreder the unconscious – as opposed to the human consciousness of reason and intellectual insight, 'thinking recognition'.[52] It is a remnant of the primal memory (*Urgedächtnis*) when, in the earliest childhood of the human race, organic life was governed by the two instincts of preservation of self and preservation of the species, and represents the synthesis of these two. Yet as humanity evolves, instinct comes to play a role increasingly subordinate to reason, and 'thinking recognition' increasingly deprives the individual of the consciousness of identity with the species in favour of a consciousness of individuality. Instinct does not, however, disappear without trace; modern men still carry with them the remains of their primitive beginnings, and one of these is the paternal instinct. Yet in the modern world there can be no regression to an earlier stage of evolution. Instead, intellect and instinct must reach a synthesis. Instinct must be made rational and thus stronger, for 'making instinct rational does not mean weakening it through the arbitrariness of understanding, but reinforcing it through insight'.[53] This means liberating this instinct from the conventional concepts of property and dominance, to let it emerge as free affection. And this is a bond, based on feelings of identity with the species, which cannot be lost by any change in society, for the basis of this feeling lies, says Mayreder, in 'the succession of the generations which is an eternal form of natural life'.[54] Thus man as father is woven into the mystery of life and of nature.

An important factor in bringing about this change is a developed sense of individuality on the part of women and children. To be a paterfamilias of the old style means 'for every man, however unfree his social position may be in other respects, to possess a small kingdom of unlimited power over wife and children'.[55] But as soon as women perceive themselves as active individuals and become increasingly independent, and children come to question the principle of 'honour your parents', this power dwindles. And vice versa: the acknowledgement of fatherly feeling as an instinct and the loosening of the paternal bonds of authority and dominance have far-reaching consequences for women and children, for they mean no less than the ultimate collapse of patriarchy. When man as father no longer finds it necessary to ascertain the legitimacy of his fatherhood as there is now trust in the faithfulness of the mother (which is in fact the only effective guarantee of legitimacy), the protectionist institutions which have evolved, including the prevailing double standards of morality, will disintegrate. The daughter released from paternal authority will demand a different morality, and not only for herself. Here the inner union of emotions and sexual desire, the result of her long obedience to traditional paternal demands and the dependence these have engendered, will prove its worth and offer the basis for a single morality for both sexes. This will not be that of masculinity, but of progressive femininity.[56] This new sexual morality in which sex relations are based on individual love rather than economic motives, religious sanction or property rights, will also have a deep effect on the morality surrounding motherhood. No longer will it be necessarily tied to marriage as the guarantor of legitimacy, as has hitherto been the case, nor, if occurring outside this institution, will it be censured, a censure which is perhaps, Mayreder claims, the most disgraceful fact in the whole of human history.[57]

Progress and Tradition

Yet how is humanity to develop to 'higher conditions of being'?[58] Mayreder answers this by suggesting yet another synthesis: of progress and tradition. Here the synthetic individual plays a significant role, for he or she is the herald not only of a new personal culture of synthesis but also of a general change in cultural norms as a whole. Because their original nature has not been deformed by culture's notions of morality, convention and duty, it is the mission of such people to 'oppose tradition, to shatter and reform petrified forms of life by the revolutionary force of an essence which deviates from the norm'.[59] This minority represents, says Mayreder, drawing an analogy from physics, the centrifugal principle in the social community, the principle of progress, whereas the majority represents the centripetal principle of conservatism. Change does however take place with the 'necessity of a natural law' through the conflict and then synthesis of precisely these two principles. 'As long as the outstanding individual is alone, he remains despised; only when he has gathered a following, a sufficient number of supporters and disciples, does the dominant norm retreat to give him scope for action,' she asserts.[60] Gradually, the progressive minority introduces new ideas which are then slowly assimilated by the majority and turned into norms. But not always, for 'only those [ideas] which correspond to the needs and abilities of the majority enter general ownership'.[61] So evolutionary development must take the form of a gradual elevation of the average type and take place 'beneath the threshold of social consciousness'.[62] The majority will never free itself from an obedience to norms; all that can happen is that the norms change to give increased individual freedom.

Yet Mayreder by no means dismisses the conservative majority as an obstacle to social evolution. Just as the centrifugal principle in the natural world needs the centripetal principle, so 'the conservative tendency of the majority forms a necessary and essential balance to the tendencies of progressive intellectuality. Without it human social life could just as little exist as the universe could exist without the effect of gravity.'[63] This retardant force is found in tradition, the only reliable organic basis of any culture. Change, claims Mayreder, is the manifestation of the natural immanent law of upward evolution, a law which is borne out by the very existence of the synthetic personality. For, as she is careful to emphasise, such representatives of the progressive principle are themselves a gift of nature; they are not the product of education and upbringing. 'New people are born, not raised, they are a work of nature, not their parents.'[64]

According to Mayreder's model, evolution, like the synthesis of *Geist* and *Geschlecht*, proceeds as a spiral of synthesis rather than a linear progression. The first phase is marked by the dominance of ideology and idealism. 'Still unsullied by the external world which brings innumerable limitations, difficulties and complications, on this level the teaching of a new order unfolds in its purest form.'[65] This phase of what should be is necessarily of limited impact amongst the majority, and followed by a phase of organisation and action rather than ideology. In this second phase what is conflicts with what should be. In order to reach the masses compromises have to be made and ideals must be tailored to reality. Such compromises are the basis of reform, and it is this rather than revolution which brings progress. This second phase gives way in turn to a third, that of power, imperialism and inner division. In this phase the desire for power becomes paramount at the expense of ideology and reform. 'If in the organisational phase the disregard for the ideological demands was in all honesty regarded as only temporary and transitional . . . then the ideological programme is [in the phase of imperialism] only a prettily decorated veil which conceals measures for the success of which secrecy is essential.'[66] Yet by corrupting the ideology which was originally its motor, the social movement initiates its own collapse. This is the essential paradox of all social movements: that their natural goal, namely gaining the power needed to push through their demands, at the same time means their uselessness as a tool of progress. But this is not to say that the reforms achieved in the second phase are worthless. Each social movement must decline and die, to make room for the next one, which can build on the reforms of its predecessors.

Problems and Contributions

On the individual level, Mayreder's goal is that of the self-determining personality, the embodiment of a 'higher humanity'.[67] This is the person who has transcended the limitations of sex teleology to achieve inner freedom and harmony. Yet each generation has to achieve this synthesis anew; it cannot be made into a norm but is 'an inexhaustible source of new possibilities of development and new forms of existence'.[68]

On the collective level such a development means a new culture dominated by the exceptional personality. This, claims Mayreder, is the ultimate goal of Western culture and determines the special direction its development has taken. If man surrenders to the elemental he is more wretched than an animal, but through the leading force of *Geist*, 'the fundamental force of culture',[69] he is able to become the master of the world, to tame the elemental and submit it to the laws he has himself created. For Mayreder it is a matter of reaching a harmonious synthesis between apparently polar pairs to achieve a culture in which the values of *Geist* hold sway over those of the material world but do not eradicate them.

Such a schematic approach is not without its problems. A major one is the abstract nature of Mayreder's design. Unlike Troll-Borostyáni and Meisel-Hess, Mayreder's essays make almost no concrete demands or suggestions for reform. Her tone is analytical rather than polemical. As she freely admits, 'I do not expect to convince opponents', and so she does not really try.[70] This difficulty was commented on by one contemporary reviewer, who accused her of using over-elaborate language and scientific-sounding terms in *Zur Kritik der Weiblichkeit*, which he nevertheless patronisingly judged a 'surprisingly peaceful and reasonable exposition of feminism'.[71] But as a result, her sharp insights, sophisticated analysis and clever criticism are not easily accessible.

In addition, Mayreder does not consistently maintain the distinction between sex and gender she herself suggests. She emphasises that those psychological characteristics which are usually considered sex specific and natural are relevant only for the majority but not for the minority of exceptional personalities, and are anyway the historical product of external conditions. The socially accepted typical images of the sexes will change as the external – social and economic – conditions that produce them change. In this analysis of the cultural origins of gender difference Mayreder joins feminists such as Troll-Borostyáni. However, unlike them, she goes a step further to question the possibility of ascertaining natural psychological differences at all, something which is for Troll-Borostyáni remarkably unproblematic. Mayreder remarks in one essay, 'As we are not able to determine with certainty what the psychological differences between the sexes are when they are divorced from all cultural influences, we must limit ourselves to looking at those differences which have so far been regarded as typical of the sexes.'[72] But it is just this awareness of the cultural evolution of what are regarded as natural sex characteristics that Mayreder cannot sustain in her vision. For she builds her anthropology on the existence of ascertainable natural sex characteristics, those of what she calls sex teleology. It is these, she suggests, which form the basis of personality for the majority of people. She thus reduces personality to a function of the reproductive process. In addition, she frequently lapses into a stereotyped allocation of characteristics and fails to question how justified this is. She calls 'feminine', for example, those characteristics usually associated with women and sets these in schematic opposition to those usually associated with men. It seems that here Mayreder undermines her own recognition of the influence of culture on what are regarded as sex (rather than gender) roles and also her own ideal of androgyny. This becomes particularly clear in her concern with *Geist*, which she obviously sees as a masculine and positive quality in contrast to feminine suggestibility and emotionality. She thus supports and perpetuates precisely the division between the sexes she is concerned to overcome. This criticism applies, too, to the way she gives social phenomena a gender – culture becomes feminine, civilisation is masculine – for this once again turns these categories into metaphysical qualities, making them rigid and eternal. It is the very tendency Mayreder wishes to counteract through her insistence on the primacy of the individual and the impossibility of completely valid generalisations. This focus on nonconformity leads her to consider those who do not submit to gender norms and to turn these into the heralds of a new culture. She issues a plea for the value of the individual who fights against authority and convention. But just as the distinction between sex and gender is unclear, so too is that between the individual and the sexual. Where does the significance of sex end and the individual begin? Is *Geist* really separable from *Geschlecht*, the human from the gender-related? These are questions she leaves unaddressed.

The significance Mayreder attaches to the intellect introduces a third set of problems. According to her design, it is largely the female intellect which will lead humanity onwards and upwards.[73] Yet this is problematic on three counts. First, Mayreder attributes too great a power and value to ideas, both in political life and in the life of the individual. This is an insight she herself admitted. Her private remarks about the women's movement and pacifism are marked by a scepticism about the ability of the intellect to effect change and by an unwilling belief in the superior strength of the irrational in human life and affairs. There is still a conflict, despite Mayreder's own synthetic ideal, between intellect and instincts. And, of course, she leaves material conditions largely out of account. Secondly, her equation of the intellectual woman with the feminist is too reductive. It was (and is) not the case that intellectuality implies sympathy with feminism and the goals of the women's movement – indeed Mayreder herself was highly ambivalent. Thirdly, she is elitist in her rejection of the possible benefits of education and in her belief that nature chooses in a quasi-religious sense a small minority of people to be the heralds of a new humanity. Nature may indeed ignore social barriers as Mayreder suggests, but she herself erects others in the name of nature and evolution. Her view of human beings is essentially determinist and damning.

Yet for all this, Mayreder's ideas must be given a special place in the history of early Viennese feminism, as they are unusual in their intellectual quality and range. While most other feminist commentators talk of what woman's role should ideally be, Mayreder talks in terms of *why* it should be so. This leads her to come to grips with the issues of the woman problem at an intellectual level unique in the movement. In spite of her own denial of interest in the movement's social and economic aspects, her contribution may be seen to be an attempt to give an argued theoretical foundation to women's common demands for the opening of opportunities, particularly for entry into the professions. It is an attempt which took her a long way from her immediate concern with employment and caused her to consider many related areas. The ideas first presented in *Zur Kritik der Weiblichkeit* led her to go far beyond the confines of the conventional debate to make a contribution to areas and themes that had largely been untouched by women, such as cultural history, anthropology, sociology, philosophy and in particular men, patriarchy and fatherhood. Her work is an attempt to break out of the widely accepted segregation of women as a problem and having a movement. It is an attempt to discuss on a par with men the necessarily wide spectrum of issues raised and to see these against a varied background which extends far beyond the debate on women's role. It is thus not surprising that when the Vienna Sociological Society (*Wiener Soziologische Gesellschaft*) was founded in 1907 by Max Adler and Karl Renner amongst others, Mayreder became an active member – and the only woman involved. Mayreder is also unusual in that she questions the possibility of identifying a natural femininity at all, even if she is not consistent in that questioning and does not go far enough. She takes up a more reticent position on upbringing, preferring non-intervention to Troll-Borostyáni's 'natural education', which would after all go against her belief in the innate personality. Also unusual is Mayreder's emphasis on the historicity of sexuality and therefore its capacity to change as a result of changes in culture and in human psychology in particular. In contrast to Troll-Borostyáni, Mayreder does not see change in the legal and institutional structure of society as the path to the realisation of her vision, although as her pacifism indicates, she does regard equal rights as a *sine qua non* of human emancipation. Instead she emphasises the less rational elements in human nature in addition to the rights of the individual and the force of cultural change. But more important is inner change, which will in turn bring about emancipatory changes in human relationships. The goal of this inner change is the harmonious, synthetic individual whose personal qualities, according to Mayreder's model, are the epitome of the human, and who represents an evolutionary avant-garde. For Mayreder some women are synthetic individuals because this is ordained by nature. For most other feminists, women are to strive for personal development because they would then be better mothers and citizens. While the latter tend to talk of women as a more or less homogeneous whole, Mayreder creates a two-tier caste system with those dominated by sexual teleology as a lower caste than those dominated by a personalised sexuality which bridges crude sexual difference. Mayreder is no Enlightenment egalitarian as Troll-Borostyáni is. Not all people are born equal in her vision. Whereas Troll-Borostyáni largely represents a rationalist feminism, Mayreder on the whole represents a Romantic one which emphasises inner change, the emotions and the individual. But just as Troll-Borostyáni manages to combine political and cultural feminism, so Mayreder, too, manages to merge her vision of the personal development of men and women with a concept of universal human qualities. The genderised individual retreats into the background to the benefit of her ideal: the truly human person, liberated from the confines of restrictive gender roles – the synthetic god.

CHAPTER 10

Eugenics and Feminism. Grete Meisel-Hess

A Monist View

Both Troll-Borostyáni and Mayreder have a vision of a new cultural order which would neither alienate its members from their true being or their surroundings nor stunt individual and collective growth by imposing a tyranny of norms. For Troll-Borostyáni this means a moral culture which is to be achieved by obeying the laws of nature, for Mayreder it means a culture of *Geist* which will become a reality when the polarities that govern human life find a synthesis. These are visions in which a solution to the woman question features only as part of the new cultural order, not as a goal in itself. Grete Meisel-Hess is no exception (see figure 15). She also cherishes a vision of a new cultural order, but unlike Troll-Borostyáni and Mayreder, her goal is human health, which is to be reached through the natural unity of spirit and matter.

Meisel-Hess claims that present civilisation is sick because it is removed from nature. People are grotesquely deformed by an unnatural way of life which is made up of suffocating judgements, the ridiculous lies of misplaced conventions, and narrow-minded conformism.[1] The mass of the population, the proletariat, is suffering from physical, mental and moral degeneration, manifested in the 'never-ending rise in the incidence of idiocy and crime',[2] while the bourgeoisie is dying of decadence, suffering from a superfluity of privileges and the lack of the need to struggle for existence. 'Just as a deficit of privileges is paralysing,' Meisel-Hess summarises, 'so their excess has an enervating effect. The result of the former is degeneration, of the latter decadence.'[3] Just how sick civilisation is, she comments, is most apparent in its sexual order. A severe sexual crisis prevails; venereal disease is rife, and as a result of the suppression of sexual desires in both sexes, sexual neuroses and psychoses abound. 'The greater part of civilised humanity suffers from this severe trauma, from this

15. Portrait photograph of Grete Meisel-Hess, *c.*1900. Österreichische Nationalbibliothek.

laborious suppression of a natural emotional state. . . . Sexual psychosis is thus also the most widely spread pathological consequence of our sexual misery,'[4] she claims, referring directly to the work of Freud and Breuer. She comes to the conclusion that 'The consistent prevention of reproduction and of sexual life in general makes people, male and female, ill; all social circles are pining as a result of this abnormal way of living.'[5] Not only is modern society sexually and emotionally diseased, it is also morally ill for it operates according to an unnatural moral code, seen above all in its obstruction of the process of selection. The social organism is, in short, so infected that it cannot be healed by piecemeal measures. It must die. It must, following the law of nature, disintegrate in order to be able to re-form.

What is to be the guiding principle of this new and healthy social organism? Like Troll-Borostyáni, Meisel-Hess states quite clearly that this is to be nature itself: 'Only through healthy conditions taken from nature itself can the sick individual and the sick organisation be healed.'[6] This, however, Meisel-Hess like Troll-Borostyáni is anxious to stress, should not be confused with any 'back to nature' philosophy or any irrationalism. 'The ideal lies not in the past,' she explains, 'but in the future, and it is not knowledge which has killed it, but instead knowledge which must bring it about.'[7] She is not a cultural pessimist. 'It is not because we have civilisation that we suffer from social evils and wrongs, but because we have too little civilisation, because we are not civilised enough to avoid many a false turn,' she claims.[8] This civilisation is to follow nature instead of working against it,

> for we cannot and do not want to build up our culture and morality according to principles which go against nature, because we would thereby unavoidably be the losers. We want to use precisely it, nature, in a thoughtful and purposeful manner as the foundation of our human organisation, as the primary measure of our system of values.[9]

Following nature in this way means acknowledging the monist principle of the unity of all things. This modern way of perceiving the world, which stands in contrast to the dualist perception of preceding generations, is the legacy of Darwin and his predecessors, Goethe, Lamarck and Spinoza, and of his apostle Ernst Haeckel. According to this view, there is no essential qualitative difference between the human and the natural spheres: the one is an extension of the other; man is the evolutionary product of a chain of being, not the isolated product of creationism. So there is no essential qualitative difference between the soul and matter, for all matter has a soul and all soul is material. There is no dichotomy between the ideal and the real, between self and others, egoism and altruism. The individual, if possessing a healthy egoism, which it will do in the natural state, will be altruistic. 'Do not let us oppose humane altruism or selflessness to egoism, for the latter is the goal of the ego looking for satisfaction, it is the most natural and valuable consequence of a healthy ego. Once again it is nature herself, the great mentor, who shows us this unity.'[10] This is a natural morality, claims Meisel-Hess, according to which the natural principle of care for others will be combined with that of egoism to give rise to the most perfect morality:

> In this lineage the 'superman' will develop, the person who is allowed to return to nature – enriched with the values of his culture and therefore without running the risk of sinking back down to his primitive beginnings and becoming a renegade – the person who has overcome pity because he no longer needs it, the natural moralist, the ego-altruist kat exochen.[11]

In this process of healing by establishing a natural order, the monist world view is again the path to health. It plays a central role by recognising that the body and above all the drive to reproduction, which Meisel-Hess calls 'the most essential natural principle',[12] and the soul, the longing for affinity, are united in the love instinct.[13] The monist world view also offers the possibility of overcoming the seeming conflicts between socialism, individualism and racial progress, the cornerstones of Meisel-Hess's design for cultural regeneration.

Socialism and Women's Emancipation

Capitalism has, quite clearly for Meisel-Hess, been responsible for human degeneration. It has exploited the physical power, the bodies, of the lower classes, accumulated wealth in only a small number of hands, kept wages to an absolute minimum, and thereby hindered intellectual middle-class men from a timely marriage and the foundation of a family. 'Capitalism,' she pithily comments, 'permits the young man to save up a few marks to be able now and then to go to the prostitute to pour his healthy life-giving seed into her artificially sterilised womb.'[14] In this way 'capitalism quite simply emasculates the citizens of its society'.[15] For her, socialism is one absolutely fundamental element of cultural regeneration; only when everyone has equal opportunities can there be any unbiased evolutionary selection and thus any improvement in human material. This, however, she is quick to point out, means neither that all are to be made 'the same' nor that the 'struggle for existence' is to be undermined. 'Only the basic conditions offered by society concerning the possibilities for human development can be equalised . . . not the goals of this development,'[16] Meisel-Hess avers, and 'in our opinion there is nothing in socialism which deprives . . . the promotion of the fitter over the less fit of a foundation . . . for socialism wants nothing more than the same starting conditions for everyone'.[17] Only a natural socialism can supply the preconditions for a fruitful individualism, for only when all have equal access to material, spiritual and intellectual benefits can the exceptional individual emerge. This socialism, Meisel-Hess maintains, is not identical to Social Democracy, which is merely the transitional step to true individual socialism. Yet it is a necessary transitional step, for the dominant conservatism of the day must first be fought and overcome by existing socialist parties before the most primitive foundations for true socialism and true individualism can at last be laid.

In Meisel-Hess's opinion, this socialist individualism is represented by the women's movement, at least as far as the reform of sexual morality is concerned. It has a number of tasks, but its most important one is to promote reproduction and racial progress. And that in turn above all implies introducing a full and efficient system of protection for mothers. This means demanding the economic emancipation of women from men, free choice of sexual partners, and campaigning for the changes in morality that go with those demands. Indeed, economic emancipation is an absolute precondition of any kind of emancipation. 'There is no kind of sexual, intellectual or emotional emancipation without economic emancipation,' Meisel-Hess asserts firmly.[18] Yet she is well aware of the negative aspects of women's paid labour, the grinding drainage of energy, which, she claims, often impairs women's reproductive capacity. 'We want freedom of profession for woman, but without compulsion to a profession,' she explains,[19] for 'when women's paid labour forces, indeed condemns, woman to celibacy, then it is almost worthless. It should mainly be a means of making marriage and motherhood easier.'[20] Harnessing women's labour to turn mother power into horse power is a mistake, and it is only under a capitalist system that human power is exploited beyond its physical limits in this way. The only viable solution is the organised protection of woman as mother. 'Only when every adult woman is sure of a profession which does not damage her female functions, when every pregnant woman and mother is sure of maintenance for herself and her children will the maintenance of woman by man become superfluous.'[21]

This form of socialism liberates woman from bourgeois morality, giving her freedom in choice of sexual partner(s). And this freedom of choice is essential for racial progress, for 'every possibility of the selection of the best, the progress of a race, stands and falls with the freedom of choice of woman (and man of course)'.[22] As Meisel-Hess goes on to explain, if woman is forced by the dowry system to pay to be made pregnant or to 'give herself' to the man who can pay the highest price, then negative selection is at work, for it does not follow that such a man will be the best father, genetically speaking. Similarly, it is also not necessarily the case that women who have the largest dowry and who are therefore the most attractive marriage partners are the healthiest in physical and moral terms. So although adaptation to existing social conditions is the norm, this in no way secures the survival of the morally and physically best, but merely of the best adapted to the status quo. 'The person who is fruitful and multiplies and asserts himself is probably the "fittest" but seldom is he noble,' Meisel-Hess caustically remarks.[23]

Yet at the same time she sees marriage and sexual union as a matter of personal affection, not merely a question of social Darwinism. 'The aim [of such union] is to bring the interests of the individual and the interests of the collective together as much as possible,' she pronounces, echoing Troll-Borostyáni.[24] The main reason for marriage is not reproduction but the completion of one individual by another. Having a child may contribute to this completion, but it cannot be a substitute for it. 'My cardinal duty to the child is to place it as "beautifully" as possible in the world! (And here it is most usually sinned against!) . . . But it must not take me from myself. I remain myself, even when I have reproduced myself . . . with my clearly felt needs and my inalienable right to my life,' Meisel-Hess explains.[25] Because of this high evaluation of sexual partnership as the union of two free and equal beings, she wishes to see a relaxation in attitudes to marriage. Although a monogamous partnership based on individualised affection remains her ideal, she sees that in such a complex matter as sexual relations it is highly unlikely that the right partner will be chosen first time off and thus pleads, like Troll-Borostyáni, for a more tolerant attitude to divorce, separation and extra-marital or other forms of sexual relationship:

> This discharging of the erotic life of the individual in a lasting sexual and social union with a being of the opposite sex is . . . the one which the individual, man and woman, will and should eternally strive for. But precisely this 'goal' can . . . be reached only after moving through many of life's phases.[26]

As a result of this attitude to marriage Meisel-Hess also launches an attack on the prevalent bourgeois morality of double standards. Like Mayreder, she sees the protection of 'decent' women and the certainty of the legitimacy of their offspring to be the underlying intent of that morality. To be sure, the protection of one class of women was once the basis of a code of chivalry but it has now degenerated to become a hypocritical official code in which male 'honour' in the public sphere plays the central role.[27] And as Meisel-Hess explains, 'A protective measure which can exist only by deceiving nature deforms those who manipulate it more than it serves them.'[28] This is particularly blatant in the case of the condemnation of unmarried motherhood and illegitimate children, who, claims Meisel-Hess, may in fact be racially better material than many a legitimate child. 'The children of strength, of youth and free selection must have the chance of being born regardless of whether the parents are mature enough to marry, able to marry, and willing to marry.'[29]

Yet the ideal marriage Meisel-Hess envisages is a possibility only when both man and woman have developed as social and erotic forces. This means for men overcoming their fear of strong, sensuous and autonomous women, for that fear is part of the problem.[30] Modern men are afraid of women who 'give' themselves to a man in free self-affirmation, and also afraid of love. What the average modern man wants, claims Meisel-Hess, is a union which 'does not absorb him erotically but in daily life gives him the necessary contact with woman, that is, marriage'.[31] Such a man also needs to have confirmation, in the form of financial investment, that a relationship is indeed valuable. And so Meisel-Hess sees that she is forced to come to the conclusion that 'a love relationship must nowadays either turn into a marriage or break up. For the whole man, the strong man, the man who can incorporate love into the fabric of his life and keep hold of it without fear is not of today.'[32] This 'unwillingness and incapacity to love of the man of today'[33] represents the tragedy of the woman of today. For her there is at present only one solution: to give, like man, her life a meaning through work in the public sphere (and in motherhood) and not to depend solely on a love relationship for her vitality. Yet at the same time, Meisel-Hess emphasises woman's deep need for both sex and motherhood; 'the healthy young woman must be allowed to become a mother, otherwise she will become neurotic. She needs not only the sexual act but also pregnancy, the "purification" achieved through giving birth, the relief achieved through breast-feeding and the feeling of love for the child.'[34]

The solution to this individual and collective sexual misery is, as Meisel-Hess sees it, the social acceptance of temporary sexual relationships which are based on mutual affection but do not necessarily consider marriage as a goal (although this does remain the ideal). This must be combined with a developed system of maternity protection and of course the acceptance of illegitimate children. Developments like these would have a number of beneficial consequences for the individual. Not only would many women find the essential emotional and sensual nourishment otherwise denied them, but man's position of tremendous power over women would be undermined, for this position rests, Meisel-Hess asserts, more on his sexual freedom than on his economic strength.[35] Such a sexual order would also lead to the eradication of prostitution, because it acknowledges men's need for sex without commitment in a way that benefits both sexes rather than denying that need as the customary moral tracts did.

However, such changes presuppose independent, completely mature, inwardly secure women who are emancipated not to turn away from sex, but towards it.[36] For them, professional life is not a substitute for sex but an addition to it, part of the liberation of the innermost personality of woman. And the mother protection movement is for Meisel-Hess the continuation of the women's movement. It builds on the foundations the movement laid as regards women's inner growth and their rights. Thus it is precisely these independent women of the women's movement who are most fitted to become mothers. For what is important, according to Meisel-Hess, is not who cares for the child, but who bears it. Acquired characteristics, in this case a free personality, are inheritable, she claims, and so genetic material takes precedence over maternal care. It should be a goal of the women's movement to enable these women to reproduce. In this connection Meisel-Hess welcomes the struggle for women's rights, for this is, she pronounces, 'a means of achieving the free self-determination of woman, in motherhood and love too, a means of extending her personality so that she can be a better person and therefore a better woman'.[37] So although she condemns suffragism along English lines as a 'side-step' of the women's movement and the product of severe female frustration,[38] she supports female suffrage in general for 'it is through suffrage that the path to the "right to love" also runs. Suffrage is an indispensable means to the liberation of the personality, of the sex, class and species.'[39] Women's rights are also a means of bringing the feminine element into the public sphere for, Meisel-Hess rhetorically asks, 'Does she [woman] not bring a new understanding into all branches of public life, that understanding which cannot be learnt, which is nature and remains nature and which must be missing in man precisely because he is man?'[40]

The Individual and Eugenics

Meisel-Hess criticises capitalist culture on two counts: not only is it an obstacle to individual development, it also runs counter to racial improvement because it prevents a true selection procedure. On both counts she is concerned to present an alternative – socialism and the reform of sexual morality – which will permit a union of the claims of the individual and the claims of eugenics. This requires the eradication of elements such as disease and poverty which weaken humanity and act as an obstacle to the creation of a happier, healthier and therefore more noble species. However, it also implies the prevention of the reproduction of 'inferior' individuals, of which there is, she admits, a lamentable abundance, and 'the terrible thing is that nothing, not a single thing, stands in the path of this inferiority being inherited'.[41] Marriage restrictions on women teachers prevented the best intellectual women from having children; similarly, young, strong army officers were barred from marriage unless they could deliver financial security. Yet the absurdity of the system did not exclude syphilitics, drunkards and similar individuals from having children.[42] Society must intervene, Meisel-Hess claims, in a way that favours racial progress, that is, it must introduce those reforms she herself suggests: mother protection, equal pay for women's work, the reform of sexual morality, and the state education of children by professionals. Yet this racial individualism which is to serve the progress of the race is not, for Meisel-Hess, to extend to the destruction of those already living. 'Once something lives then it has also a claim to protection. Only when it is a case of passing miserable characteristics on through reproduction, only then does society have the right to place its veto.'[43] This means protection from weakening, not from weakness,[44] and represents the synthesis of humanitarian ideals with the aristocratic Nietzschean ideals of the victory of the strong, the synthesis of Christian with Classical moral values.[45] Eugenics, then, is a question of upward human evolution to greater psychological as well as physical health and is to be achieved through women's sexual as well as social emancipation; it is not a question of racialist power politics, as was the case for some of Meisel-Hess's eugenicist contemporaries and successors. The rejuvenation of the joy in living of the Ancients and its synthesis with the ideal of neighbourly love and altruistic responsibility is the essence of a successful solution to the sexual crisis. It is the basis of a future sexual order which must emerge from an awakened racial consciousness and a prouder attitude to sexuality. And it is an order which will make the 'procreation of healthy, strong, beautiful people' following 'the most powerful will of nature' the only guideline for sexual mores.[46] Yet this natural will remain crippled until its consequences are protected by culture. 'For,' claims Meisel-Hess, 'the goal of all culture is the human being – the fully developed human being, who is no longer unconditionally driven by his sexual nature but ascends to the peaks of organic life.'[47] Such social engineering will give humanity more opportunities for happiness, but above all it will finally make the harmony of the individual with the universe possible: it will give birth to the monist soul.

Meisel-Hess's vision is characterised by the attempted union of individualism and eugenics. For Meisel-Hess, it is a matter of promoting both individual happiness and the happiness of the human race through reforms which are in accordance with the evolutionary laws of nature and a natural morality and which thus promote the harmonious, full life of both spirit and body. Yet do not these two pillars of Meisel-Hess's vision – individualism and eugenics – invite a tension? As Mayreder, a critic of eugenics, pointed out, the personalised desire for sexual union and the drive to reproduce do not necessarily coincide. 'The special significance of sexuality in human life,' she comments, 'rests on the fact that it is not merely a means of reproduction but also one of the fulfilment of love, that it serves the purposes of the individual just as much as those of the species. Two opposing spheres of interest are united in it.'[48] Meisel-Hess overlooks the possibility that these sets of interests, which Mayreder assumes conflict, might indeed clash. Where, for example, is the guarantee, which Meisel-Hess seems to see, that a marriage of love will lead to healthier offspring than a marriage of convenience? Mayreder allocates these two sets of interests to two different spheres, for 'love belongs to the realm of culture and not that of nature which knows nothing of the concept of the personality'.[49] Meisel-Hess on the other hand, in accordance with her pantheistic monism, relegates both love and sexuality to the sphere of the natural. Her monism here turns out to be an extension of the realm of nature to include individuality – precisely that which Mayreder is concerned to liberate from the realm of the natural. Individualised sexuality has become for Meisel-Hess another of nature's laws.

Yet as with Troll-Borostyáni's ideas, it is unclear how far nature is really reliable in Meisel-Hess's scheme of things. She claims that nature is the foundation of human organisation and sees an ideal socio-sexual organisation to be the handmaid of evolution; it is directed to promoting upward evolution. Yet that evolutionary process seems to need help, for human beings must intervene, manipulate and manage; it is not enough just to let nature take its course. Thus in fact Meisel-Hess, like Troll-Borostyáni, devises a highly interventionist system, but unlike Troll-Borostyáni, she makes the state become the guarantor of naturalness. The state is to guarantee the health of mother and child which is essential to the evolution of the race. The state is to educate the coming generation. The state is to guarantee the health of those already born – through preventive and protective measures, largely in the form of money which, as Anna Schapire-Neurath pointed out, could not, however, amount to more than negligible sums for those other than the poorest.[50] In addition, it is not always clear what the criterion of desirability is to be. Is it physical health or emotional maturity? The weight seems to be placed on the former: everything possible is to be done to promote physical health, but at the same time Meisel-Hess claims that emancipated women, that is, emotionally mature ones, are the best mothers. And quite apart from this, she does not question the highly simplistic view she has of inheritance, for again, what guarantee is there that healthy parents will produce healthy offspring, not to mention her highly questionable assumption that acquired characteristics are inheritable? In addition, she reduces femininity to woman's role in the reproductive process, a reduction Mayreder was vehemently intent on rejecting. Female sexual pleasure is important for Meisel-Hess, but it is only second best; the real pleasure is pregnancy, the physical act of giving birth to – but not rearing – a child. And it is this, and only this, which deserves state promotion in the form of maternity protection.

Yet this involves a wide range of other changes which lead Meisel-Hess away from an anti-feminist 'mother only' philosophy. In her eyes, motherhood is the path to women's full emancipation. Liberated motherhood implies being liberated from economic dependence on men, an improvement in social status, the living of femininity to the full without surrender of the self and woman's own needs to those of her child, and liberation from a constraining morality. And more than that. It also implies women's emotional emancipation, for 'the problem of the freedom of woman nowadays, so much at the centre of struggle, rests precisely on this most central question of her life. It is here that woman must become free, inwardly free, regally free if all the political and economic freedoms which she has won by fighting are to have any point at all.'[51] It is Meisel-Hess's declared goal for woman that she should not 'submit to slavery, including that of the heart, in the sense that she should not feel . . . herself to be at the mercy of someone else'.[52]

Meisel-Hess's emphasis on motherhood implies that other forms of femininity are less culturally valuable; Mayreder's intellectual woman, for example, has little place in Meisel-Hess's vision just as Meisel-Hess's vision of liberated motherhood has none in Mayreder's. And although Meisel-Hess supports the women's movement in its claims for education and suffrage, these are subordinate to the ultimate task and glory of motherhood, which celebrates the female body and above all the womb. It is this, not the mind, which is central. Motherhood is reduced to the sexual act, pregnancy, giving birth; it has a physical dimension only. There is a tension here between Meisel-Hess's emphasis on motherhood and her individualism, for giving birth cannot essentially be individualised, unlike child-rearing which offers much more scope for individuality but which Meisel-Hess largely denies woman as mother. The two strands of her argument – individualism and racial progress – are again not happily woven together.

This emphasis furthermore implies a devaluation of women who are not mothers; just being a woman seems to be of little intrinsic value. Meisel-Hess does not consider whether the emancipatory measures she suggests might be desirable for women as women and not as mothers. All is to be done for the improvement of the race in the future, rather than the present, and all is to be done for an impersonal goal. It is not primarily a question of happiness, justice, freedom, that is, of goals which can be made personal, as is the case in Troll-Borostyáni's vision, but of racial improvement, a collective goal in which the individual is submerged. Meisel-Hess may of course claim of mother protection that it liberates woman as an economic being from dependence on men at a time when she cannot earn her own living, which the new woman will be educated to do. And she may also claim that it liberates female sexuality and motherhood from the constraints of a bourgeois morality which as a precondition to motherhood demands a marriage made according to principles that run counter to both personal happiness and racial progress: the principles of money and social status. She can justifiably claim that protecting mothers undermines the patriarchal family by making the mother its centre, and that it offers the prospect of a new family life which will be ethically and socially superior to the old one, giving woman as mother power by putting sexual selection back into her hands. By making that private sphere – and its most private areas – public Meisel-Hess also makes it political. She focuses not on political equality, as Troll-Borostyáni does, nor on an abstract idea of the 'human', as Mayreder does, but on female sexuality and the need for the liberation of the private sphere. She makes clear, as Troll-Borostyáni and Mayreder do not, the centrality of sexual liberation if women's political emancipation is to have any meaning at all beyond the statute book. But this occurs at the expense of woman independent of her reproductive function. It is a high price to pay.

CHAPTER 11

Political Feminism and Spiritual Feminism

Each of these three designs for cultural renewal is characterised by a religious attitude which attempts to unite politics and spirituality. Political feminism, for example, guides Troll-Borostyáni's vision. For her, rights, legal equality and therefore justice are the paths to be trodden on the way to utopia. Present inequality is an aberration of civilisation and can be abolished by human intervention. This view is legitimised by social utility and morality; society will function better and its members will be more moral and happier if there is legal equality between the sexes. True human nature will emerge and the individual will strive for ever higher and nobler development.

Yet at the same time her political feminist vision is deeply spiritual. Ludwig Büchner, a popularist of materialism, in his preface to the second edition of *Die Gleichheit der Geschlechter* establishes a direct religious connection. There he claims that Troll-Borostyáni's work contains the religion (and philosophy) of the future and offers the perspective of 'those future Messianic times, in which general neighbourly love will take the place of the hollow and fanatical love of God and promote the well-being and salvation of humanity'.[1] The connection with religion was also indirectly established by Troll-Borostyáni herself. She chose, for example, to present a survey of the German women's movement in the form of a catechism, thus lending it the status of a truth as unassailable as that of religion.[2] And she called a study of the woman question *Die Mission unseres Jahrhunderts* (The Mission of our Century), that mission being the emancipation of women.[3] Her perception of herself as spreading the divine word of liberation emerges clearly there, and the remonstrative, fighting tone of a salvation army comes to dominate. 'Post tenebras spero lucem,' she thunders from the pulpit to her female following, 'the long night of enslavement will give way to the sun of justice, and full of pride and joy in the coming of the most noble victory your hearts will beat towards the dawn of a freedom won through toil.'[4] Similarly, the cover

16. Title page of *So erziehen wir unsere Kinder zu Vollmenschen* by Irma von Troll-Borostyáni (Oranienburg: Wilhelm Möller, 1912).

illustration to *So erziehen wir unsere Kinder* displays a Garden of Eden (see figure 16). There a female figure clad in Grecian robes leans against a flowing fountain set in a lush countryside, while the sun radiates on the horizon. She holds a torch to light the way, the symbol of enlightenment and the promise of a paradise of nature on earth. The religious associations cannot be overlooked.

The union of politics and spirituality can also be found in Mayreder's synthetic ideal, although there it takes a different form. Mayreder's politics is directed not so much at the public institutions governing gender relations, as Troll-Borostyáni's is, as at the politics of the private sphere and even the unconscious. She is concerned with the psychological mechanisms which are rooted in the sexual constitution of the individual and which govern the power relations between the sexes, not with equal rights for women, or egalitarian justice. The deep spirituality which informs her vision becomes openly apparent in her final discursive work, *Der letzte Gott* (The Final God) (1933). Yet, as Mayreder remarked in her diary, this late theodicy does not represent an essentially new development. 'Work on my book "Der letzte Gott" makes me go through my old notebooks and jottings,' she recorded, '– and there I see that this work with its basic ideas has been lying latent in me for the last 40 years without my knowing it. The material falls into an order of its own accord; it has worked on in me while my external life slowly has gone forwards to meet it.'[5] The basic motifs of this now openly religious world view can indeed be found in her essays. Right from the beginning, upward evolution is directed by an immanent spiritual force rather than the Christian God. In *Der letzte Gott* she calls this the world spirit but it is present, although without a name, in the essays. Similarly, what is called the final god in *Der letzte Gott*, the synthetic individual, is always surrounded by a religious aura. This Mayreder makes clear in *Zur Kritik der Weiblichkeit*, where she explains that the yearning for the synthetic ideal has long found expression in religious as well as profane dreams. In addition, her treatment of immortality and reincarnation is not restricted to her later work. In *Der letzte Gott* she claims that the purification that suffering brings the individual is not lost when that individual's body dies. The cell bank of humanity is enriched by that person's experiences and it is from this bank that future generations draw their genetic material.[6] Death merely marks the end of being aware of the self; the individual lives on in the cell bank, making reincarnation possible. This is the same 'succession of generations which is an eternal form of natural life',[7] the 'primal basis of Being, which lies beyond the Consciousness'[8] which Mayreder talks of in her essay on fatherly feeling in *Geschlecht und Kultur*. A characteristic feature of Mayreder's thought is that it attempts to establish a universal spiritual order and emphasises both the leading place of humanity in that order and humanity's inability to control the gradual organic process of evolution. Nature is no longer a transcendental god, but it is still guided by a force which although not omniscient and omnipotent is benevolent and with direction, for it unconsciously strives for upward evolution.

Like Troll-Borostyáni and Mayreder, Meisel-Hess asserts the spiritual nature of her vision. 'Awe of procreation is the religion of the future,' she states;[9] the new religious passion of both man and woman is to be the joint creation of the god of the earth, the new human being. Also like Troll-Borostyáni and Mayreder, she develops a politics which is to promote this religious thrust, not be weakened by it. She clearly sees that the power relations between the sexes must be changed if reproduction is to gain the spiritual value she gives it. Thus although each treats sexual politics in a different sphere – Troll-Borostyáni in the sphere of law, Mayreder that of the psyche, and Meisel-Hess that of reproduction – all combine their sexual politics with claims to spiritual significance.

All combine this union of politics and spirituality with another concern: the call for a new morality. As Meisel-Hess points out, 'The struggle for sex reform does not concern the pleasure which depraves the soul but on the contrary follows high moral goals.'[10] The new individual, who possesses an inner harmony and authenticity, is the goal for all. And for all, this means finding a new morality, a true and truthful morality in contrast to the deceitful morality of convention. For it is precisely this old morality which forcefully separates the individual from true human nature; as Troll-Borostyáni claims, 'The . . . inability of man really to be that which he wishes to be taken for . . . is the fundamental source of that lie which spreads its gigantic net over the whole of humanity in the form of social hypocrisy'.[11] This striving for a new morality offered a particularly good vehicle for the propagation of the spiritual aspects of feminism; such striving was seen to represent the deep desire of humanity to reach beyond the moment to eternity. As Meisel-Hess attempted to explain,

> The struggle of man for a morality is to be understood as . . . the struggle for an official institution which presents an obstacle to his own will at the points where it could conflict with the will to eternity. . . . In our opinion only something which extends beyond the momentary existence of the individual into eternity and at the same time is deeply and closely connected with the life of that individual . . . can point the way to a new religious goal.[12]

In each of these designs for a new humanity, nature plays a central role as a guarantor of the envisaged new morality. In Troll-Borostyáni's case this is apparent; nature itself becomes a moral category and is contrasted to the untruthfulness and disease of civilisation: 'The moral make-up and powder with which "good" society likes to make itself presentable do not replace the natural freshness of moral health.'[13] For Meisel-Hess, too, nature is the guarantor of morality, but her moral nature is that of reproduction and sexuality; it is not negatively defined as what is not civilisation, as Troll-Borostyáni's is. Mayreder's nature is not homogeneous, as Troll-Borostyáni's and Meisel-Hess's is, but, like man himself, it is polar or indeed Janus-faced. Mayreder tends to see the one pole, what is not *Geist*, as being hostile to the development of culture. 'Everywhere that the naked natural emerges barbarism too enters cultural life,' she asserts.[14] She considers that a 'natural' in the sense of instinctual approach to sexuality does not necessarily mean that the conditions surrounding sexuality improve. 'With the degeneration of culture as a general phenomenon a barbarisation of the sexual also takes place in modern life; to be sure, hypocrisy does decrease but conditions do not improve.'[15] Mayreder, unlike Troll-Borostyáni and Meisel-Hess, can see the inherent conflict between this primitive nature and culture as insoluble. While Troll-Borostyáni and Meisel-Hess devise schemes to harmonise the two, Mayreder, when she interprets nature as that which is not amenable to any laws, sees it as belonging to a sphere quite distinct from human culture. It is by necessity amoral. Yet this elemental nature can, according to Mayreder, be harmoniously united with its polar opposite, namely the world spirit. This guides evolution, is beneficent and in harmony with culture. And it is this which is the moral instance, which indeed is *Geist*, the spiritual in man and the guarantor of human divinity. So all three feminist philosophers see human progress in terms of the attempt to resolve a conflict. For Troll-Borostyáni it is that between the claims of the individual and those of society; for Meisel-Hess that between individualism and eugenics; and for Mayreder that between *Geist* and *Geschlecht*. And all endow this resolution with a spiritual and political significance.

The Stylistics of the Spiritual

How is this union of politics and spirituality expressed in the style and method of these feminists' writings? One of the most effective means employed is that of adopting the role of female prophet and Messiah. Meisel-Hess, for example, quite unabashedly asserts that 'the fact that this complete survey . . . is the investigation of a woman gives it its special position in the literature [on the subject]'.[16] By this she means not only that she presents a woman's view of the subject in the face of the ruling male monopoly but also that she follows a radically different approach, for, 'What others called scholarship became for me the office of a priest. I imbued my work with the whole of life, the doors of insight sprang open before me and my hand became the saviour of all whose diseased body it touched.'[17] It is woman's metaphysical mission, claims Meisel-Hess, to be a helper, a saviour, for 'here alone lies the great, the apparently new and yet ancient – the eternal task of woman: to become through her own purification – a mediator and finally: redeemer'.[18] Corresponding with this self-image of being a representative on this earth of higher forces, Meisel-Hess adopts the pose of being a passive go-between, not an active organiser, of her material. 'Almost involuntarily something like a new construction rose up before me . . . a fact which once again confirmed what I had intuitively sensed for a long time: that things carry the law of their form in themselves and that their morphological essence inevitably emerges when they are completely and totally honestly reduced to their basic elements.'[19] Hers is a proudly personal and anti-scientific survey of the subject, and Meisel-Hess does not hesitate to laud her own temerity in dealing with the subject in such an unusual, non-specialist manner.

This emphasis on special insight is reinforced in some cases by an openly autobiographical appeal. Meisel-Hess, for example, uses her gender to legitimise this insight and stresses that she speaks from her experience as a woman. 'The insights [into the sexual crisis] I have gained have been painfully felt, but this suffering has taught me to see the shape of the facts more clearly.'[20] The claim to suffer as a woman and therefore to speak from personal experience also plays an explicit role in some of Troll-Borostyáni's works. In *Das Recht der Frau* (The Right of Woman), for example, the narrative voice declares a deep personal interest in the rights of woman. 'I myself have suffered bitterly as a result of the position which woman has so far been allotted in human society,' she confesses, and asks for her remarks to be understood as confessions, wishes and pleas.[21]

For Mayreder, too, autobiography matters. 'I freely admit that I offer only a subjective view of the world, one which is limited by my own experience of people and books and not least of myself,' she explains.[22] Yet she uses this subjective approach in a way different to Troll-Borostyáni and Meisel-Hess. She makes no appeals to privileged insight by virtue of her sex, nor does she make any claims to courage or to doing something new. In her eyes, she writes as her own ideal of the synthetic person, making no claims that writing from any kind of personal experience leads to deeper insight, but on the contrary seeing that this sets limits which can be neither overcome nor denied. This is the superior insight of the intellectual: to recognise that subjectivity is determining and so-called objectivity an illusion which itself confines and can even tyrannise. Quite in contrast to Troll-Borostyáni, who sees her role as a missionary of reason and is convinced that through man's natural reason her reforms can be realised, Mayreder immediately presents a different view. 'I do not believe in communication by intellectual means between persons who are fundamentally different. . . . He who is experienced in the arts of thinking knows that anything can be asserted and proved, and anything doubted and refuted.'[23] This is so, claims Mayreder, because convictions are the expression of innate personality traits and are therefore the gift of nature. She is suspicious of all 'isms' and all generalisations. 'All "ists" are inaccessible to arguments which somehow do not correspond to their "conviction",' she asserted in response to a self-proclaimed Darwinist.[24]

This positive evaluation of personal experience and subjectivity is demonstrated by another aspect of these women's writings, namely the great variety of their material. Natural science, autobiography and works of literature are equal in value; there is no hierarchy along the lines that objective natural science is of a higher status than subjective insights, lived experience or the contents of the imagination. Contemporary developments in biogenetics serve Mayreder as material. To support her central idea that sex is not a primary characteristic of all living beings she cites, for example, research which had apparently shown that the simplest cells are neither female nor male.[25] Yet she also turns to current views in anthropology and sociology, draws on an impressively wide range of works of literature, and furthermore asserts that her personal experience forms the basic substance of her own works. Truth is thus not the monopoly of reason or the intellect, but is also to be found in the imagination and lived experience. Troll-Borostyáni in contrast underlines the rational, scholarly nature of some of her work. *Die Gleichstellung der Geschlechter* is studded with statistics and quotes from authorities – philosophers, historians and social economists. She rates science highly. A considerable part of *Gleichstellung* is devoted to 'the science of the real', and the subtitle of her eminently passionate *Verbrechen der Liebe* (Crimes of Love) is revealingly 'A socio-pathological study'. Yet in *Verbrechen*, for example, this bogus scientism is surrounded by an atmosphere of non-reality, even fictionality. An aura of danger and revelation, which in its pathos can hardly be taken completely seriously, is created by the dedication of *Verbrechen* to those people 'who have the courage to look truth in the eye',[26] and the voice which speaks in this pamphlet is far from unemotional, being in turn demonstrative, scolding, appealing – the voice of a preacher.

By means of these devices – playing the role of seer, emphasising personal experience and intuition, eclecticism in material, the use of a fictional framework – the visionary elements of these women's feminism are reinforced. For when used in a discursive presentation of sexual politics, such strategies can point to a transgression of boundaries and thereby to a perspective which certainly is not that of the mainstream debate on sex, gender and the 'woman question'.

The Feminist Challenge

Yet how far can this transgression promote the new, emancipated humanity which is the goal of these feminist philosophers? All three assume that nature and culture must conflict, and sex and gender also. And all three remain confined by this assumption, for their attempts to find a way of overcoming these apparent conflicts presuppose the dualisms they are concerned to bridge. None asks whether the boundaries between the elements in each of these pairs might be undefinable because they do not exist or whether the dualisms might be overdrawn. In fact, culture and nature do not exist in the complete opposition that Troll-Borostyáni and Meisel-Hess suppose in their models. Sex and gender, although different spheres, are not separate ones. It is, then, less a question of *either* nature *or* culture than of the grey zone in between. For even what is apparently most natural, the female body, is also a symbol of a particular view of nature and also of an established gender context. Yet all these thinkers work in some way or another with the assumption that there is a 'true' natural femininity and a 'false' cultural femininity. They do not consider that femininity *per se* might be a construct and that a lack of determination might offer tremendous potential to the individual. Nature itself can, as Troll-Borostyáni and Meisel-Hess inadvertently indicate, be turned into a canon which confines. Mayreder goes furthest towards this recognition when she emphasises the adaptability of both teleological and non-teleological femininity and gives individual difference a central significance. Unlike Troll-Borostyáni and Meisel-Hess, who wish to see homogeneity, Mayreder supports a radical pluralism amongst the minority of synthetic personalities. She proposes diversity not homogeneous duality for this elite and thus goes some way towards re-thinking the meaning of sex and gender. However, for the majority of 'average' persons this heterogeneous variety does not apply. Mayreder continues to use the terms 'masculine' and 'feminine' when referring to qualities, without questioning their appropriateness. But a truly emancipatory politics can be achieved only when dualisms have been dissolved and when a network of contrasts is recognised in which the importance of the spaces between the various elements is acknowledged, even if this means an absence of clear-cut definitions and a farewell to the simplicity of the egalitarianism of Troll-Borostyáni and the biologism of Meisel-Hess. It is a question of renouncing the search for criteria of 'masculinity' and 'femininity', admitting individual difference but not in terms of inadequacy, and affirming diversity rather than duality. Until then, boundaries are shifted but not overcome.

The same criticism could be made of the models of the 'new woman' which each of these three feminist philosophers presents. Each is characterised both by an attempt to present an alternative to the conventional images of woman and by a confinement. For Troll-Borostyáni the new woman of her utopia is the *citoyenne*. She participates in public political life on a par with men but does not espouse their corrupt sexual morality; she remains instead a paragon of virtue whose sexuality is inspired by love and not desire (a remarkably unproblematic distinction for Troll-Borostyáni). The intellectual woman is the model presented by Mayreder. She is the woman who lives her individuality creatively, able to do so through her disregard for the norms of femininity, the woman who displays 'masculine' strength in thought and deed. And for Meisel-Hess, different again, the 'new mother' is the new woman. She is the woman who issues a challenge to patriarchy where it hurts most, in the family, by depriving the father of his power and asserting an ancient mother-right. Yet despite the attack on the status quo each model represents, none is really satisfying or politically forceful, for each confines woman within rigid parameters. Each continues to represent prescriptions of what woman should be, and although they extend the prescriptions of the status quo they still do not break down the gender barrier.

This lack of cogency is, however, not a result of the spiritual dimension of these feminist visions. The claims to spiritual growth do not conflict with the sexual politics offered. For all three thinkers, it is change in sexual politics which is the precondition for that growth. They may have advocated utopian goals, as Mayreder herself conceded, but this, as she hinted, does not in the least reduce the political value of those goals as directives.[27] Politics and spirituality do not conflict, but complement each other.

Not only that. These designs for the future represent a courageous attempt not only to give support to the practical demands of the women's movement but also to embed those demands in a wider-ranging framework of opposition. And it is astounding with what thoroughness and vigour these feminist theorists, each in her different way, offered a challenge. For all their limitations the fact that women wrote such visionary feminist texts at all is remarkable, and all the more so when their strongly anti-feminist and anti-egalitarian environment is taken into account. It was a considerable achievement to demand equal rights in a milieu in which legal inequality was taken for granted, to be able to find the voice to retort to bestsellers like Weininger's *Geschlecht und Charakter*, with as good as no critical tradition on which to build, little supportive education, and a support network which was still fragile. Autonomous women did not remain silent or uncritical but on the contrary made an independent feminist contribution to the debate on the woman question around 1900. And they went far. Not only were anti-feminists challenged, but alternative systems of gender relations were mapped out. For all, these entailed a vigorous anti-capitalism, an attack on the nuclear family, a re-evaluation of female sexuality, and anti-clericalism. They were designs for a future which posed a serious threat to the foundations of patriarchy.

PART THREE

THE FEMINIST IMAGINATION

CHAPTER 12

Feminist Aesthetics and Imaginative Literature

Imaginative literature was of central significance to the feminists in Vienna around 1900; their concerns were not limited to practical demands and theoretical treatises, but extended to the discussion, and writing, of fiction. Both the *Dokumente der Frauen* and *Neues Frauenleben* devoted a section at the end of most issues to literature. There reviews appeared, often written by members of the General Austrian Women's Association. Books by women or those concerning the woman question were given particular attention. Sketches and short stories (often serialised) by women and men, both Austrian and foreign, and articles on leading writers were also published. So, for example, Walt Whitman (translated by Karl Federn), Ricarda Huch, Anatole France, Maxim Gorky and Anton Chekhov appeared in the *Dokumente* alongside writing by those closely connected with the General Austrian Women's Association such as Else Migerka, Robert Scheu, Margret Hönigsberg (later Hilferding, the Adlerian psychoanalyst and wife of the sociologist and economist Rudolf) and Anna Schapire-Neurath. In addition, works of literature were sometimes made the subject of the Associations' discussion evenings. Writers such as Frank Wedekind, Arthur Schnitzler, and Henrik Ibsen in particular, were given critical consideration, and in its early days the General Austrian Women's Association organised debates on, for example, Goethe's Gretchen in which different perceptions of this dramatic figure in *Faust* – is she a passive victim or an autonomous woman who affirms her sexuality? – led to a heated discussion on girls' upbringing and morality.[1] In all cases literature was read and judged with a view to the position taken by the author on the woman question. For this reason it was not difficult to make Ibsen into a leading and ideologically sound cult figure. When he visited Vienna in 1891 he was sent a telegram from 'Viennese women', including Irma von Troll-Borostyáni, in which he was apostrophised as 'the noble warrior for women's rights and women's dignity, the saviour from ancient bondage',[2] and on his death in 1906

Neues Frauenleben devoted much of its June issue to laudatory articles. For these women Ibsen was unquestionably a pioneer of a new life for women and it was this which was regarded as the main message of his work. 'That she [woman],' Erich Holm rousingly declared,

> is sacrificed to supposedly higher goals, excluded from every kind of participation in those cultural tasks which remain to be tackled, that she is not spared even in what is most holy, in her love life, that she is destroyed by the emptiness of her existence . . . this Henrik Ibsen makes the central point according to which he explains all the dangers which threaten the middle class, all the chaos of the present, the whole situation of the world.[3]

Arthur Schnitzler, too, was praised for his criticism of bourgeois morality.[4] Frank Wedekind, who in his 'three scenes', *Tod und Teufel*, makes the anti-prostitution campaigner the clichéd old maid, was applauded as an involuntary feminist who supported the mothers' protection movement without knowing it, but was considered to make unfounded generalisations in his criticism of the women's movement.[5]

Of course, women's concern with imaginative literature was not limited to reading and criticising it. The women's associations could boast of having some leading women writers as members. Marie von Ebner-Eschenbach, herself as good as appropriated by the feminists as 'our' Marie von Ebner-Eschenbach,[6] who managed to personify the dominant feminist ideal by uniting 'feminine grace with masculine strength of presentation',[7] was after all a member of the Association for Extended Women's Education in Vienna,[8] as were other successful writers, Emil Marriot, Marie von Najmájer and Bertha von Suttner. Indeed, these last three, more than Ebner-Eschenbach, directly addressed feminist issues in their works and Najmájer not only inaugurated the scholarship fund for the Association for Extended Women's Education, but also wrote poetry intended to be read at women's meetings in which she exhorted her public to display sisterly solidarity and to work to raise the intellectual level of womankind.[9] In fact, so much did 'noble, high-minded female figures who strive towards ideal goals with a far-sighted gaze' dominate Najmájer's texts that Marianne Hainisch observed with satisfaction in the *Dokumente* that 'her works are dedicated to a cult of the art of literary composition and women'.[10] For some writers, imaginative writing and feminist engagement went hand in hand as a matter of conviction rather than financial necessity. Mayreder, Meisel-Hess, Troll-Borostyáni, Helene Scheu-Riess, Anna Schapire-Neurath and Auguste Fickert, all members of the General Austrian Women's Association, were active in both spheres. Many were also productive in marginal forms of literary activity. Some translated; Marie Lang translated Maurice Maeterlinck,

Leopoldine Kulka translated Olive Schreiner and Helene Scheu-Riess Russian literature. Letters, diaries and memoirs were, of course, not neglected. In 1895, encouraged by relatives, Mayreder wrote the libretto to Hugo Wolf's only opera, *Der Corregidor*, which inaugurated a close if at times difficult working friendship between the two.[11]

Literature was, then, an integral part of the feminist project. And it was certainly not, in the feminists' view, to be relegated to the realms of the apolitical. For them, fiction could influence how the world was perceived. Meisel-Hess, for example, called Zola along with Darwin, Ibsen and Nietzsche, one of the main educators of 'our' generation.[12] He had, she claimed, shown humanity a new path in its search for liberation from the absurdity and awkwardness of convention, 'that of the most free, most unabashed naturalness, which pushes aside the barriers which cordon off reality to reveal the beauty in its gripping simplicity'.[13] And imaginative literature not only changed perception; it was a product of such change as well. Thus Zola, according to Meisel-Hess, united the ideal and the real, because his art was the product of the monist world view of the modern age. He represented the art of the 'young' along with Ibsen, Nietzsche, the Scandinavians, Russians, and also many women writers, for women, too, were socially and artistically speaking 'young'.[14] Literature was an integral part of a changed intellectual perception. For these women there were no rigid barriers between imaginative and analytical writing, as is indicated by the literary quotations and devices found in their theoretical texts. Nor was fiction seen as distinct from active engagement. Imaginative literature could be used for feminist purposes in both practical politics and theoretical writing. But just why was it given such a central place, and how does this centrality contribute to the feminist vision?

Facts and Fiction

The key to the answer is given by another question: what did the feminists consider the purpose of imaginative literature to be? The answer to this can best be approached by the path most often followed by the feminists themselves: considering what function it was not to fulfil. Obviously, literature was not merely to be innocuous verbiage, considered by the standards of literary convention to be fit consumption for the family, and above all for the adolescent daughter. It was not to supply the 'intellectual provender of the family table'.[15] Such literature was the staple of the family literary diet, and it made it its business to gloss over reality according to strict guidelines to which writers had to adhere if they wanted publication – and payment. 'The contributions published in our paper,' the editor of the popular magazine of family literature *Die Gartenlaube* (The Bower) declared in the 1880s,

> must not contain either a political or a religious message and, as far as erotic matters are concerned, must be kept so that they can be read aloud by younger members in the family circle. Neither divorce nor suicide is to appear. The plot must constantly increase in tension and in every chapter there must be some kind of turning point in the story-line, a new event or something similar. The ending must be a happy one which leaves a pleasant impression behind.[16]

It was this schematic literature which, not surprisingly, came in for the most barbed attacks from the feminists. 'The world, as it is here presented, is enclosed by a Chinese wall inside which events take place according to established rules,' Mayreder commented. 'It is a puppet's stage on which a number of stereotyped figures perform the *fable convenue* which represents human life and doings for the family table.'[17] These condemnatory sentiments were seconded by feminists like Troll-Borostyáni, who launched a spirited attack not only on this type of literature but also on her compatriots, that 'people of poets and thinkers' which allowed itself to be fed on 'sentimental literature for well-bred teenage girls, which propagates a mawkishly untruthful palaver about how perfect the world is',[18] and the literature industry, which churned out love stories according to the eternal motto, 'She loves him, she loves him not; he once loved her, loves her no longer; they love each other but cannot have each other – or get each other in the end.'[19] 'It sounds barely credible,' Troll-Borostyáni was compelled to admit, 'but it is really so: hundreds and thousands of short stories, novels, plays have been turned out according to this last and are still being produced, and delighted readers and listeners for such products can still be found.'[20] Her assumption is that the times have changed in such a way as to have made such literature redundant or at least anachronistic. Such literature may once have had an acceptable function, Troll-Borostyáni and Marriot intimate, but in the modern world that is no longer so. And indeed, not only family literature is redundant in their eyes. Great literature is so too if it presents, as Goethe's *Faust I* and Heinrich von Kleist's *Das Käthchen von Heilbronn* do, the male poetic ideal of womanhood. For those 'female figures languishing in humility before the idolized man', the Gretchen and Käthchen of Goethe and Kleist, are anachronistic in the days of the working woman, as Marriot eagerly pointed out:

> The Gretchens and Käthchens have . . . risen in value for they are beginning to become a rarity. The girl of today thinks differently. . . . Our young girls no longer gush. Modern conditions have driven that out of them. They have other ideals; instead of waiting for the most

> masterful man of all who just will not come, they now wait for a letter of appointment at a post or telegraph office.[21]

The thrust of these comments is clear. Literature is to be the 'artistic presentation of reality', a 'mission' which, as Mayreder pointed out, is irreconcilable with the goal of family literature, namely keeping adolescent girls in intellectual immaturity and sexual ignorance.[22] It is this emphasis on reality which emerges in the feminist reviews as the leading criterion of literary quality. *Der Heilige Skarabäus* (The Sacred Scarab; English title: *The Red House*) (1909), Else Jerusalem's long novel on prostitution, is, for example, criticised by Leopoldine Kulka for being 'improbable' in its portrayal of the central figure Milada, who, although born and brought up in a brothel, as an adult manages to maintain precisely those virtues 'which lie as far away as possible from the life of the prostitute' and who 'can do nothing but go and "like a good middle-class woman" save children'.[23] Christine Touaillon, in contrast, comments favourably on the 'genuine' impression made by the novel:

> Else Jerusalem however presents them [prostitutes and criminals] quite simply and obviously as they might appear to themselves. That is why everything gives the impression of being genuine. . . . It is not a tendentious work; it lets things speak for themselves, but the things it depicts speak a terrible language.[24]

But although the judgements of these two feminist literary critics differ, both start from the same assumption: that the depiction of reality is the main criterion of quality. So central was this assumption that 'reality' in an otherwise reprehensible text could act as a redeeming feature in feminist eyes. As Therese Schlesinger-Eckstein conciliatingly commented in an otherwise unfavourable review of Vera's [Betty Kris's] scandalous fictional diary *Eine für Viele* (One for Many) (1902) which took up a revelatory pose, 'The book is, you see, a cry from the heart, the lament of a creature which injures itself by knocking against the pitiless reality of life. It is at the same time a document of our times and a sign that today more than ever every privilege is felt to be an injustice.'[25]

Here, in Schlesinger-Eckstein's remark, one of the reasons for the feminists' emphasis on reality rings through, for of course this emphasis was not without an ideological dimension. What did the feminists hope to achieve through 'the artistic representation of reality'? For opportunists such as the successful actress Adele Sandrock the function claimed for the theatre, that of 'truly reflecting the natural qualities of the human being',[26] could be used as an argument for the appointment of women theatrical directors. The representation of reality was to serve to extend women's professional sphere. Yet

Schlesinger-Eckstein's comment indicates that more was at stake than professions for women. For her, as for many others, reflecting the reality of the times could point to what was wrong with those times, and so contribute to consciousness-raising. Thus Jerusalem, for example, dedicated *Der Heilige Skarabäus* to 'dancing girls – laughing brides – playing mothers' who were to hear, see, feel and think of the reality depicted in the novel and so acknowledge those 'victims of their happiness', the prostitutes.[27] But consciousness-raising was not all. Behind this emphasis lies a central feminist claim – to truth. The 'artistic representation of reality' is equated with the truth, in sharp contrast to the untruthful, glossy idealism of the family literature these women were reacting against. And with the claim to truth inevitably comes the claim to freedom. 'Only the truth can make us free,' states Camilla Theimer in the preface to her portrayal of the woman of the future.[28]

This does not mean that the feminists' aesthetics are anti-idealistic. On the contrary, as in their discursive writings there is in their fiction a strong idealistic element, but one based on a claim to realism. 'In art there is for us no longer that crude one-sidedness that reached its acme in [the artist] being either a "realist" or an "idealist",' Meisel-Hess explains. '. . . The modern artist is either both or nothing. . . . Only out of reality, out of what is natural, can those ideals emerge which mean new redemption and new bliss for humanity.'[29] This union is highly moral, for the truth that emerges from reality also leads to moral insight. Thus Touaillon comments of *Der Heilige Skarabäus*, 'And so from this grave book which probably hundreds of times offends the narrow and easily corruptible morality of the everyday resounds the voice of eternal morality.'[30] Kulka on the other hand, in keeping with her perception of a lack of realism in the novel, also laments its lack of true morality: 'True artistry would have converted all words and thoughts into life, would have known how to create a much richer, more forceful monument to our times, and deep morality does not make do with compromises,' she asserts.[31] In the eyes of these feminists, fiction was a potentially powerful ideological tool. As Touaillon claimed, the novel in comparison with 'the best known and most significant scholarly tracts' has 'a much greater power of enlisting sympathies, infiltrates into immeasurably wider circles, and has an incomparably more penetrating and sustained effect through the figures which personify its opinions than the former do through the precepts which they propose'.[32]

Yet how was this didactic potential to be realised? For some of these feminists literature could instruct by presenting role models. Works were read and reviewed with an eye to the acceptability of the female figures as didactic guides. Not surprisingly some of Ibsen's women –

Nora, Solveig, Rebekka – became cult figures of female individualism.[33] Friedrich Hebbel, too, came in for praise for involuntarily sketching the 'shape of the new woman and the outline of a new morality'[34] with the female figures in his dramas, who are intended to be truly moral individualists and are shown to suffer under a corrupt morality of outer appearances. Yet literature in this didactic function not only points to the moral path but also liberates. It is 'the first tool which demolishes one of the walls of woman's intellectual prison and opens up her view to the outside world'.[35] Literary realism was seen to offer women the possibility of making contact with the real world, of curing them of their romantic longings, and thus represented the beginning of a process of emotional healing. But as Touaillon suggested, reading was not completely without dangers, for it could also act as a substitute for living. 'Opposite the army of those who read little or nothing stands the army of those who read more than they live,' she commented. 'We women in particular are to be found on this side. As girls, we still first come into contact with life through books.'[36] She points out that literature is subject to conventions which perhaps no longer tally with reality, with the result that women are badly prepared for real life, find refuge in books and 'become increasingly blind to life'.[37]

Art and Artifice

Yet although the realism and moral message of literature should be unmistakable, literature was not to be propaganda. The 'artistic representation of reality', although a highly moral undertaking, was still to be an artistic one. And while Rudolf Lothar may have praised Bertha von Suttner's works in 1891 both for their tendentiousness – 'Every good book is a tendentious book', he asserted dogmatically – and for their quasi-scientific analysis – 'The modern novelist examines . . . the behaviour of his heroes in the same way as the natural scientist goes about solving a problem' – even he acknowledged the necessity for 'stage-lighting'.[38] Literature should still be art even if it reflected reality. But unlike Lothar, who considered the imagination to be the source of art, the feminists declared that it was emotion which was the origin of art and the morality that informed it and that it was emotion which had the power to bring about change. 'No, genuine artistry and genuine morality flow from the same spring,' Kulka explained, 'namely deepest sensibility, and in their holy fury and majestic force they tear up the prejudices which have been rooted for thousands of years . . . and implant the seed of the future into the earth of time loosened by the tempest, into receptive hearts.'[39]

That literature was essentially a matter of the emotions was an opinion held not only by feminist critics but also by feminist writers themselves (often the two were identical). Just as the philosophers of feminism emphasised the subjectivity of their texts and their basis in experience, so too did the literary feminists. So it is not surprising that autobiographical forms – diaries, letters, memoirs – were frequently chosen as frameworks for imaginative literary texts and that elements of literature and autobiography were incorporated into these women's theoretical and polemical writings; the same claims to reality, truth and personal investment mark all three areas of feminist involvement. 'Women,' the editors of the *Dokumente* declared in their leader to the first issue, 'want to experience life, the unlimited, fateful, multiform life of the free personality themselves. They no longer want to learn about life in the false guise in which it is presented to them in family literature – they want facts, they want to experience real conditions, they want to see and observe with their own eyes.'[40] Along the same lines, Suttner underlined the role of personal experience and explained in her memoirs that writing *Das Maschinenalter* gave her great pleasure, 'for in it I unburdened my soul of all the rancour and suffering regarding present conditions and all the ardours of hope regarding the promising future which had collected there'.[41] She remarks of her bestselling plea for pacifism, *Die Waffen nieder!* (English title: *Lay Down Your Arms!*), that she wrote it because she wished to serve the Peace League:

> And I thought I could do that most effectively in the form of a story. . . . I did not want to present only what I thought but also what I felt – passionately felt . . . I wanted to give expression to the pain . . . I wanted to present life, twitching life – reality, historical reality, and all that could only happen in a novel, preferably in a novel written in the form of an autobiography. And so I went and wrote *Die Waffen nieder!*[42]

Lived life is the stuff not only of politics and feminist theory but also of novels, and it is this which makes them effective in the feminists' eyes. Similarly Meisel-Hess, in the preface to *Die Stimme* (The Voice) (1907), her 'novel in leaves', claims that 'the laughter and weeping of these leaves was not only "lived" but also seen, heard, dreamed'.[43] Marie von Najmájer went so far as to establish the dictum, 'Only he who has himself experienced can portray genuinely'[44] and to explain that sensibility is the richest source of song:

> Sensibility alone is life in the universe . . .
> Only what you feel is what is most deeply yours
> Only what you feel can show what you are as a poet.[45]

For Mayreder, too, it was quite clear that her imaginative writing was *Erlebnisdichtung*, the songs of lived experience. As she exclaimed of her collection of fables (*Die Fabeleien über göttliche und menschliche Dinge*) (Fables concerning Divine and Human Things) (1921), 'This slim, small volume contains my whole being and thought, it is the result of a long life!'[46] She noted with interest and satisfaction how events of her present and past life acted as motifs for her work. The novella *Aus meiner Jugend* (From my Youth) (1896), for example, by her own admission originated in her youth,[47] and her novel *Pipin. Ein Sommererlebnis* (Pipin: A Summer Experience) (1903) she apologetically called a 'problematic book . . . which leads the reader into a bizarre milieu I was involved in years ago', adding, 'and will probably be unpalatable and incomprehensible to all who have not belonged to a similar circle'.[48]

Such insistence on the personal suggests that the inner life as well as the outer is regarded as real and true, and from there it is only a small step to seeing the psyche as the seat of a truth which is not that of objective reality. Meisel-Hess for one articulates this view; immediately after stating the autobiographical basis of *Die Stimme* she adds, 'and anyone who ever investigated the fates of such a dreamer's life knows that the vision begins precisely there where life leaves us in the lurch'.[49] The implication here is that truth is not always objective, factual reality. The basis external life can offer the imagination is limited; fantasy takes over where real life comes to a halt. But the imagination, the life of dreams, the inner life have their own truth and reality. What Meisel-Hess is saying is that there are two realities and two truths. There is the objective truth and reality of facts and external life as opposed to untruthful convention. And there is the subjective truth and reality of the inner life, which is not artistic fantasy but the 'truth of the struggling soul'.[50] This perception was shared by other feminists with the result that two, sometimes interwoven, strands in feminist fiction emerged: the strand of factual realism which displayed a socially critical and moralising element; and the strand of psychological realism which focused more on the inner life without, however, neglecting the critical political potential of the psyche.

But how were the feminists' aesthetics seen by others? For some conservative critics these feminists' works made it clear that literature had been infected by realism, a 'canker from which the present suffers and which will take its revenge yet in coming generations'.[51] Literature had been robbed of all idealism, and this was indicative of a general cultural development which could also be seen in the lamentable childlessness of modern marriages and the inconsiderate 'cult of the self'. 'In the rapidly pulsating present,' one such commentator remarked, 'people censure every sentiment which reminds them of a more idealistic view of life. They call that sentimentality and emotional wallowing and believe that the cult of the self... can give satisfaction in the long run.'[52] With such attitudes in circulation, it is not surprising that feminist writers were regarded by many as *personae non gratae.* A handful of women writers were respected. Marie von Ebner-Eschenbach was awarded an Austrian prize for art and science in 1899 and a year later was made the first female honorary doctor of philosophy of Vienna University, being 'the leading German writer in Austria today', as the professors who proposed her put it.[53] But this unqualified praise was exceptional; the status of the woman writer was generally uncertain and she was exposed to a double critical standard. In order to be accepted she was expected to toe the line of feminine delicacy in subject and style and any transgression was censured as lack of womanliness. But precisely that womanliness condemned her to inferiority in the eyes of her judges. Small wonder that some women chose to publish under a male pseudonym, or to take refuge behind an obvious pen-name. Richard Nordmann (the pseudonym of Margarethe Langkammer) for one was forced to discover that quality and being female were in the eyes of the critics an *a priori* contradiction when she finally revealed her true identity. The 'formidable theatrical talent' which one critic commented on while Nordmann was still thought to be male[54] was obviously too formidable when Nordmann was known to be female, for another critic had 'very good reasons' for thinking that her exclusive authorship of her play *Gefallene Engel* (Fallen Angels) was 'not very likely'.[55]

Such assumptions were not restricted to aesthetic conservatives, as the rumpus caused by 'Bob' illustrates. 'Bob', that is Clara Loeb, 'a girl here in Vienna', as Hugo von Hofmannsthal, a friend of the family, patronisingly called her,[56] was audacious enough to write some 'silhouettes from a girl's life'. These were published in 1897 in the *Neue Deutsche Rundschau*, largely thanks to Hofmannsthal's initiative, adorned with a prologue by Hofmannsthal himself. The scenes deal critically with the double morality and reveal how middle-class marriage is dominated by material considerations. Plans were made to publish them in book form, but Loeb's parents were so scandalised that they put pressure on Hofmannsthal and Schnitzler (also a friend of the family) to cancel publication. They obediently complied. Hofmannsthal had indeed all the time been condescending towards Loeb's work. He confided in December 1896 that her writing showed a surprising degree of observation and courage – for a woman, that is,[57] and added superciliously that perhaps he had overestimated it 'as one overestimates children's verses, because it surprises one that they have anything at all to say'.[58]

Family opposition was widespread. Even women writers who were later highly respected had to contend with it. In her memoirs Ebner-Eschenbach records how the hostility displayed by her relatives to her writing while she was a child made her feel that writing poetry was sinful.[59] Yet the more obstacles were put in her way, the more she defiantly clung to her art. Similarly, as an adolescent Mayreder found little family support for her intellectual curiosity and writing. But, like Ebner-Eschenbach, this merely strengthened her self-conviction.

Opposition to the woman writer from the literary establishment took the form of lamenting the 'effeminacy' of culture. This could be seen, it was claimed, not only in the large numbers of women writers of trivial literature but also in the spread of naturalism, the feminine literary principle. 'Naturalism is completely passive with regard to life. . . . It means the dominance of woman in literature. Every woman writer is a naturalist,' one commentator claimed.[60] Others made a distinction between women writers and feminist women writers. The former were *personae gratae*, the latter not, as the critic Fritz Lemmermeyer made clear in his otherwise positive and defensive article on women's literature in Austria when referring to Ebner-Eschenbach. 'Around her gather many women who are not blue-stocking but notable talents, genuine and proper women writers,' he remarked.[61] Feminism obviously excludes genuine literary talent for this literary commentator. But not for all, for not only did the feminist press acclaim works such as Mayreder's novel *Idole. Geschichte einer Liebe* (Idols. The Story of a Love) (1899), the general press did so too. Like her essays, Mayreder's fiction seems to have aroused almost no negative criticism and where it did it is criticised for its conventionality.[62] It seems as if the feminist aspects of her work are too deeply buried for the literary critics, who had eyes only for tendentiousness.

Yet the feminists certainly saw themselves as proper women writers, even if not as occupying woman's proper sphere. For most of them it was not only a question of talent but of morals, not only of art but of instruction. 'No art represents the whole human being and above all the moral nature of the human being so completely as imaginative literature,' was the clear working premiss shared by most.[63] And for most the didactic function of literature was also plain. 'Pride of place should always be given to those works which enlighten the adolescent girl as to her position in the family, her relationship to her husband, to her future children and to human society in general,' was one formulation.[64] For these observers, feminism's task was moral instruction, and the presentation of objective reality was the platform from which the moral message could be preached.

CHAPTER 13

Moral Feminism

The two central themes of love and hunger dominated the depiction of objective reality with which some feminists chose to present their design for a new morality. Indeed, woman's position as a sexual and economic being took over the feminist critique to such an extent that by the turn of the century one commentator was complaining of Emil Marriot's *Der Heiratsmarkt* (The Marriage Market), a play critical of the marriage market, that 'not much can be said about this play. What it wants and says has been preached to us so often that right from the start it would not enter one's head to find anything of interest in the content.'[1] The feminists, however, did not let themselves be deterred. After all, their object was not to interest the reader or spectator or to create a work of art for its own sake, but to change the world. And to this end they used mimetic realism.

Love in Literature

Unlike politics, love was eminently acceptable as a theme for female fiction writers. The love story and the historical romance adorned with a moral message were the staples of women's literature. Thus although the feminist discussion about emotions and sexual relations represented a transgression of the norms of feminine involvement in the public sphere when carried on outside literature, within the context of women's imaginative literature that discussion demonstrated obedience to the norms. Marriage, as in all the best romances, played the central role in this debate which was carried out on two levels: the purely moral, and the moral and the political combined.

Marriot's *Der Heiratsmarkt* is an unsurprising contribution to the purely moral level. It points to the fateful intermingling of marriage and money in a network of social conventions in which middle-class women are up for sale; lower-class women without family and social protection have, on the other hand, to sell themselves. Yet although this socially accepted state of affairs is vigorously condemned, there is no real consideration of why the market exists, what function it performs, and what pressures operate. Moral censure overshadows critical analysis. For Marriot marriage is sacred and love will triumph over all odds. Men will give up their licentious ways if women are faithful and loving enough. And it is the task of women to get a marriage to work through being model mothers and the 'faithful priestesses of the domestic hearth'. 'Family life disintegrates into nothing if the image of the mother is not kept pure,' Hanna, Marriot's mouthpiece in *Der Heiratsmarkt*, says.[2] It is this image which is the basis of 'a true, real marriage'.[3] Marriage is shown to be ideally an affair of the emotions not of money, and woman as the angel of the house caring for a work-weary husband. Marriot places the emphasis on love in marriage without considering how this supports the status quo of power relations. The ideals that inform her view of marriage – motherliness, faithfulness, caring for others – remain unquestioned. And although she rejects the glossy veneer spread over reality by family literature, in the last resort she averts her eyes from the reality she wishes to condemn; social criticism may be her intention, but the solution she offers neutralises that criticism by being just as unrealistic.

Auguste Fickert, although also highly unrealistic, takes a more visionary line in her fiction, seeing love, not necessarily within marriage, as an innovative rather than conservative force. But in order to bring change, love must, according to her, be freed from the prejudices, morals and laws that bind it. Only in this way will it become a love different to that experienced by most women so far, who have been brought up to believe in the holy trinity of love, marriage and material provision. Only such an emancipated love will be able to fulfil the mission of raising humanity to nobility and happiness.[4]

A treatment of love in contrast to that of both Marriot and Fickert is found in 'Sterka', a short story by Anna Schapire-Neurath, published in the *Dokumente*, which deals with a young Jewish woman's attempt to flee the marriage market.[5] Unlike Marriot, Schapire-Neurath refuses to tell a story with a happy end. Sterka, the daughter of a rabbi, is as neglected and devalued by her religion and culture as any Christian woman but is made aware of her situation by a woman teacher of revolutionary political opinions to whom she forms a deep attachment. She runs away from her parents after she has been sold in marriage for 4,500 roubles, only to realise her own helplessness in the face of the world of sheer survival. Both her family and her teacher have failed to equip her for that world, so Sterka returns in shame to her family. The strength of social conventions and the weakness of an intellectual education which blindly ignores material pressures and necessities are shown to be equally hostile to life. The alternative to the marriage market is, it is indicated, not female love within a marriage of affection as for Marriot, but female autonomy, based on financial independence. There is no moralising, no cult of virtuous womanhood in this story. Here it is a question of survival in the face of brute necessity. And that is shown to be a matter of power.

The claim to present reality as it actually is also meant that these literary feminists did not shy away from aspects of sexual morality usually concealed. Prostitution and the double standard of morality which condoned it became objects of critical attention. The former was given relatively infrequent literary treatment compared to the importance some feminists accorded it in their political involvement. Mayreder, for example, although she made the subject her *cause célèbre* in her capacity as a leading member of the General Austrian Women's Association, devoted none of her imaginative texts to it. However where it *is* treated, two attitudes can be identified. Although all commentators wish to see the prostitute as the victim of a male-dominated sexual order, some combine this with a subdued condemnation of her. Troll-Borostyáni clearly presents her as the 'blunt, worn-out tool of male desire',[6] a destroyed soul, yet at the same time intimates that no decent woman, however desperate her economic situation, would sink into the mire of prostitution. 'But she would rather die on the spot than sell herself to sin, to shame,' Troll-Borostyáni's central female figure thinks in one of the sketches on hunger, 'Anything but that, no, anything but that! And a feeling of disgust, despair, despondency overcame her . . .'.[7] Prostitution is literally a fate worse than death.

Else Jerusalem adopts a less judgemental attitude. Instead of stressing the shame for both parties, the bestiality of men and the victimisation of women (while implying their moral weakness in submitting at all), she suggests that prostitution is a profession in which women are certainly exploited but not necessarily morally ruined. For her it is a job. 'Public right – nationalised love – a stigma on the brow – my God, I have only changed profession,' an ex-piano teacher-cum-occasional prostitute exclaims.[8] Also in contrast to Troll-Borostyáni, Jerusalem perceives the roots of the problem as lying not in some external and absolute moral code, or in a quasi-religious sin that both sexes commit, but in the social conception of what sin is and in the stigma attached to the prostitute and to free female sexuality. The morality under which prostitutes (and women in general) suffer is made by men:

> They [men] are able to forget because a morality, thousands of years old, has safeguarded them against self-reproach. . . . They do not sin because world laws gave them permission right at the beginning –

> and permitted sin kills the conscience. One does not kill for what is one's right. But the lies have been engraved on our bodies. The sentimental, tender lies, embellished with unnatural, artificially cultivated feelings.[9]

It is the moral system which is at fault, not the morality of its participants. 'No, it is the soil in which they [prostitutes] are rooted,' the narrator of *Der Heilige Skarabäus* explains to the reader, 'from which they should draw up strength and life and which your pride, your hate, your indescribably tyrannical morality has thoroughly deprived of warmth, blessing, possibilities of living.'[10] In *Der Heilige Skarabäus* Jerusalem describes in detail how the brothel system operates, showing how women are procured and often destroyed – and the complicity of a society which in private colludes with the trade which in public it condemns. Unlike Troll-Borostyáni, she makes it clear in her novel that such women are not morally corrupt. Milada is a morally acceptable indeed almost exemplary figure, who founds a home for infant orphans and is capable of falling truly in love with one of the clients, who are shown as not necessarily moral monsters. Hope is the main theme here, as the title would confirm. In ancient Egyptian mythology the holy scarab, which finds nourishment in excrement, in what is least valued, is the symbol of rebirth and represents the possibility of regeneration. All is not lost, Jerusalem seems to wish to say; what is regarded as the dregs of society may rise again to achieve full moral stature. But morality is the measure of humanity, for Jerusalem as for Troll-Borostyáni.

Of course, as these realist feminists are eager to reveal, it is not only prostitutes who are the victims of the double morality of society; 'decent' women are too. And the more honest they are and the more humble their background, the more they will suffer. This Anna Schapire-Neurath makes clear in her short story 'Lorsqu'on est fille de brasserie' (If a Girl serves in a Brasserie).[11] A young woman of humble but respectable background who works as a waitress in a brasserie in Paris is raped by a customer. Convinced of her collusion and lamenting the fact that she has told him of the event, her fiancé rejects her. His woman must be pure, untouched. Her solution is suicide. As a humble girl, her chances of marriage are ruined and her feeling of self-respect likewise destroyed, thanks to her unquestioning acceptance of the tyrannical morality attacked by Jerusalem. Once again woman is the victim of the male morality at which Schapire-Neurath points an accusing finger but to which she suggests no alternative. Again Jerusalem goes a step further to suggest that the solution lies in the acceptance of women's pre-marital sexual activity. '"You must not, you must not, you must keep yourself snow white",' the ex-piano teacher-cum-prostitute says, quoting the voice of internalised social norms,

> '[you must] chastise your flesh, subdue your blood, suffocate the voice of nature. You must wait until your young, impetuous heart becomes dumb and the voice of reason alone speaks; then – he – comes, whom some lucky or unlucky coincidence leads to you, to him belongs the best, most majestic quality that you possess, to him belongs your innocence, your purity, your soul – the first trembling of your body. Then you are rewarded for your waiting and patience – then you will receive the majesty after which you have thirsted!'

whereupon, however, reality intrudes and the former piano teacher exclaims, 'My God! How does this majesty look! – Tired, bored, lackadaisical, sickly, full of cares, full of experience, – a little good-looking, a little good, a little clever and a little – man. And for that you have sacrificed the whole youthful, majestic storm and stress of your youth.'[12]

Even after marriage the double morality keeps its firm hold. 'The husband may have affairs, as many as he wants, without even keeping up appearances, yet the wife is to tolerate everything, is to suffocate her heart and voice, renounce her happiness so that the grand "world" outside does not gossip,'[13] one of Suttner's female characters says. This resolute fictional woman acts upon such feeling to rebel against this 'abominable injustice'[14] by leaving her long unloved and unloving husband for her lover. 'Moaning and making a fuss does not help: you have to shake it off. The oppressed are responsible for their oppression through their criminal patience,' she comments.[15] This woman at least shows her husband and the world that her love for another man means more to her than her reputation, and that authenticity and frankness are the true moral virtues.

It is not the case, then, that the sham moral purity of a hypocritical convention was the ideal preached by all feminists, a point often misunderstood by contemporaries. Moral purity as a goal was openly criticised by Schlesinger-Eckstein in her review of Vera's *Eine für Viele*, and the reality of women's sensual and sexual needs was emphasised by feminists as dissimilar as Troll-Borostyáni and Meisel-Hess. Yet on closer inspection a difference does emerge despite this similarity. Troll-Borostyáni may applaud the intellectual affirmation of female sensuality, but the practice causes her to balk. In her novel *Onkel Clemens* (Uncle Clemens) (1897), the new, university-educated woman, Bertha, is allowed to read literature that praises sensuality, and her aunt's criticism of it as immoral is dismissed by Bertha's uncle and mentor Clemens as 'excessively prudish condemnation'.[16] However, the practice of sensuality is kept within very strict limits. It is clear that Bertha will remain 'pure' until marriage, while the independent woman who also makes sexual freedom her key word is shown to be in the last resort unhappy and incapable of loving. And although Troll-Borostyáni may point out the hypocrisy of the double morality, she does not go so far as to condone unmarried motherhood. Her uncertainty is displayed in the short story 'Gewitter' (Storm) in her collection of sketches *Hunger und Liebe* (Hunger and Love) (1900). In this vignette a husband believes the child living in his household is not his but the fruit of a pre-marital affair of his wife. Troll-Borostyáni communicates his changing emotions and thoughts, bringing the man to the insight that this condemnation of his wife is unjust, as he has had affairs himself. But it is unclear how far this understanding is to go, for Troll-Borostyáni solves the dilemma too easily by revealing that the child is in fact his sister-in-law's. The problem is avoided. It is as if Troll-Borostyáni shrinks away from the full consequences of her own criticism. Still lurking in the background is the shameful spectre of the 'fallen' woman who has sinned against an absolute moral law. Being the model mother can, however, bring atonement and earn the respect of society, as Marie von Najmájer is anxious to point out.[17] Unlike Jerusalem, for whom it is quite clear that women must be able to lead sexual lives untrammelled by social ties and that only this can lead to fulfilled womanhood and also motherhood, feminists such as Troll-Borostyáni and Najmájer take up a more blurred position, *de facto* trying to reconcile remnants of Christian morality with insight into women's suffering.

Yet for all these feminists the leading impulse is to 'tell it straight' and to show how women – and also men – suffer under the prevailing moral code. For although women are the main victims, men, too, are seen to be constrained by a false morality of empty faithfulness and false gratitude in marriage.[18] All these feminists wish to see women occupying a different position in that moral code, but they vary as to where that position is. For those such as Troll-Borostyáni and Najmájer it is to be found in a society which obeys the ideal of bourgeois morality and which actually gives woman the place promised her. For others such as Jerusalem it lies not in the realisation of an already professed ideal but in a new ideal altogether, that of fulfilled sensuality and love of life. But for both camps the ideal is to give woman strength; the former ideal would do this by making her respected within the status quo, the latter by making her live for life not love. 'Today she understood that it would be a crime against life, which is so rich, to want to exhaust its content with this love which is so transient and often so perishable,' the main female character of a sketch published in the *Dokumente* is made to see:

It was a phase in the development of a person . . . not the sole purpose of existence. To make something of oneself, to be hard-working and noble, someone who creates to the profit and joy of self and others and thereby always climbs upwards – was that not also a goal worthy of life, the highest one perhaps, and one which only the new age had achieved for woman?[19]

The Working Woman

In contrast to love, the other central theme of the women's movement – hunger – was not supported by a long literary tradition. But as the feminists were only too anxious to point out, times had changed too much for the fact of women's employment to be ignored. Following their premiss of presenting reality, many feminist writers featured the working woman in their literature, at the same time making her the bearer of a message.

In the majority of cases that message was a plea to give woman the possibility of satisfying employment, not so much because this is a human right as because it would help to undermine the degenerate sexual morality of bourgeois society. Women whose lives are restricted to marriage and childbearing alone or who are condemned to emotional self-denial in order to survive are presented as accusations, warnings and appeals. Schapire-Neurath's Sterka is destroyed through her economic dependence as is Alice Schalek's governess, the old maid who showers her love on other people's children only to be rejected once they are adults, who wishes to marry and ends by committing suicide, not having even tasted sexual pleasure as at least the seduced maid has.[20] The proximity of economic and emotional dependence to a lack of education or the wrong education was also pointed out by these feminist writers. An education and upbringing which made marriage the only goal is shown to be a major bulwark of the double morality, of marriage for money, and of women's emotional self-mutilation. Women of both classes are denied the possibility of professional self-fulfilment. Woman exists 'just for the children', condemned to a life of self-suppression and family service, and once the children have left home, to uselessness.[21]

But economic independence and education alone are not enough for the 'new woman', as Rudolf Golm (the pseudonym of Rudolf Goldscheid) points out in his novel 'of our times of transition', *Der alte Adam und die neue Eva* (The Old Adam and the New Eve) (1895). Here, in contrast to the new Adam of his play *Lord Byron* (1888) in which the poet is the propounder of an unconventional morality,[22] the new Eve is no self-celebrating individualist. On the contrary, she is an obviously average modern woman. Of suffocating bourgeois background, she is a teacher who grimly supports herself and her parents, and who then takes refuge in a loveless marriage with an old Adam in which she is expected to subordinate herself and against which she rebels. 'Her profession, her studies had developed her into an individual; through her work she had acquired a personality. But her husband wanted to hear none of that,' the narrator explains.[23] The social context such women live in is hostile and even more so if they leave the confines of marriage, as Käthe, Golm's new Eve, does. 'Yes, I have longed to return,' she is forced to confess on coming back to her husband and family, 'the life of a woman living alone, who is neither a girl nor a widow, is a miserable one because it is enclosed on all sides by suspicions and prohibitions . . . I have merely realised that I was wrong in my belief that a woman living alone could be free. She cannot be that the way things are now.'[24] The solution offered in the novel for such a woman is 'the voluntary surrender of her freedom in love'.[25] The marriage of love is once again proposed as at least the interim goal.

Even those rare examples of women's success in achieving financial autonomy indicate that independence alone does not suffice. Troll-Borostyáni's Paula in the novel *Aus der Tiefe* (From the Depths) (1892) is one such woman. She is a single, self-supporting woman who decries the lack of women's education and professional opportunities in Austria. And she is above all a representative of Troll-Borostyáni's new morality. But such a woman, Troll-Borostyáni like Golm points out, will be the object of social suspicion, if not worse. 'The whole air was filled with hate against her,' she writes, 'for the single but very cogent reason that she was different from the others, because she was better, more rational and cultured, and because common souls hate those who are superior to them.'[26] But even here, marriage and not professional fulfilment makes the happy ending, for in wedlock Paula finds the self-fulfilment she seeks. Woman is still a moral and emotional being before she is an economic one. Golm, on the other hand, offers no happy ending. His new Eve succumbs to the force of circumstances. 'The old and the new . . . that is the great divide. That separates the generations from each other, person from person! . . . Nowadays that often separates man and woman too,' he comments. 'Without a doubt woman has made by far greater progress over the last few decades, at least she has changed a lot more than man'; and he comes to the conclusion that 'Every marriage which joins an old Adam and a new Eve means a lost paradise.'[27] And it is not only men who have to change if the longing for a paradise regained is to be realised. The ruling prejudices do, too, for 'as long as the woman living alone is not regarded with different eyes than hitherto, every young woman who is dependent on employment will long to go back to the bleakest of marriages and leave behind her lonely freedom'.[28] Marriage, even in its imperfect present form, is still preferable to a freedom which means being ostracised and going without close human relationships. And in its more perfect form, the love marriage, it is the source of female self-fulfilment and the proper sphere of women's emotional investment.

Woman's Moral Mission

The depiction of women's economic position may have been a result of feminists' wish to tear away the veil of lies which obscured middle-class women's vision of their reality. But it was secondary both to the moral function of literature which was to emerge from that depiction of reality and to the political function of initiating social change. This view of the functions of literature led to a concern with issues beyond those of sexual morality and women's employment. Feminist writers wished to present all of reality. And that included the other great question of the turn of the century: the workers' question. Yet for most this becomes in their literary texts a matter of metaphysical morality rather than politics. Poverty is presented as bringing moral superiority; the poor are good, the rich bad, but the rich can be made good by showing pity towards the poor. The impoverished seamstress is an angel of virtue in contrast to the calculating and inhuman factory owner who is her boss.[29] The story of a starving beggar boy who steals from the wealthy is intended to appeal to the reader's pity and sense of moral justice.[30] The inhumanity and immorality of the owning classes is made the central point, not the power relations which govern class relations. The poor, like women, are presented as the victims of a system designed in others' interests – the interests of those who own – and this is given a highly moral rather than political thrust. When the poor die in Troll-Borostyáni's stories, for example, they are often transfigured. Death is seen as release from the pains of this world, not as the result of poverty.[31] It is a black and white picture which Troll-Borostyáni paints, one drawn according to a system of morals that preaches virtue and neighbourly love, combined with a condemnation of decadence and luxury. Money is shown to corrupt, leading to greed, the first step on the slippery slope to gambling, dishonest dealing and ultimately the dreaded disintegration of the family.[32]

Yet although such texts are distinctly preaching a morality which is absolute, a conscious distance is placed between this morality and that of established religions. God's word is shown in Fickert's sketch with that title to be found not in the church, in the mouth of the priest, but in the mouth of the loving mother and child who give succour to each other.[33] Almost all who deal with the theme show religion, in most cases Christianity but also Judaism as in 'Sterka', as hostile to the moral progress which is the ultimate goal of these feminists. Religion supports the privilege of the wealthy and spreads a false morality, as shown by the starving beggar boy who steals and who is immediately damned by onlookers as the godless boy. True morality is not that of religion but of human nature, the only truly Christian morality. This Troll-Borostyáni makes clear by highlighting the conflict between Christian dogma and a personal secularised Christianity in a sketch in which a dying priest adamantly refuses to betray a confidence of the confessional in return for the last rites.[34]

These literary feminists used the 'artistic representation of reality' to present a critique of existing moral conditions, and a number also used it to suggest a moral vision. Some restrict themselves to homilies, and thus bring their texts into the company of those written by women critical of prevailing moral hypocrisy but not necessarily connected with the women's movement. They advocate the simple life and the values of humility, social justice, honesty, patience and forgiveness, but do not have a developed perception of how such qualities could bring about social change.[35] For many others, however, that moral vision extends to a reconsideration of gender relations. Morality is Janus-faced for these feminists. The unnatural, corrupt morality of society and most men may destroy women, but natural, uncorrupt morality is a potential strength. It is up to women of moral integrity to show men an alternative to the dominant social immorality of appearances, as Margret Hönigsberg makes clear in her sketch 'Hanna', published in the *Dokumente*. As a condition of marriage Hanna insists that her husband-to-be adopt his own illegitimate son, a son he had rejected for fear of a professional scandal. She is refused her request and forced to forgo marriage with the man she loves, for he cannot rise to her moral stature.[36] Men are shown as remaining caught in the world of appearances and convention, denying even that most natural of bonds – the bond of parentage.

For these feminists it is a question of the denial not only of natural bonds but also of natural moral duties. As Troll-Borostyáni's Uncle Clemens says, 'It is simply a question of doing your duty. Whoever does their duty at the post which fate has allotted them has done enough for themselves and their times.'[37] Yet, he continues, only a small minority know what is their duty. The others need to be issued with moral commandments. And for women, Troll-Borostyáni demonstrates, duty means above all faithfulness as a wife and mother. In that fulfilment of duty lies not only woman's strength but also her moral significance, her ability to raise the moral level of humanity and so contribute to its evolution. Thus Troll-Borostyáni makes a young wife choose to stay with her blind, much older husband instead of giving way to her reawakened love for her childhood sweetheart, thereby bringing about the moral elevation of her lover. He, as a token of their bond, takes away with him a painting of the two as children:

> And at difficult moments in the struggle between duty and desire, when the impetuous, passionate impulse of nature threatened to triumph over the soft, warning voice of higher rational insight, then he gazed up at the picture and thinking of her who had loved him and sacrificed her love to duty, he found, like her, the strength for the most difficult victory, the victory over one's own heart.[38]

Such a victory, Troll-Borostyáni teaches, will be rewarded with peaceful contentment, not ecstasy or pleasure. Reason must triumph over desire; sexual pleasure presents a great danger to morality. Even Suttner's Daniela Dormes, the embodiment of the woman who supports progress and who can confidently say of herself, 'I am neither coquette nor sentimental; I aspire to feel clearly and to think clearly',[39] is almost led so far astray by the sexual attraction she feels for the conservative, chauvinist Comte de Trelazure as to desert her intellectual and moral principles. But even where there is no such conflict, the desires of the body should be secondary to moral considerations; physical attraction must never gain the upper hand, morality must remain paramount. True love is shown to be based on moral qualities, not on erotic fascination, personal benefit or economic factors. Motherhood is also made a moral mission and a source of women's strength and influence. '"My friends",' Henri IV says as the final flourish to Marie von Najmájer's historical novel *Der Stern von Navarra* (The Star of Navarra) (1900), '"I do not know whether I am a star or not. But one thing is certain. As the stars draw their light from the sun, so do I owe everything which might be good in me to my mother!"'[40] Motherhood is woman's highest dignity, her most beautiful – and significant – office, for through motherhood she can implant her morality in the coming generation and have a lasting impact on human affairs. And while it is her heaviest burden, it is also her comfort, a balsam which heals the deepest wounds, and which, when a result of love, is the strongest bond between man and woman.

Yet marriage and motherhood, these moral feminists suggest, can only be truly uplifting for both mother and child if the mother herself is a fully developed personality. Woman's development must come first. 'Only when woman feels that she is at the peak of her development is she worthy to become the true mother of a child, not merely the chance cause of its existence.'[41] She is the representative of a true morality, unlike those 'respectable housewives'[42] who merely obey the prevailing morality and do nothing but uphold that 'rotten virtue'[43] of hypocrisy, as Ada Christen (the pseudonym of Christiane von Breden), herself a one-time prostitute, scornfully asserts. But what this new, true morality is to involve is not the same for all who attack the old, false morality. For writers such as Troll-Borostyáni and Marriot, that morality is still largely based on the repression of desire. By advocating a rigid morality of self-sacrifice and duty these feminists lend support to the ideal which informs traditional female roles. Yet it is precisely that ideal which needs to be called into question if their other ideal of an emancipated humanity is to become anything like reality. A morality based on self-control and self-denial cannot be emancipatory. For other feminists such as Jerusalem the new morality is to be life-affirming, to give room to desire and to allow for changing attachments. Yet it maintains the primacy of the highly problematic concept of true love. But for all, this moral literature should deal with life as it really is and be unashamedly didactic, indeed tendentious. The focus is placed on external reality, not on an internal one. It is the outer world which is the arena of change for these feminists.

CHAPTER 14

Psychological Feminism

The boundaries between moral and psychological literary feminism are not rigid. Elements of both can appear in one and the same text. In the former, psychological processes are not the main focus of attention; they are used as a vehicle for the moral message. In the latter, on the other hand, they are the main object of interest. This type of feminism is not primarily concerned to point out the immorality of the status quo and to plead for a natural morality which is represented above all by women. It moves away from this to concentrate on the psyche and the emotions, and on the mutual influence between these and socio-sexual relations. The life of the psyche becomes the truth to be revealed and thus the platform for another feminist vision.

Yet psychological feminism does not surrender to apoliticism and lack of criticism. On the contrary. Like moral feminist texts, psychological feminist ones point out failings and omissions in the status quo and vigorously attack rigid and inhuman social conventions to present an alternative. But unlike the moral feminists, who tend to present that alternative in moral terms in which woman plays a model missionary role, the psychological feminists highlight psychological processes, venturing into depths the former avoid. Some taboo themes are dealt with. The *Dokumente*, for example, published a sketch in which negative emotions on the part of women – hate, anger, triumphant revenge – are honestly admitted to and used to support a social order which values strength and creativity over obedience to a domesticating morality.[1] Similarly Erich Holm exposes the reality after the 'happily ever after' in her *Jenseits der Ehe* (Beyond Marriage) (1900). She critically probes her protagonists' psyche to reveal how various women react to and suffer from the reality of marriage: the docile mother and housewife who discovers sensuality and liberation with another man; the daughter of good family trapped in an unhappy marriage; the suicidal wife who poisons herself and her child on discovering her husband's infidelity; the worldly-wise wife who explains to a friend how to manage her husband.

This emphasis on the inner life is characterised by a turn away from mimetic realism and an omniscient narrator. Moral feminist writers use these techniques in order to highlight their proximity to 'the way things are' and to stress the authenticity of their criticism. For them it is a question of honest depiction, without the gloss and false harmony of sentimentally moralising family literature. Yet by choosing mimetic realism they remain within convention. Psychological feminists tend towards more experimental literary techniques, adopting a much wider use of reported interior monologue and impressionistic, associative style. The authorial voice retreats into the background to give way to a figural narrator, or to an authorial narration where one figure's inner life dominates and where all events are seen in relation to that psyche. Quoted but unspoken thoughts of various characters are brought together as in a collage. This emphasis on the inner life also leads to the self-conscious (female) narrator and narration. The reader is kept at a distance from any objective reality and led into the world of the freely speaking narrative voice. Sometimes there are direct appeals to the reader and elements of self-irony, but there is never the pretence of objective reality. The literary character of the text is openly admitted. The text's narrative voice, which is often humorous in contrast to the on the whole straight-laced tenor of the moral feminist texts, is given the opportunity to create an alternative reality. It is clear that the psyche must be approached from a vantage point other than that of observation and mimesis, namely from the imagination. As the narrative voice in Meisel-Hess's *Die Stimme* declares:

> Imagination. What is imagination? . . . Invention? Is that what it depends on? The authors of family novels have the most ability to invent things. There everything is 'made up'. . . . Is that imagination? Is it not rather perhaps that kind of seeing, that kind of hearing which sees and hears where there is something to be seen and heard, but where others perhaps see and hear nothing? To copy life in writing, that would be as hopeless as wanting to 'invent' it.[2]

How, then, is the psyche regarded in these texts? And what is the significance of this treatment for a feminist vision?

The Unconscious

Both Grete Meisel-Hess and Rosa Mayreder, the two major psychological feminist writers in Vienna of around 1900, interpret the psyche as the unconscious. In many of Meisel-Hess's texts it is shown as having the ability to liberate and thus as offering the potential for the harmonious integration of all aspects of the personality. Abilities which had been only distantly sensed can emerge from the unconscious to become part of the lived present. These were once thought to be ancient spirits which possessed the soul, but, as Meisel-Hess makes clear, 'the real spirits which govern our lives . . . are the spirits within us, the most secret drives of our innermost being, which become our fate'.[3] Her studious Anna Binder, PhD, travelling alone to the North Sea coast for a post-doctoral holiday, is possessed by such a spirit when she begins to dance in front of two men in order to convince them that she is really the professional dancer she has claimed to be. 'Had she not often heard that secret abilities which lay latent are awakened and brought to life – when the "spirit" overcomes a body and enchants the soul?!' the narrator naively asks.[4] And this is Anna's inner truth. Her fantasy identity proves to be a part of her real but hitherto only one-sidedly perceived identity. 'In this one night she had felt that she belonged to those women with a strong, bubbling femininity – to those born dancers. . . . Hidden in them lay the truth of their own essence – and it slept.'[5] This is the new woman – the one who can unite the sensual and the intellectual:

> Something new was afoot – equally far removed from depravity and inner impoverishment – something new which shattered tradition – a new femininity which possessed the strength and earnestness of the person of intellect, but also a hidden fire – the primal feminine. . . . A new femininity which – in the midst of all does not forget itself – which thinks of the salvation of – those to come. 'That is who I am', she felt with a beating heart.[6]

By letting the unconscious surface into the present such a woman can find her identity and is able to unite the intellectual, cool, northern elements in her being with the sensual, fiery, southern elements to create a unity. Anna Binder is now Annie-Bianka, north and south, intellect and sensuality. And after her wild night she almost instinctively engrosses herself in reading Suetonius' *History of the Roman Emperors*, as she serenely continues her journey, once again alone.

For Annie-Bianka the unconscious manifests itself in the discovery of her self as a sensual being. For Maja Hertz in *Die Stimme* it manifests itself in the topos of the voice and its music, the inner and outer voice which is Maja's uniting element and the uniting element of this intriguing novel. This voice of the unconscious, which is the individual's fate or inner truth, is released by ecstasy just as Annie-Bianka's unconscious is; for Annie-Bianka those whirling moments of Dionysian frenzy enable her to transgress her boundaries of cultural identity to enter a world of orgiastic dance rites, of oriental temple prostitutes. For Maja it is the ecstasy of love which liberates the melodic voice of the unconscious and allows her to enter into a life of awareness of the strength of the self. 'Voice is the strength of the soul,' the narrative voice, Maja's voice, asserts:[7]

> Full of voices is the human temperament; at times they have dried up like filled-in springs. Until a power clears away the debris under which they lie buried and the voices jump up in hundreds of manifestations.... We then feel that we are and have a presentiment of who we are. The 'voices' leap up.[8]

The unconscious leads to the sense of having a fully developed identity. It also leads to female creativity for this can, Meisel-Hess shows, be activated by dreams. These are the doors to the unconscious and can open to make the hidden truth of each individual accessible. In this way they act as triggers to creativity. Thus a dream brings a desperate, suicidal artist to the insight that it is not the loss of her financial basis which means the loss of life but the loss of the will to struggle. This insight enables her to paint again, to paint a woman, tossed by the seas of fate, but with a glow of triumph in her eyes. And this is also the solution to her desperation: '– It had come to her all the same, from where she had least expected it: from dreamland, where the secret truth of things resides, which, hidden to us, dares to cross the threshold of the conscious only when wishes and desires slumber,' the narrator reports.[9] Dreams communicate a reality deeper than that of conscious, waking life. They fulfil a compensatory function, offering the experience of what is lacking in a one-sided life; they lead to an unconscious awareness of what might be if the unconscious could be integrated, and also to an awareness of creativity. The joy in living gained by the discovery of sensuality is also the catalyst to a joy in creation, as Annie-Bianka experiences. Female creativity emerges from the union of sexuality and intellectuality, the Dionysian and Apollonian, as the young concert violinist and composer Fanny Roth (in the novel of that name) also finds out. 'She had only a blissful memory of the crazy orgy of beauty of these last months – when she had created with the somnambulant delight of the artist.... She had formed what was unconscious ... into art,' the reader is told.[10] 'And these orgiastic feverish nights were followed by days of shaping creation – of energetic, releasing, relentless, restless work.'[11] Yet creation, the sublimation of awakened sensuality, is no substitute for lived sexuality, for 'in the breaks between creation – a strange, oppressive burden on the soul ... an unconscious sob in sleep – a luxuriant dream – an ashamed awakening' disturb Fanny.[12] This is the fate, Meisel-Hess emphasises, of the virginal young woman (*Jung-Frau*) who is denied sexual fulfilment by a social and moral order hostile to life and love.

The unconscious, however, does not always offer a path to the discovery of the self and the integration of the various aspects of the personality. For Mayreder, in contrast to Meisel-Hess, the unconscious, far from being the storage vessel of sensual and creative potential, is the possible deceiver of the conscious. It is irrational, inescapable, and determines people's perception of the world, themselves and of others. As the female narrator of her novel *Pipin* says,

> Something happens; but it is not the same for all who experience it. Everyone acts according to his own hidden motives, follows his own secret goals, and the observer interprets the external signs. The inside of what is happening remains invisible and incommunicable; it has to be guessed at like solving a puzzle. Therein lies a danger of life but also its magic.[13]

In her imaginative texts Mayreder tends to focus on the dangers rather than the magic of this dominance of the unconscious. People hear what they want to hear, believe what they want to believe; they are trapped in a semi-tragic web of illusions and delusions. As she makes clear in her 'psychological sketches'[14] *Übergänge* (Transitions) (1897), they prove completely incapable of giving up obviously empty ideals that clash grotesquely with reality.[15] The unconscious is impervious to experience; indeed, it creates a comforting refuge, perpetuating and reinforcing the lies people are shown to live by. And as Meisel-Hess also demonstrates, the unconscious can even destroy the sense of self. In one of her vignettes the female protagonist, after leaving her husband, unconsciously identifies with the dragonfly her lover has trapped and killed. This fatefully leads to the total dissolution of her sense of identity, as she literally relinquishes her self and merges with the impaled insect, the symbol of the victims of male lust, greed and necrophilia.[16]

The Psychology of Love

Not only the unconscious is seen as impervious to experience. Strong emotions, above all love, are shown to be also. And here, again, the psychological feminists tread new ground by investigating an area of human experience uncritically presented in many moral feminist texts as the be-all and end-all of human relations. In Mayreder's imaginative texts love is a particularly tricky business, thanks in no small part to the fickleness of the emotion itself. It is often a delusion woven out of the illusions dreamed up by that 'artful glorious god' Eros, the god

> Full of cunning, whom no heart can escape
> As long as life's forces live there.
> He knows how to confuse the mind with masks

He comes as a friend, he wears a king's robe
Brings rich gifts, incense, gold and myrrh –
A dazzling deception which with tall flames
Blazes in the heart, until as suffering
It collapses into grey ash.[17]

In Mayreder's fiction, falling in love usually means merely creating idols who then turn out to have feet of clay. This theme is most extensively dealt with in her novel *Idole*. There Gisa, the narrator of the novel, which is presented in the form of a memoir, falls in love with the hyper-rational doctor, Raimund Lamaris. It is, however, a love which is shown to rest not on reality but on Gisa's perception of reality and her idolisation of Lamaris. But as Mayreder demonstrates, not only those like Gisa who are of a differentiated sexual constitution (to use Mayreder's terminology) need sex idols. It is a widespread phenomenon. Nelly, Gisa's socially conformist friend, idolises the 'real man', 'a man with strong arms which could protect and shelter me . . . a man with a strong will, who could make me his slave . . . a man who gives orders and does not let himself be ordered',[18] and the chauvinist lieutenant von Zedlitz idolises the counterpart, namely the 'real woman'. All wish to love according to preconceived notions of what the object of love should be rather than what it really is. Yet only Gisa suffers from her idolisation. Only she tries to live against the social norms governing the *pas de deux* of gender relations, only she feels truly and not according to the empty idolisations of convention, only she is really led by her emotions and not by reason. Nelly marries according to social convention, Lamaris finally marries his housekeeper for eugenicist reasons. For people such as Lamaris 'the imagination is a dangerous element', and he advises Gisa to live more in the real world.[19] Only for Gisa is the imagination the source of 'all that is beautiful and noble',[20] yet she suffers from this as she comes to realise how her idol deviates from the reality she is finally compelled to perceive but never fully accepts. Yet this idolisation performs a valuable function for her. It allows her to escape from the constricting world of feminine dutifulness, silence and self-denial which is her lot as a daughter of good family. 'The hopeless sobriety of this environment put a constraining pressure on my heart,' she declares,

> . . . and then I felt something like giddiness. . . . Why did I live as me, and was I my whole life long to see only the meagre small section of the world which lay within the range of this self? . . . In solemn moonlit nights . . . I would like to spread out my wings and swing upwards until the earth lies beneath me like a silver disc . . . and all pains are assuaged . . . and life is merely a gentle rocking in the infinite.[21]

Yet although she flees into a fantasy world, her imagination does allow her to enter a world of authentic identity and to find a language which is hers. 'That which had been silent in me acquired a language,' she confesses,

> I found an expression for everything which was happening in me. Breaking the long silence of my soul was a pleasure without compare. . . . This light which streamed from Raimund Lamaris illuminated my inner world with a feeling of happiness and joy in living. . . . It gave me new abilities. I had become richer, stronger, freer, I had only then become fully myself.[22]

Yet this world is still one of fantasy and is in conflict with the outer world of the objective reality represented above all by men. Gisa speaks a language which is confined to her private world and experience, to her world of idolisation. Her attempts to cross the frontier between the two worlds fail, for her feelings cannot be verbalised. The vocabulary of reality does not permit another. 'In love – an ugly word, a word with which I could not feel at ease. It aroused strange images in me, it did not belong to me. I searched for another word, for a more intimate, penetrating, subtle word, but found none,' Gisa is forced to confess.[23] The bridging leap from inner to outer is not accomplished. 'Is communication with any other being possible?' she asks. 'The depths cannot be articulated.'[24] And indeed, really deep feelings are not spoken but intimated, such as when Aunt Ludmilla cries over a twig of lilac. 'It was perhaps the most beautiful moment of her life,' Gisa comments, 'the only moment of happiness, of elevation above the everyday – but if she had talked about it in her well-bred remarks and petit bourgeois phrases, it would have been destroyed for ever. She had told me about it as she cried over the twig of lilac. And can one communicate the most sublime moments of life in any other way?'[25] Yet this is a world which is submerged and negated by the outer world. For Gisa's discovery of self, of her own language, is immediately relativised by that other world of external reality. Her articulacy within her inner world is devalued by Gisa herself as 'only conversations with myself' and her happiness is written off as the 'intoxication' of her foolish heart with fantasies.[26] She is struck dumb when she attempts to turn the inner into the outer world. 'The presence of him whom I met so joyfully and freely when I thought of him made me shy and silent. I found no words when he was there.'[27] Men and women speak two different languages. The verbal world of Lamaris is that of work, the intellect, the public world. For him language is not so much inadequate, as it is for Gisa, as dangerous, a potential betrayer of emotion. 'One never has complete control over one's words; as soon as one speaks one says more than one wishes to,' he says.[28] For men, it is a question of having power over words and over feelings.

Mayreder makes love an essentially private, incommunicable emotion which does not bring people together but isolates them. 'Ah, we stand in front of locked doors and listen,' Gisa declares, 'we hear voices that lament, voices that rejoice, voices that call, and we answer, because we believe that we can make ourselves understood, that we can come together with those who are on the other side. But the doors never open; we remain alone in the darkness, alone with ourselves and our dreams.'[29] For Gisa, love, when confronted with the reality of the outer world, means loss of self. She feels like the compass of a needle which must follow the attracting force of Lamaris's presence,[30] she feels herself subjected to his 'cold vivisector's gaze'.[31]

Meisel-Hess, on the other hand, makes her female figures see love as a means of promoting encounter and as the confirmer of identity. For Annie-Bianka love achieves the union with the animus, with the brother to whom she is sister, with the masculine parts in herself. For Maja Hertz love releases the voice and thus life's forces, bringing the individual into the world of life lived to the full. Yet this rests on a strong sense of identity, on the will to find one's true self and not to lose it to the world. 'Love means surrendering one's self. But only he who has a well-defined, aware self can surrender it,' the narrative voice explains.[32] But at the same time love releases the self from limitation. 'Love is Messianic. And it is redemptive because the one partner releases the tension of the other, the tension of his own isolated self. And that is how one can recognise the false Messiah: because he does not release this tension.'[33] Like Mayreder, Meisel-Hess accords language a central role in this encounter of the sexes, but although acknowledging the divisive role of language, unlike Mayreder, she is optimistic that communication on a deep level is possible. 'We had made conversation with each other in the interpreters' language of being in love,' Maja Hertz recalls, '... It seems to me that it is only symbolic that we made use of a foreign language in order to communicate with each other. There is a sense of belonging together which is international and builds bridges between large parts of the globe and, what is more difficult, between minds. And then it is irrelevant which language it uses.'[34] In contrast to Mayreder's pessimistic view of the deceptive nature of emotions, feelings for Meisel-Hess are the source of each person's energy. 'From the heart the thought is nourished, from the thought the mood, the voice.... From the heart comes the soul and it travels in the blood from there to the brain until it streams out as an excess of life energy, shattering, from the throat.'[35] The heart is the source of existence itself. 'Everything, everything comes from my heart: my song, my life, my being,'

Maja rejoices.[36] This happens in the state of greatest clarity, not frenzy,[37] and represents the ecstasy of love. 'Greatest awareness in the moment of possession. Greatest spirituality of sensuous experience – that is the ecstatic pleasure of love.'[38]

Here another difference immediately becomes clear. Love for Meisel-Hess is obviously inextricably linked to sexuality, an aspect Mayreder largely overlooks in her imaginative writing and most moral feminists wish to keep separate from love. And it is this which for Meisel-Hess is both the traitor and the guide. Woman, she maintains, needs to experience her sexuality in order to find her true identity and choose the father of her children. Yet to live her sexuality within the existing socio-sexual framework means making unhappy compromises. This Fanny Roth is forced to discover to her cost after she marries a man with whom deeper communion is impossible merely in order to experience her sexuality. 'A rigid social form makes of the first man who loosens the chains confining her body the one and only Mr Right to whom she has to belong for life,' Fanny comments of woman's predicament. '. . . A wild horror shook her whole body at this thought.'[39] Yet Fanny manages to free herself, being brought to awareness by a pregnancy scare. 'For now she knew that only when the blood has been calmed, when the human being in woman has come to see, – that only then . . . can she recognise, decide and choose. . . . Only now could she have chosen with recognition the man who is the complement of her own self, who belonged to her in order to create that which should be more than both.'[40] She leaves her husband to take up her musical career again, but now as a fully mature woman able to combine artistic creation with motherhood. 'Like one redeemed, she held her destiny in her own hands. . . . Thousands of possibilities lay in her awaiting fertilisation: the not yet begotten child in her womb. . . . And thousands of joys of the soul . . . which lay slumbering there in the violin.'[41] For Meisel-Hess, then, unlike Mayreder, the body is also an integral element of subjective reality; the needs of the psyche and the body must combine. Yet for both these psychological feminists, in contrast to the moral feminists, it is the inner world which is the main constituent of a reality which, when acknowledged, could lead to insight and to change.

CHAPTER 15

The Visionary Imagination

For moral feminists such as Troll-Borostyáni it was clear that literature should fulfil a visionary function. The imaginative writer was to be a doctor and a priest in one, a healer of the body and of the soul, and in this way to carry out the feminist mission of leading humanity into a new dawn. 'Let him be the champion of a better, freer, brighter future, the navigator of humanity towards this future,' she pleads.[1] It is the role of the writer to educate people to constant ethical and intellectual progress. As the servant of truth and beauty, this he or she can do by creating images based both on how things are now and on how things could be in a future in which humanity develops according to the laws of nature. The writer has an unambiguously 'sublime goal';[2] literature, for Troll-Borostyáni, is unashamedly didactic.

In moral feminist texts woman frequently appears in this missionary role. She is the moral guardian who transcends the morality of masculinity and thereby discovers her strength. She represents an alternative to the world of male moral corruption: the world of female moral purity which man must enter if he is to be redeemed. And indeed, woman is often made into a priestess figure. The pacifist Franka of Suttner's novel *Der Menschheit Hochgedanken* (English title: *When Thoughts Will Soar*) (1911) – 'no bluestocking, for heaven's sake – her bright temperament with its hunger for life, her innate grace protected her from that'[3] – is made to appear like a vestal virgin, in diaphanous white robes. Her mentor, Chlodwig, clearly determines which image she is to project. She is not to appeal to women through adherence to the women's movement but 'through the living word, through the magic, the magnetism of her person . . . devout like a priestess, transfigured like a seer . . . and the magic of youth and beauty will increase the power of the personal magnetism tenfold'.[4] Here, woman is clearly the bringer of the word of salvation. Along similar lines, a collection of Najmájer's poems is significantly called *Der Göttin Eigenthum* (What the Goddess Owns) (1901); the female voice which speaks is that of a goddess, and so the moral wisdom she imparts is also divine. Religion, not realism, is the underlying principle of these texts.

For the psychological feminists, on the other hand, the vision does not centre on morality but on the self, not on the world without but the world within. Whereas for the moral feminists the soul is largely the Christian one which must be saved and redeemed, for the psychological feminists it is the psyche. Meisel-Hess plainly considers some of her female characters to be didactic figures, not because they are the moral paragons advocated by the moral feminists but because they are representatives of a new female psyche. According to her own interpretation, some of the female figures in her novel *Die Intellektuellen* (The Intellectuals) (1911) can help her readers break with the view that the woman disappointed in marriage and motherhood is condemned to a life of emotional and material poverty.[5] It is a matter of psychology, not of morals. Meisel-Hess goes so far as to assert that 'the problem of "woman's emancipation" is only a question of fighting against psychological influences which are thousands of years old'.[6] Women's emancipation has been reduced to a matter of personal deliverance from the world of internal constraints. But for these feminists it is precisely this inner world which becomes the alternative world when it is fully realised; not morality but the fully developed self is the bringer of the new.

In these texts that self is usually female; for those who already occupy a marginal position – women – can best live according to the laws of the world within rather than those of the world without. Such a life means emancipating oneself from social conventions, which can anyway most effectively be deprived of their power by being ignored rather than by being fought directly. Thus some of Meisel-Hess's women calmly go their own way, liberating themselves from constricting norms through their refusal to conform. Annie-Bianka confidently makes her journey, both metaphorical and literal, travelling back and forth across the space between the permitted and the forbidden. The newly-wed Gusti Neuberger in the vignette 'Eine sonderbare Hochzeitsreise' (A Strange Honeymoon) quietly but firmly refuses to conform to the behaviour expected of the young bride and manages to deceive her husband and her family and get what she wants all at the same time. Others, however, do not achieve such sovereignty. The independent, feminist-orientated Olga in *Die Intellektuellen* does not find true self-fulfilment in her unconventional femininity; her university education and economic independence do not lead to real freedom. According to Meisel-Hess's own account, she can grow towards freedom, inner strength and a love of life only by experiencing poverty and pain.[7] Likewise, many of Mayreder's figures are caught in the void between the no longer and the not yet, no longer able affirmingly to conform but not yet strong enough to live beyond the norms to achieve the synthesis which is Mayreder's ideal. But as Olga declares in answer to the question where the way out of this 'realm of the intermediate' leads, 'where else but to the human being? – To the elevated human being . . .'.[8]

For both Meisel-Hess and Mayreder, this developed humanity presupposes self-realisation. And to be true to oneself means listening to the inner voice. For Meisel-Hess, this voice in artistically creative women is utterly female and comes close to the original essence of things; it is a singing echo of the secret of life.[9] These women spurn the art of men; they are women to their fingertips, able to make connections which remain concealed from rational thought. Their voice is the oracular voice of the Ancients; they are Pythia, Cassandra, Diotima. 'It is no coincidence,' Meisel-Hess maintains, 'that the prophets of the sacred oracles of myths were usually women.'[10] The anima is the soul, the immanent logical principle which is the truth.[11] For Mayreder, on the contrary, this creative voice of woman is not that of the primal feminine but of the synthetic woman, and is indeed divine. She describes her own adolescent rejection of conventional religious belief as the fall away from God, but not from *Geist*. 'I had fallen from God, but God had not fallen from me. He ruled on in me as the omnipotent will of the intellect,' she recalls.[12] This is the inner voice that calls her to defend the rights of the individual.[13] And it is this which is the voice of God, the only guiding principle which can give the self meaning in a godless age. Creative work, too, as the expression of *Geist*, becomes a divine activity. Her fable 'Die Stimme Gottes' (The Voice of God) in her collection *Fabeleien über göttliche und menschliche Dinge* is, Mayreder remarks, her 'mystical, poetic' attempt to explain why she writes.[14] There the soul is commanded by God to spread the word amongst the philistine masses, to reveal itself and dance naked on the market square at the risk of rejection and humiliation. Mayreder sees herself as such an apostle. She is called by God to expose herself in her writing. And not only that. Writing takes on the divine role of creating the world, not through the Word which is the voice of God, but through the force of the personality. 'What is concealed behind this deification of work?' she wondered in her diary:

> The desire for success, influence? The drive to be active? I think work means for me that final, highest unfolding of the personality which by virtue of its own strength can, despite all external inhibitions and negative coincidences, enter into a relationship with the world and determine it according to the immanent laws of its own essence. That is, it is the creation of the world by giving it content and form.[15]

The very act of writing has joined the cult of the self to become the expression of a religious need of which the creative woman is a prophet and disciple.

For both the moral feminists and the psychological feminists imaginative literature was to bring about change, and for both this change has a religious dimension. For the former, such as Troll-Borostyáni, the goal was ethical and intellectual progress. For the latter, such as Mayreder and Meisel-Hess, it was self-realisation. For Mayreder this was in essence a question of the intellect, for Meisel-Hess of sexuality, but for both it was a matter of aspects that traditionally have been denied woman. And for both moral and psychological feminists, despite their differences, that vision could be presented through the depiction of reality in literature: the objective reality of social constraints and the inner reality of the psyche when freed from those constraints. For neither brand of feminist, however, was it a question of simple propaganda in the sense of merely presenting positive role models.

Militant Essays and Pessimistic Fiction?

This insight into the visionary nature of feminist imaginative literature may help to explain a feature which has been noted by a number of commentators – the discrepancies between these writers' theoretical and imaginative texts. The latter apparently display a greater 'pessimism' and 'resignation'.[16] They are regarded as less militant. 'One finds only a few women who are emancipated in their imagination,' one commentator asserts. 'In the worlds of even the most enlightened, the figure of the emancipated woman remains a utopia. . . . The most militant essayists become pessimists in their works of fiction.'[17] Other interpreters see the two genres as quite distinct. They read women's texts with an eye only for the themes of the women's movement – and the more obviously those themes are there the better, it seems.[18] So Mayreder's *Idole* is chastised by one commentator for omitting 'social reality' by not treating the influence and impact of the women's movement. This critic comes to the conclusion 'that Rosa Mayreder's literary activity is not to be seen in relation to her commitment to the women's movement. These are different areas of concern which she approached with different intentions.'[19] This is apparently not only a general feature of Austrian middle-class women's literature, but also a 'regressive' feature to be lamented. 'The dominance of regressive elements is a characteristic feature of bourgeois women's literature,' it is claimed, and this is 'disappointing'.[20]

These commentators transfer modern conceptions of what feminism should be about to the early women's movement and overlook the visionary nature of the movement and the feminism which informed it. Of course, the vision did in many cases mean a highly moral tone and an exclusive concern with possibilities of self-realisation, both presented under the motto of realism. These features may appear regressive to modern readers. The tendency to pathos which is an essential element of the moral tone is for most modern readers hard to appreciate and reeks of slushy emotionalism, while the morality preached is anything but emancipatory. The concentration of the psychological feminists on the inner life and their frequent neglect of the social context can appear blind and naive, the viewpoint of comfortably off middle-class women. Meisel-Hess, for example, nowhere confronts the very real problem of how Fanny Roth in the novel of that name will manage to combine motherhood with a creative (but insecure) profession and earn her living at the same time. While fully acknowledging such difficulties in appreciating these texts, it is, however, still fruitful to look again at the apparent discrepancies that have been identified between the two genres of imaginative and discursive writing, for this closer examination leads to a deeper insight and a more differentiated appreciation.

It is true that examples of female emancipation in these texts are rare and that women's rebellion is often restricted to daydreaming, the only space for resistance offered within the reality of an oppressive marriage.[21] However, the claim that themes of the discursive texts are hardly considered in the imaginative ones can be dismissed. There is a large overlap of themes. A critique of marriage and morals, women's employment opportunities and education, woman's inner development, and love dominate both genres. In the case of Mayreder, her imaginative texts certainly deal not only with the subjectivity of perception and the nature of love and its deceptions but also with her vision of synthesis, both important themes of her discursive writing. *Pipin* and the novella 'Sonderlinge', for example, focus quite clearly on the need to find a synthesis between heart and head, while some of her fables highlight the synthesis of the ideal and the real.

But how far is it true that these imaginative texts are pessimistic, resigned and less militant than the discursive texts? A polarisation would of course be distorting. For not only do these feminists in their discursive works walk the tightrope between acceptance and rejection of the status quo, but the texts of both genres contain discrepancies and even contradictions. Nevertheless, Troll-Borostyáni's fiction does display less political awareness than her analytical writings. The moral tone, which is certainly also present in her discursive writing, comes out more forcefully in her imaginative texts but at the expense of political insight. In her fiction there is more emphasis on self-sacrifice, renunciation and duty, particularly in connection with sexual morality, than in the discursive texts. In the latter, after all, sex is affirmed as necessary to happy healthy living according to the laws of nature even if it is made to serve the benefit of the social whole, not the individual, and is kept within firm moral boundaries that imply moderation. In her imaginative literature, on the other hand, Troll-Borostyáni presents it as a danger, a seducer, a threat to morality. In the former the sex drive is acknowledged and even accepted (albeit reluctantly) as having a place in the moral system. In the latter it is precisely its negation which is given that place in the system. And so the institutionalised ideals of marriage and the nuclear family, given critical attention in *Gleichstellung der Geschlechter* for example, enjoy a positive presentation in the imaginative texts. There the state upbringing and education of children is not mentioned; child-rearing is woman's task. And noticeably, legal equality between the sexes, the central focus of Troll-Borostyáni's theoretical feminism, is hardly considered in her fiction. Paula and Bertha, the 'new women', are not those who fight for equal rights but those who are eminently moral and rational; they are not the political equals of men but morally superior to most men, and can guide men to morality or be the helpmeet of the moral man. These moral elements are also present in the discursive texts, but the emphasis is differently placed. There the spotlight falls on Troll-Borostyáni's criticism, while in her imaginative writings it is focused on the moral ideal. Troll-Borostyáni's critical view is blurred in the imaginative texts, if indeed it is not completely obscured by a third-rate narrative apparatus of sudden deaths, evil fathers, noble daughters, true lovers and gypsy passion, in which the moral message that virtue and love will triumph in the end drowns in the triviality of the narration. Troll-Borostyáni's idea that literature must be uplifting as well as realistic detracts from her critical thrust, because the two goals she sets herself but does not always reach – to present the way things are now and to outline her ideal of a moral future – work against each other. What makes her discursive writing militant is not the ideal she envisages, with which to a large extent she supports the bourgeois ideal of morality, but her criticism of how it is only half-heartedly practised. By focusing more on the ideal, her imaginative literature is necessarily more affirming of the status quo and therefore less visionary, despite her visionary intentions.

What about Mayreder? Can it be said that she shows resigned pessimism and lack of militance in her fiction as compared with her theoretical writings? One of the most striking features of her fiction is the absence of examples of a successful synthesis and emancipation from the tyranny of norms. In her imaginative texts, her synthetic vision seems to be doomed to failure. Gisa's attempt to love outside the confines of the established code of gender relations which Nelly represents founders on the sandbanks of social reality. Similarly, all attempts at synthesis are shown to come to grief in *Übergänge*, Mayreder's collection of vignettes of people in transition; society as it is is not ready for this ideal and those who represent it. Underlining this failure is a greater concern with themes which are present in Mayreder's discursive writings but which are treated there much more discreetly. Language, although seen as deceptive in Mayreder's essays when she points out the hypocrisy of terms such as 'the glories of motherhood' and 'womanly virtue', does not occupy a central place there. In some of her imaginative texts, on the other hand, language plays a pivotal role. Mayreder shows that not only does it conceal, it also divides what might be joined and is an inadequate vehicle of emotion. Likewise love plays a much larger and more significant part in her imaginative texts. In *Geschlecht und Kultur* and *Zur Kritik der Weiblichkeit* the presentation remains on a theoretical, explanatory level. The imaginative texts focus on the emotional level; there the suffering love entails is a central feature and less surrounded by the piety with which Mayreder embellishes it in her discursive texts. There is an altogether more negative view in the imaginative literature than in the discursive works. The male and female protagonists search for new forms of relationship only to fail either because the gulf in personal development is too great or because the force of social mores is too strong. It seems as if Mayreder's ideal of the synthetic personality is not made for this world.

Yet these are not the only discrepancies between the imaginative and analytical texts. The differences between the two genres are reinforced by Mayreder's use of irony, including self-irony, with regard to the ideas which characterise both. Mayreder uses irony largely by exposing the ideas' concealed and denied fantastic elements and thereby ridiculing their earnest treatment by philosophers, herself included. In the preface to *Fabeleien über göttliche und menschliche Dinge* she explains:

> To fabulate means to combine the real and the invented. Of course, then almost everything which the human intellect produces, including the image of the whole world, would be only a fable. And indeed – what were the systems of all philosophers up until now other than fables? . . . That the fables of the philosophers are meant seriously, that they, to put it in professional jargon, make claim to objective validity, does not enhance them; whoever knows a number of such ponderously serious and usually also very lengthy fables does not at the end of it all know what he is to make of the objective validity of so many unsolved contradictions.[22]

By writing fables that deal with ideas treated with a conventional seriousness in her discursive texts, Mayreder does not ridicule or contradict these ideas themselves; rather she sheds a different light on them, using them as supports in her struggle against the encroachment of reason and as confirmation of her creed of the inevitability of subjectivity, two themes vociferously expressed in the discursive works. The ideas are no longer clothed in the trappings of analytic discourse, but revealed as quite simply the 'playful inventions' they really are. Such a revelation is not intended to lead to a dismissal of all philosophy as 'mere' fiction, but to a new evaluation of the imagination and subjectivity as elements of philosophy and to philosophy's status as a playfulness to be taken to heart. The *Fabeleien* are Mayreder's very personal plea for the life of the imagination over that of the intellect and her own way of coming to terms with 'those problems which come so close to us in their awkward duality'.[23] The dualisms which are to be united in the discursive works here appear in the guise of fairytale and myth: prophets, elves, magicians, gods, the magi, Jesus-Apollo, all figure in these fantastic fables. They are taken out of the framework of analysis and psychological realism, put into an archaic dimension, and thus represent an imaginative step beyond psychological feminism. These are tales which, as Christine Touaillon pointed out, defy categorisation: 'Rosa Mayreder's "Fabeleien" lie between the genres. Is one to call them myths or legends or parables?" she asks.[24] But in them, notes Touaillon, Mayreder unites the worlds of imagination and reality. 'Rosa Mayreder does not flee from life into a distant fantasy world,' she notes. 'The world of the imagination is rather the form in which her spirit experiences reality. That is why both the spheres she presents appear to us to be one.'[25] The discrepancy to be found in Mayreder's texts is, then, not only that between optimism and pessimism, but that between reason, reality and analysis on the one hand and the imagination and invention on the other. The *Fabeleien* defy these divisions.

A discrepancy can also be seen between Meisel-Hess's imaginative literature and discursive texts. There are common central themes: the protection of mothers, the necessity for women to combine sex and intellectual life for full personal development, the justification of pre-marital sexual relations, and eugenics. Yet although not as apparently pessimistic and resigned as Mayreder's treatment of her ideal in her imaginative texts, Meisel-Hess's also leaves the reader wondering how likely the realisation of the ideal is intended to be in her fiction. Fanny Roth and Annie-Bianka may come to the insight that sex and intellect are both necessary, but the actual union remains outside the scope of the texts; the insight remains insight. Similarly Olga in *Die Intellektuellen* does not achieve the longed-for union of motherhood and intellectual life, and although Maja Hertz claims to be enjoying the ideal relationship with her lover Johannes, one through which she can find her voice, this seems to be less the ideal sexual relationship of two autonomous beings presented in Meisel-Hess's discursive texts than the traditional one of female loss of self.

What is the significance of these discrepancies? Are they really only evidence of pessimism and resignation? Or might another interpretation be possible if attention is directed towards the consciousness of the writers themselves? The widespread feminist claim to realism in fiction is a key here, for this implies that it is in the discursive and not the imaginative texts that the utopian vision which goes beyond the boundaries of the real is formulated. According to these feminists' aesthetics, the fictional framework of the novel should not be used as an opportunity to fantasise breaking out or to formulate resistance or indignation. It should not be used to create a fantasy world. On the contrary. It is reality that must stand at the centre, be exposed and used as a means of bringing change. And as involvement in the women's movement only too clearly showed, the real still imposed rigid and confining boundaries. It is not pessimism and resignation, then, that lie behind the discrepancies, but realism. And in some cases that realism may contain a stronger criticism and offer more room for optimism than any utopian fantasy.

This is true of Mayreder. Hers is a critical realism; she offers no happy endings, no easy solutions. The pictures drawn in her imaginative texts are indeed bleak, but in that bleakness lies her criticism. And although she may be resigned in the sense of offering no rousing alternative, she does not subvert that resignation into affirmation. She presents no real alternative and no role models, but also gives the reader no scope for comforting but disempowering flight. A story of failed emancipation, such as can be found in Mayreder's texts, does not necessarily mean resignation and pessimism. It could mean greater criticism by confronting the reader with reality and insisting on the need for change. For the psychological feminists this meant going one step further than the moral feminists, who remained confined to objective reality. It meant delving into the human psyche and showing how this, too, must be changed before emancipation can be achieved. This is another dimension of reality, Mayreder's work suggests, one which is archaic, which transgresses the boundaries of everyday reality to enter a realm of the intangible, the fantastic, but sometimes also the confining. Imaginative literature for these feminists is not primarily missionary work as for the moral feminists, not a question of healing or of presenting what could be, but of penetrating deeper into the human soul. What might seem escapist texts are in fact the more radical form of feminist fiction.

The discrepancies are a result of the concept of literature and its function. But they are also a result of domination by the tradition of women's romances centring on female submission, there called love. It may well have been that in order for an author to be read at all, concessions had to be made both to the female public brought up on the fare of family literature and to the male-dominated literature industry of publishers and theatre directors. Such conventions did not apply to such a great extent to women's discursive writing, as this was a new domain. There women could present a utopia free of other considerations. In addition, the two genres had a different significance for these women themselves. In accordance with the traditional values of the educated middle class, imaginative literature was regarded by Mayreder, for example, as being of a higher order; it was after all not politics but art, which for Mayreder was a form of philosophy. She was called the poet-philosopher, the *Dichterphilosophin*, a label she gladly accepted, and considered her life's work to be contained in her later imaginative texts. In her opinion, these included truths deeper than those of rational discourse, the truths of a life lived on many levels. This perhaps meant more harsh reality and failure but also more imagination, for the imagination, usually held in check by the catechist of understanding, is the path to a primeval world. This is a world in which God and the powers of yore still hold sway and one which is divorced from that so 'intolerably civilised and enlightened' world of reason and adulthood.[26] And it is in the context of this divine world that Mayreder most clearly communicates her feminist vision of synthesis in her imaginative works. Here, as in *Die Stimme*, the imagination takes over where external reality and reason are forced to come to a halt.

Modernists and Feminists

Of course these women writers were working within a heterogeneous literary context. Not only were they embedded in the tradition of innocuous women's writing taken largely from the tradition of family literature, they were also surrounded by a secession of writers and artists. Indeed, the artistic secession of Gustav Klimt and Josef Hoffmann and the secession of women, the women's movement, were at times mentioned in the same breath. Both, along with the labour movement, were out to upset the status quo. Both were part of the same unrest in the eyes of contemporaries – and to some extent also in the eyes of the feminists themselves. Fickert took up the topos of secession in her own labelling of the movement.[27] And Marie Lang was a passionate admirer of the Vienna Secession building, exulting in its provocation to the *petit bourgeois* and seeing it as a temple 'in its basic traits earnest, strict, bare and burdensome like the tasks we have to cope with', a parable not only of the women's movement but also of the joy of modern man who, like the feminists, can no longer tolerate farces and old masquerades.[28]

In their self-perception, the feminists were most definitely on the side of the new, the modern. But not necessarily on the side of those in the Viennese cultural clique who wanted to bring about change. Mayreder had little favourable to say of Karl Kraus – 'a characterless worm who nourishes himself off the leprous growths of others'[29] – and she saw Hermann Bahr as a once self-acclaimed 'free-thinking spirit' who by 1900 had landed in the haven of the most boorish, bourgeois philistinism and yet still gave himself the airs and graces of an intellectual leader.[30] Yet a distinction was made between the critic who attacked prevailing morality, and the decadent aesthete who merely languished and felt attracted, according to Meisel-Hess, not to the woman of soul, of strong and aware intellectuality, but to the *femme fatale*, the demon and the sphinx, those women 'who can most readily whip up his tired sexual energy'.[31] Not surprisingly, this enervating aestheticism clashed head-on with the feminists' robustness and reforming fervour.

What was the place of these literary feminists in the context of Viennese modernism? The modernists' characteristic tendency to focus on the self and its experience was shared by the psychological feminists and reflected in their experimentation with internal monologue and other literary techniques. For both groups, too, this hegemony of the inner over the outer life was linked to a concern with language and love, with their liability to deceive and to be deceived, and with the potential deception of perception itself. Word and referent by no means necessarily correspond for the feminists as well as for some Viennese modernists. Love is a dangerous business in which deception and self-deception play a large role. For both the modernists and psychological feminists sexual relations can be a comedy of disguise, and are the target of sharp attacks. The psychological feminists at least in many ways display characteristics of Viennese modernism.

Yet there are also significant differences. Meisel-Hess and Mayreder do not consider the self to have disintegrated, as the modernists do. For them, the self is not beyond rescue,[32] but is the director and determiner of experience. And it is this self which is the goal of personal development, the final god who has triumphed over the confines of both elemental nature and civilisation.[33] But it is above all their attitude to gender relations which is fundamentally different and the reason for the actual hostilities between the feminists and the modernists. Even if feminists like Meisel-Hess and Mayreder found themselves on the fringes of the respectable in the eyes of most other feminists, they were certainly not prepared to support the misogynist morality of many modernists who saw woman as merely a sexual being and the appendage of man.

Unlike the moral feminists, the psychological feminists do join the modernists in some respects; they may perhaps be called the feminist wing of Viennese modernism. But they are feminists before they are modernists, and visionaries before they are either: visionaries not of an apocalypse, like Kraus,[34] but of a social utopia.

CONCLUSION

The Legacy of Visionary Feminism

What did the feminists achieve in real terms? By 1914 the leaders of the General Austrian Women's Association could boast above all of the legal aid centres which had helped many impoverished and oppressed women to gain their rights, of 'Heimhof', its home for women civil servants, and of the organisation of female public employees. Other feminist groups could be proud of having launched the first girls' grammar school, having founded numerous vocational schools which certainly did much to ease the situation of a large number of women thrown back on their own resources, and of having promoted eminently practical self-help measures such as insurance and pension schemes for women in certain professions. Feminists could also point to a body of theoretical writing which supported their practical demands and to works of fiction which added new dimensions to those concerns.

Indeed, although autonomous feminism was the victim of numerous rejected or neglected petitions, internal squabbles and general political ineffectiveness, and faded almost completely from the political scene after 1918 to remain forgotten for many decades, the feminists' contribution continued to make itself felt even after the organisations had ceased to exist. In the inter-war years the Social Democrats adopted and realised many of the feminists' demands, and they were instrumental in Vienna in setting in motion a process of consciousness-raising amongst women. It was the Association which helped to pave the way for a later changed awareness of certain themes and needs: women's suffrage, the reform of regulations on prostitution and domestic service, a changed sexual morality, and above all the need for women's political education in the widest sense.

Yet judged in other terms, the feminists left an even more significant legacy in their attempt to overcome the barriers erected between the public and the private, the political and the spiritual. Politics was for them a matter of the emotions, the intellect and the imagination, as well as practical public involvement. It was an aspect of life which touched all others. And it was an aspect which inspired them with a spiritual fervour and was itself inspired by a vision. The feminists sought not only piecemeal reforms but fundamental change in the individual, in the relations of individuals to each other, and in the relations of the individual to the forces of nature. Although each leading feminist left her own personal stamp on the vision – for Fickert it meant above all the abolition of relations of exploitation, for Mayreder the emancipation of the individual from certain internal and external constraints, for Meisel-Hess physical and psychic health, for Troll-Borostyáni a more rational life – for all it meant personal growth and an affirmative attitude to life. These feminists saw precisely what many feminists today see: that feminism is not only about external reforms. And it is that similarity which makes a study of early Viennese feminism particularly rewarding and gives it a significance beyond the local and the historical. For we can see how these women attempted on all levels of experience to combine practical politics with a vision and to bring about changes which are today as pressing as ever, to ask why they in the last resort failed and what can be learnt from that failure. Such a study can help us to a greater clarity of insight. Many of the criticisms that might be levelled against aspects of the early feminist vision – the faith in the natural for example – might be levelled against some feminists today. And it also makes clearer what has changed, not only in external conditions but also in attitudes. So, for example, basic themes dealt with in the early feminists' theoretical texts – the relationship between nature and culture, body and psyche in the making of the feminine – still dominate current feminist theoretical debate. Yet the perhaps naively clear-cut beliefs and remedies of Meisel-Hess and Troll-Borostyáni have vanished. Uncertainties and yet more questions have taken their place. The subject seems to be inexhaustible. Likewise, the ideal of romantic love shared by many early feminists, their widespread assumption of heterosexuality and their acceptance of hierarchical structures in their organisations are today questioned, and alternatives to them sought. The early feminists' openness to certain authors is not shared by modern feminists. Nietzsche, Schiller, regarded as model misogynists, and to a lesser extent Goethe and Wagner figure on the current blacklist of feminist reading. Yet the first generation of feminists were open to aspects of these writers' remarks on women which are often not fully appreciated in the sometimes ahistorical readings of feminists today. The misogyny which bursts from some of Nietzsche's assertions and the insipid ideology of the dutiful mother and housewife which informs Schiller's 'Das Lied der Glocke' were perceived and rejected by this first generation of feminists, but not at the expense of other ideas to be found in these authors' writings that could very well be used for feminist purposes.

Read against the background of these women's historical situation, Nietzsche and Schiller could easily be regarded as propagators of the emancipation of humanity, which for the feminists at least included women. And the fact that the early feminists could draw on such writers to support their own ideologies in no way implies their support for the ideologies, in particular National Socialism, which later appropriated these writers. It was not in their choice of ideological support that these women went wrong.

So where did they go wrong? One possible answer might be that the union of the two levels of politics and the visionary which they attempted must necessarily fail. If real gains are to be made, the daily fray of politics might demand a hard-nosed realism which is absent in utopian visions such as those of the feminists. Perhaps it is indeed as Mayreder herself analysed, that every social movement, including feminism, must pass through the phase of pure idealism and enter that of pragmatic concessions if it is to make any mark on the world.[1] Clutching hold of a vision, according to this view, obstructs political effectiveness, although, according to another, utopianism might well be seen as a leading motive of practical political action. However, neither viewpoint explains why the changes which these feminists themselves achieved, or which have been achieved since, for example the acceptance of pre-marital sexual relations, have failed to bring about the deeper changes the feminists envisaged. Perhaps the failure of the vision lies not in any *a priori* incompatibility of political feminism and visionary feminism, but in a flaw in the vision itself and the attitudes which gave rise to it. One blind spot can possibly be found in these feminists' reluctance to investigate more closely the relationship between the psyche, the family and sexual politics. Instead, ethics, and above all sexual morality, became the central emancipatory concerns. The ideal of the nuclear family and the position of the mother in it went largely unquestioned as did the family's role as the psychological basis of much that the feminists criticised, particularly oppressive gender relations. In addition, most did not sufficiently appreciate the extent to which changes in men were necessary if their vision was to be realised. Mayreder came closest, claiming that only when men had changed as a result of cultural evolution would women have the chance of influencing that cultural development outside the family and of working against a one-sidedly masculine culture.[2] Her trust in natural evolution, however, blinded her – and others – to the great extent to which most men are bound, largely through capitalism, in the systems of values the feminists wished to see abolished or at least modified. They failed to appreciate enough the force and fear of the power hierarchy between men, and so underestimated the tenacity of the opposition and the reluctance of men to change.

Yet on a different level the early Austrian feminists also left a significant legacy by unsettling a number of often uncritically accepted notions concerning early feminism. One of the most widespread is that the early women's movement in Austria can be sharply divided into the middle-class movement on the one hand and the socialist on the other. According to this view the middle-class movement agitated for equal rights while the socialist movement campaigned for the emancipation of humanity as a whole. This in turn implies a difference in relations to men. Middle-class feminists 'limited themselves to the demand for equality with men.... They do not articulate any further-reaching goals concerning society or state policy for example. The proletarian women on the other hand see the realisation of their demands as lying in the transcendence of the social system alone and that can be achieved only through solidarity with the male workers, who are just as unfree.'[3] Such an apparent difference leads to the third claim that the Austrian middle-class women's movement was largely 'apolitical, small and limited in influence'.[4] These three seeming differences combine to create the impression that the two movements were quite incapable of mutual understanding; as one commentator asserts:

> Here too [in Austria] the interests of the two women's movements developed in such different directions that it would put it too mildly to talk of a conflict. There were not even conflicts – there was absolutely no common theme to discuss.... It was therefore hardly surprising that the bourgeois women's associations in Austria as well as in Germany regularly and emphatically dissociated themselves from every strike and every other political action of the proletarian women.[5]

An investigation of Viennese visionary feminism reveals that this divide was not as great as is supposed. First, the vision that dominated the Association's actions was never restricted to equal rights but was intensely concerned with human emancipation. Secondly, men were welcome assistants in women's struggle for self-determination and personal development; a simplistic division according to gender does not apply. Thirdly, the visionary feminists were certainly not apolitical. The leaders of the Association were very much concerned with relations of power rather than with political parties, and stressed the centrality of politics to human organisation and community. Raising women to political consciousness (and not a party political one) was the main goal of the Association. And fourthly, the alleged estrangement is certainly grossly exaggerated; some leading members of the Association sided with the proletarian women on a number of important issues, and there were many common themes to discuss. When seen in this light a more accurate labelling is called for. The restrictive label of 'middle-class' feminism could be replaced by 'autonomous'. The connotations of class struggle, which are to a large extent inappropriate to the Viennese movement, would then be avoided and the criterion of adherence to a political party made decisive, a shift of emphasis which more accurately reflects the reality of the Viennese case.

A study of visionary aspects of Viennese feminism also unsettles the notion that the autonomous feminists themselves can be divided into radicals and moderates.[6] The former, it is often claimed, were mainly concerned with legal equality and suffrage; indeed, radicalism is often equated with the demand for political and legal equality.[7] The latter supposedly espoused an ideology of cultural feminism, based in many cases on woman's motherly qualities. Viennese feminism indicates that this was not always true. Equal rights were wanted by all, but were not the ultimate goal for any. They were the means to other, wider-ranging cultural aims. But for the feminists centred around the General Austrian Women's Association, who were regarded both then and now as the radicals, the aim was not the widespread vision of social motherhood. Instead they sought a social order which would not alienate its members from themselves or each other, and which would do away with traditional relations of power and exploitation. In this way society could contribute to the natural evolution of humanity's development to a higher moral and intellectual level. The demand for equal rights cannot be taken as the sole measure of the radicalism of feminism. Indeed, as a study such as this one also shows, ideas which by modern standards are usually regarded as conservative if not reactionary, such as eugenics, an emphasis on strict moral norms and a cult of marriage and the family, could be used for radical purposes or at least connected with more radical ideas. The picture of early Viennese feminism which emerges from such a study is coloured in various shades of grey, rather than high-contrast black and white.

In addition, such an investigation contributes to a redrawing of the conventional picture of Vienna in 1900. Vienna at the end of the nineteenth century was not only the city of the joyful apocalypse, of apolitical decadence and the Oedipal rebellion of the sons against the fathers. There was in fact a flourishing culture of political opposition in which men and women worked together for a vision of a society which would not dehumanise its members but permit them to go '"in purity"' through life, 'that means without concealment and without regret'.[8] Social reform groups abounded – the monists, the pacifists, the Ethical Society, Social Politicians – and also of course the General Austrian Women's Association which acted as an important focus for female protest in particular. All these groups were fired by the conviction that the new age was coming and by the belief in the possibility of the intellectual and ethical development of the human race to freedom and love through self-awareness and inner growth. These were optimists and visionaries who represented an alternative culture to the status quo and for whom the realisation of that alternative took on the character of a quasi-religious mission. Central to this alternative culture was the feminist vision of a humanity redeemed and a Paradise regained. 'In an age deserted by God the religious need searches for expression in many different ways,' Mayreder commented.[9] The feminist vision was the form of expression of this religious need chosen by a number of women in Vienna around 1900, women inspired by the consciousness of being called to fulfil a duty, that of the work of salvation, 'the goal of all religious striving',[10] which would lead to a new age free of misery and violence.

Notes

References to published material are given in the form: author's surname, date of publication, title (where necessary), page number. A full bibliography is to be found on p. 282. Unless otherwise stated, all unpublished material is kept at the Manuscripts Department, Vienna City Library and identified here by the call mark.

All translations quoted in the text are my own.

Introduction

1. Anon., 1901f, 242.
2. See Wunberg, 1976, Vol. I, 211. See also Le Rider, 1985.
3. Liebenfels, 1911a, 1.
4. Liebenfels, 1909, 3.
5. Gruber, 1910, 3–4.
6. Hauer, 1906, 9.
7. Ibid.
8. Ibid., 10.
9. See Karl Kraus, 1906, 27–8.
10. Hauer, 1906, 6–7.
11. See Dallago, 1913.
12. Weininger, 1980, 80.
13. Ibid.
14. See ibid., 87.
15. Ibid., 447.
16. Krafft-Ebing, 1907, 297.
17. Weininger, 1980, 79.
18. Nigg, 1895, 81.
19. Ibid.
20. Ibid., 82.
21. See Engelbrecht, 1986, 279.
22. See Anon., 1897, 10.
23. See Ander, 1900.
24. Schreiber, 1893, 21.
25. See Stoerck, 1898, 394.
26. Grünwald-Zerkowitz, 1902, 9.
27. Ibid., 7.

28. See Katscher, n.d.
29. Bauer, 1894, 113.
30. See Grünwald-Zerkowitz, 1905, 13.
31. Schnitzler, 1981, 205.
32. See Verein für erweiterte Frauenbildung in Wien, 1889–1904, *2. Jahresbericht* (1890), 11.
33. See Mayreder, 1899**b**.
34. See Grünwald-Zerkowitz, 1905, 56–63.
35. Marriot, 1903, 2–3.
36. See Crepaz, 1892.
37. See Asenijeff, 1898, 6.
38. See Wiesengrün, 1897.
39. Hruschka, 1892, 39.
40. Grabscheidt, 1894, 34.
41. See Bahr, 1912, 120.
42. Bettelheim-Gabillon, 1907, 107.
43. See Bahr, 1911.
44. For further discussion of this terminology see Evans, 1986.
45. See Leichter, 1973, 376.
46. 'Wohin die Frauenbewegung führt', unpublished manuscript, Auguste-Fickert-Nachlass, I.N. 71148/57.
47. Allgemeiner Österreichischer Frauenverein, 1895, *3. Jahresbericht*, 6–7.
48. Allgemeiner Österreichischer Frauenverein, 1897, *Zur Geschichte einer Petition*, 13.
49. Fickert, 1898, 43.
50. Allgemeiner Österreichischer Frauenverein, 1893, *Stenographisches Protokoll*, 13.
51. Allgemeiner Österreichischer Frauenverein, 1893, *1. Jahresbericht*, 4.
52. 'Wohin die Frauenbewegung führt', unpublished manuscript, Auguste-Fickert-Nachlass, I.N. 71148/57.
53. Allgemeiner Österreichischer Frauenverein, 1893, *Stenographisches Protokoll*, 14.
54. Fickert, 1898, 42 and 43.
55. Allgemeiner Österreichischer Frauenverein, 1901, *8. Jahresbericht*, 2.
56. Fickert, 1898, 43.
57. Fickert, 1903**a**, 2.
58. 'Brief aus Wien an Frl. Friberg', unpublished manuscript, Auguste-Fickert-Nachlass, I.N. 71138/37.
59. 'Brief aus Wien', unpublished manuscript, ibid., I.N. 71148/38.
60. Fickert, 1896**b**, 58.
61. Allgemeiner Österreichischer Frauenverein, 1895, *3. Jahresbericht*, 7.
62. Fickert, 1898, 43.
63. See Hruschka, 1892, 39.
64. See Anon., 1901**c**, 65.
65. Ibid.
66. Hainisch, 1911**b**, 2.
67. Anon., 1914, 7.
68. Hainisch, 1892, 23.
69. Hainisch, 1896, 18–19.
70. Hainisch, 1911**a**, 26.
71. Hainisch, 1875, 24.
72. Ibid., 26.
73. See Hainisch, 1896, 3.
74. Ibid., 15.

75. E.N., 1892, 5.
76. Unpublished letter to Auguste Fickert, 8 February 1896, I.N. 70890/4. See also Anderson, 1990**b**.
77. 'Was will, was soll die Secession der Frauen?', unpublished manuscript, Auguste-Fickert-Nachlass, I.N. 71148/50.
78. See Belke, 1978.
79. Mach, 1910, 355.
80. Jodl, 1895, 4.
81. Bahr, 1912, 124.
82. Liebenfels, 1911**a**, 13.
83. Wittels, 1908, 12.
84. See Verein für erweiterte Frauenbildung in Wien, 1889–1904, *12. Jahresbericht* (1900), 18 and 19.
85. Cited in Fellner, 1986, 103.
86. See Verein für erweiterte Frauenbildung in Wien, 1889–1904, *11. Jahresbericht* (1899), 11.
87. See Brühl, 1895, 144.
88. See Ofner, 1915.
89. See Anon., 1901**a**, 6.
90. Unpublished letter to Auguste Fickert, 20 April 1895, I.N. 70889/12.
91. See Kulturpolitische Gesellschaft, 1905; Boyer, 1978.
92. See Börner, 1910, 10.
93. See Ethische Gesellschaft in Wien, 1897; Fout, 1986.
94. See Fickert, 1896**a**; Holleis, 1978.
95. See Anon., 1900**d**, 529.
96. Anon., 1901**f**, 243.
97. See Evans, 1977, 91.

Part One: Autonomous Women and Visionary Politics
Chapter 1: The First Wave

1. Urban, 1930, 25.
2. Ibid.
3. Hainisch, 1892, 24–5.
4. See Urban, 1930, 26.
5. See Wiener Frauenerwerbverein, 1987, 2.
6. See Urban, 1930, 36.
7. Mayreder, 1948, 195. See also Murau, 1895; Storch, 1989.
8. See Anon., 1906, 8; see also Schölermann, 1899**a**.
9. See Anon., 1898**c**, 4.
10. See Anscombe, 1984, 100.
11. Theimer, 1909, 249.
12. See Bund Österreichischer Frauenvereine, 1912.
13. Hainisch, 1870, 4.
14. Hainisch, 'Lebensgeschichte, Erinnerungen aus meinem Leben', 19, unpublished typescript in the private possession of Dr Marianne Hainisch and Dr Cornelia Hainisch.
15. See Petition der Wiener Frauenvereine, 1890, 174–6.
16. Verein für erweiterte Frauenbildung in Wien, 1889–1904, *16. Jahresbericht* (1904), 7.

17. Ibid., 18.
18. See ibid., *7. Jahresbericht* (1895), 25.
19. See Anon., 1900**e**.
20. See Verein für erweiterte Frauenbildung in Wien, 1889–1904, *12. Jahresbericht* (1900), 29.
21. Ibid., *16. Jahresbericht* (1904), 18.
22. Ibid., *2. Jahresbericht* (1890), 22; *13. Jahresbericht* (1901), 38.
23. Ibid., *13. Jahresbericht* (1901), 26.
24. See Engelbrecht, 1986, 284.
25. See ibid.
26. See Hainisch, 1901**c**, 174.
27. Anon., 1900**h**.
28. Anon., 1891, 239.
29. See Hainisch, 1870, 8.
30. See Verein für erweiterte Frauenbildung in Wien, 1889–1904, *16. Jahresbericht* (1904), 6.
31. See ibid., 5.
32. Petition der Wiener Frauenvereine, 1890, 175.
33. See Verein für erweiterte Frauenbildung in Wien, 1889–1904, *16. Jahresbericht* (1904), 6.
34. Ibid., *4. Jahresbericht* (1892), 5.
35. Ibid., *16. Jahresbericht* (1904), 6.
36. Ibid.
37. See Heindl and Tichy, 1990; Heindl, 1990.
38. See Bernatzik, 1900.
39. Helene Migerka, 1900, 1.
40. See Verein für erweiterte Frauenbildung in Wien, 1889–1904, *3. Jahresbericht* (1891), 17–34.
41. Spitzer, 1899, 339.
42. See Brühl, 1892.
43. See Verein für erweiterte Frauenbildung in Wien, 1889–1904, *9. Jahresbericht* (1897), 33–41.
44. Ibid., *15. Jahresbericht* (1903), 43–51.
45. Ibid., *16. Jahresbericht* (1904), 58.
46. Ibid., *10. Jahresbericht* (1898), 7.
47. See Anon., 1901**b**, 59.
48. See Urban, 1930.
49. See Anon., 1887, 1.
50. See ibid., 1–2.
51. See Fickert, 1902**b**, 183.
52. See Eine Lehrerin, 1901.
53. See Minor, 1914.
54. See Anon., 1889**a**; Anon., 1889**b**.
55. See Anon., 1898**b**.
56. Wendt *et al.*, 1889, 1.
57. Eine gute Collegin, 1889, 24–7.
58. See Czescher *et al.*, 1901; Vereinigung der arbeitenden Frauen, 1903.
59. See Vereinigung der arbeitenden Frauen, 1904, 7.
60. See Schmid-Bortenschlager, 1984.
61. Wendt, 1891, 248.
62. See Anon., 1898**a**, 2.
63. See Sigmund Kraus, 1901.

Chapter 2: Personal Politics. The General Austrian Women's Association

1. Allgemeiner Österreichischer Frauenverein, 1895–1901, *2. Jahresbericht* (1894), 7.
2. Ibid.
3. See Allgemeiner Österreichischer Frauenverein, 1894**b**, 6–7.
4. See Protokoll, 1891, 5.
5. See Turnau, 1892, 3.
6. See Protokoll, 1891, 20.
7. See Fickert, 1892**b**, 88.
8. See Kofler, 1892, 4.
9. See Anon., 1892, 59.
10. See Allgemeiner Österreichischer Frauenverein, 1893**c**, 7.
11. See ibid., 8.
12. See ibid., 11–12.
13. Ibid., 12.
14. See Allgemeiner Österreichischer Frauenverein, 1893, *1. Jahresbericht*, 11–14.
15. See Allgemeiner Österreichischer Frauenverein, 1895–1901, *7. Jahresbericht* (1900), 12–20.
16. See Anon., 1899**d**, 1.
17. See Anon., 1896**c**, 7 and 8.
18. Allgemeiner Österreichischer Frauenverein, 1895–1901, *3. Jahresbericht* (1895), 6.
19. See Allgemeiner Österreichischer Frauenverein, 1897, 6.
20. See unpublished letter from Therese Schlesinger-Eckstein to Auguste Fickert, 30 August 1897, I.N. 71018/3.
21. See unpublished letter from Rosa Mayreder to Auguste Fickert, 27 December 1898, I.N. 70890/15; for details of the *Dokumente* see Svoboda, 1989.
22. See Anon., 1899**c**.
23. See Emma Eckstein, 1899**a**, 195.
24. See unpublished letter from Therese Schlesinger-Eckstein to Auguste Fickert, 9 March 1899, I.N. 71018/8.
25. Schlesinger-Eckstein, 1902**b**, 544.
26. Fickert *et al.*, 1899, Vorwort der Herausgeberinnen, 4.
27. Lang, 1897–8, 940.
28. See Sparholz, 1986, 68.
29. Unpublished letter from Rosa Mayreder to Auguste Fickert, 9 January 1899, I.N. 70891/1.
30. See unpublished letter from Rosa Mayreder to Auguste Fickert, 21 July 1899, I.N. 70891/9.
31. See unpublished letter from Rosa Mayreder to Auguste Fickert, 25 July 1899, I.N. 70891/10.
32. Allgemeiner Österreichischer Frauenverein, 1895–1901, *7. Jahresbericht* (1900), 2.
33. See unpublished letter from Rosa Mayreder to Auguste Fickert, 29 July 1899, I.N. 70891/11.
34. Unpublished letter from Marie Lang to Auguste Fickert, 20 December 1898, I.N. 152.908, punctuation as in the original.
35. See Lang, 1930, 4.
36. Unpublished letter from Marie Lang to Rosa Mayreder, 14 August 1899, in the private possession of Martin Lang.
37. Mayreder, 1988**a**, 177.
38. Schlesinger-Eckstein, 1928, 118.

39. Lissauer, 1928, 114.
40. Jászi, 1928, 34.
41. Mayreder, 1988**a**, 177.
42. See Sparholz, 1986, 22.
43. Unpublished letter from Marie Lang to Rosa Mayreder, 29 July 1897, in the private possession of Martin Lang.
44. Mayreder, 1988**a**, 177.
45. Mayreder, 1988**b**, 283.
46. See Sparholz, 1986, 69–71.
47. See unpublished letter from Therese Schlesinger-Eckstein to Auguste Fickert, 1 March 1900, I.N. 71019/1.
48. See unpublished letter from Therese Schlesinger-Eckstein to Auguste Fickert, 5 March 1900, I.N. 71019/2.
49. See unpublished letter from Aristides Brežina to Auguste Fickert, 28 January 1902, I.N. 69904.
50. Fickert, 1902**a**.
51. Fickert *et al.*, 1899, 1.
52. Touaillon, 1918**b**, 78.
53. Unpublished letter from Rosa Mayreder to Auguste Fickert, 18 December 1893, I.N. 70889/1.
54. Unpublished letter from Rosa Mayreder to Auguste Fickert, 29 May 1894, I.N. 70889/5.
55. See unpublished letter from Rosa Mayreder to Auguste Fickert, 3 October 1895, I.N. 70889/10.
56. See unpublished letter from Rosa Mayreder to Auguste Fickert, 15 October 1895, I.N. 70889/13.
57. See unpublished letter from Rosa Mayreder to Auguste Fickert, 26 June 1902, I.N. 70894/8.
58. Unpublished letter from Rosa Mayreder to Auguste Fickert, 8 May 1902, I.N. 70894/7.
59. See unpublished letter from Rosa Mayreder to Auguste Fickert, 1 February 1903, I.N. 70895/1.
60. See unpublished letter from Rosa Mayreder to Auguste Fickert, 24 January 1908, I.N. 70896/7.
61. Unpublished letter from Rosa Mayreder to Auguste Fickert, 27 February 1907, I.N. 70896/1.
62. Unpublished letter from Rosa Mayreder to Auguste Fickert, 21 May 1894, I.N. 70889/4.
63. See ibid.
64. Unpublished letter from Rosa Mayreder to Auguste Fickert, 22 March 1894, I.N. 70889/3.
65. See unpublished letter from Rosa Mayreder to Auguste Fickert, 8 February 1896, I.N. 70890/4.
66. Unpublished letter from Rosa Mayreder to Auguste Fickert, 25 November 1896, I.N. 70890/5.
67. Fickert's diary forms part of the Auguste-Fickert-Nachlass, I.N. 70494.
68. 'Ahnungen', unpublished manuscript, Auguste-Fickert-Nachlass, I.N. 71148/17.
69. Ibid.
70. See Mayreder, 1929, 5.
71. Mayreder, 1988**a**, 17.
72. See ibid., 77.
73. See Lang, 1930.
74. Friedrich Eckstein, 1935, 9.

75. See Blavatsky, 1968, 39.
76. See Sparholz, 1986, 14.
77. Reich, 1928, 116.
78. Ibid.
79. Mayreder, 1988**a**, 185.
80. Kulka, 1910**a**, 206.
81. For details see McKittrick, 1987.
82. See Gerber, 1910, 211.
83. Mayreder, 1988**a**, 185.
84. See ibid.
85. See Baumann, 1913, 199.
86. See ibid., 192–200.
87. Mayreder, 1988**a**, 77.
88. Ibid., 70.
89. See Friedrich Eckstein, 1936, 20; See also Mulot-Déri, 1987.
90. See Friedrich Eckstein, 1936, 18–20.
91. Ibid., 15.
92. See Lang, 1930.
93. Tichy, 1989, 137.
94. See Mayreder, 1930.
95. See Lang, 1930.
96. See Tichy, 1989, 138.
97. Friedrich Eckstein, 1928, 102.

Chapter 3: Practical Politics. The Activities of the General Austrian Women's Association

1. See Allgemeiner Österreichischer Frauenverein, 1895–1901, *2. Jahresbericht* (1894), 8.
2. Mayreder, 1900**a**, 548.
3. Fickert, 1893, 6.
4. See Zuckerkandl, 1899.
5. Unpublished letter from Flora Carnegie to Auguste Fickert, no date, I.N. 112.347, English in the original.
6. Unpublished letter from Rosa Mayreder to Auguste Fickert, 27 June 1901, I.N. 70893/5.
7. Emma Eckstein, 1899**b**, 514.
8. See ibid., 515.
9. See Jodl, 1899.
10. See Hoffmann, 1900.
11. In Anon., 1893, 8.
12. Mayreder in Anon., 1894**c**.
13. Lang, 1903, 17.
14. See Kulka, 1904.
15. See Albert, 1895, 34.
16. See Anon., 1895**a**, 7.
17. See Ehrlich, 1895; Hainisch, 1896; Hannak, 1895; Kronfeld, 1895.
18. See Allgemeiner Österreichischer Frauenverein, 1895**b**.
19. See Festausschuss, 1927, 27.
20. See Anon., 1900**g**.
21. See Avicenna, 1907.

22. See Nunberg and Federn, 1962, 195–201.
23. See Anon., 1904.
24. Leichter, 1973, 373.
25. Unpublished letter from Rosa Mayreder to Auguste Fickert, 20 April 1895, I.N. 70889/12.
26. Kulka, 1908, 195.
27. See Kulka, 1910**c**.
28. See Schapire-Neurath, 1910 and 1908.
29. See Theodor Hertzka, 1896, 115; Neubacher, 1987.
30. See Fickert, 1892**a**.
31. See Hasse, 1900.
32. Schapire-Neurath, 1908, 4.
33. O.M., 1914, 113.
34. See Dora Teleky, 1914, 134.
35. See Meisel-Hess, 1901**c**.
36. See Mayreder, 1912**b**.
37. See Pollak, 1905.
38. Meisel-Hess, 1901**c**, 628.
39. Rosenthal, 1912, 135.
40. See Dora Teleky, 1914.
41. See Winter, 1901.
42. Ibid., 730–1.
43. See Key, 1899.
44. See Waldkampf, 1907.
45. See Heindl, 1981**b**.
46. See ibid., 146.
47. See Schrank, 1899, 48.
48. See Mayreder, 1988**b**, 72 and 301.
49. For details see Grün, 1907; Kocmata, 1925; Montane, 1925; Schrank, 1886, 1899, 1904.
50. See Allgemeiner Österreichischer Frauenverein, 1897, 44–5.
51. See Mayreder, 1898.
52. See Löwy, 1905.
53. See unpublished letter from Flora Carnegie to Auguste Fickert, 12 April 1894, I.N. 112.326.
54. See Anon., 1894**b**.
55. See Allgemeiner Österreichischer Frauenverein, 1897, 47.
56. Ibid., 6.
57. See Anon., 1901**e**, 767.
58. See ibid.
59. See Anon., 1901**d**.
60. See Anon., 1901**e**, 771.
61. See Anon., 1907**b**.
62. See Mayreder, 1906.
63. Schrank, 1899, vii.
64. See Winter, 1900, 585.
65. For details see Tichy, 1984, 24–58.
66. Allgemeiner Österreichischer Frauenverein, 1895**a**, 2.
67. See Anon., 1902**e**.
68. See Ofner, 1900**b**.
69. Schlesinger-Eckstein, 1900, 594.
70. Schmidt-Friese, 1900, 569–70.
71. See Gisela Teleky, 1900.

72. Allgemeiner Österreichischer Frauenverein, 1895–1901, *3. Jahresbericht* (1895), 4.
73. See ibid., 9.
74. See Appelt, 1985, 52.
75. For details see Moll and Pivl, 1903; Nawiasky, 1902; Schaufler, 1930.
76. See Anon., 1900**a**.
77. Blazeg, 1918, 72.
78. See Ofner *et al.*, 1901.
79. See Ipold, 1904, 1.
80. See Blazeg, 1918, 74.
81. See Ipold, 1904, 3.
82. See Fickert *et al.*, 1909; Bau- und Wohnungsgenossenschaft 'Heimhof', 1909.
83. See Kulka, 1911**a**, 295.
84. Ibid., 296.
85. See Kulka, 1911**b**.
86. See ibid.
87. See Kulka, 1914**b**, 167.
88. See Werner, 1906.
89. See Loos, 1902.
90. Spiegel, 1900, 727.
91. See Allgemeiner Österreichischer Frauenverein, 1894**b**, 5.
92. See ibid., 11.
93. See ibid., 15.
94. See Anon., 1896**a**, 9.
95. See Fickert and von Filek, 1907**a**.
96. See Anon., 1907**c**.
97. See Anon., 1913**b**.
98. Fickert and von Filek, 1907**b**, 7.
99. See A.G., 1901, 13.
100. See Glöckel, 1901.
101. Die antiklerikalen Frauen von Wien, 1902.
102. Fickert, 1910, 112.
103. See Steinkellner, 1985, for details of the Catholic women's movement.
104. See Kulka, 1910**b**, 1914**a**.
105. Kulka, 1910**b**, 151.
106. Fickert, 1899, 60.
107. Fickert, 1896**a**.
108. Ibid.
109. See Schlesinger-Eckstein, 1898.
110. Brief aus Wien an Frl. Friberg (no date), unpublished manuscript, Auguste-Fickert-Nachlass, I.N. 71148/37.
111. See unpublished letter from August Bebel to Auguste Fickert, 22 April 1889, I.N. 69831.
112. See Kulka, 1910**d**.
113. Allgemeiner Österreichischer Frauenverein, 1895–1901, *8. Jahresbericht* (1900), 2.
114. Fickert, 1897.
115. See Allgemeiner Österreichischer Frauenverein, 1893**a**.
116. Unpublished letter from Minna Kautsky to Auguste Fickert, 26 February 1896, I.N. 70803/9.
117. See Anon., 1896**c**, 7.
118. See unpublished letter from Therese Schlesinger-Eckstein to Auguste Fickert, 27 October 1896, I.N. 71018/1.

119. Unpublished letter from Therese Schlesinger-Eckstein to Auguste Fickert, 30 August 1897, I.N. 71018/3.
120. Fickert, 1897.
121. See unpublished letter from Therese Schlesinger-Eckstein to Auguste Fickert, 24 November 1897, I.N. 71018/4.
122. See unpublished letter from Therese Schlesinger-Eckstein to Auguste Fickert, 23 September 1899, I.N. 71018/10.
123. Letter from Therese Schlesinger-Eckstein to Karl Kautsky, 10 February 1898, cited in Tichy, 1989, 146.
124. See Anon., 1896**b**, 6.
125. Unpublished letter from Rosa Mayreder to Auguste Fickert, 19 December 1894, I.N. 70889/7.
126. Unpublished letter from Rosa Mayreder to Auguste Fickert, 5 June 1901, I.N. 70893/3.
127. Unpublished letter from Rosa Mayreder to Auguste Fickert, 25 June 1901, I.N. 70893/4.
128. Glass 1896, 3.
129. See ibid.
130. Allgemeiner Österreichischer Frauenverein, 1894**a**, 8.

Chapter 4: Equal but Different. The League of Austrian Women's Associations

1. Hainisch, 1930, 20.
2. See ibid., 21.
3. Anon., 1902**c**, 3.
4. See ibid.
5. Hainisch, 1905, 2.
6. See Anon., 1914, 9.
7. Ibid., 7.
8. See Hainisch, 1905, 2.
9. Anon., 1914, 7.
10. Herzfelder, 1907, 38.
11. Ibid., 36.
12. See Bund Österreichischer Frauenvereine, 1907, 7.
13. Ibid., 8.
14. Ibid., 7–8.
15. Anon., 1908, 5.
16. See Hainisch, 1912.
17. See Herzfelder, 1909**a**, 15.
18. See Herzfelder, 1910, 9.
19. See H.H., 1910, 6.
20. Hainisch, 1906**a**, 9–10.
21. See Robert Scheu, 1898.
22. See Hainisch, 1908.
23. See Hainisch, 1906**b**; Hainisch, 1904.
24. See Urban, 1915; Scheu-Riess, 1919.
25. See Bund Oesterreichischer Frauenvereine, 1910, 4–5.
26. Hackl, 1908, 7.
27. Urban, 1910, 5.

28. Ibid.
29. See Heindl, 1981**b**, 144–5; 1981**a**.
30. Herzfelder, 1906, 1.
31. Lonyay, 1909, 258.
32. See Herzfelder, 1909**b**.
33. See Nora, 1910.
34. Anon., 1912.
35. See Anon., 1910, 7.
36. See Hainisch, 1910, 4.
37. Ibid., 4.
38. Unpublished letter from Rosa Mayreder to Auguste Fickert, 3 May 1902, I.N. 70894/5.
39. See Anon., 1898**d**.
40. Fickert, 1906**b**, 3–5.
41. See Mossler, 1906, 24.
42. Unpublished letter from Rosa Mayreder to Auguste Fickert, 3 May 1902, I.N. 70894/5.
43. See unpublished letter from Rosa Mayreder to Auguste Fickert, 8 May 1902, I.N. 70894/7.
44. Unpublished letter from Rosa Mayreder to Auguste Fickert, 26 June 1902, I.N. 70894/8.
45. See Anon., 1902**a**, 19.
46. Fickert, 1903**b**, 20.
47. Ibid.
48. See Die Redaktion, 1906.
49. See Mossler, 1906.
50. See Franzos *et al.*, 1906.

Chapter 5: The Feminist Fringe

1. See Else Federn, 1935, 18.
2. See ibid.
3. See Anon., 1902**d**, 116.
4. Ibid.
5. Schölermann, 1899**b**, 352.
6. Else Federn, 1930, 93.
7. Else Federn, 1901, 604.
8. For details of the schools see Schwarzwald, 1902–13; Göllner, 1986.
9. See Rukschcio and Schachel, 1982, 505.
10. See Schwarzwald, 1902–13, *11. Jahresbericht* (1913), 3–18.
11. See Deichmann and Worbs, 1984.
12. See Kokoschka, 1971, 122.
13. See Rukschcio and Schachel, 1982, 191.
14. See Wellesz, 1981, 49.
15. See Schwarzwald, 1902–13, *11. Jahresbericht* (1913), 9.
16. See Herdan-Zuckmayer, 1979, 125.
17. See Schwarzwald, 1928, 121.
18. See Schwarzwald, 1902–13, *11. Jahresbericht* (1913), 10.
19. See ibid., 8.
20. See ibid., 3.

21. See ibid., 5.
22. See ibid., 25–6.
23. See Schwarzwald, 1902–13, *10. Jahresbericht* (1912), 33–45.
24. See ibid., *6. Jahresbericht* (1908), 3–38.
25. Ibid., *5. Jahresbericht* (1907), 25.
26. See ibid., *9. Jahresbericht* (1911), 4.
27. See ibid., *11. Jahresbericht* (1913), 27–39.
28. Musil, 1976, Vol. I, 631.
29. See Stefan, 1922, 15.
30. See Scheu, 1985, 49–50.
31. See Urban, 1930, 45.
32. Unpublished letter from Rosa Mayreder to Auguste Fickert, 5 June 1901, I.N. 70893/3.
33. Kassowitz, 1902, 217.
34. Ibid., 219.
35. See Klein, 1903, 33.
36. See Zuckerkandl, 1901**a**, 1901**b**.
37. See Klein, 1903, 10.
38. Letter from Auguste Fickert to Bertha von Suttner, 20 October 1891, cited in Hamann, 1986, 453. See also Hamann, 1990.
39. Letter from Bertha von Suttner to Marianne Hainisch, 14 March 1907, cited in Hamann, 1986, 454.
40. Suttner, 1912, 706.
41. See Anon., 1907**a**.
42. See Anon., February 1907**d**.
43. See Urban, 1930, 51.
44. See Waldkampf, 1911, 327–8.
45. See Anon., 1900**b**.
46. See Meisel-Hess, 1900, 542.
47. See Das Comité zur Begründung eines Frauenclubs, 1900, 70.
48. See Rukschcio and Schachel, 1982, 35–6.
49. See Anon., 1900**c**, 4.
50. Meisel-Hess, 1900, 541.
51. Ibid.
52. See Rukschcio and Schachel, 1982, 72.
53. See Anon., 1902**b**, 272.
54. For details of the women's suffrage campaign see Fürth, 1930.
55. See Minor, 1912.
56. See Anon., 1911.
57. See Österreichisches Frauenstimmrechtskomitee, 1913.
58. See Anon., 1913**a**, 1.
59. See Österreichisches Frauenstimmrechtskomitee, 1913, 7.

Chapter 6: Coda: 1914–18

1. See Herzfelder, 1914, 2.
2. Holm, 1910**b**, 2.
3. Ibid., 3.
4. See Paul Federn, 1919.
5. Roth, 1976, 938.

6. 'Stenographische Protokolle über die Sitzungen der Provisorischen Nationalversammlung für Deutschösterreich', cited in Denscher, 1989, 6.
7. Hainisch, 1918, 2.
8. See Fürth, 1930, 80.
9. See Kjäer, 1929, 2.
10. See Fürth, 1930, 81.
11. See Zaar, 1987.
12. See Eberhard, 1927, viii.
13. See Svoboda, 1984, 50.
14. Beth, 1930, 96.
15. See Fürth, 1930, 82.
16. See Beth, 1930, 96.
17. Kempny and Schnitzler, 1984, 135.
18. See Beth, 1930, 103.
19. Kjäer, 1929, 4.
20. Mayreder, 1988**b**, 185.
21. See Hainisch, 1918, 2.
22. Ibid., 3.
23. See ibid., 2.
24. See Fürth, 1918, 4.
25. See Laessig, 1949; Hoerschelmann, 1988.
26. See Hacker, 1981, 231.
27. Mayreder, 1921**a**, 3.
28. Mayreder, 1928**a**, 14.
29. Mayreder, 1928**b**, 2.
30. Mayreder, 1932, 28.
31. Ibid.
32. Ibid., 29.
33. See Svoboda, 1984, 50.
34. See Bund Österreichischer Frauenvereine, 1914, 33.
35. Ibid., 42.
36. Ibid., 43.
37. Ibid., 3.
38. See Hainisch, 1914, 11.
39. Cited in Hamann, 1986, 237.
40. Suttner, 1900**b**, 15.
41. See Anon., 1899**a**.
42. See Kulka, 1912.
43. Touaillon, 1914, 230, 231.
44. Ibid., 230.
45. See Else Migerka, 1915, 9.
46. Touaillon, 1914, 232.
47. Kulka, 1914**c**, 262.
48. Kulka, 1913, 8.
49. Internationale Frauenliga für Frieden und Freiheit, 1930, inside front cover.
50. See Hoerschelmann, 1988, 106.
51. See Mayreder, 1915**a**, 100.
52. See unpublished documents in the archive of the Vienna City Library, DZ 3627/1921.
53. Yella Hertzka, 1927, 92–3.
54. Mayreder, 1988**b**, 205.
55. Minor, 1915, 10.

56. Kulka, 1919, 13.
57. Ibid., 11.
58. Mayreder, 1988**b**, 205.
59. Ibid., 158.
60. Ibid., 155.
61. Mayreder, 1929, 8.
62. Ibid., 5.
63. Ibid., 4.
64. Unpublished letter from Auguste Fickert to Leopoldine Kulka, no date, I.N. 71159/1.
65. Kulka, 1910**a**, 206.
66. Unpublished diary of Auguste Fickert, Auguste-Fickert-Nachlass, I.N. 70494.
67. Baumann, 1913, 200.
68. Unpublished letter from Ida Baumann to Auguste Fickert, 5 March (1895), I.N. 69825.
69. See Berner, 1913, 100.
70. Mayreder, 1929, 7.
71. Kulka, 1910**a**, 208.
72. Unpublished diary of Auguste Fickert, Auguste-Fickert-Nachlass, I.N. 70494.
73. Mayreder, 1988**b**, 93.
74. Ibid., 114–15.
75. Ibid., 114.
76. Ibid., 111 (emphasis added).
77. Ibid., 107.
78. Ibid., 106.
79. Ibid., 90.
80. Mayreder, 1948, 250.
81. Schlesinger-Eckstein, 1928, 119.
82. Mayreder, 1988**b**, 226.
83. See Sparholz, 1986, 11–12.
84. See ibid., 14.
85. Else Federn, 1935, 16.
86. See Rukschcio and Schachel, 1982, 96–8; Grieser, 1989.
87. Hofmannsthal, 1959, 136.
88. Else Federn, 1935, 23.
89. See ibid., 23; Sparholz, 1986, 17.
90. Hainisch, 'Lebensgeschichte. Erinnerungen aus meinem Leben', 2, an unpublished typescript in the private possession of Dr Marianne Hainisch and Dr Cornelia Hainisch.
91. Ibid., no page number.
92. Ibid., 26.
93. Mayreder, 1988**b**, 144.
94. Hainisch, 'Lebensgeschichte. Erinnerungen aus meinem Leben', 13.

Part Two: Philosophers of Feminism
Chapter 7: Autonomous Feminism and Feminist Theory

1. See Asenijeff, 1898, 4.
2. Ibid., 3.
3. Ewart, 1895, 4.

4. See Fickert, 1906**a**.
5. Schreiber, 1893, 155.
6. Jerusalem(-Kotányi), 1902, 1.
7. See Vortmann, 1894, 13.
8. Ibid., 50, 56.
9. Druskowitz, 1905, 18.
10. Ibid., 45.
11. Ibid., 44.
12. Haag, 1893, 16.
13. Ibid., 83.
14. See 'Jemand', 1889, 79–119.
15. Ebner-Eschenbach, 1893, 61.
16. Mayreder, 1905, 2.
17. Hainisch, 1870, 15.
18. Unpublished letter from Rosa Mayreder to Marianne Hainisch, 20 September 1904, I.N. 123.714.
19. The concept of *Geist* (adjective: *geistig*) has a long tradition in German philosophy. For Mayreder it means roughly 'intellect' but it cannot be pinned down to this translation. I have therefore preferred to leave it in the original German.
20. See Widmann, 1914, 15–16.
21. See Mayreder, 1897.
22. Ibid., col.1333.
23. Ibid., col.1337.
24. Mayreder, 1988**a**, 154.
25. Mayreder, 1936, 14.
26. Wolf, 1921, 91.
27. See Mayreder, 1988**a**, 151.
28. Ibid.
29. See ibid.
30. Meisel-Hess, 1909, 400.
31. Meisel-Hess, 1917, 203.
32. Mayreder, 1988**b**, 161.
33. Mayreder, 1923, 68.
34. Reik, 1924.
35. See Fromm, 1980, 30–2.
36. Several notebooks recording Mayreder's reading form part of the Rosa-Mayreder-Nachlass at the Manuscripts Department of the Vienna City Library, call mark No. 264/51–3.
37. Quoted by Widmann, 1914, 12.
38. Unpublished letter from Rosa Mayreder to Jacqueline von Waldheim, 23 July 1876, I.N. 120.402.
39. Quoted by Widmann, 1914, 16.
40. See Hanisch and Fleischer, 1986, 137–8.
41. See Mayreder, 1905, 30–3.
42. Meisel-Hess, 1904, 64.
43. Suttner, 1909, 169–70.
44. Ibid., 178.
45. See Heymann, 1913, iv.
46. Widmann, 1914, 19.
47. L.A.W., 1897, 57.
48. See Mayreder, 1912**a**, 61.

49. See Ajax, 1914, 14.
50. Mayreder, 1905, 5.
51. Zepler, 1928, 1084.
52. Kollontai, 1977, 66.

Chapter 8: A Champion of Reason. Irma von Troll-Borostyáni

1. Troll-Borostyáni, 1912, 9.
2. Troll-Borostyáni, 1913, 38.
3. Ibid., 29.
4. Ibid., 28.
5. Ibid., 32.
6. See Troll-Borostyáni, 1914, 211.
7. See Troll-Borostyáni, 1913, 23.
8. See ibid., 131.
9. Ibid., 5.
10. See Troll-Borostyáni, 1896, 45–6.
11. See Troll-Borostyáni, 1913, 107.
12. Troll-Borostyáni, 1893, 8–9.
13. Ibid., 68.
14. Ibid., 89.
15. Troll-Borostyáni, 1913, 164.
16. Ibid., 121.
17. Troll-Borostyáni, 1914, 278.
18. Ibid., 268.
19. Troll-Borostyáni, 1878, 80.
20. Troll-Borostyáni, 1912, 5.
21. Ibid., 8–9.
22. Ibid., 6.
23. Ibid., 11.
24. Ibid., 14.
25. Ibid., 10.
26. See ibid., 12.
27. Ibid., 18–19.
28. Troll-Borostyáni, 1913, 202.
29. Troll-Borostyáni, 1911, 4.
30. See Troll-Borostyáni, 1913, 206.
31. Troll-Borostyáni, 1896, 57.
32. Ibid., 57.
33. Ibid.
34. Ibid., 58.
35. Troll-Borostyáni, 1913, 207–8.
36. Troll-Borostyáni, 1912, 24.
37. See Troll-Borostyáni, 1914, 238.
38. See ibid., 259–60.
39. See Troll-Borostyáni, 1896, 42, 52.
40. Troll-Borostyáni, 1894a, 7.
41. See, for example, Clemens 1988; Vogel, 1986.
42. See, for example, Evans, 1977.

Chapter 9: The Synthetic Ideal. Rosa Mayreder

1. Mayreder, 1988**a**, 187.
2. Mayreder, 1905, 271.
3. Ibid., 261.
4. Mayreder, 1935, 3.
5. Mayreder, 1905, 25.
6. See ibid., 35.
7. Mayreder, 1910**b**, 78.
8. See Mayreder, 1905, 293.
9. See Mayreder, 1910**b**, 79.
10. See Mayreder, 1905, 182.
11. Spencer, 1873, 373.
12. Mayreder, 1905, 52.
13. Mayreder, 1923, 119–20.
14. See Mayreder, 1905, 62.
15. See Mayreder, 1914, 24.
16. Mayreder, 1905, 93.
17. See ibid., 47.
18. See ibid., 181.
19. See Mayreder, 1923, 198.
20. See Mayreder, 1905, 102–38, 210–43.
21. See ibid., 118.
22. Ibid., 138.
23. See Mayreder, 1923, 143.
24. Mayreder, 1910**b**, 83.
25. See Mayreder, 1914, 23.
26. Mayreder, 1907, 422.
27. Mayreder, 1905, 276.
28. See ibid., 275–6.
29. 'Weiblichkeit und Genialität' (1918), unpublished manuscript, part of the Rosa-Mayreder-Nachlass, Manuscripts Department, Vienna City Library, call mark No. 264/51–53.
30. Ibid.
31. See Mayreder, 1905, 73.
32. Ibid., 72.
33. See Mayreder, 1923, 6.
34. See ibid., 10.
35. This term was coined by Ernst Horneffer in the programme of the 'Deutsche Kulturpartei' in 1908. Quoted in Hamann and Hermand, 1967, 113.
36. See Stern, 1961, 52–66.
37. See Tönnies, 1912, 303.
38. See Simmel, 1919, 254–95.
39. Mayreder, 1923, 113.
40. Mayreder, 1921**a**, 18.
41. See Mayreder, 1923, 105.
42. Ibid., 104.
43. Ibid., 107.
44. Ibid., 108.
45. See ibid., 110.
46. Mayreder, 1916, 650–1.
47. Mayreder, 1921**a**, 12.

48. See ibid., 19.
49. Mayreder, 1917, 640.
50. Mayreder, 1923, 37.
51. See Mayreder, 1912, 'Mutterschaft und doppelte Moral'; Mayreder, 1923, 75–82.
52. Mayreder, 1923, 46.
53. Ibid., 73.
54. Ibid., 74.
55. Ibid., 64.
56. See ibid., 81.
57. See Mayreder, 1912**b**, 156.
58. Mayreder, 1923, 331.
59. Mayreder, 1905, 87.
60. Ibid., 88.
61. Ibid., 96.
62. Ibid.
63. Ibid., 94.
64. Ibid., 83.
65. Mayreder, 1926, 10.
66. Ibid., 34.
67. Mayreder, 1905, 282.
68. Ibid., 298.
69. Mayreder, 1923, 89.
70. Mayreder, 1905, 5.
71. Colby, 1913, 874.
72. Mayreder, 1910**b**, 79.
73. See Mayreder, 1905, 85–101.

Chapter 10: Eugenics and Feminism. Grete Meisel-Hess

1. See Meisel-Hess, 1901**b**, 112–13.
2. Ibid., 80.
3. Ibid., 97.
4. Meisel-Hess, 1909, 397.
5. Ibid., 400.
6. Meisel-Hess, 1901**b**, 102–3.
7. Ibid., 106.
8. Meisel-Hess, 1914, 231.
9. Meisel-Hess, 1901**b**, 51–2.
10. Ibid., 58.
11. Ibid., 67.
12. Ibid., 33.
13. See ibid., 34.
14. Meisel-Hess, 1909, 366.
15. Ibid., 365.
16. Meisel-Hess, 1914, 3.
17. Meisel-Hess, 1909, 309.
18. Ibid., 236.
19. Ibid., 272.
20. Ibid., 275.

21. Ibid., 201.
22. Ibid., 6.
23. Ibid., 129.
24. Meisel-Hess, 1907**b**, 9.
25. Ibid., 8.
26. Meisel-Hess, 1909, 16.
27. See ibid., 42–3.
28. Ibid., 13–14.
29. Ibid., 49.
30. See ibid., 24.
31. Ibid., 23.
32. Ibid., 24.
33. Ibid.
34. Ibid., 383–4.
35. See ibid., 383.
36. See ibid., 218.
37. Ibid., 263.
38. See Meisel-Hess, 1914, 170.
39. Ibid., 255.
40. Ibid., 165.
41. Meisel-Hess, 1909, 288.
42. See ibid., 288.
43. Ibid., 292.
44. See ibid., 315.
45. See ibid., 316.
46. Ibid., 413.
47. Meisel-Hess, 1914, 4.
48. Mayreder, 1923, 163–4.
49. Ibid., 165.
50. See Schapire-Neurath, 1911, 238.
51. Meisel-Hess, 1911**b**, 156.
52. Meisel-Hess, 1914, 105.

Chapter 11: Political Feminism and Spiritual Feminism

1. In Troll-Borostyáni, 1913, xii.
2. See Troll-Borostyáni, 1903.
3. See Troll-Borostyáni, 1878.
4. Ibid., 164.
5. Mayreder, 1988**b**, 270.
6. See Mayreder, 1933, 216–17
7. Mayreder, 1923, 74.
8. Ibid., 71.
9. Meisel-Hess, 1909, 324.
10. In Rosenthal, 1912, 86.
11. Troll-Borostyáni, 1914, 206.
12. Meisel-Hess, 1909, 323.
13. Troll-Borostyáni, 1914, 211.
14. Mayreder, 1923, 159.
15. Ibid.

16. Meisel-Hess, 1917, vi.
17. Ibid., xxi–xxii.
18. Ibid., 203.
19. Meisel-Hess, 1909, ix.
20. Ibid., viii–ix.
21. Troll-Borostyáni, 1893, 3.
22. Mayreder, 1923, iv.
23. Mayreder, 1905, 5.
24. Mayreder, 1899**a**, 198.
25. See Mayreder, 1910**a**.
26. Troll-Borostyáni, 1896, 5.
27. See Mayreder, 1923, 113.

Part Three: The Feminist Imagination
Chapter 12: Feminist Aesthetics and Imaginative Literature

1. See Anon., 1894**c**.
2. Wiener Frauen, 1891.
3. Holm, 1910**a**, 75.
4. See Wesely, 1913.
5. See Grünes, 1909.
6. Hainisch, 1901**b**, 632.
7. Minor, 1900, 408.
8. See Verein für erweiterte Frauenbildung in Wien, 1889–1904, *1. Jahresbericht* (1889), 11.
9. See Najmájer, 1901, 50.
10. Hainisch, 1901**b**, 633.
11. For more on the Mayreder–Wolf collaboration see Mayreder, 1900**b**; Wolf, 1921; Walker, 1951, 353–407; Cook, 1976.
12. See Meisel-Hess, 1901**a**, 9.
13. Ibid., 9–10.
14. See Meisel-Hess, 1901**b**, 48–9.
15. Mayreder, 1905, 189.
16. Cited in Strecker, 1969, 17.
17. Mayreder, 1905, 189.
18. Troll-Borostyáni, 1891, 1006.
19. Ibid., 1005.
20. Ibid.
21. Marriot, 1895, 6.
22. See Mayreder, 1905, 190.
23. Kulka, 1909, 217, 218.
24. Touaillon, 1909, 187.
25. Schlesinger-Eckstein, 1902**a**, 1.
26. See Sandrock, 1897–8, 505–7.
27. Jerusalem, 1909, 1.
28. Theimer, 1898, 5.
29. Meisel-Hess, 1901**b**, 47.
30. Touaillon, 1909, 188.
31. Kulka, 1909, 218.
32. Touaillon, 1918**a**, 47.

33. See Holm, 1906.
34. Meisel-Hess, 1913, 171.
35. Grossmann, 1899, 366.
36. Touaillon, 1913, 20.
37. Ibid., 21.
38. Cited in Wunberg, 1976, Vol. I, 187.
39. Kulka, 1909, 218.
40. Fickert *et al.*, 1899, 2.
41. Suttner, 1909, 169–70.
42. Ibid., 180.
43. Meisel-Hess, 1907**a**, preface (no page number).
44. Najmájer, 1901, 23.
45. Ibid., 48.
46. Mayreder, 1988**b**, 204–5.
47. See unpublished letter from Rosa Mayreder to Auguste Fickert, 12 December 1895, I.N. 70889/14.
48. Unpublished letter from Rosa Mayreder to Oskar Grohe, 21 November 1902, I.N. 128.900.
49. Meisel-Hess, 1907**a**, preface (no page number).
50. Reuter, 1902, 231.
51. Weissenthurn, 1911, 45.
52. Ibid., 91.
53. See Bettelheim, 1990, 245.
54. Mauthner, 1893–4.
55. David, 1895.
56. Hofmannsthal, 1984, 314.
57. Ibid.
58. Ibid., 315.
59. See Ebner-Eschenbach, 1906, 151.
60. Hans Landsberg cited in Wunberg, 1971, 173.
61. Lemmermeyer, 1890.
62. See Fred, 1899.
63. Necker, 1899, 206.
64. Filek, 1904**b**, 6.

Chapter 13: Moral Feminism

1. G.L., 1897, 517.
2. Marriot, 1897, 115.
3. Ibid., 120.
4. See 'Ahnungen', unpublished manuscript, Auguste-Fickert-Nachlass, I.N. 71148/17.
5. See Schapire-Neurath, 1900.
6. Troll-Borostyáni, 1900, 131.
7. Ibid., 30.
8. Kotányi(-Jerusalem), 1899, 43.
9. Ibid., 48.
10. Jerusalem(-Kotányi), 1909, 406.
11. See Schapire-Neurath, 1901.
12. Kotányi(-Jerusalem), 1899, 48.

13. Suttner, 1919, 152.
14. Ibid., 190.
15. Ibid.
16. Troll-Borostyáni, 1897**a**, 53.
17. See Najmájer, 1901, 144.
18. See Else Migerka, 1900.
19. Zitelmann, 1900, 43.
20. See Schalek, 1905, 190.
21. Merk, 1901, 778.
22. See Golm, 1888.
23. Golm, 1895, 162.
24. Ibid., 367.
25. Ibid., 406.
26. Troll-Borostyáni, 1892, Vol. I, 72.
27. Golm, 1895, 397.
28. Ibid., 395.
29. See Troll-Borostyáni, 1900, 19–31.
30. See ibid., 138–44.
31. See Troll-Borostyáni, 1898, 44–54.
32. See ibid., 3–15; Troll-Borostyáni, 1900, 159–71.
33. See 'Gottes Wort', unpublished manuscript, Auguste-Fickert-Nachlass, I.N. 71148/3.
34. See Troll-Borostyáni, 1900, 199–207.
35. See Christen, 1892; Nordmann, 1895.
36. See Hönigsberg, 1899.
37. Troll-Borostyáni, 1897**a**, 18.
38. Troll-Borostyáni, 1898, 123.
39. Suttner, 1900**a**, 197.
40. Najmájer, 1900, Vol. II, 236.
41. See Filek, 1904**a**, 18.
42. Christen, 1870, 33.
43. See Beutner, 1985, 27.

Chapter 14: Psychological Feminism

1. See Müller, 1899, 346–9.
2. Meisel-Hess, 1907**a**, 220.
3. Meisel-Hess, 1912, 3–4.
4. Meisel-Hess, 1903, 60.
5. Ibid., 69.
6. Ibid., 71.
7. Meisel-Hess, 1907**a**, 246.
8. Ibid., 247.
9. Meisel-Hess, 1905, 26.
10. Meisel-Hess, 1902, 6–7.
11. Ibid., 10.
12. Ibid.
13. Mayreder, 1903, 15.
14. Steiner, 1900, 80.
15. See Mayreder, 1908**a**, 122.

16. See Meisel-Hess, 1905, 1–14.
17. Mayreder, 1908**b**, 1.
18. Mayreder, 1899**c**, 48.
19. Ibid., 63.
20. Ibid.
21. Ibid., 21–2.
22. Ibid., 34.
23. Ibid., 53.
24. Ibid., 28.
25. Ibid., 123–4.
26. Ibid., 34.
27. Ibid., 35.
28. Ibid., 160.
29. Ibid., 91.
30. See ibid., 67.
31. Ibid., 56.
32. Meisel-Hess, 1907**a**, 239.
33. Ibid., 122.
34. Ibid., 98–9.
35. Ibid., 268.
36. Ibid., 410.
37. See ibid., 292.
38. Ibid., 332.
39. Meisel-Hess, 1902, 123.
40. Ibid., 123–4.
41. Ibid., 133.

Chapter 15: The Visionary Imagination

1. Troll-Borostyáni, 1891, 1022.
2. Ibid.
3. Suttner, 1911, 9.
4. Ibid., 117.
5. See Meisel-Hess, 1914, 268.
6. Ibid., 270.
7. See ibid., 271.
8. Meisel-Hess, 1911**a**, 197.
9. See Meisel-Hess, 1909, 270.
10. Ibid., 271.
11. See Meisel-Hess, 1907**a**, 107.
12. Mayreder, 1988**a**, 29.
13. Ibid., 18.
14. Ibid., 48.
15. Mayreder, 1988**b**, 188–9.
16. See Le Rider, 1982, 166.
17. Ibid.
18. See Dopplinger-Loebenstein, 1987.
19. Ibid., 104.
20. Ibid., 255.
21. See Schnabel, 1900.

22. Mayreder, 1921**b**, 5.
23. Ibid., 6.
24. Touaillon, 1923, 7.
25. Ibid.
26. Mayreder, 1921**b**, 5.
27. See 'Was will, was soll die Secession der Frauen', unpublished manuscript, Auguste-Fickert-Nachlass, I.N. 71148/50.
28. Lang, 1897–8, 940.
29. Mayreder, diary entry for 31 January 1919, in the Rosa-Mayreder-Nachlass, Manuscripts Department, Vienna City Library, Zuw. Prot. No. 264/51–3.
30. See unpublished letter from Rosa Mayreder to Auguste Fickert, 18 October 1900, I.N. 70892/8.
31. Meisel-Hess, 1909, 355.
32. See Mach, 1903, 20.
33. See Mayreder, 1933.
34. See Timms, 1986.

Conclusion: The Legacy of Visionary Feminism

1. See Mayreder, 1926.
2. See Mayreder, 1905, 63.
3. Gutt, 1978, 156-7.
4. Lafleur, 1978, 219.
5. Borneman, 1981, 22–3.
6. See Evans, 1977; Schenk, 1980.
7. See Evans, 1977, 95.
8. Suttner, 1919, 191.
9. Mayreder, 1988**a**, 187.
10. Suttner, 1894, 216–17.

Dramatis Personae

Adler, Max, sociologist and leading theorist of Austromarxism.

Adler, Victor, doctor and leading Social Democratic politician.

Altenberg, Peter, Viennese modernist writer.

Andreas-Salomé, Lou, writer of fiction and theoretical essays on the 'woman problem' and a disciple of Sigmund Freud.

Bahr, Hermann, modernist writer and cultural critic.

Bebel, August, leading German Social Democrat and author of the influential *Die Frau und der Sozialismus* (Woman and Socialism).

Bernatzik, Edmund, Professor of Law at the University of Vienna.

Brühl, Carl, Zoologist.

Diederichs, Eugen, socially critical and influential German publisher.

Ebner-Eschenbach, Marie von, respected and successful writer.

Federn, Else, leading organiser of the Vienna Settlement.

Fickert, Auguste, primary schoolteacher and the most prominent representative of the visionary wing of the Austrian women's movement.

Glöckel, Leopoldine, active member of the Austrian women's movement.

Goldscheid, Rudolf, writer, pacifist and Darwinist. He propagated the idea of human economy in Austria.

Gomperz, Theodor, classicist and professor at the University of Vienna.

Haeckel, Ernst, German zoologist and propagator of monism, the pantheistic belief that spirit and matter are one and that therefore the Christian belief in a transcendent God is false.

Hainisch, *Marianne*, leading figure of the pragmatic wing of the Austrian women's movement.

Hartmann, *Ludo Moritz*, left-liberal teacher of history at the University of Vienna and active promoter of adult education classes in Vienna.

Herzfelder, *Henriette*, active supporter of the pragmatic wing of the Austrian women's movement.

Hofmannsthal, *Hugo von*, Viennese modernist writer.

Jodl, *Friedrich*, Professor of Philosophy at the University of Vienna and founder of the free-thinking Viennese Ethical Society.

Klein, *Hugo*, gynaecologist who was active in the dress reform and mother protection movements.

Kautsky, *Karl*, socialist politician and theorist.

Kautsky, *Minna*, successful writer of socialist popular literature and sympathiser of the Austrian women's movement.

Klimt, *Gustav*, artist and a leading member of the Vienna Secession, a movement which broke away from Vienna's art establishment.

Kraus, *Karl*, founder, writer and editor of the satirical journal *Die Fackel* (The Torch).

Kronawetter, *Ferdinand*, leading member of the left-liberal Democratic Party and member of Parliament.

Kulka, *Leopoldine*, pacifist and active member of the visionary wing of the Austrian women's movement.

Lang, *Marie*, leading member of the visionary wing of the Austrian women's movement and founder of the Vienna Settlement.

Lueger, *Karl*, conservative Mayor of Vienna and opponent of the women's movement.

Loos, *Adolf*, avant-garde architect.

Mach, *Ernst*, Professor of Physics at the University of Vienna.

Marriot, *Emil* (pseudonym of Emilie Mataja), successful fiction writer.

Mayreder, *Karl*, architect and husband of Rosa Mayreder.

Mayreder, *Rosa*, leading member of the visionary wing of the Austrian women's movement; writer, feminist theorist, painter, pacifist.

Meisel-Hess, *Grete*, writer and feminist theorist.

Najmájer, *Marie von*, successful fiction writer and supporter of women's education.

Ofner, *Julius*, left-liberal politician and member of Parliament. Active supporter of the Austrian women's movement.

Pernerstorfer, *Engelbert*, Social Democratic member of Parliament and supporter of the Austrian women's movement.

Philippovich, *Eugen von*, economist and left-liberal politician.

Popp, *Adelheid*, leading figure in the Social Democratic women's movement in Austria.

Renner, *Karl*, Social Democratic politician.

Roller, *Alfred*, avant-garde artist and stage designer.

Schapire-Neurath, *Anna*, social worker, writer and commentator on the 'woman problem'.

Schlesinger-Eckstein, *Therese*, active member of the visionary wing of the Austrian women's movement who then joined the Social Democratic women's movement.

Schnitzler, *Arthur*, doctor, dramatist and fiction writer who experimented with narrative technique.

Schwarz, *Marie*, the first school headmistress in Vienna and veteran supporter of women's education.

Schwarzwald, *Eugenie*, pedagogue, founder of the Schwarzwald schools, and promoter of avant-garde culture.

Suttner, *Bertha von*, pacifist and founder of the Austrian Peace Society.

Touaillon, *Christine*, supporter of the visionary wing of the Austrian women's movement, literary historian and teacher of German at the University of Vienna.

Troll-Borostyáni, *Irma von*, fiction writer and feminist theorist.

Wedekind, *Frank*, avant-garde dramatist.

Weininger, *Otto*, author of the bestselling and influential *Geschlecht und Charakter* (Sex and Character) who committed suicide soon after its publication, at the age of 23.

Zuckerkandl, *Berta*, hostess of a salon frequented by cultural and political celebrities.

Zuckerkandl, *Emil*, Professor of Anatomy at the University of Vienna. Husband of Berta.

Bibliography

Unless otherwise stated, place of publication of independent works is Vienna.

Ajax (1914) 'Der synthetische Mensch', *Neues Frauenleben*, 26, nos. 1–2 (January–February), pp. 14–22.

Albert, Eduard (1895) *Die Frauen und das Studium der Medicin.*

Allgemeiner Österreichischer Frauenverein (1893; 1895–1901) *Jahresberichte.*

——— (1893**a**) Anmerkung, *Die Volksstimme*, 20 August, p. 6.

——— (1893**b**) *Statuten.*

——— (1893**c**) *Stenographisches Protokoll über die Constituierende Versammlung des Allgemeinen Österreichischen Frauenvereines, abgehalten am 28. Jänner 1893 im Sitzungssaale des alten Rathhauses zu Wien.*

——— (1894**a**) Anmerkung zu 'Reinliche Scheidung', *Die Volksstimme*, 6 May, p. 8.

——— (1894**b**) *Zum Frauenstimmrecht in Österreich. Bericht über die am 9. Dezember 1893 im alten Rathhaussaale stattgehabte allgemeine freie Frauenversammlung.*

——— (1894**c**) Zweiter Jahresbericht, *Die Volksstimme*, 25 November, pp. 7–10.

——— (1895**a**) *Ein Beitrag zur Lösung der Dienstbotenfrage.*

——— (1895**b**) *Hohes Abgeordnetenhaus! Petition um Zulassung der Frauen zur ärztlichen Praxis.*

——— (1897) *Zur Geschichte einer Petition gegen die Errichtung öffentlicher Häuser in Wien. Protokoll der Frauenversammlung vom 20. Februar 1897 im alten Wiener Rathhause. Nebst fünf Gutachten.*

——— (1901) Petition des Allgemeinen Österreichischen Frauenvereines an das Abgeordnetenhaus um eine Enquete über die Sanitätscontrole, *Frauenleben*, 13, pp. 132–5.

Ander, M. (1990) 'Zur Frauenfrage in Österreich', *Die Wage*, 3, pp. 131–3.

Anderson, Harriet (1985) 'Beyond a Critique of Femininity. The Thought of Rosa Mayreder', unpublished doctoral dissertation, University of London.

——— (1987) 'Neues zu Karl Kraus und dem Allgemeinen Österreichischen Frauenverein', *Kraus-Hefte*, 41 (January), pp. 1–5.

——— (1988) Einleitung, in Rosa Mayreder, *Tagebücher 1873–1937*, ed. Harriet Anderson (Frankfurt am Main), pp. 10–40.

——— (1989**a**) '"Uns handelt es sich um weit Höheres . . .". Visionäre Entwürfe von bürgerlichen Feministinnen in Wien um 1900', in *Aufbruch* *ins Jahrhundert der Frau? Rosa Mayreder und der Feminismus in Wien um 1900*, exhibition catalogue, Historisches Museum der Stadt Wien, pp. 19–27.

——— (1989**b**) 'Zwischen Modernismus und Sozialreform. Rosa Mayreder und die Kultur der Wiener Jahrhundertwende', in *Rosa Mayreder 1858–1938. Mitteilungen des Instituts für Wissenschaft und Kunst*, 44, pp. 6–12.

——— (1990**a**) 'Feminism as a Vocation. Motives for Joining the Austrian Women's Movement', in *Vienna 1900. From Altenberg to Wittgenstein*. Austrian Studies Yearbook 1, ed. Edward F. Timms and Ritchie Robertson, Edinburgh, pp. 73–86.

——— (1990**b**) '"Mir wird es immer unmöglicher, 'die Männer' als die Feinde der Frauensache zu betrachten...". Zur Beteiligung von Männern an den Bestrebungen der österreichischen Frauenbewegung um 1900', in *'Das Weib existiert nicht für sich'. Geschlechterbeziehungen in der bürgerlichen Gesellschaft*, ed. Heide Dienst and Edith Saurer, pp. 189–201.

——— (1991) 'Rosa Mayreder', in *Major Figures of Turn-of-the-Century Austrian Literature*, ed. Donald G. Daviau, Riverside, California, pp. 259–90.

——— (1992) 'Psychoanalysis and Feminism: An Ambivalent Alliance. Viennese Feminist Responses to Freud, 1900–30', in Austrian Studies Yearbook 3, ed. Edward F. Timms and Ritchie Robertson, Edinburgh, pp. 71–80.

Anon. (1887) Bericht, *Mittheilungen des Vereines der Lehrerinnen und Erzieherinnen in Österreich*, 2 (January), pp. 1–2.

——— (1889**a**) Correspondenzen und Mittheilungen, *Der Lehrerinnen-Wart*, 1, no. 6 (June), p. 8.

——— (1889**b**) Correspondenzen und Mittheilungen, *Der Lehrerinnen-Wart*, 1, no. 7 (July), pp. 10–11.

——— (1891) Correspondenzen und Mittheilungen, *Neuzeit*, 3, no. 11 (November), pp. 239–40.

——— (1892) 'Der österreichische Frauentag verschoben', *Allgemeine Frauen-Zeitung*, 1, pp. 58–9.

——— (1893) Mittheilungen des allg. österr. Frauenvereines, *Die Volksstimme*, 10 December, pp. 7–8.

——— (1894**a**) Discussion über 'Ein Handschuh', *Die Volksstimme*, 23 December, p. 7.

——— (1894**b**) Mittheilungen des allg. österr. Frauenvereines, *Die Volksstimme*, 22 April, p. 8.

——— (1894**c**) 'Über das Gretchen in Goethe's Faust', *Die Volksstimme*, 18 November, p. 6.

——— (1895**a**) Mittheilungen des allg. österr. Frauenvereines, *Die Volksstimme*, 10 November, pp. 7–8.

——— (1895**b**) Mittheilungen des allg. österr. Frauenvereines, *Die Volksstimme*, 22 December, pp. 6–8.

——— (1896**a**) 'Das Wahlrecht der Frau', *Frauenleben*, 8, no. 2 (May), pp. 9–10.

——— (1896**b**) 'Ein Frauenabend in Wien', *Die Volksstimme*, 5 January, pp. 6–8.

——— (1896**c**) Mittheilungen des allg. österr. Frauenvereines, *Die Volksstimme*, 19 April, pp. 7–8.

——— (1897) 'Neues von den heiratsfähigen Töchtern', *Neue Freie Presse*, 25 December (Morgenblatt), p. 10.

——— (1898**a**) 'Der Verein der Schriftstellerinnen und Künstlerinnen in Wien und die Frauenbewegung', *Frauenleben*, 10, no. 3 (June), pp. 1–3.

——— (1898**b**) 'Die Lehrerinnen gegen den Stadtrath', *Frauenleben*, 10, no. 2 (May), p. 5.

——— (1898**c**) 'Neues für Frauen und

von Frauen', *Frauen-Werke*, 5, no. 11 (no month given), p. 4.

——— (1898**d**) 'Wem zum Nachtheil?', *Frauenleben*, 9, no. 12 (March), p. 83.

——— (1899**a**) 'Die Internationalen Friedenskundgebungen der Frauen, *Dokumente der Frauen*, 1, pp. 162–3.

——— (1899**b**) 'Die k.k. Telegraphen-Manipulantinnen', *Dokumente der Frauen*, 2, pp. 443–8.

——— (1899**c**) 'Documente der Frauen', *Neue Freie Presse*, 10 March (Morgenblatt), p. 5.

——— (1899**d**) 'Nachtrag zum II. praktisch-socialen Curs', *Österreichische Frauen-Zeitung. Zeitschrift für die christliche Frauenwelt*, 2, no. 27 (29 July), p. 1.

——— (1900**a**) 'Das Budget der erwerbenden alleinstehenden Frau', *Dokumente der Frauen*, 3, pp. 101–5.

——— (1900**b**) 'Der Wiener Frauenclub. Begrüssungsabend und Eröffnung', *Neues Wiener Journal*, 15 November, p. 3.

——— (1900**c**) 'Der Wiener Frauenclub. (Sein erster Abend)', *Neues Wiener Tagblatt*, 15 November, pp. 4–5.

——— (1900**d**) 'Frauenpolitik', *Dokumente der Frauen*, 4, pp. 529–33.

——— (1900**e**) 'Gymnasiale Mädchenschule', *Dokumente der Frauen*, 3, pp. 288–90.

——— (1900**f**) 'Herr Dr Carl Lueger und das Frauenwahlrecht', *Dokumente der Frauen*, 2, p. 728.

——— (1900**g**) 'Unsere Universitätsprofessoren', *Dokumente der Frauen*, 4, pp. 480–2.

——— (1900**h**) 'Zulassung der Frauen zum medicinischen Studium', *Neue Freie Presse*, 15 September (Morgenblatt), p. 5.

——— (1901**a**) 'Aufruf zur Gründung eines Volksheims', *Neue Freie Presse*, 12 February (Morgenblatt), p. 6.

——— (1901**b**) 'Ausschluss der Frauen aus dem Postbeamtenverein', *Frauenleben*, 13, no. 3 (March), pp. 58–9.

——— (1901**c**) 'Die österreichische Frauenbewegung an der Jahrhundertwende', *Dokumente der Frauen*, 5, pp. 63–5.

——— (1901**d**) 'Eine Polizei-Affaire', *Neue Freie Presse*, 5 March (Abendblatt), p. 1.

——— (1901**e**) 'Eine Protestversammlung', *Dokumente der Frauen*, 4, pp. 766–71.

——— (1901**f**) 'Pöbel', *Dokumente der Frauen*, 5, pp. 241–3.

——— (1902**a**) 'Allg. österr. Frauenverein', *Neues Frauenleben*, 14, no. 6 (June), pp. 19–20.

——— (1902**b**) 'Der Wiener Frauenclub', *Dokumente der Frauen*, 7, pp. 271–2.

——— (1902**c**) 'Ein Frauenbund in Österreich', *Frauen-Werke*, 9, no. 7 (no month given), pp. 2–3.

——— (1902**d**) 'Verein "Settlement"', *Dokumente der Frauen*, 7, pp. 116–17.

——— (1902**e**) 'Zur Dienstbotenfrage', *Neues Frauenleben*, 14, no. 3 (March), pp. 18–19.

——— (1904) 'Das gemeinsame Universitätsstudium der Geschlechter', *Neues Frauenleben*, 16, no. 2 (February), pp. 1–5 and no. 3 (March), pp. 5–12.

——— (1906) 'Die Kunstschule für Frauen und Mädchen', *Der Bund*, 1, no. 4 (March), pp. 8–9.

——— (1907**a**) 'Der österreichische Bund für Mutterschutz', *Neues Frauenleben*, 19, no. 1 (January), p. 11.

——— (1907**b**) 'Der Prozess Riehl und Konsorten in Wien', in *Archiv für Kriminal-Anthropologie und Kriminalistik*, ed. Hans Gross, 27, pp. 1–111.

——— (1907**c**) 'Die Thronrede', *Neues Frauenleben*, 19, no. 7 (July), p. 6.

——— (1907**d**) 'Mutterschutz. Die konstituierende Versammlung des österreichischen Bundes für Mutterschutz', *Neues Frauenleben*, 19, no. 2 (February), p. 21.

——— (1907**e**) 'Österreichischer Bund für Mutterschutz', *Mitteilungen der österreichischen ethischen Gesellschaft*, 17 (February), pp. 198–200.

——— (1908) 'Sexuelle Erziehung', *Der Bund*, 3, no. 4 (April), pp. 3–5.

——— (1910) 'Der erste katholische Frauentag in Wien', *Der Bund*, 5, no. 4 (May), pp. 7–8.

——— (1911) 'Der Frauentag', *Zeitschrift für Frauen-Stimmrecht*, 1, no. 4 (April), p. 2.

——— (1912) 'Das Jubiläum der Staatsbeamtin in Österreich', *Der Bund*, 7, no. 2 (February), pp. 6–7.

——— (1913**a**) 'Die Internationale Frauenstimmrechtskonferenz in Wien', *Zeitschrift für Frauen-Stimmrecht*, 3, no. 6 (July), pp. 1–5.

——— (1913**b**) 'Ist das Frauenstimmrecht gerecht und notwendig? Ist es kulturfördernd oder kulturhemmend? Eine Enquete', *Neues Frauenleben*, 15, no. 6 (June), pp. 145–53.

——— (1914) 'Ziele und Erfolge des Bundes österreichischer Frauenvereine', *Der Bund*, 9, no. 4 (April), pp. 6–9.

Anscombe, Isabelle (1984) *A Woman's Touch. Women in Design from 1860 to the Present Day*, London.

Appelt, Erna (1985) *Von Ladenmädchen, Schreibfräulein und Gouvernanten. Die weiblichen Angestellten Wiens zwischen 1900 und 1934.*

Asenijeff, Else (1898) *Aufruhr der Weiber und das dritte Geschlecht*, Leipzig.

——— (1901) *Unschuld. Ein modernes Mädchenbuch*, Leipzig.

Avicenna [Fritz Wittels] (1907) 'Weibliche Ärzte', *Die Fackel*, 225, pp. 10–24.

Bahr, Hermann (1911) *Wienerinnen. Lustspiel in drei Akten*, Bonn.

——— (1912) 'Frauenrecht', in *Inventur*, Berlin, pp. 119–25.

Bau- und Wohnungsgenossenschaft 'Heimhof' (1909) 'Statuten der Bau- und Wohnungsgenossenschaft "Heimhof"', *Neues Frauenleben*, 21, no. 11 (November), pp. 369–74.

Bauer, Rhoda (1894) 'Preisfrage: Woher kommt es, dass so viele gutsituirte Männer nicht heiraten, und inwieferne liegt die Schuld hieran auch an den Frauen der Gegenwart?', *Frauenleben*, 6, no. 6 (August), pp. 111–13.

Baumann, Ida (1913) 'Aus meinem Leben', *Neues Frauenleben*, 25, nos 7–8 (July–August), pp. 192–200.

Bebel, Ferdinand August (1910) *Die Frau und der Sozialismus*, 50th edn, Stuttgart. First published 1879.

Belke, Ingrid (1978) *Die sozialreformatorischen Ideen von Josef Popper-Lynkeus (1838–1921) im Zusammenhang mit allgemeinen Reformbestrebungen des Wiener Bürgertums um die Jahrhundertwende*, Tübingen.

Bernatzik, Edmund (1900) *Die Zulassung der Frauen zu den juristischen Studien. Ein Gutachten.*

Berner, E. (1913) 'Ida Baumann', *Neues Frauenleben*, 25, no. 4 (April), pp. 99–100.

Bertin, Célia (1989) *La femme à Vienne au temps de Freud*, Paris.

Beth, Marianne (1930) 'Die Stellung der Frau im Recht', in *Frauenbewegung, Frauenbildung und Frauenarbeit in Österreich*, ed. Martha Stephanie Braun *et al.*, pp. 95–103.

Bettelheim, Anton (1900) *Marie von Ebner-Eschenbach. Biographische Blätter*, Berlin.

Bettelheim-Gabillon, Helene (1907) *Lilith und Eva und andere unmoderne Betrachtungen.*

Beutner, Eduard (1985) 'Widerstand und Resignation. Zur Lyrik der österreichischen Schriftstellerin Ada Christen', in *Unterdrückung und Emanzipation. Festschrift für Erika Weinzierl*, ed. Rudolf G. Ardelt *et al.*, Salzburg, pp. 15–37.

Blavatsky, Helene (1968) *The Key to Theosophy. Being a clear Exposition in the Form of Question and Answer of the Ethics, Science and Philosophy for the Study of which the Theosophical Society has been founded*, London. First published 1889.

Blazeg, Marie (1918) 'Die Beamtinnenorganisation', *Neues Frauenleben*, 30, no. 4–5 (April–May), pp. 71–4.

Blomowa, O. (1900**a**) 'Die Gemeinderathswahlen und die Wiener Frauen', *Dokumente der Frauen*, 3, pp. 161–2.

——— (1900**b**) 'Die Wiener Christliche Frauenbewegung', *Dokumente der Frauen*, 3, pp. 1–4.

Bock, Eva (1987) 'Therese Schlesinger-Eckstein (1863–1940). Eine Untersuchung über ihr politisches und publizistisches Wirken in der sozialdemokratischen Frauenbewegung', unpublished doctoral dissertation, University of Vienna.

Bölsche, Wilhelm (1898) *Das Liebesleben in der Natur. Eine Entwickelungsgeschichte der Liebe*, Leipzig.

Borneman, Ernest (ed.) (1981) *Arbeiterbewegung und Feminismus. Berichte aus vierzehn Ländern*, Frankfurt am Main.

Börner, Wilhelm (1910) 'Die österreichische Ethische Gesellschaft von 1894 bis 1909', *Mitteilungen der Ethischen Gesellschaft in Wien*, 1–2 (February), pp. 8–37.

Boyer, John W. (1978) 'Freud, Marriage, and Late Viennese Liberalism. A Commentary from 1905', *Journal of Modern History*, 50 (March), pp. 72–102.

Brühl, Carl (1892) 'Einiges über die Gaben der Natur an die Frauen und die Konsequenzen hieraus für Bedeutung, Stellung, Aufgaben und Rechte der Frau in der menschlichen Gesellschaft', in *4. Jahresbericht des Vereines für erweiterte Frauenbildung in Wien*, pp. 33–64.

——— (1895) 'Naturhistorische-ethische Cultur-Abende für gebildete Frauen und Mädchen', *Frauenleben*, 7, no. 6 (September), p. 144.

Bubeniček, Hanna (1986) 'Wider die Tyrannei der Norm. Impressionen zu Rosa Mayreder', in Rosa Mayreder, *Wider die Tyrannei der Norm*, ed. Hanna Bubeniček, pp. 9–25.

Bund Österreichischer Frauenvereine (1907) 'Die Frauenbewegung gegen die Legalisierung der Unzucht', *Der Bund*, 2, no. 1 (January), pp. 6–8.

——— (ed.) (1909) *Marianne Hainisch zum 25. März 1909.*

——— (1910) Zwei Eingaben des Bundes Österr. Frauenvereine, *Der Bund*, 5, no. 5 (June), pp. 3–6.

——— (1912) *Wegweiser zur Berufswahl für Mädchen.*

——— (1914) *Frauenkriegskalender 1915.*

——— (1962) *Sechzig Jahre Bund Österreichischer Frauenvereine.*

Byrnes, John (1979) 'Emil Marriot Bibliography', *Modern Austrian Literature*, 12, nos 3–4, pp. 59–76.

——— (1983) *Emil Marriot. A Re-evaluation Based on her Short Fiction*, New York, Berne, Frankfurt am Main.

Cella, Ingrid (1981) 'Die Genossen nannten sie die "rote Marlitt". Minna Kautsky und die Problematik des sozialen Romans, aufgezeigt an "Die Alten und die Neuen"', *Österreich in Geschichte und Literatur*, 25, pp. 16–29.

Christen, Ada [Christiane von Breden] (1870) *Aus der Asche. Neue Gedichte*, Hamburg.

——— (1892) *Jungfer Mutter. Eine Wiener Vorstadtgeschichte*, Dresden.

Christmann, Hans Helmut (1980) *Frau und 'Jüdin' an der Universität. Die Romanistin Elise Richter (Wien 1865–Theresienstadt 1943)*, Wiesbaden.

Clemens, Bärbel (1988) *'Menschenrechte haben kein Geschlecht!' Zum Politikverständnis der bürgerlichen Frauenbewegung*, Pfaffenweiler.

Colby, F.M. (1913) 'The Book of the Month', *North American Review*, 198, pp. 874–80.

Cook, Peter (1976) *Hugo Wolf's 'Corregidor'. A Study of the Opera and its Origins*, London.

Crepaz, Adele (1892) *Die Gefahren der Frauen-Emancipation. Ein Beitrag zur Frauenfrage*, Leipzig.

Czescher, Clara (*et al.*) (1901) 'Aufruf!', *Dokumente der Frauen*, 6, pp. 492–3.

Dallago, Carl (1913) 'Verfall der Geschlechter', *Der Brenner*, 3, pp. 825–33.

Das Comité zur Begründung eines Frauenclubs (1900) 'Lebhafter denn je . . .', *Dokumente der Frauen*, 3, pp. 69–70.

David, Jakob Julius (1895) 'Geistiges in Wien', *Magazin für Litteratur*, 64, col.163.

Deichmann, Hans and Worbs, Dietrich (1984) 'Eine Wohnungseinrichtung von Adolf Loos. Das Haus Schwarzwald 1909–1938, Josefstädterstrasse 68, Wien 8', *Bauforum*, 17, no. 105, pp. 28–32.

Denscher, Bernhard (1989) *Wahljahr 1919. Katalog der 215. Wechselausstellung der Wiener Stadt- und Landesbibliothek.*

Die antiklerikalen Frauen von Wien (1902) 'Aufruf an die Frauen Wiens!', *Neues Frauenleben*, 14, no. 10 (October), p. 21.

Die Redaktion (1906) 'Verraten!', *Neues Frauenleben. Beamtinnen-Sektion*, 18, no. 1 (January), p. 3.

Dohnal, Johanna (1980) 'Bürgerliche und proletarische Frauenbewegung', in *Das geistige Leben Wiens in der Zwischenkriegszeit*, ed. Norbert Leser, pp. 105–19.

Dopplinger-Loebenstein, Andrea (1987) 'Frauenehre, Liebe und der abgesetzte Mann. Bürgerliche Frauenliteratur in Österreich (1866–1918) am Beispiel von Franziska von Kapff-Essenther, Julie Thenen, Rosa Mayreder, Dora von Stockert-Meynert und Emilie Mataja', unpublished doctoral dissertation, University of Vienna.

Druskowitz, Helene von (1905) *Pessimistische Kardinalsätze. Ein Vademekum für die freiesten Geister*, Wittenberg.

Dworschak, Hertha (1949) 'Rosa Obermayer-Mayreder', unpublished doctoral dissertation, University of Vienna.

Eberhard, E.F.W. (1927) *Feminismus und Kulturuntergang. Die erotischen Grundlagen der Frauenemanzipation.*

Ebner-Eschenbach, Marie von (1893) *Aphorismen*, in Marie von Ebner-Eschenbach, *Gesammelte Schriften*, Vol. I, Berlin.

——— (1906) *Meine Kinderjahre. Biographische Skizzen*, Berlin.

Eckstein, Emma (1899**a**) 'Die Fackel- und Dokumente der Frauen. Revuen', *Socialistische Monatshefte*, 5, pp. 194–5.

——— (1899**b**) 'Vorbereitung der Frau zur Lebensarbeit', *Dokumente der Frauen*, 2, pp. 512–16.

——— (1900) 'Das Dienstmädchen als Mutter', *Dokumente der Frauen*, 2, pp. 594–8.

——— (1904) *Die Sexualfrage in der Erziehung des Kindes*, Leipzig.

——— (1908) 'Aus eines Mannes Mädchenjahren', *Neues Frauenleben*, 20, pp. 238–40.

Eckstein, Friedrich (1928) 'Ein Gruss aus längst vergangenen Tagen', in *Der Aufstieg der Frau. Zu Rosa Mayreders 70. Geburtstag am 30. November 1928 als Ehrengabe dargebracht vom Verlag Eugen Diederichs in Jena*, Jena, pp. 101–3.

——— (1935) 'Die erste Begegnung mit Marie Lang', in *Marie Lang, Gedenkblatt des Settlement für seine Mitglieder und Freunde*, pp. 8–10.

——— (1936) *'Alte unnennbare Tage!' Erinnerungen aus siebzig Lehr- und Wanderjahren.*

Ehrlich, Eugen (1895) 'Zur Frage des Frauenstudiums', *Deutsche Worte*, 15, pp. 703–12.

Eine gute Collegin (1889) 'Die gute Collegin!', *Der Lehrerinnen-Wart*, 1, no. 1 (January), pp. 24–7.

Eine Lehrerin (1901) 'Ehe und Eheconsense', *Dokumente der Frauen*, 5, nos 9–10 (August), pp. 270–4.

Engelbrecht, Helmut (1986) *Geschichte des österreichischen Bildungswesens. Erziehung und Unterricht auf dem Boden Österreichs*, Vol. IV, *Von 1848 bis zum Ende der Monarchie.*

Ethische Gesellschaft in Wien (1897) *Die Arbeits- und Lebensverhältnisse der Wiener Lohnarbeiterinnen. Ergebnisse und stenographisches Protokoll der Enquete über Frauenarbeit abgehalten in Wien vom 1. März bis 21. April 1896.*

Ettel, Konrad, (n.d.) *Die Frau in der Gesellschaft. Ein Wort zur Frauenfrage.*

Evans, Richard J. (1977) *The Feminists. Women's Emancipation Movements in Europe, America and Australasia 1840–1920*, London.

——— (1986) 'The Concept of Feminism. Notes for Practicing Historians', in *German Women in the Eighteenth and Nineteenth Centuries. A Social and Literary History*, ed. Ruth-Ellen B. Joeres and Mary Jo Maynes, Bloomington, Indiana, pp. 247–58.

Ewart, Felicie [Emilie Exner] (1895) *Die Emancipation in der Ehe. Briefe an einen Arzt*, Hamburg.

——— (1906) *Eine Abrechnung in der Frauenfrage*, Hamburg.

Federn, Else (1901) 'Settlement in Österreich', *Dokumente der Frauen*, 4, pp. 596–605.

——— (1930) 'Die Entwicklung der modernen Fürsorge', in *Frauenbewegung, Frauenbildung und Frauenarbeit in Österreich*, ed. Martha Stephanie Braun *et al.*, pp. 87–94.

——— (1935) 'Zur Erinnerung an Marie Lang', in *Marie Lang. Gedenkblatt des Settlement für seine Mitglieder und Freunde*, pp. 15–26.

Federn, Paul (1919) *Die vaterlose Gesellschaft. Zur Psychologie der Revolution.*

Fellner, Günter (1986) 'Athenäum. Die Geschichte einer Frauenhochschule in Wien', *Zeitgeschichte*, 14, pp. 99–115.

Festausschuss (ed.) (1927) *Dreissig Jahre Frauenstudium in Österreich 1897 bis 1927.*

Fickert, Auguste (1892**a**) 'Die Frauenfrage in "Freiland"', *Neuzeit*, 4, pp. 2–6.

——— (1892**b**) 'Rundschreiben', *Neuzeit*, 4, p. 88.

——— (1893) 'Bildungsgang eines jungen Mädchens', *Die Volksstimme*, 17 May, pp. 6–7.

——— (1896**a**) 'Die Socialpolitiker und die Frauen', *Die Volksstimme*, 15 November, p. 7.

——— (1896**b**) 'Meinungsaustausch', *Frauenleben*, 8, p. 58.

——— (1897) 'Zum Brüsseler Frauencongress', *Die Volksstimme*, 24 October, p. 7.

——— (1898) 'Ziele der Frauenbewegung', *Die Wage*, 1 (15 January), pp. 42–3.

——— (1899) 'Das Frauenwahlrecht in Österreich', *Dokumente der Frauen*, 1, pp. 55–61.

——— (1902**a**) 'An die Leser!', *Neues Frauenleben*, 14, no. 1 (January), inside front cover.

——— (1902**b**) 'Der Stand der Frauenbildung in Österreich', in *Handbuch der Frauenbewegung*, ed. Helene Lange and Gertrud Bäumer, Berlin, Vol. III, pp. 160–90.

——— (1903**a**) 'Sozialdemokratie und Frauenbewegung', *Neues Frauenleben*, 15, no. 12 (December), pp. 1–3.

——— (1903**b**) 'Zur zweiten Generalversammlung des Bundes Österreichischer Frauenvereine', *Neues Frauenleben*, 15, no. 6 (June), pp. 19–21.

——— (1905**a**) 'An die Wiener Schulkinder zur Schiller-Feier', *Neues Frauenleben*, 17, no. 4 (April), pp. 9–10.

——— (1905**b**) 'Hohes k.k. Justizministerium', *Neues Frauenleben*, 17, no. 5 (May), pp. 1–6.

——— (1906**a**) 'Eine Abrechnung in der Frauenfrage', *Neues Frauenleben*, 18, no. 10 (October), pp. 18–20.

——— (1906**b**) 'Ziele und Aufgaben der Frauenbewegung', *Neues Frauenleben*, 18, no. 1 (January), pp. 1–6.

——— (1910) 'Was ist Grösse?', *Neues Frauenleben*, 22, no. 4 (April), pp. 109–12.

——— (with Enna von Filek) (1907**a**) *Das Frauenstimmrecht*, 19, no. 6 (June), pp. 8–10.

——— (with Enna von Filek) (1907**b**) 'Der §30 des Vereinsgesetzes', *Neues Frauenleben*, 19, no. 6 (June), pp. 7–8.

——— *et al.* (1899) Vorwort der Herausgeberinnen, *Dokumente der Frauen*, 1, pp. 1–4.

——— *et al.* (1909) 'Aufruf zur Schaffung eines Einküchenhauses', *Neues Frauenleben*, 21, no. 5 (May), pp. 117–19.

Filek, Egid von (1904**a**) 'Blühen und Reifen', *Neues Frauenleben*, 16, no. 7 (July), pp. 16–19.

——— (1904**b**) 'Mädchenlektüre', *Neues Frauenleben*, 16, no. 12 (December), pp. 3–8.

Flich, Renate (1987) 'Frauen und Frieden. Analytische und empirische Studie über die Zusammenhänge der österreichischen Frauenbewegung und der Friedensbewegung mit besonderer Berücksichtigung des Zeitraumes seit 1960', in *Überlegungen zum Frieden*, ed. Manfred Rauchensteiner, pp. 410–61.

——— (1990) 'Der Fall Auguste Fickert – eine Wiener Lehrerin macht Schlagzeilen', *Wiener Geschichtsblätter*, 45, no. 1, pp. 1–24.

Fout, John C. (ed.) (1984) *German Women in the Nineteenth Century. A Social History*, London.

——— (1986) 'The Viennese Enquete of 1896 on Working Women', in *German Women in the Eighteenth and Nineteenth Centuries. A Social and Literary History*, ed. Ruth-Ellen B. Joeres and Mary Jo Maynes, Bloomington, Indiana, pp. 42–60.

Frank, Herbert (1970) 'Friedrich Jodl (1849–1914). Seine Lehre und seine Rolle in der bürgerlichen Reformbewegung Österreichs und Deutschlands', unpublished doctoral dissertation, University of Freiburg im Breisgau.

Franzos, Marie (*et al.*) (1906) 'Aus dem allgemeinen österreichischen Frauenvereine', *Der Bund*, 1, no. 6 (June), pp. 10–11.

Fred, W. (1899) 'Idole, Roman von Rosa Mayreder', *Das literarische Echo*, 1, cols. 1304–5.

Freismuth, Elisabeth (1984) 'Die Frau im öffentlichen Recht', in *Die Frau im Korsett. Wiener Frauenalltag wischen*

Klischee und Wirklichkeit 1848–1920, exhibition catalogue, Historisches Museum der Stadt Wien, pp. 30–40.

Freundlich, Emmy (1922) *Die Hausfrau, der Einkaufskorb und der Konsumverein.*

Friedrichs, Elisabeth (1981) *Die deutschsprachigen Schriftstellerinnen des 18. und 19. Jahrhunderts. Ein Lexikon*, Stuttgart.

Fromm, Erich (1980) *Greatness and Limitations of Freud's Thought*, New York.

Fürth, Ernestine von (1918) 'Wahlpropaganda', *Der Bund*, 13, no. 10 (December), pp. 3–4.

——— (1930) 'Geschichte der Frauenstimmrechtsbewegung', in *Frauenbewegung, Frauenbildung und Frauenarbeit in Österreich*, ed. Martha Stephanie Braun *et al.*, pp. 65–83.

G., A. (1901) 'Aus der Frauenbewegung', *Frauenleben*, 12, no. 1 (January), pp. 13–14.

Gerber, Adele (1910) 'Auguste Fickert und die österreichische Frauenbewegung', *Neues Frauenleben*, 22, no. 7 (July), pp. 208–14.

Glass, Charlotte (1896) 'Zur Frauenfrage des Bürgerthums', *Arbeiterinnen-Zeitung*, 19 November, pp. 2–5.

Glöckel, Leopoldine (1901) 'Nach den Wahlen', *Dokumente der Frauen*, 4, pp. 658–62.

Goldscheid, Rudolf (1909) *Darwin als Lebenselement unserer modernen Kultur.*

——— (1913) *Frauenfrage und Menschenökonomie.*

——— (1921) *Frauen, Freiheit und Friede.*

Göllner, Renate (1986) 'Mädchenbildung um 1900. Eugenie Schwarzwald und ihre Schulen', unpublished doctoral dissertation, University of Vienna.

Golm, Rudolf [Rudolf Goldscheid] (1888) *Lord Byron, Ein Drama.*

——— (1895) *Der alte Adam und die neue Eva. Ein Roman unserer Übergangszeit*, Dresden.

Grabscheidt, Franz von (1894) 'Ein Wort zur Frauenfrage', *Frauen-Werke*, 1, no. 5, pp. 33–4 and no. 6, pp. 41–2.

Grieser, Dietmar (1989) 'Ein unbedachtes Wort. Lina Loos und Heinz Lang', in *Eine Liebe in Wien*, St Pölten, pp. 46–58.

Grossmann, Stefan (1899) 'Seelische Heilprocesse', *Dokumente der Frauen*, 2, pp. 365–8.

——— (1931) *Ich war begeistert. Eine Lebensgeschichte*, Berlin.

Gruber, Max (1910) 'Mädchenerziehung und Rassenhygiene', *Neue Freie Presse*, 2 October (Morgenblatt), pp. 3–4.

Grün, Heinrich (1907) *Prostitution in Theorie und Wirklichkeit.*

Grünes, Willy (1909) 'Frank Wedekind', *Neues Frauenleben*, 21, no. 10 (October), pp. 367–8.

Grünwald-Zerkowitz, Sidonie von (1902) *Die Schattenseiten des Frauenstudiums*, Zurich.

——— (1905) *Wie verheiratet man mitgiftlose Mädchen?*

Guschlbauer, Elisabeth (1974) 'Der Beginn der politischen Emanzipation der Frau in Österreich 1848–1919', unpublished doctoral dissertation, University of Salzburg.

Gutt, Barbara (1978) *Emanzipation bei Arthur Schnitzler*, Berlin.

H.H. (1910) 'Das Universitätsstudium der Frauen und die Lyzeen', *Der Bund*, 5, no. 3 (March), pp. 4–6.

Haag, Ella (1893) *Die physische und sittliche Entartung des modernen Mannes*, Berlin.

Hacker, Hanna (1981) 'Staatsbürgerinnen. Ein Streifzug durch die Protest- und Unterwerfungsstrategien in der Frauenbewegung und im weiblichen Alltag 1918–1933', in *Aufbruch und Untergang. Österreichische Kultur zwischen 1918 und 1938*, ed. Franz Kadrnoska, pp. 225–45.

——— (1987) *Frauen und Freundinnen. Studien zur 'weiblichen Homosexualität' am Beispiel Österreich 1870–1938*, Weinheim.

Hackl, Louise (1908) 'Von und über Dienstboten', *Der Bund*, 3, no. 5 (June), pp. 7–8.

Hainisch, Marianne (1870) *Zur Frage des Frauen-Unterrichts. Vortrag gehalten bei der dritten General-Versammlung des Wiener Frauen-Erwerb-Vereines.*

——— (1875) *Die Brotfrage der Frau.*

——— (1892) 'Ein Mutterwort über die Frauenfrage. Vortrag gehalten am 1. Februar 1892 zu Wien im Verein für erweiterte Frauenbildung', in *4. Jahresbericht des Vereines für erweiterte Frauenbildung in Wien*, pp. 21–32.

——— (1896) *Seherinnen, Hexen und die Wahnvorstellungen über das Weib im 19. Jahrhundert. Vortrag gehalten im Vereine für erweiterte Frauenbildung in Wien am 14. Jänner 1896.*

——— (1901**a**) *Bericht über den International Council mit einem Rückblick auf die österreichische Frauenbewegung der Jahrhundertwende.*

——— (1901**b**) 'Ein neuer Roman und ein Band Gedichte. Beiträge zur Familienliteratur Österreichs', *Dokumente der Frauen*, 4, pp. 632–4.

——— (1901**c**) 'Die Geschichte der Frauenbewegung in Österreich', in *Handbuch der Frauenbewegung*, ed. Helene Lange and Gertrud Bäumer, Berlin, Vol. I, pp. 167–88.

——— (1904) *Aufwand und Erfolg der Mittelschule vom Standpunkte der Mutter. Vortrag gehalten am 25. Jänner 1904.*

——— (1905) 'Geleitwort', *Der Bund*, 1, no. 1 (November), pp. 1–2.

——— (1906**a**) 'Zur Mittelschulreform', *Der Bund*, 1, no. 7 (November), pp. 9–10.

——— (1906**b**) 'Zur Schulreform', *Die Wage*, 9, pp. 736–9.

——— (1908) 'Die Mittelschul-Enquete', *Der Bund*, 3, no. 2 (February), pp. 1–3.

——— (1910) 'Katholische Frauenbewegung', *Der Bund*, 5, no. 3 (March), pp. 3–4.

——— (1911**a**) *Frauenarbeit.*

——— (1911**b**) 'Zur Frauenbewegung', *Der Bund*, 6, no. 4 (April), pp. 1–2.

——— (1912) 'Die Enquete über das Kinematographenwesen', *Der Bund*, 7, no. 5 (May), pp. 1–3.

——— (1913) *Die Mutter.*

——— (1914) 'Die Friedensbestrebungen und die Frauen', *Der Bund*, 9, no. 8 (October), pp. 10–12.

——— (1918) 'An unsere Leser!', *Der Bund*, 13, no. 10 (December), pp. 1–3.

——— (1930) 'Zur Geschichte der österreichischen Frauenbewegung. Aus meinen Erinnerungen', in *Frauenbewegung, Frauenbildung und Frauenarbeit in Österreich*, ed. Martha Stephanie Braun *et al.*, pp. 13–24.

Hamann, Brigitte (1986) *Bertha von Suttner. Ein Leben für den Frieden*, Munich.

——— (1990) 'Österreichische Frauen in der Friedensbewegung', in *Aufbruch ins Jahrhundert der Frau? Rosa Mayreder und der Feminismus in Wien um 1900*, exhibition catalogue, Historisches Museum der Stadt Wien, pp. 134–41.

Hamann, Richard, and Hermand, Jost (1967) *Deutsche Kunst und Kultur von der Gründerzeit bis zum Expressionismus*, Vol. IV, *Stilkunst um 1900*, Berlin.

Hanisch, Ernst, and Fleischer, Ulrike (1896) *Im Schatten berühmter Zeiten. Salzburg in den Jahren Georg Trakls (1887–1914)*, Salzburg.

Hannak, Emanuel (1895) *Prof. E. Alberts*

Essay. Die Frauen und das Studium der Medicin. Kritisch betrachtet.

Harriman, Helga H. (1985) 'Marie von Ebner-Eschenbach in Feminist Perspective', *Modern Austrian Literature*, 18, pp. 27–38.

Hasse, Else (1900) 'Arbeit und Ewigkeit', *Dokumente der Frauen*, 3, pp. 305–16.

Hauer, Karl (1906) 'Weib und Kultur', *Die Fackel*, 213, pp. 5–10.

Heindl, Waltraud (1981**a**) 'Ehebruch und Strafrecht. Zur bürgerlichen Moral in Österreich um 1900', in *Das ewige Klischee. Zum Rollenbild und Selbstverständnis bei Männern und Frauen*, ed. Autorinnengruppe der Uni Wien, pp. 155–78.

——— (1981**b**) 'Frau und bürgerliches Recht. Bemerkungen zu den Reformvorschlägen österreichischer Frauenvereine vor dem Ersten Weltkrieg', in *Politik und Gesellschaft im alten und neuen Österreich. Festschrift für Rudolf Neck*, Vol. I, pp. 133–49.

——— (1990) 'Die Studentinnen der Universität Wien. Zur Entwicklung des Frauenstudiums (ab 1897)', in *'Das Weib existiert nicht für sich'. Geschlechterbeziehungen in der bürgerlichen Gesellschaft*, ed. Heide Dienst and Edith Saurer, pp. 174–88.

——— and Tichy, Marina (eds) (1990) *'Durch Erkenntnis zu Freiheit und Glück . . .'. Frauen an der Universität Wien (ab 1897).*

Helperstorfer, Irmgard (1984) 'Die Frauenrechtsbewegung und ihre Ziele', in *Die Frau im Korsett. Wiener Frauenalltag zwischen Klischee und Wirklichkeit 1848–1920*, exhibition catalogue, Historisches Museum der Stadt Wien, pp. 21–9.

Herdan-Zuckmayer, Alice (1979) *Genies sind im Lehrplan nicht vorgesehen*, Frankfurt am Main.

Hertzka, Theodor (1896) *Freiland. Ein sociales Zukunftsbild*, Dresden. First published 1889.

Hertzka, Yella (1927) 'Die Frau in der Politik', in *Das Buch der Frau. Eine Zeitkritik*, ed. Helene Granitsch, pp. 91–3.

Herzfelder, Henriette (1906) 'Die Wahlrechtsversammlung der Wiener Frauen', *Der Bund*, 1, no. 2 (January), pp. 1–2.

——— (1907) *Die gemeinsame Erziehung der Geschlechter*, Leipzig.

——— (1909**a**) 'Frauenbewegung und Sexualethik', *Der Bund*, 4, no. 6 (September), pp. 14–15.

——— (1909**b**) 'Frauenemanzipation und Erziehung', *Der Bund*, 4, no. 8 (December), pp. 5–7.

——— (1910) 'Mehr Mutterschutz', *Der Bund*, 5, no. 6 (October), pp. 6–9.

——— (1914) *Die organisierte Mütterlichkeit*, Leipzig.

Heymann, Lida Gustava (1913) 'Biographische Angaben', in Irma von Troll-Borostyáni, *Die Gleichstellung der Geschlechter und die Reform der Jugenderziehung. Die Mission unseres Jahrhunderts*, ed. Bayerischer Verein für Frauenstimmrecht, Munich, pp. ii–vi.

Hoerschelmann, Klaudia (1988) 'Pazifismus und Frauen in Österreich von 1918 bis 1934', unpublished M.A. thesis, University of Vienna.

Hoffmann, Elisabeth (1900) 'Weibliche Einjährige', *Dokumente der Frauen*, 4, pp. 425–8.

Hofmannsthal, Hugo von (1959) *Aufzeichnungen*, in Hugo von Hofmannsthal, *Gesammelte Werke in Einzelausgaben*, ed. Herbert Steiner, Frankfurt am Main, Vol. XV.

——— (1984) *Gedichte*, ed. Eugene Weber, in Hugo von Hofmannsthal, *Sämtliche Werke*, Frankfurt am Main, Vol. I.

Holleis, Eva (1978) *Die Sozialpolitische Partei. Sozialliberale Bestrebungen in Wien um 1900.*

Holm, Erich [Mathilde Prager] (1900) *Jenseits der Ehe*, Dresden.

——— (1906) 'Henrik Ibsen', *Neues Frauenleben*, 18, no. 6 (June), pp. 1–3.

——— (1910a) *Henrik Ibsens politisches Vermächtnis. Studien zu den vier letzten Dramen des Dichters*, Leipzig.

——— (1910b) 'Wandlungen', *Neues Frauenleben*, 22, no. 1 (January), pp. 1–5.

Hönigsberg, Margret (1899) 'Hanna', *Dokumente der Frauen*, 1, pp. 252–4.

Hruschka, Ella (1892) *Der Wirkungskreis des Weibes. Ein Beitrag zur Lösung der Frauenfrage.*

Hubenstorf, Michael (1981) 'Sozialmedizin, Menschenökonomie, Volksgesundheit', in *Aufbruch und Untergang. Österreichische Kultur zwischen 1918 und 1938*, ed. Franz Kadrnoska, pp. 247–65.

Internationale Frauenliga für Frieden und Freiheit (1930) *Fünfzehn Jahre Frauenliga. Tätigkeit und Organisation der Internationalen Frauenliga für Frieden und Freiheit 1915–1930.*

Ipold, Maja (1904) 'Der erste österr. Beamtinnentag', *Neues Frauenleben*, 16, no. 12 (December), pp. 1–3.

Janssen-Jurreit, Marielouise (1979) 'Nationalbiologie, Sexualreform und Geburtenrückgang. Über die Zusammenhänge von Bevölkerungspolitik und Frauenbewegung um die Jahrhundertwende', in *Die Überwindung der Sprachlosigkeit. Texte aus der neuen Frauenbewegung*, ed. Gabriele Dietze, Darmstadt, pp. 139–75.

Jászi, Oskar (1928) 'Rosa Mayreder – die Revolutionärin', in *Der Aufstieg der Frau. Zu Rosa Mayreders 70. Geburtstag am 30. November 1928 als Ehrengabe dargebracht vom Verlag Eugen Diederichs in Jena*, Jena, pp. 33–5.

'Jemand' [Bertha von Suttner] (1889) *Das Maschinenalter. Zukunftsvorlesungen über unsere Zeit*, Zurich.

Jerusalem(-Kotányi), Else (1902) *Gebt uns die Wahrheit. Ein Beitrag zu unserer Erziehung zur Ehe*, Leipzig.

——— (1909) *Der Heilige Skarabäus. Roman*, Berlin. English title: *The Red House*. London, 1932.

Jodl, Friedrich (1895) *Über das Wesen und die Aufgabe der Ethischen Gesellschaft. Rede zur constituierenden Versammlung der Ethischen Gesellschaft in Wien (10. Dezember 1894).*

——— (1899) 'Höhere Mädchenbildung und die Gymnasialfrage', *Dokumente der Frauen*, 1, pp. 141–6.

Jušek, Karin J. (1990) 'Ein Wiener Bordellroman. Else Jerusalems "Heiliger Skarabäus"', in *'Das Weib existiert nicht für sich'. Geschlechterbeziehungen in der bürgerlichen Gesellschaft*, ed. Heide Dienst and Edith Saurer, pp. 139–47.

Kancler, Emma (1947) 'Die österreichische Frauenbewegung und ihre Presse. (Von ihren Anfängen bis zum Ende des Ersten Weltkrieges)', unpublished doctoral dissertation, University of Vienna.

Kassowitz, Julie (1902) 'Die moderne Frau und die Antialkoholbewegung', *Dokumente der Frauen*, 7, pp. 217–25.

Katscher, Leopold (n.d.) *Wunde Punkte unseres Frauenlebens.*

Kempny, Hedy and Schnitzler, Arthur (1984) *'Das Mädchen mit den dreizehn Seelen'. Eine Korrespondenz*, ed. Heinz P. Adamek, Reinbek bei Hamburg.

Key, Ellen (1899) 'Weibliche Sittlichkeit', *Dokumente der Frauen*, 1, pp. 171–84.

Kjäer, Illy (1929) 'Zehn Jahre parlamentarische Frauenarbeit in Österreich', *Die Österreicherin*, 2, no. 2 (February), pp. 2–4.

Klein, Hugo (1903) *Über die Frauenkleidung vom Standpunkte der Hygiene.*

Kocmata, Karl F. (1925) *Die Prostitution in Wien. Streifbilder vom Jahrmarkt des Liebeslebens*.

Kofler, Viktoria (1892) 'Der erste österreichische Frauentag und die Arbeiterinnen', *Arbeiterinnen-Zeitung*, 3 June, pp. 3–4.

Kokoschka, Oskar (1971) *Mein Leben*, Munich.

Kollontai, Alexandra (1977) *Die neue Moral und die Arbeiterklasse*, Munster. First published 1918.

Kotányi(-Jerusalem), Else (1899) *Venus am Kreuz*, Leipzig.

Krafft-Ebing, Richard (1907) *Psychopathia Sexualis mit besonderer Berücksichtigung der konträren Sexualempfindung. Eine medizinisch-gerichtliche Studie für Ärzte und Juristen*, Stuttgart. First published 1886.

Kraszna, Hermann (1907) 'Ein Strafrechtsfall', *Neues Frauenleben*, 19, no. 11 (November), pp. 14–17.

Kraus, Karl (1906) 'Sittenrichter', *Die Fackel*, 212, pp. 26–8.

Kraus, Sigmund (1901) 'Zur Lage der Lehrerinnen in Österreich', *Dokumente der Frauen*, 4, pp. 610–13.

Kristan, Etbin (1900) 'Durst', *Dokumente der Frauen*, 3, pp. 300–2.

Kronfeld, Moritz (1895) *Die Frauen und die Medicin. Professor Albert zur Antwort. Zugleich eine Darstellung der ganzen Frage*.

Kulka, Leopoldine (1904) 'Lyzeen oder Gymnasien?', *Neues Frauenleben*, 16, no. 10 (October), pp. 1–3.

——— (1905) 'Die dritte Generalversammlung des Bundes österreichischer Frauenvereine', *Neues Frauenleben*, 17, no. 5 (May), pp. 14–18.

——— (1907) 'Bis zur Dozentur und – nicht weiter!', *Neues Frauenleben*, 19, no. 9 (September), pp. 1–5.

——— (1908) 'Wozu brauchen wir weibliche Juristen?', *Neues Frauenleben*, 20, no. 8 (August), pp. 193–5.

——— (1909) 'Noch einmal "Der Heilige Skarabäus"', *Neues Frauenleben*, 21, no. 8 (August), pp. 216–18.

——— (1910**a**) 'Auguste Fickert', *Neues Frauenleben*, 22, no. 7 (July), pp. 205–8.

——— (1910**b**) 'Der erste österreichische katholische Frauentag', *Neues Frauenleben*, 22, no. 5 (May), pp. 145–51.

——— (1910**c**) 'Mädchenerziehung und Rassenhygiene', *Neues Frauenleben*, 22, no. 9 (September), pp. 263–5.

——— (1910**d**) 'Was bedeutet Bebel der bürgerlichen Frauenbewegung?', *Neues Frauenleben*, 22, no. 3 (March), pp. 78–81.

——— (1911**a**) 'Die Eröffnung des "Heimhofes"', *Neues Frauenleben*, 22, no. 11 (November), pp. 293–6.

——— (1911**b**) 'Heim und Staat', *Neues Frauenleben*, 22, no. 10 (October), pp. 259–60.

——— (1912) 'Teuerung und Kriegsgefahr', *Neues Frauenleben*, 24, no. 10 (October), pp. 266–8.

——— (1913) 'Gegenseitige Hilfe als Naturgesetz und Entwicklungsfaktor', *Neues Frauenleben*, 25, no. 1 (January), pp. 2–8.

——— (1914**a**) 'Der 2. österr.-katholische Frauentag', *Neues Frauenleben*, 26, no. 5 (May), pp. 136–41.

——— (1914**b**) 'Hausfrauenbewegung und Frauenbewegung', *Neues Frauenleben*, 26, no. 6 (June), pp. 165–9.

——— (1914**c**) 'Der Wille zum Frieden', *Neues Frauenleben*, 26, no. 12 (November), pp. 261–2.

——— (1919) 'Zur Wiedererweckung der Fraueninternationale', *Der Bund*, 14, no. 2 (March), pp. 11–13.

Kulturpolitische Gesellschaft (1905) *Protokolle der Enquete betreffend die Reform des österreichischen Eherechts (vom 27. Jänner bis 24. Februar 1905).*

Kupec, Ingrid (1963) 'Die Eheschranken für die berufstätige Frau seit Beginn der industriellen Gesellschaft am Beispiel Österreichs', unpublished doctoral dissertation, University of Vienna.

L., G. (1897) 'Der Heiratsmarkt', *Wiener Rundschau*, 2, p. 517.

Laessig, Hildegard (1949) 'Marianne Hainisch und die österreichische Frauenbewegung', unpublished doctoral dissertation, University of Vienna.

Lafleur, Ingrun (1978) 'Five Socialist Women. Traditionalist Conflicts and Socialist Visions in Austria 1893–1934', in *Socialist Women. European Socialist Feminism in the Nineteenth and Early Twentieth Centuries*, ed. Marilyn J. Boxer and Jean H. Quataert, New York, pp. 215–48.

Lang, Marie (1897–8) 'Das Secessionsgebäude', *Wiener Rundschau*, 2, pp. 939–40.

——— (1903) 'Über Erziehung', *Die Zeit*, 21 May (Familienbeilage), pp. 15–18.

——— (1930) 'Wie ich zur Arbeit an der Frauenbewegung kam', *Die Österreicherin*, 3, no. 3, p. 4.

Langer, Marie (1986) *Von Wien bis Managua. Wege einer Psychoanalytikerin*, Freiburg im Breisgau.

Langer-Ostrawsky, Gertrud (1984) 'Erziehung und Bildung. Eine Untersuchung zum Schulwesen für Mädchen 1848–1920', in *Die Frau im Korsett. Wiener Frauenalltag zwischen Klischee und Wirklichkeit 1848–1920*, exhibition catalogue, Historisches Museum der Stadt Wien, pp. 54–60.

Leichter, Käthe (1973) *Käthe Leichter. Leben und Werk*, ed. Herbert Steiner.

Leistner, Sofie (1897) 'Kämpfe', *Frauenleben*, 9, no. 4 (July), pp. 25–6.

Lemmermeyer, Fritz (1890) 'Zur Frauenliteratur in Österreich', *Moderne Dichtung*, 1, p. 383.

Le Rider, Jacques (1982) *Le cas Otto Weininger. Les racines de l'antiféminisme et de l'antisémitisme*, Paris.

——— (1985) 'Modernismus/Feminismus – Modernität/Virilität. Otto Weininger und die asketische Moderne', in *Ornament und Askese. Im Zeitgeist des Wien der Jahrhundertwende*, ed. Alfred Pfabigan, pp. 242–60.

——— (1989) '"Vielleicht ist eine der wichtigsten Entstehungsbedingungen der Frauenbewegung in Veränderungen innerhalb des männlichen Geschlechts zu suchen". Rosa Mayreder und die Krise der modernen Männlichkeit', in *Rosa Mayreder 1858–1938. Mitteilungen des Instituts für Wissenschaft und Kunst*, 44, no. 1, pp. 12–16.

Liebenfels, Lanz von (1909) *Die Gefahren des Frauenrechts und die Notwendigkeit der mannesrechtlichen Herrenmoral*, Rodaun.

——— (1911**a**) *Die Komik der Frauenrechtlerei. Eine heitere Chronik der Weiberwirtschaft*, Rodaun.

——— (1911**b**) *Die Tragik der Frauenrechtlerei. Eine ernste Chronik der Weiberwirtschaft*, Rodaun.

——— (1912) *Die soziale, politische und sexuelle Weiberwirtschaft unserer Zeit*, Rodaun.

Lissauer, Ernst (1928) [no title] in *Der Aufstieg der Frau. Zu Rosa Mayreders 70. Geburtstag am 30. November 1928 als Ehrengabe dargebracht vom Verlage Eugen Diederichs in Jena*, Jena, pp. 113–15.

Lonyay, Gräfin Elemer von (Princess Stephanie of Belgium), (1909) 'Frauenemanzipation und Erziehung', *Österreichische Rundschau*, 21 (October–December), pp. 255–8.

Loos, Adolf (1902) 'Damenmode', *Dokumente der Frauen*, 6, pp. 660–4.

Löwy, Wilhelm (1905) 'Konkubinate in Wien', *Österreichische Rundschau*, 3 (May–July), pp. 591–6.

M., O. (1914) 'Gründung der neuen Sektion "Mutterschaftsversicherung"', *Neues Frauenleben*, 26, no. 4 (April), pp. 113–14.

Mach, Ernst (1903) *Analyse der Empfindungen und das Verhältnis des Physischen zum Psychischen*, Jena. First published 1885.

——— (1910) *Populär-wissenschaftliche Vorlesungen*, Leipzig.

Marriot, Emil [Emilie Mataja] (1895) 'Das braune Mädchen', *Neues Wiener Abendblatt*, 21 January, p. 6.

——— (1897) *Der Heiratsmarkt. Sittenbild in drei Akten*, Berlin.

——— (1903) 'Nietzsche und das "neue Weib"', *Neues Wiener Tagblatt*, 3 May, pp. 2–3.

Mauthner, Fritz (1893–4) 'Theater', *Die Nation*, 11, p. 760.

Mayreder, Rosa (1896) *Aus meiner Jugend. Novellen*, Dresden.

——— (1897) 'Richard Wagner, der Heide', *Magazin für Litteratur*, 66, cols. 1333–8.

——— (1898) *Die Abolitionisten-Föderation*.

——— (1899**a**) 'Antwort auf einen Darwinianer', *Dokumente der Frauen*, 1, pp. 198–9.

——— (1899**b**) 'Frau Grünwald-Zerkowitz', *Dokumente der Frauen*, 1, pp. 71–2.

——— (1899**c**) *Idole. Geschichte einer Liebe*, Berlin.

——— (1900**a**) 'Familienliteratur', *Dokumente der Frauen*, 2, pp. 543–50.

——— (1900**b**) 'Über Hugo Wolf und seine Oper. Erinnerungen', in '*Der Corregidor' von Hugo Wolf. Kritische und biographische Beiträge zu seiner Würdigung*, ed. Edmund Hellmer, Berlin, pp. 22–61.

——— (1903) *Pipin. Ein Sommererlebnis*.

——— (1905) *Zur Kritik der Weiblichkeit. Essays*, Jena. English title: *A Survey of the Woman Problem*. Translated by Herman Scheffauer. London, 1913.

——— (1906) 'Die Frauen und der Prozess Riehl', *Neues Frauenleben*, 18, no. 11 (November), pp. 7–17.

——— (1907) 'Zur Kritik der Weiblichkeit', *Kunstwart*, 21, pp. 420–2.

——— (1908**a**) *Übergänge*, Jena. First published 1897.

——— (1908**b**) *Zwischen Himmel und Erde. Sonette*, Jena.

——— (1910**a**) 'Das Urphänomen der Geschlechtlichkeit', *Die neue Generation*, 6, pp. 351–5.

——— (1910**b**) 'Die Kultur der Geschlechter', *Frauenzukunft*, 1, pp. 77–83.

——— (1912**a**) 'Irma von Troll-Borostyáni', *Neues Frauenleben*, 24, no. 3 (March), pp. 61–3.

——— (1912**b**) 'Mutterschaft und doppelte Moral', in *Mutterschaft. Ein Sammelwerk für die Probleme des Weibes als Mutter*, ed. Adele Schreiber, Munich, pp. 156–62.

——— (1914) Nachwort, *Neues Frauenleben*, 26, nos. 1–2 (January–February), pp. 22–4.

——— (1915**a**) 'Der Haager Frauenkongress im Lichte der Frauenbewegung', *Neues Frauenleben*, 27, no. 5 (May), pp. 98–101.

——— (1915**b**) 'Die Frau und der Krieg', *Internationale Rundschau*, 1, pp. 516–27.

——— (1916) 'Kriegsphrasen', *Internationale Rundschau*, 2, pp. 585–90, 648–52.

——— (1917) 'Sozialistische Betrachtungen zum Weltkrieg. Zwei Schriften Max Adlers', *Internationale Rundschau*, 3, pp. 638–40.

——— (1921**a**) *Die Frau und der Internationalismus*.

——— (1921**b**) *Fabeleien über göttliche und menschliche Dinge*.

——— (1923) *Geschlecht und Kultur. Essays*, Jena.

——— (1926) *Der typische Verlauf sozialer Bewegungen*.

——— (1928**a**) 'Kann man von einer Dekadenz der Frauenbewegung sprechen? Äusserungen führender Frauen', *Neue Freie Presse*, 6 (January), p. 14.

——— (1928**b**) 'Gleichstellung und Ehe', *Die Österreicherin*, 1, no. 2 (February), pp. 1–2.

——— (1929) 'Ihr Charakterbild', in *Auguste Fickert. Zur Enthüllung ihres Denkmals am 22. Juni 1929*, pp. 4–9.

——— (1930) 'Wie ich zur Arbeit an der Frauenbewegung kam', *Die Österreicherin*, 3, no. 3 (March), p. 3.

——— (1932) 'Bürgerliches Vorurteil', *Die Bereitschaft*, 12, no. 4 (August), pp. 27–9.

——— (1933) *Der letzte Gott*, Stuttgart.

——— (1935) 'Mensch und Natur', *Die Glocke*, 1, no. 18 (November), pp. 3–7.

——— (1936) 'Von Wagner zu Nietzsche. Ein Jugenderlebnis', *Die Glocke*, 2, no. 23–4 (February), pp. 8–15.

——— (1948) *Das Haus in der Landskrongasse. Jugenderinnerungen*, ed. Käthe Braun-Prager.

——— (1988**a**) *Mein Pantheon. Lebenserinnerungen*, ed. Susanne Kerkovius, Dornach.

——— (1988**b**) *Tagebücher 1873–1937*, ed. Harriet Anderson, Frankfurt am Main.

For a full list of Rosa Mayreder's writings see Aufbruch ins Jahrhundert der Frau? Rosa Mayreder und der Feminismus in Wien um 1900, *exhibition catalogue, Historisches Museum der Stadt Wien, 1989, pp. 211–13.*

McGrath, William J. (1974) *Dionysian Art and Populist Politics in Austria*, New Haven.

McKittrick, Brigid Mary Ursula (1987) 'Women – The Borderline Case. Karl Kraus and the Role of Women in turn-of-the-century Vienna', unpublished doctoral dissertation, University of Exeter.

Meditz, Johanna (1979) 'Die "Arbeiterinnen-Zeitung" und die Frauenfrage. Ein Beitrag zur Geschichte der österreichischen Frauenbewegung der Jahre 1890–1918', unpublished doctoral dissertation, University of Vienna.

Meinel-Kernstock, Gertrude Josefine (1948) 'Dora Stockert-Meynert und der Verein der Schriftstellerinnen und Künstlerinnen in Wien', unpublished doctoral dissertation, University of Vienna.

Meisel-Hess, Grete (1900) 'Zur Frauenclub-Eröffnung', *Dokumente der Frauen*, 4, pp. 541–4.

——— (1901**a**) *Generationen und ihre Bildner*, Berlin.

——— (1901**b**) *In der modernen Weltanschauung*, Leipzig.

——— (1901**c**) 'Liebelei', *Dokumente der Frauen*, 4, pp. 625–8.

——— (1902) *Fanny Roth. Eine Jung-Frauengeschichte*, Leipzig.

——— (1903) *Annie-Bianka. Eine Reisegeschichte*, Leipzig.

——— (1904) *Weiberhass und Weiberverachtung. Eine Erwiderung auf die in Dr Otto Weiningers Buche 'Geschlecht und Charakter' geäusserten Anschauungen über 'die Frau und ihre Frage'.*

——— (1905) *Eine sonderbare Hochzeitsreise*.

——— (1907**a**) *Die Stimme. Roman in Blättern*, Berlin.

——— (1907**b**) 'Ehe und Ehegesetze', *Die Freiheit*, 28 October, pp. 8–9.

——— (1909) *Die sexuelle Krise. Eine sozial-psychologische Untersuchung*, Jena. English title: *The Sexual Crisis. A Critique of Our Sex Life*. New York, 1917.

——— (1911**a**) *Die Intellektuellen*, Berlin.

——— (1911**b**) 'Mutterschutz als soziale Weltanschauung', *Die neue Generation*, 7, pp. 150–9.

——— (1912) *Geister*, Leipzig.

——— (1913) 'Hebbel und die Frauen', *Die neue Generation*, 9, pp. 170–84.

——— (1914) *Betrachtungen zur Frauenfrage*, Berlin.

——— (1917) *Die Bedeutung der Monogamie*, Jena.

Meissner-Diemer, Fanny (1897) 'Frauenrecht in Österreich', in *Der Internationale Kongress für Frauenwerke und Frauenbestrebungen in Berlin*, ed. the Redaktions-Kommission, Berlin, pp. 312–27.

Merk, Emma (1901) 'Nur für die Kinder' *Dokumente der Frauen*, 4, pp. 774–8.

Meyer-Renschhausen, Elisabeth (1984) 'Radikal, weil sie konservativ sind? Überlegungen zum "Konservatismus" und zur "Radikalität" der deutschen Frauenbewegung vor 1933 als Frage nach der Methode der Geschichtsforschung', in *Die ungeschriebene Geschichte. Historische Frauenforschung*, ed. Wiener Historikerinnen, pp. 20–36.

Migerka, Else (1900) 'Die Getreuen', *Dokumente der Frauen*, 3, pp. 120–3, 153–6.

——— (1915) 'Was der Krieg in uns reift', *Der Bund*, 10, no. 1 (January), pp. 8–11.

Migerka, Helene (1900) 'Die Zulassung der Frauen zum Rechtsstudium', *Frauenleben*, 12, no. 5 (May), pp. 1–2.

Minor, Daisy (1900) 'Marie von Ebner-Eschenbach', *Dokumente der Frauen*, 4, pp. 406–9.

——— (1912) 'Die erste österreichische Frauenstimmrechtskonferenz', *Der Bund*, 7, no. 4 (April), pp. 5–7.

——— (ed.) (1913) *Literatur zur Frauenfrage, im Auftrage des Bundes österreichischer Frauenvereine.*

——— (1914) 'Das solidarische Eintreten der Frauen für die Lehrerinnen', *Der Bund*, 9, no. 3 (March), pp. 8–9.

——— (1915) 'Über den internationalen Haager Frauenkongress, *Der Bund*, 10, no. 6 (June), pp. 8–10.

Moll, Fritz and Pivl, Anton (1903) *Die Berufswahl der Frauen im Staatsdienste und im öffentlichen Leben. Ein Ratgeber und Führer für jene Frauen, welche sich eine selbständige Existenz gründen wollen.*

Montane, H. (1925) *Die Prostitution in Wien. Ihre Geschichte und Entwicklung von den Anfängen bis zur Gegenwart.*

Mossler, Ida (1906) 'Allg. österr. Frauenverein', *Neues Frauenleben*, 18, no. 4 (April), pp. 20–4.

Müller, Klara (1899) 'Rache', *Dokumente der Frauen*, 1, pp. 346–9.

Mulot-Déri, Sibylle (1987) *Sir Galahad. Portrait einer Verschollenen*, Frankfurt am Main.

Murau, Karoline (1895) *Wiener Malerinnen.*

Musil, Robert (1976) *Tagebücher*, ed. Adolf Frisé, Reinbek bei Hamburg.

N., E. (1892) 'Arbeiterinnenbewegung', *Arbeiterinnen-Zeitung*, 1 April, pp. 4–6.

Najmájer, Marie von (1900) *Der Stern von Navarra. Historischer Roman in zwei Bänden*, Berlin.

——— (1901) *Der Göttin Eigenthum.*

Nawiasky, Hans (1902) 'Die Frauen im

österreichischen Staatsdienst', *Wiener staatswissenschaftliche Studien*, 4, pp. 1–246.

Necker, Moritz (1899) 'Die Literaturgeschichte in der höheren Töchterschule. Brief an eine Freundin', *Dokumente der Frauen*, 1, pp. 203–9.

Neubacher, Franz (1987) *Freiland. Eine liberalsozialistische Utopie.*

Neyer, Gerda (1984) 'Sozialpolitik von, für und gegen Frauen. Am Beispiel der historischen Entwicklung der Mutterschutzgesetzgebung in Österreich', *Österreichische Zeitschrift für Politikwissenschaft*, 13, pp. 427–41.

Nigg, Marianne (ed.) (1893) *Biographien der österreichischen Dichterinnen und Schriftstellerinnen. Ein Beitrag zur deutschen Literatur in Österreich*, Korneuburg.

——— (1985) 'Die Enterbten der Arbeit', *Frauen-Werke*, 2, no. 11 (November), pp. 81–3.

Nora (1896) 'Abwege in der modernen Frauenliteratur', *Die Volksstimme*, 27 September, pp. 7–8.

——— (1910) 'Also sprach die Prinzessin', *Neues Frauenleben*, 22, no. 1 (January), p. 14.

Nordmann, Richard [Margarethe Langkammer] (1895) *Die Überzähligen. Ein Stück aus dem Volksleben in vier Akten.*

Nunberg, Herman and Federn, Ernst (eds) (1962) *Minutes of the Vienna Psychoanalytic Society*, New York, Vol. I.

Ofner, Julius (1900**a**) 'Die Christlich-Socialen und die Frauen', *Dokumente der Frauen*, 4, pp. 561–3.

——— (1900**b**) 'Zur Dienstbotenfrage', *Dokumente der Frauen*, 2, pp. 580–4.

——— (1905) 'Die Zivilehe', *Neues Frauenleben*, 17, no. 5 (May), pp. 6–7.

——— (1915) *Julius Ofner zum siebzigsten Geburtstag. Festschrift.*

——— (*et al.*) (1901) 'Die Frage der Beamtinnen im Abgeordnetenhaus', *Frauenleben*, 13, no. 3 (March), p. 57.

Österreichisches Frauenstimmrechtskomitee (ed.) (1913) *Das Frauenstimmrecht. Festschrift.*

Pappenheim, Wilhelm (1901) 'Der Schutz des ungeborenen unehelichen Kindes in Österreich', *Dokumente der Frauen*, 5, pp. 265–70.

Pataky, Sophie (ed.) (1898) *Lexikon deutscher Frauen der Feder. Eine Zusammenstellung der seit dem Jahre 1840 erschienenen Werke weiblicher Autoren nebst Biographien der Lebenden und einem Verzeichnis der Pseudonyme*, Berlin.

Pauli, Bertha (1911) *Mädchenerziehung und Kampf ums Dasein. Ein Vortrag gehalten in der Versammlung forschrittlicher Frauenvereine Wiens am 16. November 1910.*

Petition der Wiener Frauenvereine (1890), *Lehrerinnen-Wart*, 2, no. 7 (July), pp. 174–6.

Philippovich, Eugen von (1896) *Das Programm der Socialpolitiker.*

Pitter, Viktor (1911) *Die rechtliche Stellung der Frau in Österreich.*

Pollack, Melanie (1905) 'Die Vernichtung des keimenden Lebens', *Neues Frauenleben*, 17, no. 11 (November), pp. 8–11.

Popp, Adelheid (1909) *Jugend einer Arbeiterin*, Munich.

——— (1910) *Schutz der Mutter und dem Kinde.*

——— (ed.) (1911**a**) *Der Frauentag.*

——— (1911**b**) *Die Arbeiterin im Kampf ums Dasein.*

——— (1929) *Der Weg zur Höhe. Die sozialdemokratische Frauenbewegung Österreichs. Ihr Aufbau, ihre Entwicklung und ihr Aufstieg.*

Prost, Edith (1983) 'Weiblichkeit und bürgerliche Kultur am Beispiel Rosa

Mayreder-Obermayer', unpublished doctoral dissertation, University of Vienna.

Protokoll einer Frauenversammlung am 14. Mai 1891 im Sitzungssaale des alten Rathhauses in Wien (1891).

Rabenlechner, Michael Maria (1898) 'Das Weibliche im literarischen Wien', in *Literaturbilder Fin de Siècle*, ed. Anton Breitner, Leipzig, Vol. III, pp. 94–141.

Reich, Emil (1891) 'Ibsen und das Recht der Frau. Vortrag gehalten von Dr. Emil Reich am 19. März 1892', in *3. Jahresbericht es Vereins für erweiterte Frauenbildung*, pp. 17–34.

——— (1928) [no title] in *Der Aufstieg der Frau. Zu Rosa Mayreders 70. Geburtstag am 30. November 1928 als Ehrengabe dargebracht vom Verlag Eugen Diederichs in Jena*, Jena, pp. 115–18.

Reik, Theodor (1924) 'Rosa Mayreder. Die Krise der Väterlichkeit', in *Imago*, 10, p. 353.

Reiss, Mary-Ann (1984) 'Rosa Mayreder. A Pioneer of Austrian Feminism', *International Journal of Women's Studies*, 7, pp. 207–16.

——— (1989) 'Rosa Mayreder and the Vienna School of Aphorists 1880–1930', in *Rosa Mayreder 1858–1938. Mitteilungen des Instituts für Wissenschaft und Kunst*, 44, no. 1, pp. 23–8.

Reuter, Gabriele (1902) 'Verlästerte Bücher', *Dokumente der Frauen*, 7, pp. 229–34.

Richter, Elise (1977) *Kleine Schriften zur allgemeinen und romanischen Sprachwissenschaft*, ed. Yakov Malkiel, Innsbruck.

Rigler, Edith (1976) *Frauenleitbild und Frauenarbeit in Österreich vom ausgehenden 19. Jahrhundert bis zum Zweiten Weltkrieg.*

Roller, Alfred (1902) 'Gedanken über Frauenkleidung', *Dokumente der Frauen*, 6, pp. 649–54.

Rosenthal, Max (ed.) (1912) *Mutterschutz und Sexualreform. Referate und Leitsätze des 1. Internationalen Kongresses für Mutterschutz und Sexualreform in Dresden*, Breslau.

Roth, Joseph (1976) *Die Kapuzinergruft*, in Joseph Roth, *Werke*, ed. Hermann Kesten, Cologne. First published 1938.

Rozenblit, Marsha (1983) *The Jews of Vienna 1867–1914. Assimilation and Identity*, Albany, NY.

Rukschcio, Burkhardt and Schachel, Rolånd (1982) *Adolf Loos. Leben und Werk*, Salzburg.

Sandrock, Adele (1897–8) 'Die Regisseurin', *Wiener Rundschau*, 2, pp. 505–7.

Sauer, Walter (1980) *Katholisches Vereinswesen in Wien. Zur Geschichte des christlichsozial-konservativen Lagers vor 1914*, Salzburg.

Schalek, Alice (1905) *Das Fräulein.*

Schapire-Neurath, Anna (1900) 'Sterka', *Dokumente der Frauen*, 3, pp. 187–90, 215–22, 248–53.

——— (1901) 'Lorsqu'on est fille de brasserie', *Dokumente der Frauen*, 6, pp. 498–504.

——— (1908) *Die Frau und die Sozialpolitik*, Leipzig.

——— (1909) *Abriss einer Geschichte der Frauenbewegung*, Leipzig.

——— (1910) 'Noch einmal "Mädchenerziehung und Rassenhygiene"', *Neues Frauenleben*, 22, no. 10 (October), pp. 294–9.

——— (1911) 'Zwei Lager', *Neues Frauenleben*, 23, no. 9 (September), pp. 232–9.

Schaufler, Rosa (1930) 'Die Kanzlei- und Verwaltungsbeamtin', in *Frauenbewegung, Frauenbildung und Frauenarbeit in Österreich*, ed. Martha Stephanie Braun *et al.*, pp. 267–73.

Schenk, Herrad (1980) *Die feministische*

Herausforderung. 150 Jahre Frauenbewegung in Deutschland, Munich.

Scheu, Friedrich (1985) *Ein Band der Freundschaft. Schwarzwaldkreis und Entstehung der Vereinigung sozialistischer Mittelschüler.*

Scheu, Robert (ed.) (1898) *Was leistet die Mittelschule?*

——— (1901) *Culturpolitik.*

——— (1947) 'Die österreichischen Fabier', *Arbeiter-Zeitung*, 31 July, p. 2.

Scheu-Riess, Helene (1919) 'Das Dienstjahr der Frauen', in Helene Scheu-Riess, *Wege zur Menschenerziehung*, pp. 9–13.

Schlesinger-Eckstein, Therese (1898) 'Bürgerliche und proletarische Frauenbewegung', *Socialistische Monatshefte*, 2, pp. 459–66.

——— (1898–9) 'Camilla Theimer: "Die Frau der Zukunft"', *Die neue Zeit*, 17 (Vol. 1), pp. 632–4.

——— (1899) 'Zu dem Kampfe gegen die Reglementierung der Prostitution', *Die neue Zeit*, 17 (Vol. 2), pp. 365–74.

——— (1900) 'Die Arbeitstheilung im Haushalte', *Dokumente der Frauen*, 2, pp. 591–4.

——— (1902**a**) 'Die geschlechtliche Moral in der neuesten Wiener Literatur', *Arbeiter-Zeitung*, 19 July (Morgenblatt), pp. 1–3.

——— (1902**b**) 'Die Wiener Frauenpresse', *Socialistische Monatshefte*, 6, pp. 542–6.

——— (1919) *Die geistige Arbeiterin und der Sozialismus.*

——— (1928) 'Rosa Mayreder als Erweckerin', in *Der Aufstieg der Frau. Zu Rosa Mayreders 70. Geburtstag am 30. November 1928 als Ehrengabe dargebracht vom Verlag Eugen Diederichs in Jena*, Jena, pp. 118–20.

Schmid-Bortenschlager, Sigrid (1984) 'Der Verein der Schriftstellerinnen und Künstlerinnen in Wien 1885–1938', in *Jahrbuch der Universität Salzburg 1981–83*, Salzburg, pp. 124–37.

——— (1987) 'Der Fall "Vera". Diskurstheoretische Überlegungen zu einem Literaturskandal aus dem Wien von 1902', in *Frauenbilder – Frauenrollen – Frauenforschung*, ed. Christa Gürtler *et al.*, Salzburg, pp. 63–77.

Schmid-Bortenschlager, Sigrid, and Schnedl-Bubeniček, Hanna (eds) (1982**a**) *Österreichische Schriftstellerinnen 1880–1938. Eine Bio-Bibliographie*, Stuttgart.

——— (eds) (1982**b**) *Totgeschwiegen. Texte zur Situation der Frau von 1880 bis in die Zwischenkriegszeit.*

Schmidt-Friese, Johanna (1900) 'Unsere Dienstboten', *Dokumente der Frauen*, 2, pp. 567–73.

Schnabel, Jenny (1900) 'Siestaträume', *Dokumente der Frauen*, 2, pp. 703–6.

Schnedl-Bubeniček, Hanna (1981**a**) 'Grenzgängerin der Moderne. Studien zur Emanzipation in Texten von Rosa Mayreder,' in *Das ewige Klischee. Zum Rollenbild und Selbstverständnis bei Männern und Frauen*, ed. Autorinnengruppe der Uni Wien, pp. 179–205.

——— (1981**b**) 'Von der Dame zur Bürgerin. Ansätze zur Frauenemanzipation', in *Anatols Jahre. Beispiele aus der Zeit vor der Jahrhundertwende*, exhibition catalogue, Historisches Museum der Stadt Wien, pp. 69–77.

——— (1982) 'Rosa Mayreder. Eine Sympathisantin des Lebendigen', in Rosa Mayreder, *Zur Kritik der Weiblichkeit*, ed. Hanna Schnedl, Munich, pp. 9–32.

——— (1984) 'Pazifistinnen. Ein Resumee zu theoretischen Ausführungen und literarischen Darstellungen Bertha von Suttners und

Rosa Mayreders', *Wiener Beiträge zur Geschichte der Neuzeit*, 11, pp. 96–113.

Schnitzler, Arthur (1966) *Das Wort. Tragikomödie in fünf Akten. Fragment*, ed. Kurt Bergel, Frankfurt am Main.

—— (1981) *Jugend in Wien. Eine Autobiographie*, ed. Therese Nickl and Heinrich Schnitzler.

—— and Waissnix, Olga (1981) *Liebe, die starb vor der Zeit. Ein Briefwechsel*, ed. Therese Nickl and Heinrich Schnitzler.

Schölermann, Wilhelm (1899a) 'Die zweite Schulausstellung des Vereines Kunstschule für Frauen und Mädchen in Wien', *Dokumente der Frauen*, 1, pp. 188–91.

—— (1899b) 'Settlements', *Dokumente der Frauen*, 2, pp. 351–62.

Schorske, Carl E. (1978) 'Generational Tension and Cultural Change. Reflections on the Case of Vienna', *Daedalus. Journal of the American Academy of Arts and Sciences*, 107, pp. 111–22.

—— (1980) *Fin-de-Siècle Vienna*, London.

Schrank, Josef (1886) *Die Prostitution in Wien in historischer, administrativer und hygienischer Beziehung*.

—— (1899) *Die amtlichen Vorschriften betreffend die Prostitution in Wien, in ihrer administrativen, sanitären und strafgerichtlichen Anwendung*.

—— (1904) *Der Mädchenhandel und seine Bekämpfung*.

Schreiber, Clara (1893) *Eva. Naturalistische Studien einer Idealistin*, Dresden.

Schwarzwald, Eugenie (1902–13) *Jahresberichte der Schulanstalten der Frau Dr. phil. Eugenie Schwarzwald*.

—— (1928) 'Geliebte Rosa Mayreder!', in *Der Aufstieg der Frau. Zu Rosa Mayreders 70. Geburtstag am 30. November 1928 als Ehrengabe dargebracht vom Verlag Eugen Diederichs in Jena*, Jena, pp. 120–2.

Simmel, Georg (1919) 'Weibliche Kultur', in Georg Simmel, *Philosophische Kultur*, Berlin, pp. 254–95. First published 1911.

Sparholz, Irmgard (1986) 'Die Persönlichkeit Marie Lang und ihre Bedeutung für die Sozialreformen in Österreich im ausgehenden 19. Jahrhundert', unpublished M.A. thesis, University of Vienna.

Spencer, Herbert (1873) *The Study of Sociology*, London.

Spiegel, Else (1899) 'Allerseelen', *Dokumente der Frauen*, 2, pp. 430–2.

—— (1900) 'Abrüsten!', *Dokumente der Frauen*, 2, pp. 725–7.

Spitzer, Marie (1899) 'Professor Dr Carl Bernhard Brühl', *Dokumente der Frauen*, 1, pp. 339–42.

Stefan, Paul (1922) *Frau Doktor. Ein Bildnis aus dem unbekannten Wien*, Munich.

Steiner, Herbert (1980) 'Käthe Leichter. Arbeiterfunktionärin und Kämpferin für die Rechte der Frau', *Weg und Ziel*, 38, pp. 283–5.

Steiner, Rudolf (1900) 'Rosa Mayreder', *Die Gesellschaft*, 16 (Vol. 2), pp. 79–87.

—— (1925) *Mein Lebensgang*, Dornach.

—— (1955) *Briefe*, ed. Edwin Froböse and Werner Teichert, Dornach.

Steinkellner, Friedrich (1985) 'Emanzipatorische Tendenzen im Christlichen Wiener Frauen-Bund und in der Katholischen Reichsfrauenorganisation Österreichs', in *Unterdrückung und Emanzipation. Festschrift für Erika Weinzierl zum 60. Geburtstag*, ed. Rudolf G. Ardelt *et al.*, Salzburg, pp. 55–67.

Stern, Fritz (1961) *The Politics of Cultural Despair. A Study in the Rise of the Germanic Ideology*, Berkeley, California.

Storck, Emil (1898) 'Warum heiratet "man" nicht?', *Mitteilungen der Ethischen Gesellschaft in Wien*, 29, pp. 393–5.

Storch, Ursula (1989) '"...hübsche Blumenstücke und Stilleben...". Rosa Mayreder und andere bildende Künstlerinnen in Wien um 1900', in *Aufbruch in das Jahrhundert der Frau? Rosa Mayreder und der Feminismus in Wien um 1900*, exhibition catalogue, Historisches Museum der Stadt Wien, pp. 90–101.

Strecker, Gabriele (1969) *Frauenträume, Frauentränen. Über den deutschen Frauenroman*, Weilheim.

Suttner, Bertha von (1891) *Die Waffen nieder! Eine Lebensgeschichte*, Dresden and Leipzig. English title: *Lay Down Your Arms. The Autobiography of Martha von Tilling*. London 1892.

——— (1894) *Vor dem Gewitter*.

——— (1900a) *Daniela Dormes*, Dresden. First published 1886.

——— (1900b) *Die Haager Friedenskonferenz. Tagebuchblätter*, Dresden.

——— (1909) *Memoiren*, Stuttgart.

——— (1911) *Der Menschheit Hochgedanken. Roman aus der nächsten Zukunft*, Berlin. English title: *When Thoughts Will Soar. A Romance of the Immediate Future*. London, 1914.

——— (1912) 'Die Mütter und der Weltfrieden', in *Mutterschaft. Ein Sammelband für die Probleme des Weibes als Mutter*, ed. Adele Schreiber, Munich, pp. 704–8.

——— (1919) *Marthas Kinder. Eine neue Folge von 'Die Waffen nieder!'*, Berlin. First published 1903.

Svoboda, Silvia (1984) 'Die Soldaten des Hinterlandes', in *Die Frau im Korsett. Wiener Frauenalltag zwischen Klischee und Wirklichkeit 1848–1920*, exhibition catalogue, Historisches Museum der Stadt Wien, pp. 50–3.

——— (1989) 'Die "Dokumente der Frauen"', in *Aufbruch in das Jahrhundert der Frau? Rosa Mayreder und der Feminismus in Wien um 1900*, exhibition catalogue, Historisches Museum der Stadt Wien, pp. 52–9.

Teleky, Dora (1914) 'Die Pflichten des Staates gegenüber den Müttern', *Neues Frauenleben*, 26, no. 5 (May), pp. 131–5.

Teleky, Gisela (1900) 'Geehrte Redaction!', *Dokumente der Frauen*, 2, pp. 695–6.

Theimer, Camilla (1898) *Die Frau der Zukunft*.

——— (1909) *Frauenarbeit in Österreich*.

Tichy, Marina (1984) *Alltag und Traum. Leben und Lektüre der Wiener Dienstmädchen um die Jahrhundertwende*.

——— (1989) '"Ich hatte immer Angst, unwissend zu sterben". Therese Schlesinger. Bürgerin und Sozialistin', in *'Die Partei hat mich nie enttäuscht...'. Österreichische Sozialdemokratinnen*, ed. Edith Prost, pp. 135–84.

Timms, Edward F. (1986) *Karl Kraus. Apocalyptic Satirist. Culture and Catastrophe in Habsburg Vienna*, New Haven and London.

Tönnies, Ferdinand (1912) *Gemeinschaft und Gesellschaft. Grundbegriffe der reinen Soziologie*, Berlin. First published 1887.

Touaillon, Christine (1909) 'Der heilige Skarabäus', *Neues Frauenleben*, 21, no. 7 (July), pp. 186–8.

——— (1913) 'Vom Umgang mit Büchern', *Neues Frauenleben*, 25, no. 1 (January), pp. 19–23.

——— (1914) 'Weltkrieg', *Neues Frauenleben*, 26, no. 8–9 (August–September), pp. 229–32.

——— (1918a) 'Der abgesetzte Mann', *Neues Frauenleben*, 20, no. 3 (March), pp. 47–50.

——— (1918b) 'Unsere Zeitschrift', *Neues Frauenleben*, 20, no. 4–5 (April–May), pp. 76–9.

——— (1923) 'Rosa Mayreders Fabeleien über göttliche und menschliche Dinge', *Neue Freie Presse*, 5 March, pp. 7–8.

Troll-Borostyáni, Irma von (1878) *Die Mission unseres Jahrhunderts. Eine Studie über die Frauenfrage*, Pressburg.

——— (1891) 'Die Liebe in der zeitgenössischen deutschen Literatur', *Die Gesellschaft*, 7, pp. 1004–22.

——— (1892) *Aus der Tiefe*, 2 vols. Dresden.

——— (1893) *Das Recht der Frau. Eine soziale Studie*, Berlin.

——— (1894a) 'Die Frauenfrage im Lichte der ethischen Entwicklung', *Die Volksstimme*, 16 September, p. 7.

——— (1894b) 'Die Sittlichkeit der Wiener Frauenvereine', *Die Volksstimme*, 20 May, p. 8.

——— (1896) *Die Verbrechen der Liebe. Eine sozial-pathologische Studie*, Leipzig.

——— (1897a) *Onkel Clemens*, Erfurt.

——— (1897b) *Das Weib und seine Kleidung*, Leipzig.

——— (1898) *Was ich geschaut. Novellen.*

——— (1900) *Hunger und Liebe*, Leipzig.

——— (1903) *Katechismus der Frauenbewegung*, Leipzig.

——— (1911) 'Frauenpflicht', *Neues Frauenleben*, 23, no. 1 (January), pp. 1–5.

——— (1912) *So erziehen wir unsere Kinder zu Vollmenschen. Ein Elternbuch*, Oranienburg.

——— (1913) *Die Gleichstellung der Geschlechter und die Reform der Jugenderziehung. Die Mission unseres Jahrhunderts*, ed. Bayerischer Verein für Frauenstimmrecht, Munich. First published 1884 as *Im freien Reich. Ein Memorandum an alle Denkenden und Gesetzgeber zur Beseitigung sozialer Irrtümer und Leiden*, Zurich.

——— (1914) *Ausgewählte kleinere Schriften*, ed. Wilhelmine von Troll, Leipzig.

Turnau, Ottilie (1892) *Über die Notwendigkeit eines Frauentages.*

Urbach, Annie (1972) 'The Federn Family', *Journal of Clinical Psychology*, Monograph Supplement no. 32, January: '35 Years with Freud in Honour of the Hundredth Anniversary of Paul Federn, MD', pp. 12–17.

Urban, Gisela (1910) 'Die neue Dienstbotenordnung für Wien', *Der Bund*, 5, no. 7 (December), pp. 3–6.

——— (1915) 'Das Frauendienstjahr. Ein praktischer Anfang', *Der Bund*, 10, no. 7 (July), pp. 10–11.

——— (1930) 'Die Entwicklung der österreichischen Frauenbewegung. Im Spiegel der wichtigsten Vereinsgründungen', in *Frauenbewegung, Frauenbildung und Frauenarbeit in Österreich*, ed. Martha Stephanie Braun *et al.*, pp. 25–64.

Velde, Henry van de (1901) 'Die künstlerische Hebung der Frauentracht', *Die Zeit*, 27, pp. 42–3.

Vera [Betty Kris] (1902) *Eine für Viele. Aus dem Tagebuche eines Mädchens*, Leipzig.

Verein für erweiterte Frauenbildung in Wien (1889–1904) *Jahresberichte*, 1–16.

Vereinigung der arbeitenden Frauen (1903) Mitgliederverzeichnis, *Mitteilungen der Vereinigung der arbeitenden Frauen*, 1, no. 2 (April), p. 3.

——— (1904) 'Auszug aus den Statuten', *Mitteilungen der Vereinigung der arbeitenden Frauen*, 2, no. 17 (November), p. 7.

Vogel, Ursula (1986) 'Rationalism and Romanticism. Two Strategies for Women's Liberation', in *Feminism and Political Theory*, ed. Judith Evans *et al.*, London, pp. 17–46.

Vogelsang, Marie von (1896) 'Frauenarbeit in Wien', *Die Zukunft*, 4, pp. 113–24.

Vogt, Christa, and Pleschberger, Werner (1980) 'Frauenemanzipation und sozialistische Bewegung in Österreich. Kritische Bemerkungen zu parteiinternen Bedingungen der Frühgeschichte', in *Internationale Tagung der Historiker der Arbeiterbewegung. 14. Linzer Konferenz 1978. Die Frau in der Arbeiterbewegung 1900–1939*, Vol. XIII, part 1, pp. 262–82.

Vortmann, Thusnelda (1894) *Die Reform der Ehe*, Zurich.

W., L.A. (1897) 'Frau Irma von Troll-Borostyáni', *Frauenleben*, 9, no. 8 (November), pp. 57–8.

Wagner, Nike (1982) *Geist und Geschlecht. Karl Kraus und die Erotik der Wiener Moderne*, Frankfurt am Main.

Waldkampf, Marianne Tuma von (1907) *Zur Reform des österreichischen Eherechts*, Leipzig.

——— (1911) 'Mutterschutzbestrebungen in Österreich', *Die neue Generation*, 8, pp. 322–30.

Walker, Frank (1951) *Hugo Wolf. A Biography*, London.

Weiland, Daniela (1983) *Geschichte der Frauenemanzipation in Deutschland und Österreich. Biographien, Programme, Organisationen*, Düsseldorf.

Weininger, Otto (1980) *Geschlecht und Charakter. Eine prinzipielle Untersuchung*, Munich. First published 1903.

Weinzierl, Erika (1975) *Emanzipation? Österreichische Frauen im 20. Jahrhundert*, Munich.

——— (1986) 'Österreichische Frauenbewegungen um die Jahrhundertwende', in *Wien um 1900. Aufbruch in die Moderne*, ed. Peter Berner *et al.*, pp. 221–5.

Weissenthurn, Max von [Maximiliane Franul von Weissenthurn] (1911) *An die Frauen! Gesammelte Essays*.

Wellesz, Egon and Emmy (1981) *Leben und Werk*.

Wendt, F.M. (*et al.*) (1889) 'Unser Ziel', *Lehrerinnen-Wart*, 1, no. 1 (January), pp. 1–2.

——— (1891) 'Die österreichische Volkshymne', *Neuzeit*, 3, no. 11, pp. 248–50.

Werner, Gabriele (1906) 'Konsumenten-Moral', *Neues Frauenleben*, 18, no. 6 (June), pp. 5–14.

Wesely, Jary (1913) 'Arthur Schnitzler', *Neues Frauenleben*, 25, no. 2 (February), pp. 47–51.

Widmann, Hans (1914) 'Irma von Troll-Borostyáni. Das Leben einer Dichterin und Denkerin', in Irma von Troll-Borostyáni, *Ausgewählte kleinere Schriften*, ed. Wilhelmine von Troll, Leipzig, pp. 5–32.

Wiener Frauen (1891) 'Begrüssungstelegramm', *Moderne Rundschau*, 3, no. 3, p. 131.

Wiener Frauenerwerbverein (1987) 'Die Geschichte unserer Schule', *Jahresbericht 1986/87*, pp. 2–4.

Wiesengrün, Paul (1897) 'Gegen die Emanzipation des Weibes', *Wiener Rundschau*, 2, pp. 387–91, 431–7, 503–10.

Winter, Fritz (1900) 'Statistisches', *Dokumente der Frauen*, 2, pp. 584–7.

——— (1901) 'Der Heiratsmarkt', *Dokumente der Frauen*, 4, pp. 725–31.

Wittels, Fritz (1908) 'Die Feministen', *Die Fackel*, 248, pp. 9–14.

Wittmann, Maria (1950) 'Die österreichische Frauenstimmrechtsbewegung im Spiegel der Frauenzeitungen', unpublished doctoral dissertation, University of Vienna.

Wolf, Hugo (1921) *Briefe an Rosa Mayreder. Mit einem Nachwort der Dichterin des 'Corregidor'*, ed. Heinrich Werner.

Wunberg, Gotthart (ed.) (1971) *Die literarische Moderne. Dokumente zum Selbstverständnis der Literatur um die Jahrhundertwende*, Frankfurt am Main.

——— (ed.) (1976) *Das junge Wien. Österreichische Literatur- und Kunstkritik 1887–1902*, 2 vols. Tübingen.

Zaar, Birgitte (1987) 'Dem Mann die Politik, der Frau die Familie. Die Gegner des politischen Frauenstimmrechts in Österreich 1848–1918', *Österreichische Zeitschrift für Politikwissenschaft*, 16, pp. 351–62.

Zepler, Wally (1928) 'Rosa Mayreder', *Socialistische Monatshefte*, 34, pp. 1084–9.

Zitelmann, Katharina (1900) 'Einst – und Jetzt!', *Dokumente der Frauen*, 3, pp. 40–3.

Zuckerkandl, Berta (1899) 'Cultureller Dilettantismus', *Dokumente der Frauen*, 1, pp. 231–3.

——— (1901**a**) 'Die künstlerische Hebung der Frauentracht', *Die Zeit*, 27, pp. 42–3.

——— (1901**b**) 'Künstlermoden. Zum Vortrage Van de Velde's in Wien', *Die Zeit*, 26, pp. 168–9.

Index